Wishing you

"*To forget how to dig the earth and tend the soil is to forget ourselves.*"

MOHANDAS KARAMCHAND GANDHI

Copyright

DREAMING IN SPICE
A Sinfully Vegetarian Odyssey

FIRST PRINTING
Copyright © 2020 Global Cooking School, LLC
All Rights Reserved. No part of this publication may be reproduced, stored in a retrieval system, or transmitted in any form or in any means – by electronic, mechanical, photocopying, recording or otherwise – without prior written permission.
ISBN: 978-0-9862727-1-4
390 pages

Published by Global Cooking School, LLC
Designed and Produced by Hari Pulapaka, Ph.D., C.E.C.
Editorial Services by Megan O'Neill, Ph.D.

Printed by E. O. Painter Printing Company, DeLeon Springs, Florida, USA

Dedication

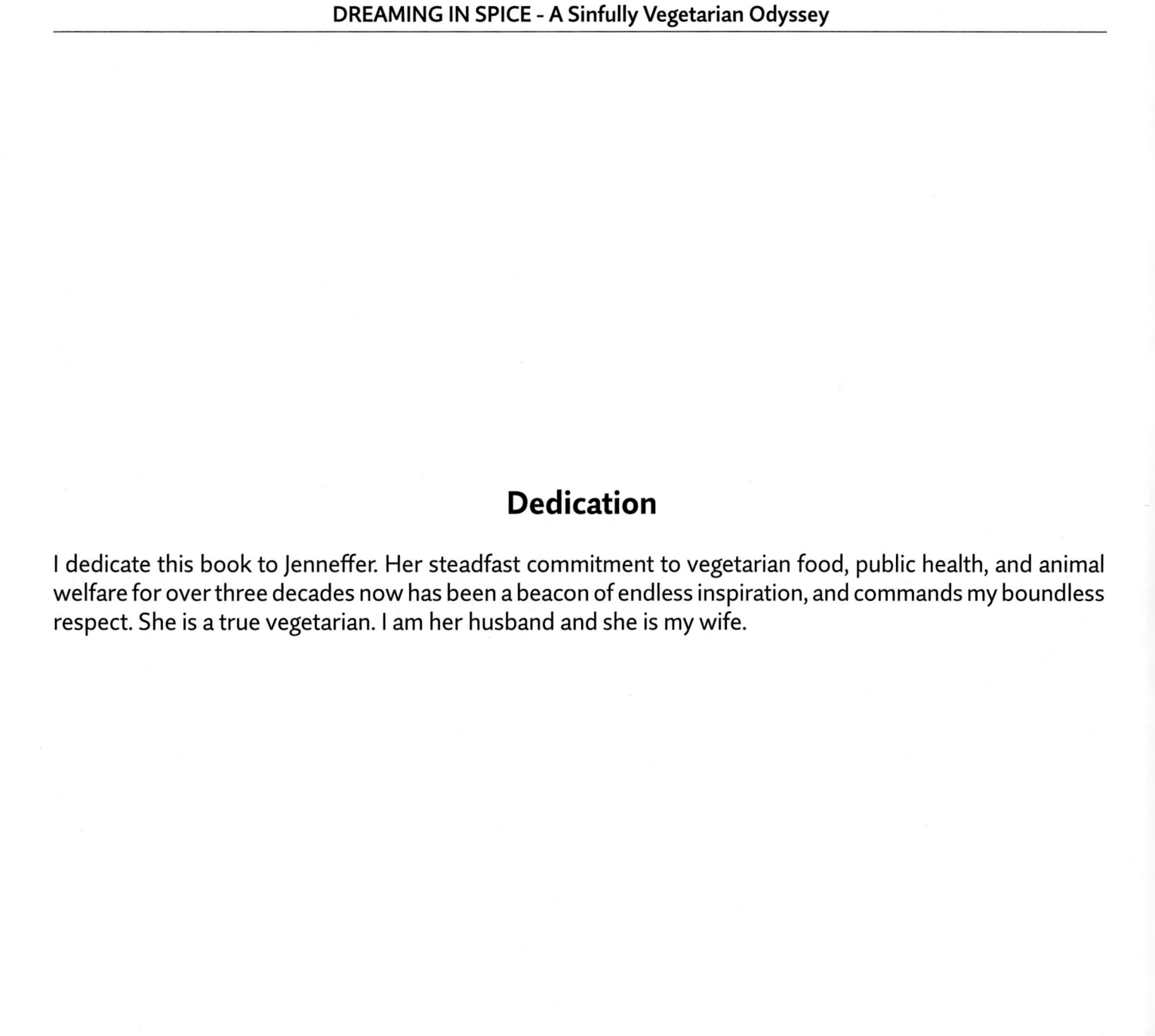

I dedicate this book to Jenneffer. Her steadfast commitment to vegetarian food, public health, and animal welfare for over three decades now has been a beacon of endless inspiration, and commands my boundless respect. She is a true vegetarian. I am her husband and she is my wife.

Table of Contents

FOREWORD (Danielle Nierenberg, *President*, Food Tank)	pp. 5-6
PEARLS OF SUPPORT	pp. 8-9
PREFACE	pp. 10-11
Chapter 1 - A LONG FORAGING ROAD (2014)	pp. 12-13
Chapter 2 - A TORRID PACE (2015)	pp. 14-16
Chapter 3 - GLOBAL TABLE, SUNSHINE STATE (2016)	pp. 17-19
Chapter 4 - RE-FOCUSING ENERGIES	pp. 20-22
Chapter 5 - CERTIFIED MASTER CHEF PRACTICAL (2017)	pp. 24-25
Chapter 6 - SEVEN COURSES SEVEN COUNTRIES (2017)	pp. 26-28
Chapter 7 - SOLIDARITY SUNDAY (2018)	pp. 30-31
Chapter 8 - NEW BEGINNINGS	pp. 32-34
Chapter 9 - BEING VEGETARIAN: WHY & HOW	pp. 35-46
Chapter 10 - POUR YOURSELF A BEVERAGE	pp. 47-57
Chapter 11 - LET'S COOK	pp. 58-65
PAGE NUMBERS & LIST OF RECIPES	pp. 66-70
1) Spice Blends & Marinades	pp. 73-87
2) Chutneys & Relishes	pp. 88-105
3) Sauces	pp. 106-121
4) Hors d'oeuvres	pp. 122-142
5) Soups	pp. 144-162
6) Salad Dressings	pp. 164-170
7) Composed Salads	pp. 171-184
8) Flour-Based	pp. 186-206
9) Hand-Helds	pp. 209-221
10) Street-Inspired	pp. 222-239
11) Rice Dishes	pp. 241-258
12) Grains	pp. 260-270
13) Legumes	pp. 272-283
14) Pasta	pp. 284-300
15) Curries	pp. 301-315
16) Global Fusion	pp. 316-342
17) Sides & Condiments	pp. 344-365
18) Sinfully Vegan Degustation in 15 Acts	pp. 366-383
GLOSSARY	pp. 384-385
INDEX	pp. 386-388
AUTHOR BIOGRAPHY	p. 390

Foreword
by
DANIELLE NIERENBERG
President & Founder, *Food Tank*; 2020 Julia Child Award Winner

As I write this, the world is about 6 months into the global pandemic of COVID-19 and Hurricane Isais is barreling up the Eastern Seaboard. It seems fitting that the book you hold in your hands could be part of the solution to not only a post-pandemic environmentally sustainable world, but one that also respects land and animals and the people who care for them both. Vegetarian and plant-forward diets are a critical tool that nutritionists, chefs, and eaters are using to improve both human health and the health of the planet.

The author, Chef and Ph.D. Hari Pulapaka, has created a way to take a culinary journey through the world of vegetables, beans, grains, and of course spices. And he's used both sides of his brain as both a lover of food and a mathematician to create something truly extraordinary in "Dreaming in Spice: A Sinfully Vegetarian Odyssey"

A book that appeals to both omnivores and vegetarians alike; a book that satisfies cravings both large and a small; and a book that doesn't talk down to the reader but provides a rich landscape and practical set of tools for cooking and eating tasty food.

One of the things I admire most about Chef Pulapaka's approach to cooking—and writing about food—is that he recognizes the need for making do with what you have in your own kitchen. The recommended substitutions list he provides is *the* most useful and innovative section of any cookbook I've ever used. I want to tear out that page and hang it on my wall. He understands that not every cook has the wealth and variety of different spices or other ingredients that he has in his own kitchen.

And while some of his recipes have intimidatingly long lists of ingredients, once you dive in, you realize that they're not that complicated. Much like the equations he teaches his students at Stetson University in Florida, the combinations of flavors he creates are complex and simple at the same time. At the same time, there are very simple ingredient recipes for spices and foods that will help any cook, no matter what their ability in the kitchen. The only rule is deliciousness.

Chef Pulapaka is a teacher at heart and he provides readers with a way to envision recipes that I've never seen in any other cookbook. He gives instructions on how to develop flavors and tastes that balance one another and that the art of being prepared is the best tool a cook can have at their disposal.

He is an expert at combining so many different flavors, from South Asia to the Southern United States. These are recipes that honor and respect the cultures from which they came and the people who developed them. No matter what part of the world you call home, there's something that will appeal to you in this book.

Chef Pulapaka also recognizes that his work is not separate from his home life. His wife, Dr. Jenneffer Pulapaka, is not only his life partner, but also business partner and a significant character in this book. She provides her own chapter on wine. I love wine but am not an expert and her writing is an excellent primer for anyone who wants to learn how to delightfully pair different flavors. It's the perfect companion to the recipes.

This book doesn't dictate or preach to the reader about the right or wrong way to cook. He says that he's offering "guidelines" of ways to cook his recipes, but he's not dictating to all of us as cooks and eaters. Instead, he's offering a cornucopia of ways to enjoy food. And he reminds the reader that mistakes in the kitchen are rarely mistakes—again, as an educator, he wants us to learn something new in the kitchen every day. Ultimately, he wants us to be excited about creating satisfying, harmonious dishes in our own kitchens that bring joy.

There's never been a better time for a book like "Dreaming in Spice: A Sinfully Vegetarian Odyssey"—one that reminds us that good food, delicious food is not only for chefs to create in professional kitchens, but something that we can all do at home. I hope you write notes in this book about variations that worked for you, I hope you share the recipes with friends and family, and I hope it becomes dog eared and stained with your efforts to create incredible meals.

Danielle Nierenberg

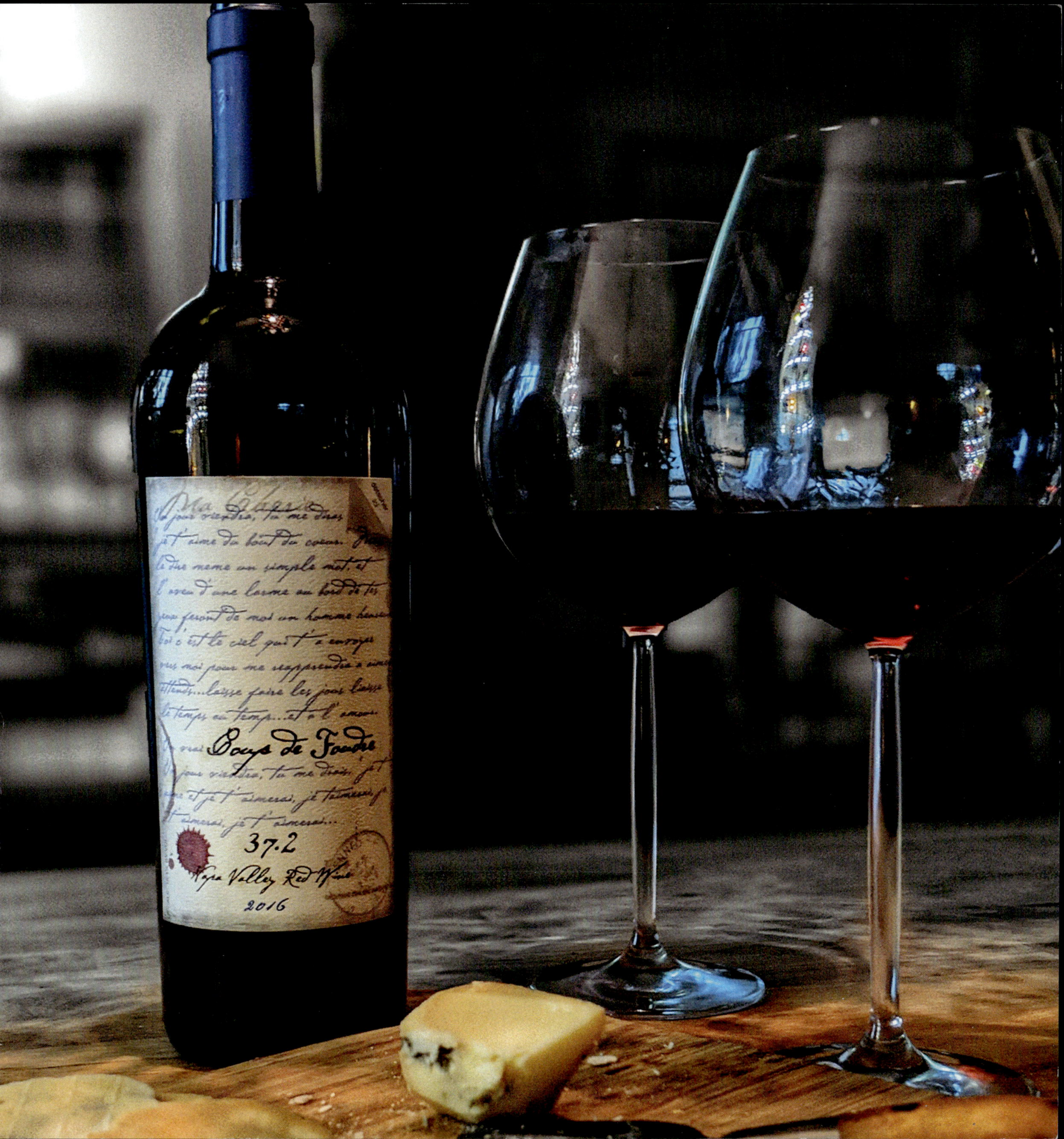
Coup de Foudre
37.2
Napa Valley Red Wine
2016

Pearls of Support

RICK BAYLESS
Humanitarian, Award-Winning Chef, Multiple James Bear Award Winner, 2016 Julia Child Award Winner, Author

Hari Pulapaka is crazy in love with spices and the way they weave together in an almost alchemical way, launching even a simple dish to new heights. Cooks from India have perfected that spice sorcery, and Hari builds on their (his!) tradition, adding an accomplished chef's perspective and an openness to the delicious variety and complexity that is found in all the world's kitchens. And he does all that relying only on the great diversity the plant kingdom offers.

CHIP GILLER
Founder GRIST, Heinz Award Winner, TIME Environment Hero, Author

Hari Pulapaka's nuanced and inventive recipes are remarkable in their own right -- but knowing the journey that he undertook to develop them, as well as the ethical underpinnings of all his work, only adds to the deliciousness. Sinfully Vegetarian is a feast for the mind and the taste buds.

MARY SUE MILLIKEN
Humanitarian, Trailblazing and Award-Winning Chef, 2018 Julia Child Award Winner, Author

Hari is an incredible teacher and storyteller, not to mention, uber creative chef. His mathematical/scientific mind juxtaposed with a no boundaries approach, make for an amazing collection of unique, mouthwatering recipes. If you're looking for exciting ways to eat a more plant-forward, planet-friendly diet - this book is for you. There are hundreds of innovative ideas in this book.

Pearls of Support

ART SMITH
Humanitarian, Former Chef to Oprah Winfrey, James Beard Award Winner

Hari Pulapaka is a professor and a chef whose mission has been to educate the student and the diner about whole delicious foods. Chef Hari is a Florida gift on a mission to eat our vegetables and promote vegetarian cuisine, but with thought and delicious creativity. A Sinfully Vegetarian Odyssey is so much more than a cookbook with serious and thoughtful recipes. In many ways, it is a testament to the American Dream.

NORMAN VAN AKEN
Pioneering Chef, James Beard Award Winner, James Beard Who's Who in Food, Author

"Dreaming in Spice - A Sinfully Vegetarian Odyssey" is a very personal, warm, and engaging cookbook written by a highly accomplished Mathematician who eventually became a professor and then became an acclaimed chef as well. Here in this book Hari shares his abiding love of cuisine. It is the beautiful confluence of how immigrants enrich the lives of all by providing a new way of looking at things, cooking things, thinking of things, and adding dimension to the world around us. I am privileged to know Hari personally as well as professionally. We've shared a few stages and kitchens too. He is open to life, socio-politically engaged, and connected to the world and the changes it brings us and bring it. I also enjoy that his wife Jenneffer is his life partner and business partner. They complement each other perfectly with her peerless abilities to match his dishes with the correct beverages. Hari's sincere, self-effacing dedication to the craft of cooking is something you will learn along the way as you read "Sinfully Vegetarian". You won't be able to read it in one sitting...because you will be too inspired to get in your kitchen and cook out of it!

Preface

Greetings. I am a professional chef and a professional mathematician. I was born and raised in the bustling metropolis of Mumbai, India. On August 12, 1987, at the impressionable age of 21, I boarded a Pan Am jumbo jet and arrived in the United States to pursue graduate education in Mathematics. My journey has been one of modest comfort, conformity, survival, perseverance, excitement, and opportunity. On my 54th birthday this year, I was on tap to present a 10-course vegan dinner at the vaulted James Beard House in New York City. But a global pandemic had other plans. For more than 15 years I've led a dual professional life consumed with an insatiable urge to please. In 2004, while going through what I now refer to as a *professional midlife crisis*, after having obtained tenure at a prestigious private university in DeLand FL, I embarked on the serious journey of training as professional chef. In 2015, I wrote my first book, and almost immediately, I was already planning a sequel of sorts. The following year, I launched a project titled *Sinfully Vegetarian*. At the time, I was primarily interested in teaching others how to cook more flavorful vegetarian food. You see, I was a vegetarian for every day of the first 21 years of my life. And then, suddenly, after coming to America, it went downhill for me. The reasons why I stopped remaining vegetarian are complex and numerous. However, their common denominator is the undeniable fact that, at least in the United States, vegetarian food in everyday society including restaurants is--how should I put this gently-- generally pretty lame. I wasn't much of a cook when I arrived in the United States. However, the three dishes that I knew how to make, partly thanks to the spice blends I brought with me from India, were always full of flavor and thoroughly enjoyable. Not surprisingly, pizza became a favorite of mine when I didn't feel like cooking for myself. My pizza always had lots of spicy green chiles. Part of the reason for that is that while I didn't always chase the capsaicin, I always chased the flavor and freshness. Undeniably, America was and is a melting pot of cultures and ethnicities. And while there were instances of diverse ethnic food in the communities where I've lived, even they were woefully inadequate in their celebration of vegetarian food. I could not understand why a soup that was supposed to be a celebration of greens or beans or peppers or even potatoes needed a chicken stock. Years later I conjectured that this reality was either a direct result of cultural and culinary habits or a complete lack of knowledge regarding flavor development in food. Bacon makes everything better, they say. To that I respond, no, it does not.

For years, I've relished in opportunities to create thoughtful, vegetarian tasting menus for guests who requested such experiences. Even I, with all my experience and confidence, would sometimes find myself facing creative dead ends in my attempts to be continually original and expansive. So I get it. It's hard enough to be creative when presented with a fully loaded arsenal of ingredients and options. When the restrictions increase, only the willing survive. In theory, most chefs could be more thoughtful about vegetarian food. In reality, most chefs choose not to. With this book, it is my hope that professionals and amateurs alike will become more energized and confident in becoming more inclusive about the foods they eat. I have only barely scratched the surface of what might constitute a globally-inspired, professionally-edged vegetarian cookbook. I've observed a complete breakdown of culinary education in this country when it comes to teaching students how to cook and embrace vegetarian food. As a glaring example, in the same amount of time it takes to perfectly tournée a pound of potatoes, one could become more proficient in creating a delicious plant-based sauce.

Naturally, in this book, I've drawn from many parts of the world. Doing so is an honest reflection of how I view the world. I don't have a culinary specialty, *per se*, but I do have a culinary style. And in this book, I believe that is represented well and inclusively. I've adopted classical cooking techniques universally when developing flavor in dishes. After all, the foundations don't lie. The number of ingredients that can be derived from plants greatly outnumbers those that are not from plants. So, the notion that requiring a dish be vegetarian restricts/requires restricting one's ability to make something tasty is both incorrect and misinformed. Furthermore, today's grocery stores are lined with ingredients from all over the world. When compounded with the fact that most towns and cities of any size boast at least one ethnic store, our potential pantry grows even more tantalizing. Furthermore, most mainstream grocery stores have an ethnic aisle. They seem more fully stocked than other aisles.

It is my hope that American society will embrace vegetarian food just as ubiquitously as it has embraced pizza or tacos. This book is a small step towards an overarching project aimed at adding to a body of culinary knowledge and inspirations that furthers vegetarian food. It is my hope that this baby step will empower a fuller and more mindful existence through food. In writing this book, I have taken a deep dive into myself as a human being. For me, the intersection of mindful eating and being a food industry professional creates an existence that contains vast amounts of sinfully vegetarian food.

I invited you to join me on this journey of exploration and vegetarian decadence, taking inspiration from near and distant corners of the world. I hope you will tolerate my meandering storytelling because it testifies to my decision-making, my very existence, when it comes to food. It is my chef-prof life.

With much love and mad respect for the plant world,

I remain, sincerely,

Hari
DeLand, Florida
USA

Chapter 1: A LONG FORAGING TRIP (2014)
"If I had to do it all over again, I wish I had met Jenneffer earlier in my life."

By now I had a decade of professional cooking under my belt, including a fast-paced year of formal culinary training, two years of being a private chef, two short yet impactful experiences in restaurants, and six years of running my own kitchen. I developed a weathered look and a broadened outlook from opening and running a successful kitchen in the midst of both the 2008 financial crisis and being a full-time academic. You see, I have this insatiable, almost gluttonous desire to push the envelope, as it were. My wife Jenneffer had planted the thought of driving up to New York City, shopping for a few ingredients along the way, and cooking a meal for the New York food elite. That idea blossomed into something so amazingly elevated that even we were impressed and taken back at the outcome.

Certainly, many chefs specialize in foraging for the ingredients that inspire their creations. But we had other plans. In June of 2014, a few of us from Central Florida decided that we would travel by road to NYC to cook a special dinner at the prestigious James Beard House. Initially, the idea was to be able to transport the ingredients that we were going to use. But then, and quickly, we became inspired by the notion of procuring most of the ingredients we needed as we meandered from town to farm to highway. Growing up, I was used to helping my family shop for ingredients every single day for a freshly made meal that was to be consumed that day. Shop as you go, and cook as you go, with both parents working full-time. What a concept! And even after I came to this country, I've essentially practiced the same sort of model. At the restaurant, I had already made a habit of sourcing in-season ingredients and procuring them several times a week. And since I never contracted from a large distributor for any length of time, I found myself going to the grocery store every single day. As exhausting as that was, in some ways, it was the only choice I thought I had. I still don't know how I did it all. Today, I dread most grocery stores. Not because I hate fresh produce and great ingredients or shopping, but because they have a way of reminding me of a time and pace that made hours seem like seconds and years like months. For years, I maintained a frenetic pace trying to shop for ingredients in order to be ready for dinner service in between teaching, prepping, receiving deliveries, etc. The endless grind, as it were, had taken its silent toll.

In early June 2014, Jenneffer Pulapaka, Geraldine Fowler, Bram Fowler, Kevin Fonzo, and I embarked on a journey for our collective ages. Each of us could recall growing up knowing where our food came from. I was raised in Mumbai, Kevin in New York state, Bram in South Africa, Geraldine in Mauritius, and Jenneffer in Orlando. As youngsters, each of us had vivid memories of going to the market every day and buying fresh ingredients that would end up on our dinner tables that evening. This trip would return us to our childhood memories about food and ingredients as we chose sustainable farms and artisans to visit along the way to procure ingredients to be showcased on the Beard House dinner menu. We were a motley crew of personalities, palates, and styles, bound together by the common bond of friendship, camaraderie, and love—love for food, hospitality, and humanity. Our goal was simple, singular, and focused: we were going to showcase our culinary talent and prowess using the bounty of the East Coast of the United States in probably the most illustrious kitchen in the United States. We began this once-in-a-lifetime journey in Central Florida and meandered our way up through Georgia, South Carolina, North Carolina, Virginia, Maryland, Pennsylvania, New Jersey, and ultimately New York. Over 1200 miles of American roadways, both major and not so much, and over 20 hours of driving later, we arrived in NYC, champing at our bits to do our thing. The James Beard House is one of the world's preeminent culinary performance spaces. It was not my first time at the House, but the pure energy, history, and significance of this space gives me tummy butterflies to this day. Amazingly, barring a small leak in one of our containers, it was a flawless road trip of seeing farms and meeting an array of producers and passionate practitioners of good food in North America. From an eccentric bivalve specialist in South Carolina, to an academic turned shepherd in Virginia, to a philanthropist and JBF trustee making us burgers, it was a memorable road trip for sure. To list a few our stops: Clammer Dave, SC, Charleston Farmers' Market, SC, Joyce Foods, NC, Border Springs Farm, VA, Rappahannock Cellars, VA, Barboursville Vineyards, VA, Dupont Circle Farmers' Market, Washington DC, Chelsea Market, NYC.

When we reached NYC, I was out for the count, thanks to one too many a celebratory beverage along the way. I found a quiet room in our accommodations in Soho and lay tucked in a fetal position, to recover as I needed to. Jenneffer left me some food as the rest of the gang hit the city.

The day of the event had arrived, and I was raring to be in that kitchen, head down, yet again trying to prove that I belonged. The day of prep and execution is all a blur to me today, even though there's a plethora of video footage. All I can remember is that we had sufficient professionals in the kitchen. Mind you, I was used to working essentially by myself back home. So I welcomed the extraordinary hands (kitchen lingo). From all indications, we had represented and represented well. It's always a reminder at these sorts of events of exactly what keeps us going as chefs and wine professionals. Sure, there's a fair bit of ego, but the pure joy of seeing one's work appreciated almost instantaneously is the reward that's simultaneously both unique and challenging. It was by all measures an incredibly successful event. We were certainly not the first group of chefs from Central Florida to cook at the James Beard House. But the way we executed our plan was quite likely the first of its kind. I'm not sure whether how we did it has ever been replicated. One hears of pop-up restaurants and dinners all the time, but we went on a long and thoughtful shopping trip in addition to popping-up for one night only, 1200 miles from home. We had successfully foraged along the way and prepared a meal that was quite easily greater than the sum of its parts.

Chapter 2: A TORRID PACE (2015)

I was a stone's throw away from turning 50, in early 2015, when a fourth semifinalist recognition for the prestigious James Beard – Best Chef South award came my way. I was beginning to accept these national accolades as being deserved. Admittedly, I was excited about expanding my influence and recognition in the world of food, and I was hoping to progress further, toward the self-proclaimed Oscars of the food world. Later that year, I submitted my first book *Dreaming in Spice* for consideration of a James Beard Award Best Book in the Food Advocacy Category. A month later, much to my disappointment, I received notice from the committee that my book was to be re-assigned in the General Cooking category instead. *Dreaming in Spice* was so much more than a cookbook. It was my life's story melded together with passionate focus on improving local food systems through practice and perseverance. I had secured a coveted invitation to cook my food at the prestigious James Beard House in New York City in April 2016. There was some stability in my restaurant kitchen with a sous chef and assistant sous chef who were able to hold down prep and some of the creativity needed to maintain the standards we were establishing. As far as I could gauge, I was starting to peak in my momentum as a professional chef. More on that feeling in a moment.

Meanwhile, on the academic front, Stetson University granted my application for a sabbatical leave of absence for the 2015-2016 academic year. During my sabbatical, I primarily undertook a path of research, connecting my mathematical background with an ongoing interest in food sustainability. I wrote a manuscript titled "A Traceability Index for Food" which I presented by invitation at the 2016 Farm to Table Experience & Conference in New Orleans. It is a research project I hope to revisit during my next sabbatical.

During that year, I also explored a long-standing unsolved problem in Mathematics: prove or disprove the non-revisiting path conjecture for polyhedral maps on the connected sum of three projective planes. That problem remains unsolved to this day. Also that year, I was actively involved in several high-profile events representing myself as a faculty member of Stetson University as well as a food system improvement advocate, which included lobbying the United States Congress on the issue of healthy food in schools. With my good friend, Chef William Dissen, I helped organize a gathering of chefs, farmers, food writers, and government officials at a James Beard Foundation mini boot camp for policy and action in Asheville, NC. Having contributed to some of the behind-the-scenes ranking system for the program, I was also regarded as a Senior Advisor for the James Beard Foundation Smart Catch Program.

I was firing on all cylinders as both professional chef and professional mathematician. At least, it seemed that way. Then, slowly, the curve started to flatten. I was left off the 2016 Beard Awards list, my book wasn't winning any awards although I sold every copy I printed and even left unmet demand, my assistant sous chef was getting complacent, and my sous chef was losing his drive and commitment for the restaurant life.

It seemed as if my chef life was starting to lose some mojo. From my vantage point, 2015 was an incredible year and the thought of not formally moving forward professionally was unsettling, to say the least. So, where did I go from here? Should I repetitively cruise along, braise more lamb, make more crème brûlée, create popular and even edgy specials every weekend, etc., or should I pause to reflect on where all this was going? I began to question my incessant need for recognition and for validation. I think part of it was that I began so late in life as a professional chef that I was constantly trying to prove myself as deserving of serious acknowledgment. The academic in me never stopped probing deeper into my chef mind. But chasing awards and recognitions was having a detrimental effect on my overall sense of happiness and fulfillment. Also, I was aging ever so slightly. Yet, I had a business to run, a classroom to control, and a complete commitment to continue the path of advocacy. In April of 2016, we took the show on the road one more time to cook at the prestigious James Beard house in NYC. This time, my fifth time there, it was going to be my food, exclusively. But in the true spirit of teaching and collaboration, I included my sous chef in the creation of the menu, to the extent that he wanted to be involved.

At this point, I was convinced that I was no longer obsessed with chasing awards and recognitions. However, I still needed to set purpose and direction in my professional lives. I've often asked myself: What exactly kept me going all these years as a chef? That question needed an honest answer. In fact, many of my friends and acquaintances had lost bets on how long I could keep this dual life going. Sometimes I got the feeling that outsiders looking in had the misguided impression that, you know, I would come into the restaurant, dabble a bit in the kitchen, cook some dishes, and call it a day. So, in return, I would incessantly promote my investment and dedication to the craft of cooking. I'm sure many around me thought this was pompous and arrogant. But frankly, I knew of no other way to try to make people understand that I was completely hands-on and that there were no magical switches to put necessary restaurant and business tasks on autopilot. Something had to give. I needed assistance identifying the direction of my life. The irony of preaching about sustainability to others--when my own professional life was incredibly unsustainable--was not lost on me. I guess I could have hired more staff, kept going, and kept the restaurant open. But frankly, I couldn't see how to ensure that every standard that we had worked so hard to uphold would be upheld in our absence. Others would remind me that there are scores of examples all over the world of businesses sustaining the highest of standards without the complete involvement of the founders. But as I reflected on my inability to do that, I came to realize that the answer lay in the fact that for over three decades, I had been a teacher without assistants in charge of my own work. I was never able to outsource my teaching. Despite my efforts, I've never been able to outsource my cooking.

So, while on the one hand my chef-prof life seemed to be firing on all cylinders, internally, I knew that my life was a path that could not be sustained. But I couldn't just hang it up. Why, that would be failure. The same people who advised me not to open a restaurant years ago would point to me and say, "See, we told

DREAMING IN SPICE - A Sinfully Vegetarian Odyssey

you." It was becoming apparent to me that I was continuing for others. I think that's a common way of life for many. It is something of a luxury to be able to do in life just what one wants to do for one's self. By this time, I was a much better cook than when we first opened the restaurant. I was much more informed about food systems, and most importantly, I was completely invested in the notion that through food, we can change the world for the better. So closing the restaurant was not an option. And to be sure, we would not be closing the restaurant because it wasn't successful. Instead, we would be closing the restaurant because we were so successful that our full-time dual lives were becoming unsustainable. So, we continued...

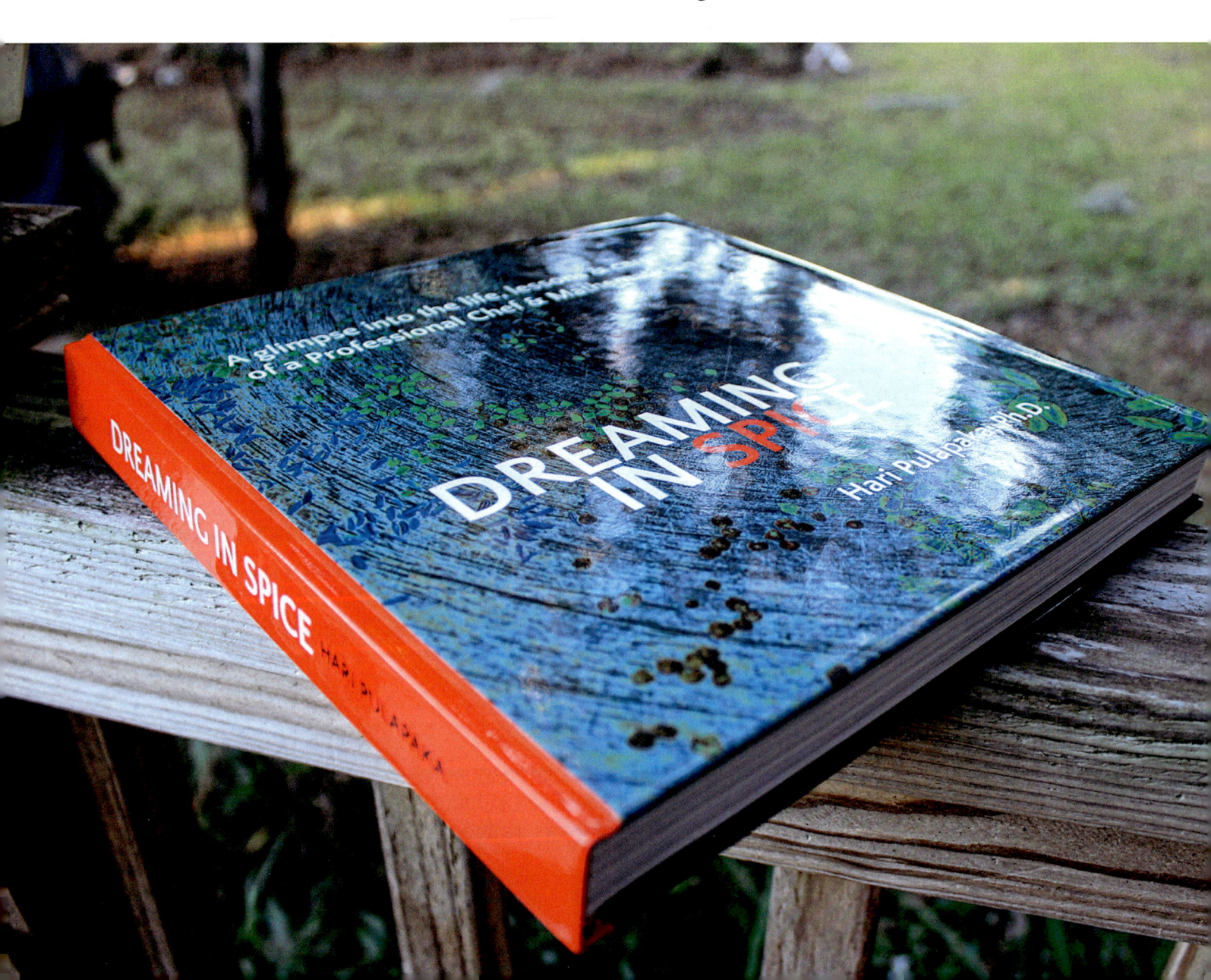

Chapter 3: GLOBAL TABLE, SUNSHINE STATE (2016)

It took me an unexpectedly long time to visit NYC for the first time. But once I did, it was love at first sight. And why wouldn't it be? I was born and raised in Mumbai, a metropolis like no other. NYC reminds me of home but not in the way one might imagine. Sure, they both have tall buildings, with New York's skyline evoking wonderment among lovers of such views, but Mumbai is catching up. It's more about the energy. The inhabitants possess a calm intensity. The word *cosmopolitan* doesn't adequately describe the demographic makeup of the two mega cities. Mumbai's history is a bit older than that of NYC, but what Mumbai has in history and indigenous culture, NYC more than makes up for in vibrancy, style, and panache. The James Beard House is an incredibly grounding space that reminds chefs that ultimately, when we cook for our guests, we are essentially welcoming you into our homes. For years, the James Beard House has been a showcase and performance space for chefs from all over the world. To be invited to cook there is an honor bestowed on only a handful of chefs. So, to have had the opportunity to cook at the house on more than one occasion--let alone five, six, or perhaps even seven times--is an honor that falls in the category of "did not see that coming."

The promotion to the event reads "Outside of operating their critically acclaimed Central Florida restaurant, powerhouse husband-and-wife team Hari and Jenneffer Pulapaka pursue ambitious careers and advocate for improving local food systems. Join us as this duo combine their enlightened outlooks and culinary prowess for a night of globally inspired, regional American cuisine." We had to pull out all the gastronomic stops. So, we did. While the formal menu was not 100% vegetarian, it could easily have been curated that way. And that is the way I think about food. To me, dishes are templates. Recipes are important and necessary, but they are rooted in templates. This is the single most significant intersection between my mathematician brain and my chef brain: the ability to use abstraction as a guiding principle in my creativity. To complement the vast globally-inspired menu, Jenneffer curated amazing wine pairings as well as three spectacular cocktails that were fitting, delicious, and elevated. Mind you, this is not an easy task for any wine and beverage professional. But Jenneffer is no ordinary sommelier. Her ability to process information, flavor profiles, and contrasting textures knows no bounds. I've met many sommeliers in my life, but easily, Jenneffer is the best of the best when it comes to pairing foods with the perfect beverages. Her vegetarian palate has been trained to chase flavor and nuance. Sometimes, less is more, and being a vegetarian allows Jenneffer to have a greater ability to detect nuances on her finely tuned taste buds.

It was Monday, April 4th, 2016. By 4:00 a.m., I was already tossing and turning in the hotel bed because I knew that it was going to be a long and exciting day in the Beard House kitchen. By 6:00 am, I had kissed Jenneffer good morning and left the hotel. After loading up some of the provisions that I had brought with me from DeLand, I headed to the West Village in Manhattan. Access to the kitchen normally starts at 8:00

a.m. But by 7:00 a.m., I was already pacing in front of 167 West 12 Street, eager to enter, organize, and just sit down quietly to find the focus I needed for the day. The passing minutes led to half hours; half hours led to hours. By 1:00 pm, it was a buzzing kitchen with my sous chef, student volunteers, of course Jenneffer, our friends Melissa and Jim, and my chef friend, Aarthi Sampath. It was a complex menu for any culinary team, let alone our modest team. The formal start time of the event was 7:00 p.m. But by 5:30, there were already visitors from the James Beard Foundation, friends, and well-wishers. By 6:00 p.m., photographers started pouring in, bloggers started chatting, and many wanted a moment of my time for a quick interview. I, of course, was singularly focused on what I needed to do, what we needed to do, for the next several hours. In some ways this felt like a last hurrah, even though it clearly was not. As the passed hors d'oeuvres started making their way out of the kitchen, the journey had begun. For the next three hours, the 60 or so guests were going to be subjected to globally-inspired, thoughtfully-sourced food that didn't come out of any playbook. Rather, the dishes represented the sensibilities of my own taste buds honed over time, kissed by global inspirations, and ultimately, they evolved into creations that represented a sum of my parts as a chef and human being. I reached for the stars and dug deep within my mind and soul as a chef. I represented my style of cooking and my need for honest story-telling via deep and bold flavors. Looking back, I would not change an iota. It is exactly the menu I would curate today, years later.

Every dish was meticulously described and conceived. Hors d'oeuvres like spring onion tartlet with dill, wildflower honey and coarse mustard; Mumbai samosa chaat with date-smoked tomato chutney; Meyer lemon ricotta and spinach gnudi with green garbanzo bean hummus, tomato jam and spiced almonds; and Hudson Valley French toast with apple compote, bourbon caramel, and pistachio creme fraîche represented only a small sample of the sinfully vegetarian options that night. Many non-vegetarian components and dishes were on the menu. But every one of them was easily adaptable to being decadently vegetarian. And that is how I like to think about food. Ingredients inspire me in very specific ways. But the ingredients are not entirely necessary for the creations. I always imagine dishes conceptually. The recipes and the execution come later.

By all indications, it was a wildly successful evening. During the wrap-up chat with the guests, I became somewhat emotional. In the moment, my mind flashed back to growing up modestly, the kid from Kalina, Mumbai, dreaming about making something of myself someday, living up to my mother's expectations. In my teenage years, that desire formalized into a tangible plan of coming to America someday. How did this culinary journey come about? I mean, I never planned to be a chef. I simply wanted to study, make my parents and family proud, and justify the trust they placed in me. How on earth did my life follow this path? I was consciously feeling these thoughts while standing in front of all the guests... including the leadership of the James Beard Foundation. Somehow, I found the words to thank them for being present and to thank everyone who helped make the event the success that it was. But on a broader level, my mind

DREAMING IN SPICE - A Sinfully Vegetarian Odyssey

was wandering into hitherto unknown places. As was customary, we shared a glass or two of wine at the end of the night to toast the spectacular day, in a spectacular venue, for a spectacular cause. But at some level, I imagined that my chef life was going to change moving forward. I didn't know exactly how, but I did know why. I was no longer interested in doing the same old cooking in my kitchen. From the day I entered this profession in 2004, everything I've done has had a sense of urgency. The restaurant opened during the toughest economic crisis of many generations. But for eight straight years, we stuck through it, elevating our game every single day. Yet the thought of continuing along the same path seemed, at the very least, unsustainable. Something had to give. Changes had to be made. Passions had to be revived. So we went back to the drawing board.

Chapter 4: RE-FOCUSING ENERGIES

I was still dashing to the local farms every week, scrambling to the grocery store almost every day, and schlepping everything here and there, both with the restaurant and my teaching. Something had to give. I seemed to have the energy, but it seemed to be expelled by partaking in minutiae. Even I could see that it was a matter of time before a shutdown would be inevitable. But we had to mitigate against that stage. We returned to the drawing board. As an introspective exercise, some questions needed honest answers. What did I enjoy the most about cooking? This was at the heart of any resolution towards my chef life sustainability moving forward. What did I really enjoy? Where exactly was the joy? What was I hanging on to?

Then, one day, it came to us. From the outset, we've had a chef's table option on the menu. In the beginning, it was as whimsical and brash as opening a new restaurant with no restaurant experience. But I was stubborn then and I had become even more stubborn now. The greatest joy engulfed me when I was able to cook food with the attention to detail that I knew it took and then present the food myself to a guest, while sharing with them both the journey of my thought process as well as the logistics and technicalities of execution, all of which culminated in a summarized description of the composition. Pshew. Of course, these were quick conversations. After all, I was a teacher, so I'd become very adept at summarizing my thoughts... although I suspect others might suggest that I tend to ramble. Yet in my mind, the next sentence has a purpose just as much as the current one does. Nevertheless, we concluded that we were at our happiest at the restaurant when we were able to articulate to our guests our vision, inspirations, passions, and values. We then determined that the restaurant would phase into a concept in which we were going to be serving food and wine, curated and developed via menus rooted in themes and special events.

Wait. What? Why couldn't we leave a good thing alone? The restaurant was wildly successful and here we were about to make some dramatic changes again! But then again, maybe that's the point. Maybe that's why this restaurant was so well-received and so beloved (albeit sometimes despised) not just in little old DeLand, but throughout Central Florida. We remained relevant every single day of our existence, but when we made changes, they came from a place driven by a sincere desire to improve. We were making changes not simply for our convenience. Rather, we were making changes so that we could continue to improve as professionals. By now, we had already moved to a service-included pricing structure. There was no more tipping at the restaurant. But now we were going to do something even more focused. For sure, since the restaurant's inception in 2008, we were pushing for sustainable sourcing, environmentally conscious business practices, an inclusive environment, an opposition of bigotry, and bold public stances on hotbed political and social issues. None of it was because we thought they would make our business more profitable. Rather, all of them were because we always believed that what we did could not define who we were; rather, *how* we do defines who we are. We had clearly not subscribed to the adage that politics and business should not mix. Every business decision we made, we understood to be intertwined with politics on many levels. It is the nature of food and beverage. But ultimately, we were in the business of creating a special occasion restaurant that delivered on quality and value, night in and night out. The accolades had been wonderful and were much appreciated, but we could not imagine that we would change anything even without them.

By September 2016, we had begun Year 9, and I was alone in my kitchen, again. I could just hear our friends and foes alike, muttering among themselves, "this can't last...". We began curating events that featured cuisines of lands near and far, reacting with nimble perseverance when there was a need predicated by circumstance, disaster, injustice, and even, celebration. The restaurant had formally transitioned to an events-only concept. It took about a year for some folks to comprehend that our events were not exclusive and private but, almost always, open to the public. Event tickets had to pre-purchased and service was included. We had already eliminated tipping. Every restaurant employee was being paid at least double the minimum hourly wage, even as the work expectations had become much less stressful for all. Almost every event sold out, ensuring guaranteed profits and minimal food waste. If there is a model for restaurant efficiency, we had developed one. Everything inspired us, but nothing felt like work. I was cooking with joy and purpose again. Vegetarian and vegan-only events sold out alongside predictably popular themes that were not in the slightest bit plant-forward. In almost every instance, I offered a vegetarian version of the menu, for which there always were takers. Interestingly, I would often observe guests who were not vegetarian sample some of the vegetarian options on our tasting menus, only to discover that were they not only delicious but often fascinatingly creative and ultimately satisfying. It just reminded us that placing plant-forward food in a focused manner on our menus was not only the correct approach, but, gastronomically, made all the sense in the world. Our menus were degustation menus consisting of three, five, and chef's choice tasting menus. But moving forward, even that routine began to weigh on me. Why couldn't we have a somewhat normal life and continue to feed our community thoughtfully and deliciously? It's becoming increasingly difficult for me to fathom how chefs are able to pass their menus off to others to cook their food. I didn't get into professional cooking to just own restaurants. One of the very first events in our new concept was a Sunday brunch at a local farm, which we followed with a sinfully vegetarian feast. Slowly, word got around about what we were doing. Mind you, the press was having a hard time featuring us in their usual style of reviewing restaurants. After all, we no longer had a set schedule even though we publicized upcoming events well in advance. We had gained an immeasurable amount of creative freedom. If a flower inspired us, we could create an entire event based around that. Evidently, my cooking improved even more. How could it not?

Being a consummate academic, I was secretly intrigued by the idea of attaining the highest formal certification in the culinary arts in North America. The need for professional formality mirrored some of the same reasons I went to culinary school. Perhaps it was yet another attempt to prove that I belonged. For a couple of years leading up to this point, I had laid down the foundation, with the American Culinary Federation, that I was interested in pursuing the CMC exam. My application was complete, and it was being considered for the candidate pool for the next time the exam would be offered. It had been years since the organization put out a call for candidates for this highly prized certification. Just as we had dared to open a restaurant during the toughest economic crisis of our generation, my general sense of boredom with the same old routine dared me to attempt the rigorous eight-day certification exam. The passing rate was historically low. By some measures, the test was antiquated. Yet I valued the foundational rigor built into the exam. So, by May of 2017, I was sure that I was going to attempt the exam.

That summer, I was informed by the ACF that I was chosen to be a candidate for the exam and that the exam was scheduled for November 2017. The stars had aligned. Even though we were not going to be open for regular hours anymore, by placing the CMC on my plate as it were, the pressure was on and my chef life again had purpose. I began practicing in the solitude of my kitchen. We even hosted a couple of events grounded in some of the competencies of the exam. On the one hand, I had never practiced for anything in the culinary world as I was doing for this exam. But on the other hand, I knew that surprises were in store for me, especially given the formality wrapped in old world expectations. Nevertheless, there was no turning back, and thousands of dollars later, Jenneffer and I boarded a flight from Orlando to Detroit. All my kitchen tools fit in one bag, a small one at that. I ordered a few more all-white chef coats, some white aprons, a white toque, and a few tall white chef hats. I didn't own any of this, so that in and of itself was an indication of how different my candidacy was going to be relative to the others at the testing center. We arrived in Detroit and I felt like I was back in culinary school. It appeared I had everything to gain and nothing to lose. Yet, when it came to my drive as a chef, I had quite a bit to lose. And I didn't know what I would gain.

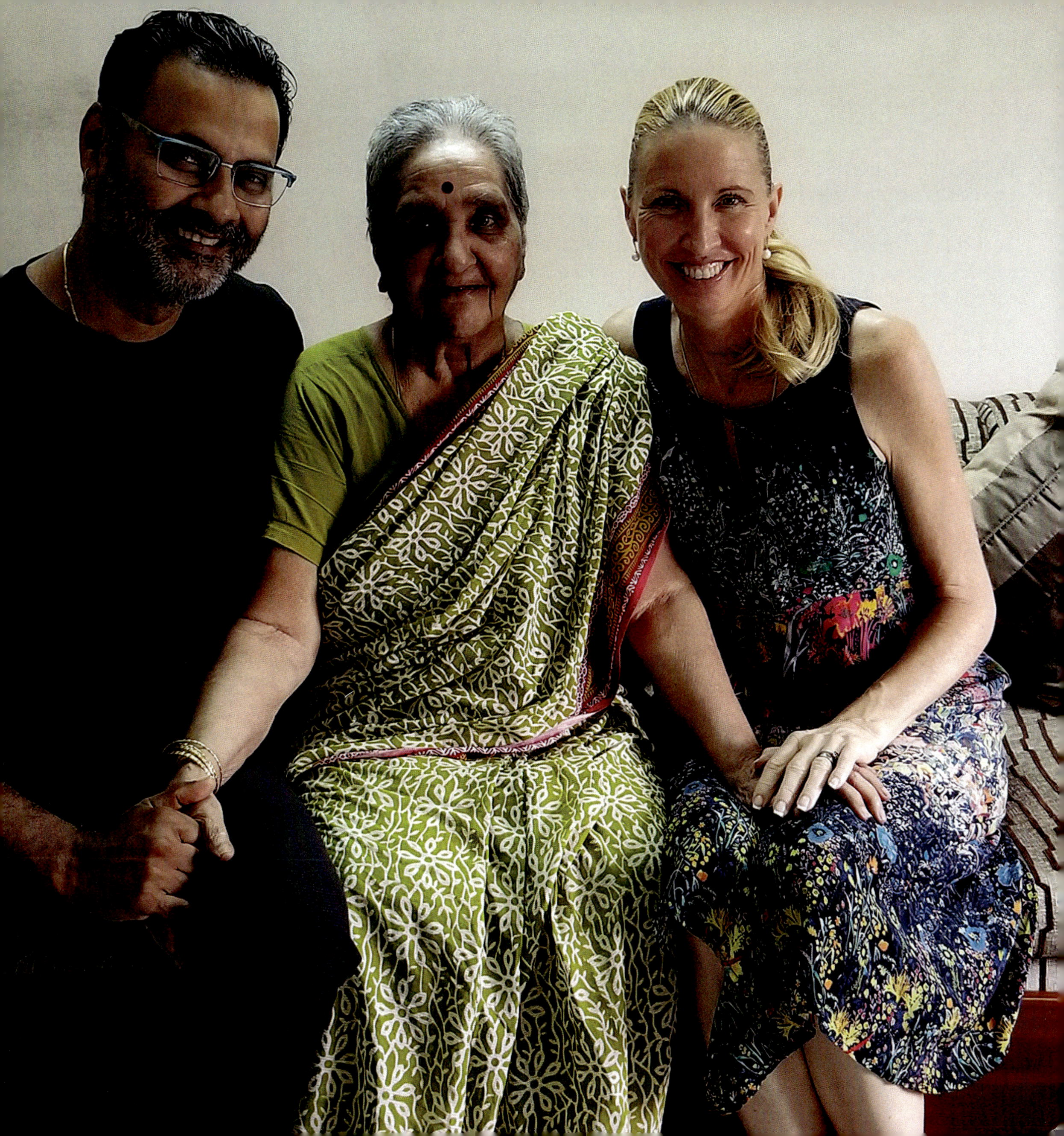

Chapter 5: CERTIFIED MASTER CHEF PRACTICAL (2017)

To be clear, the certification exam is not a competition, or at least it's not intended as such. It comprises a series of hurdles and tasks aimed at evaluating professional chef competencies at the highest formal level. However, it's challenging to be unaffected in a kitchen when there are so many watchful eyes and, sometimes, voices. Day One was an orientation of sorts. The entire atmosphere sent me right back to culinary school. In many regards, I was the least experienced when it came to certification processes and expectations. I was confident in my ability to cook creative and tasty food. However, after having gone through the Certified Executive Chef (CEC) exam twice, I knew that it was equally important that every step I took and every decision I made was consistent with the expectations of the many chefs evaluating us. There were only 67 CMCs in the United States and it seemed as though they were all in the room. At the end of the day, of course, I could only do what I was going to be able to do. But, come what might, I was going to dig deep and stay focused. The least I could do would be to overcome obvious inadequacies. Failure (to put forth my best effort) was not an option.

Day One: Healthy Cooking
The night before, I had already submitted recipes and a nutritional analysis of my menu. My basket included a whole leg of lamb with the bone in and a whole Arctic Char (a fish like salmon). I remember wondering why, if we really want to be healthy, are we forcing these meats on the menu? But I understood the intent. I was going to be evaluated on my ability to quickly and efficiently break down the leg of lamb and the fish. I struggled with the lamb. Partly because I was using knives I had never used before, wearing clothes I had never worn before, hadn't practiced nearly as much as I needed to, and was overly eager to please and impress. In other words, I was out of my comfort zone. Within the first 10 minutes of my working on the lamb leg, I cut myself. It was sort of downhill from there. I burnt the farro and overthought the garnishes. Dishes were to be presented using proper Russian platter service. Again, a first for me. The price I was paying for not having practiced obsessively for months on end, sometimes years, under the mentorship of certified master chefs, was clearly showing. Nevertheless, I presented all my dishes on time and completely. I was hoping that the evaluators would be impressed by the way I rebounded from my early setbacks. During the feedback interview that afternoon, it became apparent to me that mistakes were going to prove costly. Just as during the CEC, the greatest criticism related to my lack of organization relative to the standards. I guess after I cut myself, the instinctive cook in me came out and I just started cooking. But the expectations of the CMC are a bit different. When my score was revealed, it was obvious that I had dug a bit of a hole for myself. If I were to continue on to the next competency, I would have to ace the next task. Day 2 would be about classical, fussy, mostly overrated food. But I was going to give it my all, because what other option was there? And fundamentally, the techniques illustrated more complete utilization of ingredients in a kitchen. Who could argue with that ideal?

Day Two: Buffet Catering

Over the next two days, I was expected to produce a lavish display of charcuterie prepared in some of the oldest traditions of classical French cuisine. There was nothing vegetarian or comfortable about this. It's not the food I eat, even though it is food that I learned to prepare in culinary school. Evidently, this task was not in my comfort zone. During the first day, even though I was feeling great about the flavor development and the instinctive cooking I was doing, some of the supervising evaluators were correcting me often. I felt somewhat bullied. Yet I held my own. I justified every decision I had made. I kept cooking. At the end of the first day of the second test, while everybody else had already prepared their aspic-coated platters, I poured my aspic--but not without spilling most of it in the walk-in cooler, with only two minutes to spare in the allotted time window. It was becoming increasingly clear that only through grit and determination would the next day culminate in a successful buffet display that lived up to the minimum standards of the examination. Surprising myself, I held on to a glimmer of hope. At the end of Day 3 of the exam, I was called into the proverbial principal's office for a conversation. The testing administrator and head of certification for ACF began in the usual but seemingly genuine way of telling me all the things that I did well. Still, at the end of the day, my average combined score was below the minimum necessary to continue in the exam. As one chef pointed out, they were confident that the next time I would be successful. They also recognized that I never got to cook my food. But that's OK, because I didn't come here to cook my food. I understood that the exam was focused on technical ability and proficiency. Certainly, if a few missteps could have been avoided, I might have continued. Compared to my colleagues, I clearly wasn't equipped or prepared. While they were rolling in pre-set carts of *mise en place* during the setup window, I was trying to remember where I had left my backpack. I made some mistakes from which I thought I recovered, but at this level, mistakes are not permitted. There was still some subjectivity. After all, as artists, we are going to differ, but the journey had toughened me.

Life is about moving forward, not looking back. Life and death happen whether we like them or not. I believe we should always reflect and think back, because doing so helps us derive inspirations and motivations to do better, both in the moment and moving forward. So I wasn't going to blame anyone but myself. I really did my best. I accomplished some tasks I didn't think I could. I might not have passed the exam, I might have been chopped early, but I had clearly improved as a chef. I dared to choose a journey in my professional chef career that undoubtedly made me a better chef, improved my technique, and, in a strange way, gave me some closure. I will never be a certified master chef, but I will also never shy away from a challenge that gives me the opportunity to improve as a human being. So we returned to DeLand and I dug in stirring another pot of grits.

Chapter 6: SEVEN COURSES SEVEN COUNTRIES (2017)

It was Sunday, January 29, 2017. We had just completed a wonderfully creative and inspiring event with the MIND Institute, a non-profit dedicated to improving Mathematics education for children of all ages. We were flying back from John Wayne Airport in Orange County, CA to Hartsfield-Jackson Airport, in Atlanta, en route to DeLand. After landing, our plane had come to a stop on the tarmac in Atlanta because of weather-related delays, and we waited for a long time. As was my habit, I turned on my cell phone and began mindlessly perusing the headlines of the day. Shortly, I was caught off guard by a "breaking news" headline which read, "President Bars Refugees and Citizens from 7 Muslim Countries." My jaw dropping, I had to re-read the headline to believe my eyes before being able to read the full article. As it sank in, I felt my irritation growing. I turned to Jenneffer and may have said "f*&% that!" I had to vent in defiance somewhere, somehow, so I turned to social media (Facebook), chose a bright purple background, and, choosing my word length carefully, typed "I'm inspired to create a special event showcasing the cuisine of Syria, Sudan, Libya, Iran, Iraq, Somalia, and Yemen." And I sat there quietly...Hundreds of comments and reactions later, our pilot still waiting to taxi to a gate, I responded "Great to see all the support. We're stuck on a runway in Atlanta having landed for 2 hours with no relief in sight. Nationwide computer issues with Delta Airlines. We were supposed to return to DeLand tonight which is looking doubtful. Regarding the event, you can bet I will be contacting many of you!" This was the beginning of the inspiration for what was to become our "7 Courses 7 Countries" dinner on the street.

Over the years, I've been frequently reminded to shut up and cook. But every instance of that kind of reprimand stimulates deeply rebellious feelings against servitude. As a food advocate, I am of the firm belief that some of us cannot just *shut up and cook*. We are not defined by what we do but rather, we are defined by how we do and who we are as human beings. It is something I stand up against, the idea that we don't have a voice because we're workers.

Not unexpectedly, the decision to protest peacefully by celebrating the foods of the regions involved was overwhelmingly well-supported. However, there was the occasional example or two of opposition and boycott. One such reaction reminded me "politics is not good for business." Many local food writers interviewed me about my intentions and goals. So many of them asked me a version of the question "what do you say to people who tell you that it's foolish and self-destructive to mix business and politics?" And my answer is (essentially) always the same: It's all politics, folks. The decisions we make as consumers make their way into the marketplace as a sign of the overall demand. Producers, on the other hand, react to the demand and, in many cases, lead consumers with creative marketing. Amidst all this interplay, the extent of lobbying by special interest groups in Washington, DC, and other world centers of political influence is of an order of magnitude unimaginable for most consumers. So, yeah, food and politics are strongly connected.

The seven countries were Iraq, Iran, Libya, Somalia, Sudan, Syria, and Yemen. The seven courses, however, needed some careful thought and organization. Because I am from India, I never once felt that I was out of my comfort zone, to take a deep dive into the cuisines of these countries. If anything, at times it seemed I would have to temper my natural instincts to go big and bold. I would need to learn to finesse the ingredients and delicate spices to honor the culinary traditions of these great regions of the world. When word got around about the dinner, many farmers and producers of sustainable fruits, vegetables, meats, and seafood reached out to me, offering donations of ingredients to help with costs. The strength of their support elevated my energy and commitment to my belief. Jenneffer was, always, the wind beneath my sails. The attendees of the sold-out 300+ street event came for a myriad of reasons. Some came to express their solidarity and support to our stand. Others came to support friends and family. A few were curious about the event itself. But almost every guest was intrigued by the notion of tasting flavors from countries that they probably hadn't imagined as sources of food inspirations, let alone places that they might visit someday. I have not been to any of these countries. But chefs routinely dig deep and explore our own culinary creativity through the time-tested specialties of lands near and far. So I went for it. The food served family-style was a long and winding road, touching tradition, interpretation, honesty, and resistance.

As I began studying the cuisines of the countries involved, I quickly realized that developing the correct flavor was not going to be an issue for most of it. However, without having traveled to these faraway lands, how could I possibly be authentic? But was that really the point? The event was aimed at bringing the cultures of these countries to our little community through the medium of food, and even if I missed on the exact flavors, we would take the time to learn just a little bit more about cultures and societies in ways that we perhaps would not have otherwise. That was enough. Just as I design any menu, I became inspired by seasonal and local ingredients and ways to use them in dishes that were indigenous to these countries. This is where formal training helps a lot. At the end of the day, recipes are different, flavors are different, but there are only so many cooking techniques around the world. That, singularly, is the power of educating oneself in sound cooking techniques. Mind you, one doesn't have to go to culinary school for that. Nowadays it is possible to teach oneself formal cooking techniques, for free, using a vast array of online and other resources. But don't be wrapped up in the recipes. Extract, more importantly, the technique and the layering of flavors--and, to some degree, the relative proportions among ingredients.

As I wove my way through the cuisines of Syria, Yemen, Sudan, Iraq, Iran, Libya, and Somalia, the menu for this important event in my chef career began unfolding in a natural and meaningful way. The task of making so much food from our tiny restaurant kitchen with the modest equipment and storage space we had was challenging enough. I would also have to decide how service would unfold, especially when we had allotted only two hours for over 300 guests to be served seven dishes. Then it came to me. How about if I placed room temperature food at the table before the guests even arrived? And that's how I began planning the menu. After an iteration or two, I landed on the following menu: Ocala honey labneh (Syria), split pea and fresh garbanzo hummus (Syria), flatbread (Yemen), ful, spices, and parsley (Sudan), wagyu beef and potato kubba (Iraq), local tomato and English cucumber shirazi salad (Iran), polow, saffron, raisins, cashews (Iran), roasted corvina, spices, olive oil (Iraq), camel-duck kebab, cilantro (Libya), lamb maraq, spices (Somalia), local veggies, couscous (Syria), saffron rice pudding, rose water, and dates (Iran).

I scratched and borrowed, spending close to a week in between teaching classes to make all the food. I made more food than we needed, which was picked up by a local church. When the dust settled, we were able to donate $10,000 to the International Rescue Committee (IRC), a long-standing non-profit with a stated mission to respond to the world's worst humanitarian crises and help people to survive, recover, and gain control of their future. I have no idea how we pulled it off. But what I do know is that the human spirit, civility, and decency triumphed. And perhaps most of all, integrity and democracy triumphed.

Between April 2017 and April 2018, we exploded with creativity, philanthropy, and style through our special events. I was cooking some of my best food. Dinners showcased sinfully vegetarian options, classic French dishes in the style of Escoffier, soulful and deep-flavored Indian food, a jaunt through Europe in 12 culinary acts, sustainable seafood, flavors from the islands near and far, food from a recent trip to Mexico, an event showcasing some of our greatest hits from the restaurant, Native American food on the street on the eve of the Trail of Tears, a love affair with Tuscany, fall harvest in Central Florida, holiday celebrations, etc. Interspersed through such events were events that were meaningful beyond the food - a fundraiser to support local women's projects, a fundraiser to support an organization dedicated to celebrating women inspiring change and community development, a fundraiser for the hurricane-ravaged island of Puerto Rico, a fundraiser to aid the rescue efforts to combat the damaging fires in California and especially to benefit animal rescues, a fundraiser to support a local fourth-generation farmer we purchased from regularly. (Said farmer would later scold me because he inferred that I didn't care about raising funds for local causes. In the spirit of killing with kindness, we followed with a fundraiser brunch on his farm.) Rounding off our philanthropy was a fundraiser to help kick off a local community garden amid what might be considered a food desert. But what was to transpire in early 2018 changed everything.

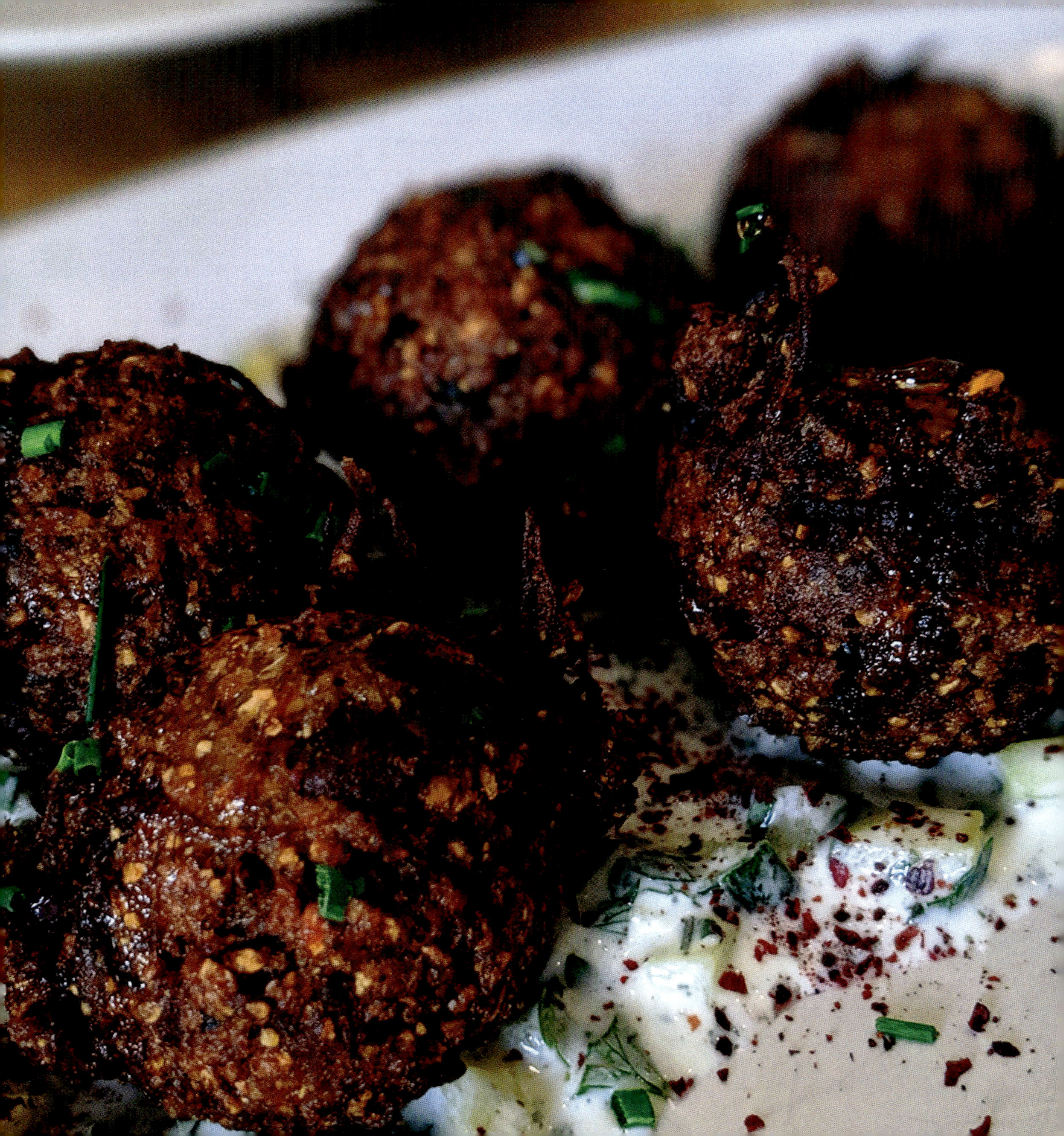

Chapter 7: SOLIDARITY SUNDAY (2018)

You can't make this up. It seemed like the Twilight Zone. Barely a year had passed since the Seven Courses, Seven Countries dinner when the President riled up yet another global controversy by referring to Haiti, El Salvador, and several countries from Africa as "shithole" countries. News of this blasphemy began to spread like a fungus among us. While the media was getting wrapped up in how to challenge this, all I could think was, my gosh, a person with so much influence just passed a broad, sweeping brush over the humanity, culture, and incredible food history and tradition from a large swathe of the world's population. In an encore extension of "f*&% that!", I was determined, once again, to dive into cuisines that evidently spoke to me but are largely unfamiliar to the North American audience. Of course, my ulterior motive was to take a stand against what was becoming routine occurrences of condescension and tyranny. So, in my usual way, I began studying the cuisines of countries that might help me develop a composed, family-style menu.

We put out a call that we were going to host another street event outside the restaurant and this time, we were going to name it the "Shithole Dinner." The ensuing reactions extended beyond my wildest expectations. News about our announcement spread rapidly and was, dare I say, trending. Overnight the announcement drew thousands of likes, some dislikes, and hundreds of shares. Then we became aware of a growing sense of anger within our own community in Central Florida from the very same constituency that we were supporting. It became apparent to us that the term "shithole" in the title of our dinner was perpetuating the very same damagingly derogatory language that we were supposedly standing up against.

One activist threatened to protest during our dinner. I reached out to this individual to allay his fears, to introduce myself, and to provide some context and history about our work. Once it became apparent to him that we were on the same side, doing this dinner was no longer an issue. But the culprit term needed to be changed. So, we agreed to rename the event *Solidarity Sunday*. This time, we hosted over 400 guests on the little street outside our restaurant. But the event didn't come to fruition without additional challenges along the way. We were required to obtain insurance for our event, naturally. Our existing insurance agent for the restaurant was, let's just say, politically conservative. He and his office provided no assistance whatsoever. In fact, the verdict was that no company would be able to provide insurance for our event because, in his words, it was a "racially charged" event. He blamed it on the parent insurance company yet showed no desire to shop elsewhere on his loyal client's behalf. So, we changed insurance agents, switching to a company that came through for us, and the rest is history.

I decided on a menu featuring ten dishes from nine countries in a family-style dinner. All proceeds were to be donated to the Florida Immigrant Coalition, a statewide alliance of immigrants' rights organizations. We sold 400 tickets in about a week. This dinner was already larger than the Seven Courses, Seven Countries dinner from the prior year, and that event had severely tested my tiny kitchen and our resources. But experience taught me that this time we needed to make an even stronger statement. We pushed ourselves and I dug deep while thinking through logistics, execution, and efficiency. I knew that there was going to be a dish from Haiti and a dish from El Salvador, which left seven dishes to be chosen... from all of Africa. Trying to choose seven dishes from the continent of Africa is like choosing your favorite bean from hundreds of varieties of legumes. So, I resorted to an academic way of thinking about food. We needed to have small bites, medium bites, and large bites. And the flavors needed to range from gentle and approachable to robust. Ultimately, I chose an iconic dish from each of the following nine countries: Ethiopia, Haiti, Kenya, Somalia, Ghana, Liberia, Nigeria, Cameroon, and El Salvador. Mind you, I haven't been to any of these countries because I don't count on a cruise stop at Disney's private island in Haiti to represent the country. How dared I? I didn't know, I was just going to read and learn and do my best. And if someone was going to challenge me on whether a specific dish was authentic or traditional, I was simply going to look them in the face and say "I did my best. Thank you for being here." Fortunately, I did not have to use that passive-aggressive language with anyone before, during, or after Solidarity Sunday. I presented these dishes, to be served family-style, alongside the note "These dishes represent the inspirations for my creations. I do not pretend to claim authenticity, but rather, only my interpretation of and respect for tradition, culture, and flavor. Thank you for your love and support."

Dirik ak Pwa (Haiti) Doro Wat (Ethiopia), Misr Eat (Ethiopia), Sukumi Wiki, (Kenya), Ayamese (Nigeria), Jollof (Ghana), Ndole (Cameroon), Pupusa (El Salvador), Kelewele (Ghana), Songi (Senegal). Six of these dishes were already vegetarian, and the remaining had versions that were. This is how I think about vegetarian food. (More on that in Chapter 11.) And after it was all said and done, we had raised $10,000 for a regional non-profit organization with a mission to protect the rights of immigrants and other marginalized workers in the United States. Food brings people together. Food also transports us to places we may never visit. Thanks to the information age we find ourselves in, recipes and stories about food are practically at our fingertips. While it is true that the information is only as good as the provider of that information, there is no questioning the fact that with each passing day, we are learning more and more about each other as human beings. Food is truly a universal language. You don't have to understand any spoken word *per se*. Simply reading about and tasting proper food--food grounded in culture and tradition--gives us a meaningful glimpse of a people.

The final two years of our existence at the restaurant in its current incarnation gave us a chance to truck around the globe as we featured cuisine and story-steeped special events. Of course, I have my favorites. And I also have my comfort zones. But I took the opportunity to explore new cuisines and new flavors. And in doing so, I became a better chef. I also became a better human being. And if I haven't, it's my own fault.

Chapter 8: NEW BEGINNINGS

By now, I was being recruited to develop and teach food-related courses at Stetson University. The first example was an Honors course that explored food systems and empowered others to become more knowledgeable about sustainable practices. The end goal was to provide tangible tools leading to positive behavior among students. I urged the students to create a sinfully vegetarian potluck dinner at the end of the course. I was impressed by the initiative, creativity, and excitement students brought to this assignment. Cauliflower crust pizza, zoodles, and lentil stew were the highlights of our time together. The experience got me thinking. Why couldn't I meld my dual professional lives into one? What if I implored the university to pursue food studies in the curriculum?

This was the beginning of several semesters in a row of my teaching both first year seminars as well as junior seminars on food-related topics. The experiences were rewarding because I began learning again. On the other hand, the usual dose of student lethargy and apathy was hard to digest. When it comes to food, I can't imagine even a single individual not being invested in one way or another. As unrealistic as that is, that is how I've conducted myself as a working chef for all this time. With each instance of a food-related course, I was discovering that academia is fraught with bureaucracy, not unlike certain aspects of government. Academia is not particularly nimble. So, after noting the writing on the wall in relation to the half-hearted approach to a food studies program, I threw in the towel and continued back to the Mathematics classroom and to the restaurant kitchen. And just like that, of my own volition, out went any aspirations of combining the two professions in a very formal and high level way. At least, for now.

I've juggled this dual-profession life for the past 15 years and, to ad lib for a moment, I've learned a thing or two because I've seen a thing or two. My cooking brain is an amalgamation of abstract mathematical thoughts and applied cooking experience. However, yet again, I could not see a light at the end of the proverbial tunnel. I mean, did I really need to make another batch of tikka masala sauce? Or make another batch of crème brûlée? I didn't need to, but I felt as though I had to. Often, we are faced with forks in the road that are either self-defined or imposed. In my case, it felt as though I was meandering through the tree trunk of life, an enviable path. Yet more and more frequently, I was being tempted with the branches of life. I knew that my intensity was waning. Furthermore, I didn't see the point, and my motivation was suffering. It was becoming increasingly difficult to sustain the pace of the past 15 years, by reasonable estimates 20% of my expected life span. Sure, I could continue for another year or maybe two, but at what cost? What else was there to prove? We had certainly showed them, and they--or rather, their opinion--didn't matter anymore. It seemed like the perfect time to make a bold decision and carve out the most meaningful path for moving forward. Perhaps because of paranoia, or perhaps because of over three decades of a prof life in charge of classrooms with no teaching assistance, I suffer from control issues. This explains why both my books have been self-published. I've never understood how chefs can outsource their food. It's not that I don't trust others. Well, maybe a little. But more, it's that when the art is not standardized, how can one replicate it? In fact, maybe that's the point. Maybe there's no need to replicate it. So, it was time to look for a way to keep the core of what we had built but allow for new ideas and new energy to sustain its future.

By introspective reflection, I've often tried to better understand the interplay between Mathematics and cooking. Are you ready?

Nerd Alert!

LEFT BRAIN versus RIGHT BRAIN?
What is the connection between cooking and Mathematics, you ask? Mathematics is the queen of all sciences because it is the foundation and language of the scientific world. At its core lies an ever-increasing set of facts (theorems) which have been proved without a shadow of scientific doubt. For every theorem, there exist multiple, equally interesting, and significant unsolved problems. To explore Mathematics, one often needs only imagination, some skill, and a bare minimum list of gadgets (pen, paper, pencil). We are what we eat (are we?), and food is my metaphor for life. To prepare good food, one often needs only imagination, some skill, and a bare minimum set of (good) ingredients. There are fundamental food-based facts, and while most Mathematics is developed outside the context of food, my life weaves its way through both worlds.

Here are my 10 food theorems inspired by well-known theorems of Mathematics. I present them light-heartedly and without proof because unlike Mathematics, when it comes to food, one person's proof is another's counterexample.

1. FUNDAMENTAL THEOREM OF CALCULUS
Differentiating unique flavors is inverse to integrating additional ingredients.

2. TRAVELING SALESMAN PROBLEM
A traveling salesman's biggest problem is that he rarely enjoys a home-cooked meal, but he can rest assured that his travel is efficient and easy on the wallet.

3. CENTRAL LIMIT THEOREM
Upon slow roasting in a dry pan, the average flavor of a sample of spices from a large collection of stale spices is within acceptable standards, despite the inadequacy of each individual spice.

4. L'HÔPITAL'S RULE
Challenging the limit of a recipe's ratios can sometimes land you in a hospital.

5. HANDSHAKING LEMMA
In any food system network, the total number of instances of inflow & outflow of ingredients is equal to twice the number of collaboration links. The vertices consist of consumers, producers, and distributors.

6. FUNDAMENTAL THEOREM OF ARITHMETIC
Every dish is a product of ingredients and steps, including repetitions. The final flavor is unique, up to the order of steps and proportions of ingredients.

7. FUNDAMENTAL THEOREM OF LINEAR PROGRAMMING
Consider the problem of optimizing the flavor of food subject to the constraints of varying but bounded palates. An optimal solution is the result of adding an extreme ingredient or lies along a balanced approach with optimal ingredients and techniques.

8. CANTOR'S THEOREM
For any pantry of ingredients, the number of dishes possible is always greater than the number of ingredients in the pantry.

9. DEMOIVRE'S FORMULA
The five senses (salty, sweet, sour, bitter, and savory) of any food-related experience contribute to the most important consideration of good food: taste. In the equation that relates these five senses, it is reasonable to assume that salty=essential (e), savory=i (the imaginary unit), sweet = π, sour = 1, and bitter = 0. In the mathematical world, $e^{i\pi}+1=0$. So, it remains to be inferred that salty$^{(savory)(sweet)}$+sour=bitter. The difficulty will be in defining the operations in the formula as they relate to food and/or its consumption.

10. BINOMIAL THEOREM
The sum of all possible choices made in a mom and pop restaurant is a result of the collective power of the two forces.

Chapter 9: BEING VEGETARIAN: WHY AND HOW

Vegetarianism is practiced around the world for several reasons--some historic and traditional, others contemporary and progressive. Here, I've laid out only a few.

Religion

Many major religions of the world prescribe a meatless life. Respect for the sanctity of all sentient beings is a cornerstone of Jainism (mainly in India) practiced by approximately 7 million people around the globe. Buddhism and Hinduism also have interpretations that dictate a vegetarian diet. Certainly, even Christianity and Islam preach abstinence from consuming meat during certain religiously and spiritually significant times of the year. It should be no surprise, then, that India has the most vegetarians of any country in the world. According to new research, conservative estimates reveal that approximately 20% of India's population is strictly vegetarian, which translates to about 275 million individuals. Compare that with the approximately 20 million vegetarians (including vegans) in the United States.

Health

Even though I've been a professional chef for over 15 years, I will be the first to tell you that scratch cooking at home, using clean and unprocessed ingredients, is invariably healthier than dining out in a restaurant. In my view, the purpose of the restaurant is to allow culinary and social experiences that are difficult and sometimes infeasible to attain at home. The purpose of this book is to encourage you to cook at home and create deep-flavored vegetarian food laced in satisfaction and even decadence. So, the idea that it is impossible to make restaurant-style luxurious meals at home is misleading for sure. It is well-documented medical fact that a vegetarian diet includes many health benefits, such as reducing one's risk of heart disease, diabetes, and certain types of cancers. Having noted that, it is important to realize that even a vegetarian diet heavy in processed foods, sugars, fats, and sodium can be just as damaging as a non-vegetarian diet. So the goal is to learn how to cook more vegetarian food while being mindful of those unhealthy triggers. Vegetarian diets come in many forms, but in this book, I've focused primarily on vegetarian dishes, where if my recipe calls for animal, dairy, or eggs, they can be left out or easily substituted with a functionally alternate ingredient that promotes better health.

Choosing a meatless diet provides a smaller risk for obesity, high blood pressure, and Type 2 diabetes. A wholesome vegetarian diet, compared to diets containing meat and other foods derived from animals, inherently has less cholesterol, more dietary fiber, more magnesium, vitamins C & E, and many phytonutrients. A vegetarian diet can be beneficial in the prevention and treatment of cardiovascular disease, hypertension, diabetes, cancer, osteoporosis, renal disease, dementia, and even rheumatoid arthritis. The emerging field and scope of lifestyle medicine in the United States and other countries is a testament to the notion that we can improve our health, especially as we age, by increasing the percentage of plant-based ingredients in our diet and combining that with exercise and subtle yet impactful changes to our lifestyle. In addition to her prowess handling diabetic limb salvage cases, Jenneffer is also a certified lifestyle medicine practitioner. Plants do not contain cholesterol, while meat is deficient in many vitamins and in carbohydrates, particularly the starches which are so essential to proper health. Plant-based diets using minimally or unprocessed ingredients and scratch-cooking has been shown to be highly beneficial for human and planet health. Animal foods contain far higher concentrations of agricultural chemicals than plant foods, including pesticides, herbicides, etc. A host of bacteria and viruses, some quite dangerous, are common to animals. Ahem...2020 has shown the world that for perpetuity. Have I mentioned that during the writing of this book, we are in the thick of a global pandemic thought to have emanated from contaminated animal meat? Fiber absorbs unwanted excess fats, cleans the intestines, provides bulk, and aids in peristalsis. Plant food is high in fiber content; meat, poultry, and dairy products have none. It is possible to consume too much protein (one of the main health-related risks of animal consumption). Consuming protein that is well beyond recommended dietary levels on a routine basis causes excess nitrogen in the blood, which creates a host of long-term health problems.

Environment
The global food system accounts for a significant share of fossil fuel consumption because of the demands created by production and consumption practices. Research shows that a minimal shift in our diets towards plant-based ingredients could decrease the overall energy consumption of food systems by several percentage points. In general, meat production places severe demands on available water resources and energy. This is especially true in animal agriculture: a 2017 USDA study showed that the fossil fuels needed to produce the foods and beverages consumed by Americans accounted for almost 14% of all carbon dioxide emissions from fossil fuels into the atmosphere. In other words, food production--and the type of food being produced--are significant contributors to greenhouse gas emissions, which cause long-term environmental damage and even climate change. Several well-known studies evaluating the environmental impacts of our dietary choices have shown that typically, animal-based products such as meat or dairy are more demanding on the resources needed to produce food compared to plant-based ingredients. In other words, our environment is less healthy when we produce food obtained from animals than when we rely on food obtained from plants. By default, a vegetarian diet--and even more, a vegan diet--is more sustainable for the near- and long-term future of a healthy and vibrant planet. It should be pointed out that some studies that claim hybrid ecosystems and regenerative agriculture include animals in the life-cycle. However, the point here is raising animals for consumption versus promoting healthy soils.

Animal production requires more water and land than plant production, and it does so less efficiently. Free grazing of animals requires significant land with a diversity of plant growth. Additionally, the pressure to produce vast amounts of food that can quickly make it to the marketplace inevitably requires animals to be housed in inhumane conditions, fed unnatural diets at a hurried pace, and sometimes injected with necessary antibiotics to prevent disease and contamination. And let's not forget that a tremendous amount of the arable land in developed countries is being used to produce food for animals that are being raised as food for human beings. This is the age-old dilemma of optimizing human efficiency against natural forces which are, by default, sustainable. While using animals for food production is not the sole contributor to climate change, the factory farming of animals has been, damaging to say the least. Raising animals for food on a large industrialized scale is counterproductive to saving and preserving the planet's overall environment through water conservation, soil conservation, preserving our forests, and, ultimately, allowing natural life cycles to complete.

It is important to note that many mindful small and independent farmers use best practices to raise animals and complete the natural cycle to the best of their abilities, and it would be unreasonable to expect an overnight shift in our food habits. So, farmers who grow thoughtfully with a sensitivity and understanding of their impacts on the environment must be encouraged and even rewarded.

Ethics

Clearly, living a healthy, productive, long life is possible without ever consuming animals or even animal-based ingredients. An aspect of our evolution is the ability to question daily the ethics and morality of our decisions. Eating animals purely for pleasure and taste can be fraught with contradictions in relation to the value we place on life. Some make distinctions between human life and animal life. An argument that I've heard often is that it is wrong to kill and eat animals with whom we have a social contract. Under this argument, our pets are protected. At some level, however, this is a self-serving definition of the protection of life. We need pets for a variety of reasons, and of course our pets, in turn, depend on us. My brother always says that if you're going to eat animals, there should be no boundaries, beyond likes and dislikes related to flavor, on what one should or should not eat. My brother has been a life-long vegetarian.

Finances

The health benefits of a vegetarian diet immediately imply that by eating more plant-based ingredients in our daily lives, we reduce the risk of health problems, and hence our health care costs are reduced. But what about the cost of a vegetarian diet to begin with? In most developing and underdeveloped countries, meats are considered luxury items and often are used in much smaller quantities to enhance flavor or indulge in decadence. Furthermore, meats and seafood cost significantly more per pound than plant-based ingredients. To be fair, vegetarian ingredients labeled as organic or otherwise certified tend to have a higher price tag than factory-farmed meats and dairy. However, considering just the normal vegetarian ingredients against the normal animal ingredients, significant savings at the end of the year could be expected.

Myths about Vegetarian Food

One of the challenges of the western world's perceptions of "vegetarian food" is the fact that it's labeled as such. The irony of this book's subtitle is not lost on me. At the end of the day, isn't vegetarian food simply food prepared using a well-defined set of ingredients? Labeling food is of course necessary, but that same label has been corrupted to suggest--at least in the meat-eating world--a lack of flavor, and that's the least of the corruption. Ah, but to the contrary! As a chef, I've cooked an incredibly wide variety of dishes using a spectacular array of ingredients. I've been fearless when it comes to using ingredients in my dishes, even though I do draw the line in certain instances. But I can safely say that if I compiled two columns of ingredients at our everyday disposal--one vegetarian and the other not--the vegetarian column would lap the non-vegetarian column. So why is it that, as a profession and industry, we've been unable to truly laud and celebrate the column which gives us so much? I can already hear the explanations. We descended from cave men and cave women, so of course, our genetic heritage is to eat meat. Especially meat over open fires. Well, we are long generations away from that version of ourselves. Very few of us hunt for our food. Subsistence farming has been around for a very long time. Most of the world does not really have access to vast amounts of meat. But the mainstream food industry has, in pushing a false narrative, made it seem as though a festive meal is incomplete without a centerpiece animal protein, one that was pampered for days and cooked slowly and infused with complementary flavor—derived, ironically, from plants.

Via this book, I want to dispel several myths about vegetarian food. I also want to promote the use of more plant-based ingredients in our daily lives. And equally, my intent is to teach you ways of making delicious, satisfying, creative, and nutritious meals that will greatly expand your own portfolio of go-to vegetarian dishes. I don't expect carnivores to give up meat because of the dishes in this book. However, if someone reduces their meat consumption because of this book, then I will have succeeded.

Bacon is a crutch used in cooking under the pretext of infusing better flavor. But vegetables, rice, beans, and legumes without bacon are so boring, they bellow! Bacon is a crutch for many chefs. Its obsessive use in Western cooking is also a fault in formal culinary education. Certainly, I am sensitive to the old practice of using rendered fats from animals as a cooking medium, but highly processed bacon from large food service companies is in no way necessary for everyday cooking. And that is just one example. Every ingredient in the world has some flavor, and the flavor depends to a large degree on our taste buds. If we are programmed to always seek those familiar accents like smoked meats in the food we consume, then I agree that it's a little bit of a challenge at first to do without them. There is a time and a place for every ingredient. If you are trying to showcase squash, tomato, and eggplant, why on earth would you need to start the dish with bacon? If anything, I would argue that doing so mucks up the flavors. With bacon, the result may be richer, but frankly, not nearly as delicious, focused, thoughtful, or healthy. By leading with the word "delicious," what I am proposing is that the inclusion of bacon makes the dish less delicious!

My use of the word meat includes seafood as well. After all, we've all heard of the terms *crab meat, lobster meat* etc. I did not eat any meat until I came to the United States at the age of 21. My taste buds were only programmed to accept vegetarian ingredients. But what we're talking about here is not necessarily giving up familiar and comforting ingredients from meatland. Liking meat and eating more plant-based ingredients are not mutually exclusive. In many cuisines, meat is an accent, used in small quantities, almost as a luxury item. If we can systematically reduce our consumption of large quantities of meat, it will serve at least two purposes: our food systems and agriculture will become more sustainable for future generations, and we will give plant-based ingredients a chance to shine. And I can assure you that they will rise to the taste challenge beyond your wildest expectations. From a purely gastronomic and molecular point of view, meats have less complex flavor than aromatics and essential oils that comprise the flavonoids of plant-based ingredients. We don't marinate with chicken or beef or even a shrimp stock. We marinate with olive oil, garlic, herbs, ginger, spices, citrus, etc. And we must ask ourselves: why we do that? If meats were already so tasty, there would be no need to help them along. I recognize that purely raised meats and fresh, wild-caught seafood don't need much more. But, as composed dishes, they still need complementary accents that are plant-based. That's more evidence that plant-based ingredients naturally have a tremendous amount of flavor. We simply need to learn how to leverage that flavor thoughtfully and skillfully. For anyone who feels as though they need meat for taste, it is a simple exercise to change their mind.

I've often tried to imagine exactly what a dedicated meat eater dislikes about a plant-based dish. Of course, in some instances, it's simply the flavor profile of the dish. But it goes deeper than that. In and of itself, IMHO, most meat really has no fulfilling flavor. There is flavor, but not a lot. Secondly, in many instances, both meat and seafood (barring ceviche, sushi, sashimi, etc.) needs to be cooked. Likewise, most plant-based ingredients also need to be cooked. Of course, raw diets and preparations exist. But mostly, food around the world is cooked. So, where exactly is the seeming source of deprivation? Why is an omnivore or carnivore unsatisfied with plant-based food? Let's dissect some perceived shortcomings of vegetarian food.

Protein
The notion that plants do not contain enough protein--which the human body needs for good health, growth, and sustenance--is false and misleading. Many sources of protein are found in plants. For example, legumes, grains, nuts, seeds, and even vegetables contain significant amounts of protein. In terms of chemical composition, proteins derived from animals are not that different from proteins derived from plants. Both have amino acids, and both contain the same number of amino acids. However, the difference lies in the ratio of these amino acids in animal protein versus plant protein. A common criticism of plant proteins is that they are not complete, which is false because complete protein sources are found in plants such as quinoa and soybean. It is completely flawed thinking to expect to get all that your body needs in every meal

that you consume. It is more important that the body receives the requisite nutritional components over a reasonable cycle of time and body functions. So, while you might have more of one thing in one meal, it would make sense to have more of another thing in the next meal. Eating a good variety of ingredients with different flavor profiles and nutritional characteristics is the best recipe for long-term health.

Fats

All through culinary school, we are taught that fat is flavor. I get it. But I also believe that plant-based fats can be just as satisfying to the taste as animal-based fats. Here's a radical fact. For a life-long vegetarian, as I was for the first 21 years of my life, the aroma of meat cooking is somewhat stomach-churning. Furthermore, meat is notoriously high in cholesterol and saturated fat, which we know are significant contributors to poor health. While fat is fat is fat, there's a distinct difference between saturated fats and unsaturated fats. In terms of cooking delicious food, I have never felt held back in flavor development just because I could not or did not start with bacon grease or butter. In fact, after you've taken a break from animal-based fats for a while, your body tends to detox a bit. I speak from firsthand experience when I note this: after laying off for a significant while, if you find yourself tasting animal fat again, it can seem unpleasantly rich.

Dairy

The dairy industry is up in arms about the labeling of plant-based extractions as "dairy." From a purely technical point of view, plant and nut-based extractions that simulate traditional dairy do not serve the same physiological function as milk does in mammals. So, there is clearly a difference. However, when it comes to the contribution in terms of flavor, I believe that there are many delicious and nutritious plant-based alternatives to animal milk-based ingredients. Coconut, grains like oat and rice, legumes like soy, and nuts like cashew and almond are incredible sources of plant-based milks that serve the same gastronomic function in dishes as animal milk products. Manufacturers need to do a better job of developing products intended for straight consumption versus products suitable for cooking, since applying heat to a plant-based dairy substitute can have a detrimental outcome. I hope that increased demand will drive innovation and dairy substitutes will become more cooking-friendly. Cheese, however, is another matter altogether. In my experience, non-dairy "cheeses" are lacking on many levels.

An Incredible Pantry

What prevents us from reveling in the cornucopia of possibilities is the systemic pigeonholing of plant-based ingredients as only elements of accents, accoutrements, or side dishes. Imagine turning that philosophy inside out. Culinary education needs to empower cooks with the gumption and tools to lead the way. Chefs need to sustainably inspire and facilitate the work. Many more interesting dinner table centerpieces (should that be a desired outcome) can be created using only vegetarian ingredients. In fact, it is quite the travesty that vegetarians find themselves at the short end of the holiday meal stick, as it were. Purportedly, the holidays are a time for family reflection and socializing over traditional food and beverage. You know, being thankful for the good in our lives and all. Yet, all too often, at least in the Western world, a holiday meal's featured dish is a big piece of meat, while the vegetables and grains are sides and, even then, prepared with meat-based accents.

Almost every classical culinary technique which may have been developed and refined for meats and seafood may easily be adapted or employed directly for vegetables. So, why then has refined and thoughtful vegetarian cuisine been resigned for the extremes of the restaurant industry? One either finds rustic, simple, and humble versions of dishes or extremely fussy, edgy, and (dare I say) point-missing versions at the other end of the spectrum. Whatever happened to developing a wide swathe of focused, thoughtful, and satisfying vegetarian cuisine in restaurants? Maybe the time has come for chefs to lead and for guests to discover all the possibilities of globally-inspired vegetarian cuisine. I realize that television and media give the audience what they think they want or, in some instances, what they wish they would want. So, in some sense, there is an onus on good education, research, and the dissemination of that information in culinary schools, mainstream media, and the corporate world.

With my glass-full point-of-view glasses on, I suggest that this mindset is changing. Each year, the percentage of vegetarians and vegans increases around the world. In my lifetime I expect to see a more mainstream adoption of vegetarianism, even in hardcore meat-consuming countries. Systemic, meaningful, and lasting change will come about only if culinary professionals lead the way with an honest and informed practice of their craft applies to vegetarian food. If it is progressive to continually move the limits of meat-based foods forward, then I believe that it is equally, if not more so, progressive to continually move the limits of vegetarian food forward. When it's all said and done, I think progressive changes will stick in society only if it can be shown that vegetarian food is not only good for you for all of the reasons mentioned earlier, but also this diamond in the rough just needs a bit of polishing, a bit of chopping, and a bit of a showcase to promote open-mindedness in traditionally reluctant societies. My frustration with uninspired vegetarian food is inversely proportional to my age. It is my hope that more chefs will take deeper dives into what is possible from a global perspective with vegetarian dishes. When every known cooking technique may be applied to vegetarian ingredients, theoretically it is just a matter of time before that will happen. The balancing of complementary and contrasting flavors and textures is so much more interesting with vegetarian ingredients than is currently being accomplished in mainstream dining. Certainly, many talented chefs are at the leading edge of where we should be. I only hope that their work and vision will inspire an entire generation of chefs, and then ultimately diners, to radically alter their perception and experience with vegetarian food. Part of the challenge is that because we are not exposed to enough thoughtful vegetarian food at a young age, our propensity for meat-based dining lingers in our psyche and cravings all through our formative, teen, and adult years.

Start Them Young

I remember my first real meal (the accidental Whopper with cheese notwithstanding) in the United States. It was in Radford, VA. My host, from a Blacksburg, VA church group, had invited me to dinner and chose a massive all-you-can-eat kind of place. Slightly overwhelmed by all the options, I opted for what seemed like a safe bet: the salad bar. When I piled my first plate (which also ended being my only plate) with every vegetable I could spot, my host seemed amused, but pointed out that I could return for seconds. I didn't think much of it at the time, but our plates looked drastically different. Mine was colorful and his was pale and "brown." In retrospect, my host composed a tasty plate of food whereas I struggled through my plate because the flavors really didn't jive. And how could they? As my mother likes to point out, it was like eating hay and grass. I had piled pickled veggies on top of salad dressings (note the plural) on top of various legumes which were mostly flavorless and decidedly under-cooked for my Indian palate. Mind you, I was used to Dal Makhani, Chana Masala, and Sambhar. If I had been a kid here, I too would never eat my veggies again.

As a chef, when I am handed a ticket with a modifier that reads "Child's Pasta" or "Child's Chicken," the implication is that I am to not season the dish as I would for an adult. Maybe I could use salt, but for sure no pepper. And no other spice blend or fresh herbs are to be added. And the last thing I should be serving the youngster is a vegetable of any kind. My staff can attest to my reaction every time. It is one of frustration and downright indignation. "This is why kids don't eat their vegetables," I rant. So, I've begun to contemplate this more reasonably. Can you imagine a world where children desire vegetables over fried foods and desserts? Can you imagine the demand they would generate in the schools for healthier and more vegetable-friendly meals? I am certainly not an expert on discerning the palate of a child. While I do know how to prepare dishes they would enjoy, I also believe that as a society, we are doing a disservice to both the vegetables and the children with the way vegetables are presented for consumption. They don't have to be simply steamed. And for sure, they need not be devoid of flavor. Let's better understand what savory flavors appeal to a youngster's palate; let's complement vegetables with those flavors. Let's roast, grill, "confit," and puree. Let's not hide vegetables as if we are afraid that a child might see them. Instead, let's dream of and realize a time when a child asks for broccoli because they know that it's in season and that it's delicious. If the child prefers it steamed, so be it, but let's not sell short their ability to enjoy adult flavors and diverse cooking techniques. Studies show that children are more likely to emulate an adult they admire and respect. So, are we setting a bad example? Are there not enough adults who eat their veggies?

To repeat *ad nauseum*, I was a vegetarian for 21 years; now I am not, but over 95% of my diet is plant-based. My wife has been a vegetarian for the past 30 years; earlier, she was not. The cuisines that best feature vegetables have done so for centuries because of religious, economic, geographic, and moral factors. According to a 2012 UN FAO Study, out of 177 countries, India had the lowest annual average per person meat consumption (about 7.4 lbs.) whereas the United States had the highest (about 250 lbs. on average per person, per year). The most staggering aspect of this comparison is that India's population is more than four times that of the United States. Furthermore, most African nations rank very low in per capita meat consumption. There is no denying the immense pressures on the land, resources, and environment of a largely animal-based diet versus that of a plant- and vegetable-based one. This note is not meant to provide any overnight magical solutions (because frankly, there aren't any) to reducing the consumption of meat worldwide. Rather, it's an attempt, from a chef's point of view, to point out some simple ways in which vegetables can provide dietary satisfaction, nutrition, and even preference. Here are some specific techniques for treating plant-based ingredients.

SMOKING: Bacon, barbecue, kālua titillates the taste buds because of their deep connections to decadent and rich flavors. Smoking vegetables is underutilized. Season them as you would an animal protein, even marinating them overnight, and smoke them covered for a while. Finish uncovered. Some vegetables that are great when smoked are tomatoes, peppers, cauliflower, greens, summer squash, winter gourds, cabbage, and onions. Generally, juicy vegetables do well under this preparation, but par-cooking firmer vegetables prior to the barbecue steps yields amazing results. After smoking the vegetables, use them as is or incorporate them into other dishes.

ROASTING: Not everyone has a smoker, but almost everyone in North America has an oven. At the restaurant, we roast an assortment of vegetables every day before service and they accompany many of our entrees. Roasting intensifies the flavor and showcases the natural sugars, providing a tasty snack or satisfying way of incorporating the vegetables into other preparations.

USING SPICES: Indian cuisine, better (and more) than any other cuisine, specializes in the use of spices. The reason Indian cuisine is so satisfying for vegetarians worldwide is that the dishes are fraught with deep and savory flavors, thanks to the knowledgeable and experienced use of spices. For the record, spicy doesn't necessarily mean hot (pungent). So, anyone who thinks they don't like spices perhaps just doesn't like the pungency of capsaicin. By layering the flavors of vegetables during the cooking process with a variety of spices, the result can be both nutritious and delicious. Many spices are even known to have a medicinal value.

SAUCES: Vegetables lend themselves to sauces just as animal proteins do. Instead of simply stir-frying them and accompanying them with a starch or grain, develop a repertoire of sauces that complement the flavor of the prepared vegetable. Treat the vegetable as the centerpiece rather than an accompaniment.

SEASONALITY: In most grocery stores in the United States, many vegetables are available year-round, which is unthinkable in many vegetarian-forward countries. Because the consumers demand them, they are supplied, somehow, partly thanks to long supply chains. Unfortunately, the cost of omnipresent availability is the flavor. Staging vegetables at various levels of ripeness in temperature-controlled facilities before supplying them to the market has sucked the flavor out of most of them during the off-season. By focusing on the seasonal vegetables, one can better enjoy the benefits of their flavor and nutritional value.

At the end of the day, we can espouse all the virtues of limiting meat consumption; by not offering some viable alternatives, however, the chance for a tangible change in the tide is minimal. Chefs have a tremendous role to play in this regard. I welcome that responsibility, one coriander-spiced, roasted, cauliflower-stuffed, smoked tomato with grilled ramp chimichurri starter at a time.

Composing a Vegetarian Dish
As a chef, when I'm developing and executing dishes, I don't think of them as being vegetarian. In fact, what inspires me are vegetables. So, I look at a set of ingredients. I evaluate their place and role in either a one-pot dish or a dish with several components. I then try to imagine competing and complementing flavors and textures. One of the founding principles of good cooking is to understand and subsequently match the appropriate cooking technique to each ingredient. So, when an ingredient is already delicate and fresh, processing it beyond what is necessary would be somewhat detrimental. As an example, let's consider a simple ingredient like fresh basil. Of course, one can simply tear up the basil and garnish the dish so that a bite of food which has that basil will pop with its freshness and floral qualities. Some might say it's a travesty to cook that basil. Agreed, to a point. So let's think of that basil as being composed of at least three distinct parts. First, there is the stem. Then, there are the large leaves. And finally, there are often smaller leaves, and, towards the end of the season, the flowers. As a chef, I imagine different applications for those parts. The stem is a great resource for infusing the flavor and aroma of basil into a dish. The larger leaves can be handled with some abandon. The small leaves and any flowers can be used as the garnish, which envelops the dish with the flavor and aroma of basil.

I've never understood why well-trained and obviously experienced chefs experience such a difficult time composing a non-routine vegetarian dish. I see them, when it comes to a meat-based dish, taking great pains and deriving great joy in finessing and infusing flavor while imagining and developing something from nothing. But those same chefs are woefully lacking in their ability to imagine a similar composition that is just as thoughtful and balanced when presented with a basket of only vegetarian ingredients. That is a staggering reality in the West. Is it simply because chefs themselves think of vegetarian food as lacking? My experience suggests that to be the case for many chefs. Where have we failed in the industry? I think at least some of the limits in imagination and desire are culturally grounded. If we don't eat it, we don't care.

Maybe that is why so many full-flavored vegetarian dishes seem to gravitate towards those cuisines with a long and storied history of using only plant-based or vegetarian ingredients. Those cuisines embrace them, so they've learned to innovate. There's something about necessity being the mother of invention.

Frankly, composing a vegetarian dish is exactly like composing any dish. In classical cuisine, the formulaic approach consists typically of some sort of an animal protein as a centerpiece, accompanied by a starch, vegetable, sauce, and perhaps some garnishes. So even if chefs simply emulate this template for a composed dish, a vast majority of them will have already done so without being particularly innovative. This is an ideal first step for professional chefs: develop at least one composed vegetarian dish on their menus. For someone who is not already well-versed in the nutritional composition of plant-based ingredients, a good idea is to become a student of that kind of information. Once that becomes second nature--perhaps through practice--then it's quite amazing how seamlessly one can compose a thoughtful, delicious, seasonal, and creative vegetarian dish. As the so-called professionals in this world, we owe it to ourselves not just to think outside the box with traditional dishes but also to reimagine dishes with an entirely different set of ingredients.

Furthermore, I'm of the firm belief that classical vegetarian dishes from cuisines that do them well can serve as inspiration for meat-based dishes. Yes, I am speaking of turning the tables. Vegetarian cuisine need not always take a backseat to non-vegetarian cuisine. In fact, I find many traditional meat-based dishes quite uninspired. We have a reliable crutch when it comes to flavor: Start with bacon. Sure, but other than smoke and salt, why? You see what I mean? I can already see my colleagues shaking their heads in disagreement. We really must step back for a moment, and I'm convinced that, if we do, the need to label a dish vegetarian will become a thing of the past. In fact, I believe labeling a dish as vegetarian immediately raises the back hairs of certain people to the point where they won't even try it. Restaurant menus are notoriously at fault for this kind of separation of dishes, and ethnic (southeast Asian) restaurants are even more culpable. Having noted that, I completely understand it. When I was growing up in India, if there was even the slightest chance that the food might be contaminated with non-vegetarian ingredients, my family and other vegetarian friends and acquaintances would, without hesitation, walk away. In fact, I think when someone is a vegetarian, they are even more likely to be antagonized, and angry, should cross-contamination occur. For example, should an individual who is not vegetarian find out that the bacon or shrimp in a dish was contaminated by a tomato, they are far less likely to be upset than if it was the other way around. (Except, of course, if they're allergic to a tomato or just completely averse to it.) Do you see my point? Being a vegetarian is quite the commitment. It is an assertively dedicated lifestyle.

The notion that there are not enough vegetarian ingredient choices world to make enjoyable meals is both ridiculous and systemically flawed. It really is a matter of trying just a bit harder to step away from levels of comfort. Doing so will not just radically change the quality of our diet, but also help us be the change that we claim we want to see. Mind you, I am not naive enough to think that within my lifetime, more people around the world will be vegetarian than not. However, a disproportionate and damaging concentration of poor and uninformed food production and consumption dominates some of the most advanced societies on this planet. It seems counter intuitive, given that knowledge is power. At some level, it is the age-old conundrum of measuring personal freedom against the good of society. However, in this case, there is enough evidence to suggest that eating more vegetarian food is not only good for society, but also has benefits for self. It is a win-win proposition. The disconnect is related to the myth that vegetarian food lacks flavor. Aggressive anti-marketing in some parts of the world means that vegetarian food is seen as flavorless or just plain boring. The same individuals who laud the virtues and decadence of meat-based dishes attack dishes without meat as being lacking. This further makes my point that vegetarian dishes need not be labeled as such. Simply prepare a dish, present it for what it is, and the rest will follow. At some level, the label vegetarian limits the potential for greater acceptance.

Over the last three decades in the United States, I have noticed a disdain for alternative options that would welcome vegetarians to the table. Traditionalists wrinkle their nose and fuss under their breaths when individuals who don't eat meat are at the holiday table. When the holidays are intended to bring families together to a common table over food, love, and merriment, the ironic outcome is often the opposite. Either there's disgruntlement or there's complete disregard. Either way, it is very troubling. Preparing a range of meal choices seems like a small sacrifice for a family unit, especially when such a myriad of possibilities exist for creating flavorful and interesting food without falling back on non-vegetarian ingredients.

This seems like a good place to get cracking with taking a deep dive into the incredible world of vegetarian food. Naturally, I will have barely scratched the surface by the end of this book. But it is my hope that you will be inspired to think outside the box, to challenge traditionally false norms, and to romp around in the playground of full-flavored, nutritious, inspired, and just plain delicious food. Are you ready to cook a sinfully vegetarian feast? Excellent! First, pour yourself a beverage.

Chapter 10: POUR YOURSELF A BEVERAGE
by
JENNEFFER PULAPAKA
physician, sommelier, entrepreneur, advocate

I am a podiatric surgeon with a private practice in DeLand, FL. In 2008, I also became the co-owner and General Manager of Cress Restaurant with my husband, Chef Hari. I did not take a traditional path in the hospitality industry. I did not take the traditional path during my wine education. I jumped into this bizarre world with my medical scrubs & lab coat on and I remain curiously fascinated by people. I initially read book upon book about wines, winemaking, and wine pairings prior to Cress' opening. I remember the moment when reading about all the glittery ways to pair chocolate and Cabernet Sauvignon (both of which we had in the house) and I tried it. "What the heck? That's horrible!" So much for books. I needed a redirect, and books for me seemed to miss the dance between wine and food. They were focused on details: vineyards, wine makers, vintages, seasons, and ratings. While all very important, the marriage of wine and food was my focus in the restaurant, as it should be. So, I began the task of tasting everything I could and comparing it to the wines we had. I would use different varietals to taste with green apples, Tikka sauce, Cress grits, bleu cheese, aged Manchego, sherry vinaigrette, beurre blanc, Kosher salt, roasted grapes, green peppers, any hot pepper, plain black pepper, and on and on. Most wine books "thought" they talked about sauces and pairing, but they did not have enough respect for a sauce's power to transform a dish. Consequently, the kitchen became my classroom, the food became my color palate, and I had to figure out how to paint and remember which style of art each individual guest liked. Several years later, I finally formalized my focus in wine with The Wine & Spirit Education Trust and with other individual Societies/Appellations.

Wine is a social and culinary experience. Because of this, our palates are always changing and evolving. Like many wine drinkers, one might remember starting out with sweet white wines, then into reds, followed by the big California Cabs. As my taste continues to change, I have transitioned into switching between reds, whites, rosés, and sherries—from one course to the next and back. I find the lateral play between one pairing to the next to be refreshing and a break in the monotony. I love the harmony wine can contribute to the food and the power a wine can have in changing the character of a dish.

My love and fascination for wine fully extends into Cress. As the Wine Director, I wanted to have a dynamic wine menu, one that matured with the food. After a decade of food and wine pairings, my focus remains constant, and I enjoy exploring how the *terroir* of the land plays with the *terroir* of wine. I remember the first moment *terroir* awoke my consciousness of the land. It was in India--not California, Germany, France, or walking the wine fields of the Virginia, but India.

Let me begin by stating that a recipe is merely a road map. Many recipes have amounts of ingredients followed by a step by step method of preparation. For me, the amount of each ingredient represents an abstract notion of proportion relative to the whole. In most cases, even if I'm following a recipe I respect, I allow myself some flexibility, as should you. In fact, the only way you can personalize the food you make is by adapting a recipe tailored to your own palate and the taste buds of your guests. One should never cook scared. Although that's easier said than done. After all, when we serve our guests the food that we may have made, the evaluation happens almost instantaneously. To complicate matters, even when the food is as delicious to you as you can possibly make it, there is always the chance that someone else consuming it might find it less than spectacular. For cooks like me who put their heart and soul into every dish we make, as much as we've become accustomed to facing criticism with a grain of salt (pun intended), it is never easy to be on the receiving end of less-than-flattering commentary.

For years now, I've seen restaurant menus with vegetarian options that are clearly afterthoughts. It doesn't take much to dissect how little thought may have gone into a vegetarian option on the menu. Some of the reasons are cultural, while other reasons are professional. There's a lack of training and there's a lack of sensitivity. But above all, there is a lack of foundational knowledge about the vast bounty of plant-forward ingredients at our disposal. Clearly the world has more fruits and vegetables and grains and legumes and spices and herbs than edible forms of non-plant-based ingredients. So why is it that there is such a paucity of creative vegetarian cooking in the western world? For the most part. vegetarian and vegan-friendly restaurants seem inspired by cuisines from just a few countries around the world. Countries like India. That's no surprise because after all, by sheer volume, India has the greatest number of vegetarians in the world. Is it any surprise that Indian food is full flavored? Of course, it is the land of spices, but it is also the land of thousands of years of vegetarian dining. Practice makes perfect.

Notes from Nasik Wine Trip
I remember hearing myself say, "I hope I get to see the monsoons this time in India." Just two days after returning from Kanha Tiger Preserve and being subjected to nonstop rain, I realized I may have misspoken. But with bags packed, we run down three flights of stairs from Mummy's flat to get to our driver and escape Mumbai. The Western Ghats flank the side of the vehicle through the monsoon highway as we head out to Nasik. It's amazing how clean Mumbai looks during the rains. The countryside is a pleasant change. As we advance through the mild, sloping mountains, the golden earth has already started to sprout new green life. Farmers have plotted out their land for the growing season. The hillside is covered with checkerboard patterns, small square knee walls constructed with cow dung patties. Such a convenient way to partition off land, and at the same time, the farmers get instant fertilizer in convenient application packs.

We reach the city center of Nasik, which is covered in a swamp of construction traffic; slowly we make progress and then head northeast for approximately 45 minutes to a small town, Niphad. One can't help but notice the vineyards lined up alongside the road. India is among the top 10 countries in the world in the production of table grapes and raisins. The peak production of the growing season is during the month of February, March and April., when the crops benefit from the warm days and cool nights that assist in the slow maturation of the grapes.

Grape cultivation is one of the most remunerative farming enterprises in India. Cultivated grapes are believed to have been introduced into the north of India by Persian invaders around 1300 AD. Currently, India has three distinct agro-climatic zones: Sub-tropical Region, Mild Tropical Region, and Hot Tropical Region. Nashik, which lies in this Hot Tropical Region, is the major viticulture region, accounting for approximately 75% of the grapes grown in the country. The Western Ghats provides this region with laterite soil, which is rich in iron and provides good drainage. Drainage is what the ground needs after those long monsoon rains.

We approach the outstretched land where our first vineyard, Reveilo Wines, waits, and I realize we've beaten the rain clouds, which are still advancing in the West. I excitedly open the door, and the scents of the land engulf me as we enter the main production plant. Yet, there is something unsettling in Nashik. My mind has begun to wander, discerning and evaluating, looking for that thing that is eluding me when Ramesh, the Commercial Manager, walks in and greets us.

Reveilo Wines was incorporated, in late 2002, by Vintage Wines. It is one of the few estate vineyards in India with the primary objective of producing quality wines. They have their own vineyards on which they grow table grapes and wine grapes, have a testing lab, do pressing, and have bottling and maturing facilities. All of these are within a single estate.

I grab a notepad from my bag, pull out my pen, and I am back in medical school: ready to take notes. As we begin our tour, Ramesh is wonderfully open and pleasant, taking the edge off the long drive in. I hate driving, hate it completely. I am like a little impetuous child when a trip exceeds my inner limit of 2 hours. But now we are out of the car, strolling through the architecture of steel tanks. A clean smell of the approaching rain blends with the smoked cherry fragrance of the room rising to greet me. The monsoons are here early this year.

We make our way out into the flat field of vineyards and walk among the vines' labyrinth. They are under the supervision of an Italian winemaker, Andrea Valentinuzzi. Andrea uses the sunshine to add great aromas to white varietals and lets the red grapes develop soft tannins. He also notes that harvesting in warmer weather plays with the acid content of the grapes. The white grapes are especially sensitive to this, where pH value is essential for preserving the aromas in the resulting wine. While I look over rows of variant Guyot trained vines, that gentle nudge starts again, almost as irritating as a tenacious mosquito. My mind keeps asking, "What is it?" Along our walk, we discuss their status as the first vineyard to successfully produce Chardonnay and Grillo among their whites in India. Along with the Italian Grillo, the 215-acre estate also grows Nero D'Avalo and Sangiovese.

The angry border of gun-grey clouds warns us of an approaching wave of a monsoon storm, so we head back to the production plant to begin our tasting in the vineyard's laboratory. Here is the perfect setting for me to sit down and roll back in the chair, comfortable. Several of the groundskeepers come in and help Ramesh assemble an array of ten wines. We start to partake in the tasting. However, there it is again, the unsettling puzzle I cannot put my finger on. As soon the first pour of wine hits the glass, though, the bouquet rises in the air and I make the connection. The land is in the air. It's in the wine. It's the yeast. The key factor to this vineyard's wine flavor is the native yeast, which I've tasted in India's wines before, and now I realize it's everywhere. I can taste India's countryside just by breathing in.

It remained all around me during this trip, and I saw how some vineyards celebrated their land, terroir, and other vineyards stripped it away. It was in those few days I grew to love and appreciate the meaning of a vigneron, one who cultivates a vineyard for wine. The spirit of the grape comes from the land. Respect it and celebrate it.

Bare Bone Basics of Wine
Where does much of the flavor of wine come from? Simply put, the tannins, acidity, alcohol, sugar, yeast, and the vigneron's skill with the grape. A wine grape has four components: stems, skin, flesh/pulp, and seeds. Green and unripe stems can produce an herbaceous or cut grass component to the wine. As they ripen, the palate can discern wood, spice, pepper, and clove. Finally, they age to the point of becoming brittle and over ripe, creating the unique flavors of tea and dry leaves. The skin is the most important factor of red wine, as it imparts its color. It contributes much to the flavor of the finished wine and the tannins in the wine. Hence, most white wines have low tannins, as they are usually crushed and pressed the same day, giving little time for the tannins to have contact and develop in the must/juice. The skin is also the host for native yeast that may or may not contribute to the wine's fermentation process. The flesh or pulp is another major contributing flavour, along with acidity, sugar, and water. Finally, seeds can express hard aggressive tannins. Seeds contain bitter oils, and during alcohol fermentation, the increasing alcohol can increase the unsavory amount of seed tannin extraction.

Alcohol gives the wine body. As the alcohol viscosity increases, so does the body of the wine. Grapes with the highest sugar content, Brix (°Bx), have the highest alcohol. Alcohol contributes to a wine's astringency. Just like alcohol, tannins contribute to wine's astringency. Tannins are a sensation in the mouth that creates dryness. They are not a taste. Tannins bind to proteins, and one's own saliva can affect the individual perception of the tannin's strength. This sensation can be appreciated if you taste the inside of a banana peel. With time, however, tannins are believed to bind to the color pigments in wine and settle out in the sediment.

Acid is a crisp, tart, mouth-watering sensation. Acid contributes to the liveliness of the wine. Cool climate grapes have high acid and low sugar, while warm climate grapes have low acid and high sugar. Low acid wine is flat or insipid.

Sweetness in wine comprises several interacting components: sugar, acidity, tannins, and alcohol. Wines can range from very sweet--Pedro Ximénez Sherry-- to dry with hints of sweetness--Barossa Valley Shiraz-- to bone dry--Nebbiolo. Sugar and alcohol enhance the sweetness in wine, whereas acidity and tannins counteract it.

Wood is usually the main profile that oak, the most commonly used wood, gives to wine. Grape stems also contribute to the wood flavoring in wine. French oak is a finer/tighter grain and contributes a subtle refined spice flavor and silky tannins. American oak, in contrast, is coarse grain and denotes bold tannins with the flavour of soda, vanilla, and coconut.

Fruit in wine is what you are paying for. Fruits are the tasting notes most people describe as "lushness of the black fruit," "brightness of red fruit," and vibrant tropical whites."

While writing the wine portion of this book, I realize science tells us a lot about the production and components of wine. Only a small fraction of science can explain our palate's associations with wine, however, and therefore the keys to successful wine pairings remain personal. I have narrowed it down to five simple guidelines I follow. These core principles are easy to navigate and will make your wine experience real and spectacular.

1. *Pair sweet wine with sweet foods.* Sweetness in food will increase the intensity of a given wine's bitterness and alcohol burn. When you eat food, those bitter flavors flood the palate. It's like a lock and key system. The lock is the sugar receptors on the tongue and the key is the sugary food. Once the key is placed in the lock, no other key can communicate with the lock, even while you still have the other functioning locks of salty, bitter, sour, and umami. Now, however, when you sip your wine after eating a dessert, those sweet "receptors" are blocked and the receptors for bitter and sour are open, allowing the harshness that may have been hidden in the wine to come front and center on the tongue. I despise chocolate and Cabernet Sauvignon; I never understood what the fuss was about. A dry red wine, like a Cabernet Sauvignon, loses the sweetness of the grapes/fruit, and what remains is alcohol burn and bitter tannins. But pair a sweet dessert with a sweeter wine and you have harmony. I love a beautiful aged Pedro Ximénez Sherry with vanilla ice cream, marcona almonds, and a dash sea salt.

2. *Match the acidity of the wine with the acidity in the food.* Acidity, a powerful flavour component in wine, contributes to fresh, tart, and sour qualities. But where does acidity come from? The three common acids in wine are tartaric, malic, and citric acids; also, acidity is higher in grapes that are grown at higher altitudes. During the process of wine fermentation, the winemaker can emphasize malic acid or allow that acid to go through a second fermentation process to change malic acid to lactic acid. Lactic acid is milder acid that gives chardonnay its buttery feel and "milky" character. This is known as malolactic fermentation. Most red wines go through malolactic fermentation, and this gives notes of chocolate milk to wine. Acidity envelops the palate and provides a "richness in mouth" feel to the wine. Highly acidic foods, like pickled vegetables, will knock out a wine with medium to low acidity, and the wine will become insipid or flat. Salads with vinaigrette pair best with, for example, an Albariño from the Rias

Baixas. A light, buttery chardonnay both illustrates the difference in acidity and pairs well with a creamy ranch dressing.

3. *Salt softens bitterness and the alcohol burn.* The best example of salt's power can be seen when a young bold varietal, such as a Shiraz, is opened prematurely and the tannins have not softened. Salted meats, like prosciutto or a salted steak, help pull an unpleasant wine (that you shouldn't have opened, but too late now) into richness and soften the tannin's bitterness, allowing the fruit to shine. More recently, cocktail salts have been used to soften the burn of alcohol in drinks.

4. *Bitters heighten bitterness.* When cooking with spiced and spicy dishes, stay away from the components in wine that contribute to bitterness like tannins, alcohol, and oak. In other words, sweet wines help to balance the harshness of the pungent dish. Stay away from dry red fruit wines, such as Nebbiolo.

5. *Umami foods need sweet wines or a slash of acid.* This is the most difficult pairing, as the term "umami" refers to food that has become all it can be, food in a perfect state of grace. Wine, in all its elegance, is not subtle; it is a player in the culinary scene. It is hard to pair an aggressive partner with a perfect dish. With that in mind, I rely on a subtly sweet wine like a Gewürztraminer or controlled Muscatel for umami foods.

The pairing of food and wine can be harmonious. These rules can help improve wines' faults or blend them luxuriously together. Over the last several years, I have been walking the delicate line of allowing the food to shine and letting the wine be an elegant partner. Pairing remains a dynamic experience. Embrace a state where food, wine, and friendship flow. Let go of trivial restrictions, escape the rhetoric of dining, and relax in the surroundings of the moment with close friends. Indulge in food, enjoy wine, and get lost in conversation. Wine is a brilliant way to explore the terroir of lands, the terroir of the plate, and the *terroir* of your palate. The table on the next page contains summarized observations that I have made after years of tasting an incredible diversity of wines. Ultimately, the focus is on pairing wine and food. That's where it can get even more magical.

Probing deeper...Woodiness and structure are the main profiles that oak gives to the wine. The flavor of wood, along with spice, can also come from the grape stems, as they are fermented as whole grape clusters and not destemmed. Different barrel constructs or staves have distinct qualities, such as, French oak with a finer/tighter grain, contributes a subtle, refined spice flavor and silky tannins. In contrast, American oak is a coarse grain and denotes bold tannins with the flavor of soda, vanilla, and coconut. The aging period will vary, along with the use of new or used barrels to infuse flavor and texture. Through it all, the fruit in wine is what you are paying for, and land and culture dictate their delicate or dominant differences.

Jenneffer's WHITE WINE Basic Tasting Notes

Herbaceous Notes & Lightly Floral	Tropical Fruit & Melon	Stone Fruit & Apple
Sauvignon Blanc, Pinot Blanc, Semillon, Grüner Veltliner, Pinot Grigio, Pinot Gris, Chenin Blanc	Albariño, Pinot Blanc, Pinot Gris, Gewürztraminer, Torrents, Riesling, Chardonnay, Muscat, Semillon	Chablis, unoaked Chardonnay, Marsanne, Pinot Blanc, Roussanne
Light Body White	**Medium Body White**	**Heavy Body White**
Soave, Pinot Grigio, Pinot Gris, Kabinett, Viño Verde	Graves, Chablis Premier (1er), unoaked Chardonnay, Sauvignon Blanc, Roussanne, Gewürztraminer	California oaked Chardonnay, Burgundy Premier (1er) & Grand Cru, Viognier

BLACK GRAPE Varietals

Red Fruit	Pinot Noir, Gamay, Grenache, Zinfandel, Tempranillo, Pinotage, Barbera, Barbaresco, Merlot
Black Fruit	Cabernet Sauvignon, Cabernet Franc, Syrah, Petite Syrah, Malbec, Nero d' Avalo

Jenneffer's RED WINE Basic Tasting Notes

Red Fruit	Strawberry, Raspberry, Cranberry, Pomegranate, Cherry, Red Plum, Lingonberry
Black Fruit	Blackberry, Black Cherry, Blueberry, Black Currant, Raisin, Fig, Prune/Jam

Light Body Red	Medium Body Red	Heavy Body Red
Beaujolais, Pinot Noir, Rioja, Sangiovese, Gamay, Cinsaut	Crianza, Burgundy, Côtes du Rhône, Merlot, Barbera, Bordeaux Crus, Garnacha, Chateauneuf du Pape	Washington Syrah, Shiraz, California Cabernet Sauvignon, Malbec, Zinfandel, Barbaresco, Barolo

Ergo, not all wines can be created equally. Therefore, welcome and enjoy the expression of different regions and flavors when building a wine pairing menu. First, begin to focus on the dish's direction, determining its overall levels of salt, richness, acid, umami, and sweetness. Next, consider the amount of contribution a chutney, relish, or sauce confers on the dish. Then, evaluate the main ingredient's dower to a pairing and determine if it has an airy or robust role on the plate. Lastly, pin down the overall sweeping mouthfeel a wine will have compared to its food partner. For instance, match the clean brightness in the Ceviche of Hearts or the Watermelon Gazpacho with a Washington State Sauvignon Blanc or Txakoli from Spain. This match builds complexity in the overall dish, adding another depth to our plate.

Whenever we travel, we eat and drink the flavors of the land. This celebration held true on our Foraging trip, up the East Coast, to the James Beard House in New York City. The climate moved from the prickly heat of Florida through the spirits of the Carolinas. Finally, Virginia led the way through the Blue Ridge Mountains that watched over Thomas Jefferson's Monticello Wine Trail, offering flavors reminiscent of the Napa and Sonoma of the past.

Virginia is one of the top ten wine-producing states in the USA. Many of the produced red varietals use a French-style technique. Therefore, their Cabernet Franc brings aromatics of sweet tobacco, white flowers, pepper, and spice. They possess a softer tannin feel in the mouth and emphasize red plummy fruit on the palate, which pairs nicely with Italian, Mediterranean, and European dishes. The Cabernet Franc's elegance is on display in Virginian wines, and a similar refined red streak can be noted in the Cabernet Sauvignon, Merlot, Barbera, and Nebbiolo. At the same time, the darker black fruits of blackberry and black cherry shine through in the Petit Verdot, Malbec, and Norton.

Virginian white varietals display clean grassiness and salinity in the Viognier, Pinot Gris, Riesling, Chardonnay, Sauvignon Blanc, and Albariño. Virginia's white wines can provide an accent to composed salads or legumes dishes and put an uplifting spin on food that would fall flat with a red wine.

Hunting out the graceful attributes in a wine and boosting those subtle notes is similar to Hari infusing saffron or fresh fennel into a dish. This is refined restraint. The play on the palate is a French or European style of wine and food design, allowing a connection to the cultivated food qualities.

A prime example of this connection is found in France's beautiful region along the coastline of Nice, beside Monte Carlo. With Hari's family, we spent a lovely lunch in the sophisticated appellation of Provençe, at *Le Relais Des Moines*, Les Arcs sur Argens. We took the recommendation of their Sommelier to visit the Château Gasqui, in the Gasqui valley that extends north of the last foothills of the Massif des Maure. Sheep filled the vineyard as we arrived in the early afternoon, and spent several hours chatting with their vigneron,

François Miglio, about the topic of biodynamic wine production. Here, the red wines sing of lilies and red currants. There has been a recent trend within France to regain a connection with the land and translate that connection into wine. The vignerons draw attention to their wine's unique regional qualities without modifying the yeast or blending beyond balancing.

Food pairings should address this subtle nature of an appellation. In this case, connect with the floral while respecting the bravado in some of Provençe's tannin levels; they can sneak up on you and be very assertive with bold edges. To deal with an austere wine, I gravitate to foods with higher salt qualities and more earthy notes, such as the Toasted Barley and Mirepoix Stew or Duxelle Filled Quinoa Buttermilk Crepe. On the other hand, the Provençal Rose's grace is alluring to show off by itself or with Signature Passion fruit composed salad.

We shift now from grace to power, on the West Coast of the USA with Washington and California's wines. Several years ago, I participated in the Washington State Wine Road Trip, experiencing this state's wine's diversity as we drove through Yakima Valley, Horse Heaven Hills, Red Mountain, and Walla Walla Valley. There remains a signature aroma in Washington red wines that note a smokiness joined by black fruit, plum, and dark chocolate. Another side of wine comes from the rouge yeast, Brettanomyces. Brett can take up residence in a wine cellar or winemaking facility with its robust profile of burnt wood, leather, sweaty saddle, or wet dog, with metallic, antiseptic, and tin bandage can notes in certain red wines.

One should examine the tannins, which can be assertive when Merlot's percentage is high. Washington Merlot seeds must be tempered with care because they contribute to the wine's robust nature with more intensity than the Washington Cabernet Sauvignon. Therefore, the winemakers avoid agitating their seeds when designing wines. This attention to detail shines in one of my favorite wines of the region, the Pedestal by Longshadow. The richness in Paella, Jambalaya, and Pulao work well with dark fruit wines and accents that hint at smokiness in the Washington reds.

It was there in Washington that I realized the vast magnitude of blending. It is not just within the land, varietals, or barrels but also through the yeast strains and the winemakers' imagination that great wines are developed. This revelation occurred at Goose Ridge Estate Vineyards and Winery near Benton City, adjacent to the famed Red Mountain AVA. During our winery tour, a winemaker taught us how she prepares and feeds yeast in the barrels, as we tasted along at various stages. I was sampling a rich body Chardonnay that was flat on the palate against one with brightness but no backbone. These barrels were from the same vineyard row, with the same grapes, but aged with different yeast strains. The winemaker mentioned she might blend the barrels. I jumped on that opportunity, inquiring if I could take samples of each barrel and mix them on my own. From that moment on, I realized the dynamism and skill of the winemaker. Diversity shines in Washington's Rieslings, such as Chateau Ste. Michelle Winery, which strives to show their flexibility of bone-dry to dessert sweet. I applaud Riesling's excellent acid structure, which comes from their cooler climates' growth that is accented with struggle, and why they are chosen to pair with spicy Indian and Mexican creations, since their sweetness complements the spice.

Napa Valley remains the powerhouse of intensity. This was a diversity challenge on our trip. I wanted to experience excellently edgy winemakers and decadent food pairings while discussing what makes Napa exciting. And that is exactly what happened, from magnificent Malbecs to sparkling Cabernet Sauvignon. Our sit-down conversation with Andrew Dickson gave us insight into the barrel's character as we spent hours chatting about designing a perfect wine. The invaluable input of his father and mother contributed to his development as a winemaker. It was an afternoon of tasting *Andrew Lane Winery*'s 2008, 2010, 2011, and 2012 Cabernet Sauvignon vertical, as we walked through a discovery of oak and acid's vexation on wine. Over the next few days, we continued to focus on pairing powerful Napa reds with vegetarian options that included uninspiring dishes of roasted squash and grilled mushrooms, with little creatively influenced vegetarian foods.

Hari alluded to this problem during his late morning lecture at the Culinary Institute of America in Napa Valley. The infusion of flavors from the land is powerful. It is a pivotal point in the development of cuisine by skilled chefs. We debated the confounding reasons around creating avant-garde meat-free menus, at *Cindy's Backstreet Kitchen*, in St. Helena, with a vegetarian meal that delivered complexity. At the same time, we sipped on a beautiful wine, Six Sigma Tempranillo, coming from the north in Lake County. Our prattle wrapped up around this newly advancing wine region that delivers crisp, glittery, and refined California reds; only time will tell what happens in Lake County.

As our time faded in Napa, we participated in a spectacular afternoon at Robert Sinsky's Napa vineyard. Their property focuses on biodynamic techniques and a chef-driven kitchen, with vibrant white wines, like Abraxas. This wine accented the brightness in their locally grown vegetables. Through this vineyard, the expression of the land shines. It is about the earth, the lives, and the people that bring us to the table. Science tells us tremendous information about wine production and components, but the human element is missing. Only a small fraction of science can explain our palate's associations with wine; however, the keys to successful wine pairings remain personal. From these samples, I draw down or narrow pairings into the five simple guidelines (refer pages 52-53) that I follow. These easily navigated core principles will make your wine experience real and spectacular.

Chapter 11: LET'S COOK

I will preface this chapter by noting that my musings on this topic are general tips for cooking and not necessarily unique to vegetarian cooking. So, in some instances I will allude to the handling and cooking of non-vegetarian ingredients. I hope that will not deter you from reading past this point.

Mis En Place
Mise en place doesn't simply apply to the preparation of food; it is the culinary variation of efficient project management and execution. Not surprisingly, the term harks back to the writings and teachings of formal French cuisine by Antoine Marie Carème and Auguste Escoffier, both of whom had deep connections with the French royalty and military. "Everything in Place" or "Put in Place" is a recipe for leading an efficient and somewhat prepared life. As a preteen, I was in the Boy Scouts in Mumbai under our troop leader Makhi Sir. "Be prepared" was our motto, so when I was taught the meaning of *mise en place* in culinary school, I thought it to be common sense. I would tell my best friend Satish that I could anticipate when things would happen; I thought I had a special skill or virtue. In retrospect, I think it was simply my desire and ability to be prepared, grounded in a fear of failure. In professional cooking, the kitchen must be ready to offer every single item on the menu when the doors open. The only way that is possible, day in and day out, is if the kitchen staff is organized and methodical about every single ingredient needed to perfectly execute the dishes on the menu. Being an academic at heart, my first purchase for the restaurant kitchen was two white boards. They are unquestionably our best media to communicate what needs to be done to get ready for service. These boards speak also to servers and ultimately, our guests, showcasing information relevant to our mission, craft, and practice. I write everything on those boards. To this day, if I am prepping for an event, I write down my shopping list and order of preparation on the board. Just as dishes and bowls start disappearing into the dish pit during a multi-course dinner, items leave the prep list indicating increasing readiness. Also, when tasting spoons start disappearing, it's a sure sign that the food is being tasted religiously and in stages, as it should.

In a perfect world, seasons give birth to ingredients, inspiring us to bring forth a dish or several dishes. A dish may be as one-dimensional as grilled fish with a wedge of lemon. Or it could be composed and layered with seasonings, accompaniments, and garnishes. In my world, everything on a plate, except perhaps the dinnerware and silverware, should be edible. But beyond that, the different elements should complement each other and result in a variety of sensory experiences. When creating a multi-course menu or holiday meal, the dishes themselves, as composed as they may be, must complement one another. A good idea is to list out the proteins, starches, vegetables, ideal serving temperatures, and of course, portion sizes to gauge exactly where one is in the planning of a multi-course meal or a restaurant menu. When developing new menus at the restaurant, I imagine a guest looking to dine who will indulge in at least two courses, sometimes more. To meet that desire, I must create a large enough variety of composed dishes so that a diner experiences a two or three course meal without ever feeling a sense of repetition, as if they received the same flavors, ingredients, and overall experience with every course. Being organized is critical, since the accompaniments to each dish are in fact unique even while they complement most of the other dishes. The same kind of thinking goes into the planning of a successful family-style holiday meal. Now imagine going through this complete mind and body exercise every time you cook.

Once you have gathered all your ingredients, visualize and write down your precooking prep list. If something needs to be oven-roasted, get it going while you continue prepping for other dishes. Even the number of pots and pans on the stove should be a function of only the items that need immediate cooking. Collecting ingredients or utensils before needing them creates unnecessary clutter, which takes up valuable space. A cluttered environment causes avoidable stress in a kitchen.

Another benefit of a list is that it facilitates multi-tasking. As a simple example, if you need onions for both a braised dish and some polenta, prepare enough onions to satisfy both needs. Say that you need a medium to large dice for the braised dish and a mince for the polenta. By doing the onion all at once, you are prepping the same ingredient, using the same knife and cutting board and using one bowl to hold both cuts (separated of course). *Mise en place* constitutes a way of life where every action is enacted—consciously at first, instinctively over time--to save space, prepping time, cleaning time, and increase efficiency. The overarching benefits are, of course, timely task completion, meaning that one is left with enough time to enjoy the fruits of the labor in the company of your guests over thoughtful food and wine.

I am often asked, "How do you know which flavors to combine?' Frankly, I don't always know. But I have a strong foundation of finding balance in food. That is the key - *balance*. *Balance* in no way means that every bite taste the same or that a spoonful is simply a miniature version of the bowl. Rather, I mean that there are sufficient complementary flavors that highlight each other. Too many flavors can result in a muddled composition. Sometimes, the simplicity of an in-season, perfectly ripe tomato with a touch of sea salt is a magical experience. The sea salt offers the perfect foil to the natural sweetness, acidity, and texture of the tomato. And other times, a complex Hyderabadi biryani with its thoughtful layering of vegetables, aromatics, spices, proteins, rice, and garnishes provides the satiation we seek. Some common rules of thumb can help develop powerful flavor combinations from the simple and serene to the complex and intriguing. For example, acidity and sodium naturally whet our taste buds to receive more flavor, so many chefs finish their dishes with a pinch of coarse salt. That first impression should be one of satiation and full flavor. When we season food, it must be done in stages rather than all at once. This is one of the main reasons that chefs prefer to use a coarse salt like Kosher salt: they can feel, within their fingers how much salt is being added at what stage. And every time salt hits a newly added ingredient, flavor is naturally drawn out into the combined dish. This is just one aspect of the important art and science of layering flavors.

To develop flavor is to facilitate the transformation of an ingredient with time and proper handling so that it hits peak flavor at the same time it is ready to be consumed. Reduction is the most common technique to help develop and intensify the flavors of sauces and soups. The conventional wisdom is to cover a simmering dish. Well, if the purpose is to simply cook the ingredient, then as long as the cooking liquid is properly seasoned, that technique is valid. Most deep flavors, however, are achieved by cooking things low and slow. Almost always, this is done uncovered, except in the case of a braised dish. Even then, after the braising is complete, chefs commonly skim off any excess fat, remove the liquid, and puree parts of the braising liquid to thicken the dish naturally and intensify the flavor.

An important key is to taste the dish at periodic stages. Reduction is simply to evaporate the neutral water and intensify all the flavors in the dish. So, if one fully seasons a dish early in the cooking process and then simmers it for a while, one runs the risk of crossing over the balanced line. On the other hand, flavors develop in stages and layers, so that you need to season as you go. In a nutshell, achieving a layered yet developed flavor involves the proper methodology of cooking and seasoning ingredients in stages coupled with tasting as you go. It all sounds very simple and with enough practice and repetition, it really can be. For that element of surprise, I always think of a component for the final composition which can stand up to the rest of the elements in the dish, but at the same time lies in complete contrast with the flavor profiles of the rest of the dish. The contrast must be along the lines of sweet versus salty, acidic versus fatty, and crisp versus smooth. The receptors on a human tongue can perceive five primary tastes: sweet, salty, sour, bitter, and umami. So, the goal for me is to make intermittent and harmonious connections between these areas of the tongue with layered and developed flavors.

The best chefs in the world, however, have made mistakes with food preparation. Burning a steak, overcooking a piece of fish, over salting a sauce, undercooking a soufflé--the list goes on. But the best chefs also learn from their mistakes. I require this in my kitchen. I ask kitchen staff every day, "What did you learn today?" And if they are not able to articulate something reasonable, it raises a red flag. I learn something new every single day. I do so in the classroom and in the kitchen. There are very few instances when a mistake in the kitchen cannot be fixed. If something is burnt, make a dip. If something is over salted, add a dairy or stir it into a bland starch like rice or potatoes. If something is too spicy (although I don't think that's really a mistake), add some natural sweetness and again, dairy to take the edge off. Almost all food is edible. Except, of course, when unredeemable spoilage occurs.

In this book are 251 recipes and they are all vegetarian. Nerd Alert: I could have stopped at 250 recipes in the book, but I added one to make it 251. What's so special about 251? It's a prime number. It's a Sophie Germain prime (because 2*251+1=503 is also a prime). It's the sum of three consecutive primes: 79 + 83 + 89. It's the sum of seven consecutive primes: 23 + 29 + 31 + 37 + 41 + 43 + 47. One gets the idea. I like numbers.

The recipes progress in the natural way from spices to chutneys, to sauces, and beyond. These recipes are simply guidelines to prepare a dish. Even when exacted, the outcome is one that the creator of the recipe desired or at least imagined. Of course, as chefs, we hope that all our guests enjoy everything we create. But, obviously, our taste buds and palates are as different as they are unique. So, the main purpose of a recipe should be to teach and share the joy of being able to achieve excitement, intrigue, balance, harmony, and satisfaction with ingredients. But it should also acknowledge the variability in what we taste and like. The amount of salt, spice, garlic, and so for this all subject to interpretation and preference. Yet, by using appropriate and proper cooking techniques and layering soulfully developed flavors, the outcomes serve as useful canvasses for further individualized experimentation and fine-tuning. If a general recipe calls for eggplant, I can tell you from experience that not all eggplant tastes the same. The eggplant in India tastes different from the eggplant in a specific Central Florida farmers' market or grocery store. The soil, water, fertilizer, seed variety, growing cycle, etc. all have some effect on the final flavor. In that case, why bother with recipes, one might wonder? Well, there is a lot of value in knowing proportions and certainly the chemical reactions significantly affect the outcome. Measurements are more about the relative proportions. In many of the recipes that follow, I tell a personal story about my inspiration for the dish. I also try to offer some modifications should there be an ingredient one cannot use, is averse to, or simply isn't available. The inspiration sometimes comes from knowing the farmer who grew that vegetable.

The recipes are rated "Basic," "Intermediate," or "Pro." These labels are simply meant to indicate that an "Easy" recipe may be more forgiving and takes fewer steps (not necessarily ingredients); one labeled "Intermediate" may require a sequence of steps and some attention to timing and the handling of the ingredients; "Pro" requires focus, care, and a deeper understanding of the development of the dish. In any case, as I tell my students, practice makes perfect, so if you like a recipe and it seems tedious at first, make it more than once. And most importantly, try to make every recipe your own by changing the ingredients, seasonings, or proportions to fit your preference after tasting it the way I have prescribed it. Only then can you unlock the full potential of what that dish can mean for you. And then, someday, those of you who have considered the possibility will write your own recipes and possibly even a cookbook. It may be one that preserves treasured family culinary traditions for future generations. After all, that is one of the greatest gifts we can give someone: the gift of food made with love.

Cooking with Spices
Generally, spices are aromatics that are used to flavor and season ingredients and sauces. Technically, a spice can be any part of a plant except the leaves (which are called herbs). Hence, spices may be derived

from stems, roots, flowers, seeds, and bark. The single most important thing to do is to either dry-toast spices to release the essential oils or to bloom them in warm oil (not water).

According to the Oxford English Dictionary, the word spice can be used to refer to "an aromatic or pungent vegetable substance used to flavor food." This is an extremely broad definition; by this measure a vegetable itself could be a spice. But most of us would agree that not all vegetables are spices. The most common misconception is that spices are spicy. When a dish has a lot of capsaicin, we would refer to it being pungent because of the sensation it stimulates. India may be the land of spices, but that doesn't mean that all Indian cuisine uses spices. For the most part, Indian cuisine is stereotyped in the tourist sections of major Indian cities, as well as outside India with all too familiar dishes. North Indian cuisine has done a masterful job of marketing itself around the globe, and recently, South Indian cuisine (what I grew up with) has made a debut on the world stage. I suppose the same could be said about the growing understanding that Indian cuisine is diverse and regionally influenced. Spices were historically used for preservation because of the general lack of refrigeration, especially in remote areas. I remember using turmeric on my wounds as an antiseptic. At home, we used numerous whole spices and just a few ground varieties. The word masala refers to a spice mix; however, it could also refer to a mix of fresh ingredients to make the base of a sauce or to marinate ingredients. Everyday cooking did not involve the use of excessive spices and was always simple and highlighted the vegetables. In Telugu, the word "kamma" refers to something being savory (not the herb). This is akin to the notion of "umami" and usually involved the use of a minimal amount of spices.

It is very important to bloom spices using consistent, low to medium heat in a fat-based medium. This process releases their essential oils. (The same is true for nuts.) Spices can certainly get stale sitting unused on kitchen shelves for months on end. They lose their aroma and, to some degree, their flavor. Dry toasting them before use helps bring them back to some life. It is still difficult to achieve the fine grind of a store-bought spice because commercial grinders are obviously more powerful. Investing in a high-powered coffee grinder is useful for the sole purpose of grinding freshly toasted spices. In North American cuisine, while it is common to add spices to a simmering soup like a chili, in Indian cuisine the spices or masalas would be added to heated oil or during the sauté stage. This is a fundamental step which must not be omitted.

For beginners, a simple staple blend is one part ground cumin, one part ground coriander (the seed of the cilantro plant), half part ground turmeric, and half part ground paprika (or cayenne depending on how pungent one likes it). Curry powder sold in grocery stores is heavy on the turmeric and distinctive in flavor and aroma. Even in India, home cooks do use store bought blends of spices, but the varieties and combinations are targeted at specific dishes rather than a generic "curry" flavor profile. I am a big fan of fresh ginger, while most people might not think of ginger as a spice.

Whole spices are a great way to infuse the intoxicating aroma and flavor of spices in a dish without the fear of overpowering it. Once again, blooming the spices early in the cooking process is important. The advantage is once the dish is finished, one can remove the whole spices. In classical French cooking, the use of a *bouquet garni* accomplishes the same result. A *bouquet garni* consists of aromatics like bay leaves, thyme, peppercorns, and parsley tied into a cheese cloth pouch with a butcher's twine. It fortifies stocks, soups, and sauces. Upon completion of the dish, the pouch is fished out and discarded. Certainly, one could use bouquet garni filled with various combinations of whole spices. If whole spices are left in the dish overnight, they have a propensity to intensify the flavor of the dish, but they will also soften, potentially resulting in inadvertently consuming them whole, which might be somewhat unpleasant--although growing up, I used to eat whole cinnamon bark and cloves just for the fun of it. For the beginning user of spices, I would recommend buying only small quantities. Unfortunately, even small quantities are extremely expensive in grocery stores. For those who grow herbs, drying them is a great way to save money. Just leaving them on a flat sheet in a dry area for a few days will naturally dry them. Doing so on the lowest setting in an oven works as well. For the experienced user of spices, it is a matter of developing a deeper understanding of the interactions between them and how they react to cooking. Ultimately, it is a matter of personal taste. But to truly develop the flavor of a dish which uses spices, using the proper amount of heat, blooming, and resting is important. A dish with spices usually tastes better after it has rested for a bit because the spices have had a chance to harmonize.

Plant-Based Alternatives
Many ingredients that serve a functional purpose need plant-based alternatives. In this section, I present a few. In general, I am not a fan of plant-based "meats." However, for classic dishes, for which a diner expects a certain texture and feel, I can see the benefit. One will notice that, in this book, there are only a handful of such instances. And that is the point. Vegetarians in India aren't craving burgers.

Egg Alternatives as Binders
AQUAFABA
Aquafaba is the left-over liquid obtained after cooking legumes like chickpeas. A preserved version is the gelatinous liquid found in canned legumes. When possible, re-hydrate dried legumes and cook them yourself for a more unadulterated version. To use aquafaba to make, say, a vegan alternative for traditional mayonnaise, simply season with salt, lemon juice, some neutral oil, and a high speed hand blender for about 10 minutes.

FLAXSEED (aka LINSEED)
An antioxidant-packed seed, flaxseed is useful in baking as a binder. Simply mix ground flaxseed with three times the volume of water and let the mixture sit for 10 minutes.

CHIA SEED
Chia seed is similar to flaxseed. Either the seed itself or a ground version can be used. Typically, a 2.5 water to 1 part chai seems to do a consistent job. Again, allow the mixture to sit for 10 minutes before using as a binder.

TAPIOCA STARCH SLURRY
Tapioca starch is a consistent gluten-free flour, and when mixed with water to make a paste or slurry, it may be used as a thickener for sauces, fillings, and even for baking.

CHICKPEA PASTE OR FLOUR
Just like Tapioca Starch, chickpea (garbanzo) flour offers a way to thicken sauces without using dairy or eggs. Simply mix with an equal amount of water to make a paste. There is no need to let the paste rest. One must also be aware of the inherent nutty flavor of chickpeas.

Milk Alternatives
NUT-BASED
There has been quite the uproar and push back from the dairy industry regarding the use of the word "milk," for any product not derived from animals. Nevertheless, there is no denying the impact of coconut milk and soy milk, specifically, and to a lesser degree, almond milk or cashew milk, as a non-dairy option. From a cooking point of view, coconut milk is the most versatile and, frankly, delicious. However, coconut milk tends to be higher in saturated fats, which explains its decadent mouthfeel. None of the nut-based milks are particularly stable under the duress of high heat or long cooking times required in certain dishes. Nut-based dairy alternatives are most effective when used to finish cooked sauces or dishes. Additionally, their flavor is distinctive, and one needs to account for that in any given dish.

GRAIN-BASED
Oat milk is delicious and extremely versatile. Its higher fat content translates as a good approximation to traditional dairy. Its flavor is extremely conducive to cooking. Other types of grain-based dairy substitutes are derived from rice and even quinoa.

SOY-BASED
Sometimes, it's best if tofu doesn't quite taste like tofu. There is no mistaking the distinctive flavor of tofu. Young soybeans, on the other hand, have a different flavor profile. Yet, blended silken tofu mixed with a bit of water is thick and may be used in place of heavy cream. The flavor is another matter. Functionally, it works well. Commercial soymilk is available in a variety of flavors and sweetness levels.

Meat Alternatives

As I've noted, life-long vegetarians don't crave meat because, well, they don't know the difference. On the contrary, the presence, aroma, and certainly texture of meat is extremely off-putting for one who has never tasted it. A useful analogy is that of native wild-life in the Galapagos Islands, who have no fear of humans because of the safe association with humans. We are influenced by our experiences. So, in order to turn the tide and satisfy a palate which is used to and even craves meat, we have to, at least in the interim, determine plausible alternatives to meat. In this book, I recognize that need and have in certain instances proposed a plant-based alternative to meat.

TOFU

Tofu is sold in a variety of textures ranging from silken to extra-firm. Depending on the application, choosing an appropriate texture is just as important as marinating the tofu before using. Despite what some prescribe, tofu is somewhat resistant to taking on other flavors. The trick is to puncture the tofu with a fork and then rubbing on a wet marinade before marinating for many hours, preferably overnight.

Alternately, dry roasting firm or extra-firm tofu shreds in the oven at, say, 325F for about an hour will dehydrate it to a texture reminiscent of tofu crumbles without any of the factory processing.

SOYA NUGGETS

My mother used to rehydrate soya nuggets in warm water for 30 minutes before squeezing out the extra water. We found it interesting and tasty when used in bhajis or curries. My mother did this purely as a nutritional supplement. Lately, I've re-discovered this product which is widely available in Indian grocery stores. Jenneffer is a fan.

TEMPEH

I am a fan of tempeh, a fermented soy-based product. Its texture is already interesting, and it marinates well, so it grills and pan-roasts really well. Its naturally nutty flavor offers richness and decadence.

SEITAN

Seitan is made by hydrating, forming, and cooking wheat gluten mixed with other flavorings and seasonings. Wheat gluten is the essential protein found in wheat. Think of it as a chewy and spongy bread. Its flavor is rather neutral and, consequently, makes for a versatile alternative to mild flavored meats like chicken and pork.

Welcome to my kitchen.

Some Recommended Substitutions for Recipe Ingredients
when an ingredient is unavailable or if you are seeking a substitution

INGREDIENT	SUBSTITUTION	INGREDIENT	SUBSTITUTION
Ajwain	Dried Thyme	Kaffir Lime	Lime/Lemon
Allspice	Cinnamon/Cloves/Nutmeg	Kokam	Tamarind/Lemon/Lime
Anise	Dried Fennel	Lavender	Tarragon
Arrowroot	Tapioca/Potato Starch	Lemon Balm	Lemon Zest
Asafoetida	Garlic/Onion Powder	Lemon Grass	Lemon/Lime Zest
Basil	Oregano	Lemon Thyme	Lemon/Thyme
Bay	Thyme	Lemon Verbena	Lemon Grass/Lemon Zest
Borage	Bay Leaves/Nasturtium	Loomi	Dried Lime/Lime Zest
Caraway	Cumin/Dill	Lovage	Celery/Parsley/Chervil
Cardamom	Nutmeg/Cinnamon	Mace	Nutmeg
Cayenne	Any Spicy Pepper	Marjoram	Oregano
Chervil	Fennel	Mint	Parsley/Basil/Shiso
Chinese Five Spice	See Recipe	Mustard	Wasabi
Chinese Parsley	Celery Leaves	Nasturtium	Watercress/Arugula
Chives	Onion/Garlic	Nutmeg	Mace/Cinnamon
Cilantro	Parsley/Mint	Oregano	Basil
Cinnamon	Nutmeg/Allspice	Paprika	Cayenne (much less)
Clove	Allspice	Parsley	Celery Tops/Cilantro
Coriander	Cumin	Pink Peppercorns	Green Peppercorns
Culantro	Cilantro/Cumin	Rosemary	Sage/Thyme
Cumin	Coriander	Saffron	Turmeric/Paprika
Curly Parsley	Cilantro	Sage	Rosemary
Curry Leaves	Bay/Lime/Basil	Savory	Thyme/Sage
Curry Powder	Turmeric/Cumin/Coriander	Shiso	Lemon Zest/Mint
Dill	Tarragon/Fennel	Sorrel	Spinach/Lemon Zest
Epazote	Oregano/Savory/Cilantro	Star Anise	Fennel/Allspice
Fennel	Dill	Sumac	Lemon/Salt/Coriander
Fenugreek	Coriander	Tamarind	Lime/Lemon/Sugar
Galangal	Ginger	Tarragon	Lavender/Dill/Fennel
Garlic Powder	Onion Powder	Thai Basil	Basil
Ginger Powder	Turmeric/Fennel	Thyme	Sage/Rosemary
Grains of Paradise	Cardamom	Turmeric	Mustard Powder
Herbs de Provence	See Recipe	Za'tar	Thyme/Sesame/Salt

DREAMING IN SPICE - A Sinfully Vegetarian Odyssey

Page Numbers & List of Recipes - I

SPICE BLENDS & MARINADES
73 Garam Masala
74 Tandoori
75 Malabar
76 Xacuti
77 Berbere
78 Bahārāt
80 Ras El Hanout
81 Herbs de Provençe
81 Tuscan
82 Sichuan
82 Chinese Five Spice
84 Togarashi
85 Jerk
86 Adobo
87 Creole

HORS D'OEUVRES
122 Jumbo Cauliflower Cake
123 Exotic Mushroom & Goat Cheese Crème Brûlée
125 Onion & Carrot Top Pakora
127 Not Your Average Falafel
129 Roasted Cabbage Momo
130 Zucchini Rockefeller
131 Samosa Spring Roll
133 Roasted Tomato, Spinach, Leek Quichelet
135 Oregano & Fontina Arancini
136 Basil & Brie Wonton
138 Rapini & White Bean Crostini
139 Cured Hearts
140 Asparagus and Tofu Egg Roll with Peanut Sauce

CHUTNEYS & RELISHES
88 Salsa Verde
90 Manchurian
91 Harissa
92 Muhammara
93 Pepperonata
94 Chimichurri
94 Coconut Cilantro
95 Mango Masala
96 Moroccan Ratatouille
97 Zaalouk
98 Romesco
99 Arugula & Tomato Pesto
100 Tomatillo Salsa Fresca
100 Roasted Pepper Coulis
102 Grilled Eggplant & Fava Bean Hummus
103 Peanut Coriander
103 Beet & Cardamom
104 Sofrito
105 Tamarind Date
105 Chermoula

SOUPS
144 Gumbo
147 Chili
148 Sopa de Mani
150 Green Chile and Coconut
151 Assorted Greens Stew
152 Provençal White Bean
153 Cream of Root Vegetables
154 Turnip & Parsnip Vichyssoise
155 Watermelon Gazpacho

SAUCES
106 Leche de Tigre
107 Creole
108 Tikka Masala
110 Saag Masala
112 Green Curry Concentrate
113 Rendang
114 Vindaloo
116 Mojo
116 Marcela Hazan Inspired
117 Mole
118 Mushroom Demi
119 Beurre Blanc
120 Pineapple Habanero
120 Truffled Gorgonzola Cream
121 Smoked Onion Cream

SALAD DRESSINGS
164 Sesame Sherry
164 Passion fruit Lemon Balm
165 Cranberry
165 Orange Ginger
166 Herb Truffle
166 Caramelized Shallot Cider
168 Green Goddess
169 Pomegranate Walnut
169 Turmeric Miso
170 Creamy Caesar

COMPOSED SALADS
171 Signature with Passion fruit
172 Kale with Apple Cider
174 Caprese with Basil Pistou

DREAMING IN SPICE - A Sinfully Vegetarian Odyssey

Page Numbers & List of Recipes - II

HORS D'OEUVRES (...)
141 Char Siu Turnip
142 Cashew Cutlet

FLOUR-BASED
186 No Knead Covid-19 Table Bread
191 Aloo Paratha
192 Naan
193, 196 Gnocchi & Gnudi
194 Injera
197 Pizza Dough
200 Blue Corn Tortilla
201 Quinoa and Buttermilk Crêpe
203 Pupusa
205 Tarragon Buttermilk Biscuit
206 Pesarattu

RICE DISHES
241 Paella
242 Pulao
244 Jambalaya
245 Biryani
246 Bengali Porridge
247 South of the Border Risotto
248 Basil & Edamame Fried Rice
249 Pulihara
250 Khichidi
252 Coconut Habanero
253 Red Beans & Rice
255 Eggplant & Tamarind
256 Pongal
257 Daddojanam (Curd Rice)
258 Umami Rice Pilaf

SOUPS (...)
156 Roasted Poblano and Corn Chowder
157 Lentil Veracruz
158 Ginger Butternut Squash
160 Tunisian Lentil Stew
161 Sorrel & Daikon Sambhar
162 Masala Lentils (Dal)

HAND-HELD
209 Ultimate Burger
211 Sloppy Joe
212 Torta
213 Mumbai Sandwich
216 Reuben
217 Banh Mi
218 Falafel Döner
219 Croque Madame
220 Po'boy
221 Ultimate Grilled Cheese

GRAINS
260 Heirloom Grains & Fiddlehead Fern Risotto
261 Bulgur Kachori
263 Quinoa, Garbanzo, Corn Pilaf
264 Freekeh Tabbouleh
264 Shiitake & Thyme Grits
265 Toasted Barley and Mirepoix Stew
266 Sorghum Roti & Dal
268 Buckwheat Crepe
268 Roasted Corn Salsa
270 Wild Rice & Cranberry

COMPOSED SALADS (...)
175 Grilled Asparagus
176 Arugula with Cranberry
178 Heirloom Grains with Sesame Sherry
180 Fennel with Orange Ginger
181 Spinach & Roasted Cherries
182 Roasted Beets & Carrots
184 Seasonal Berries & Herbs

STREET-INSPIRED
222 Pomegranate & Pakora Chaat
223 Pav Bhaji
225 Bhel
226 Ragda Pattice
228 Vada Pav
230 Arepa
231 Poutine
232 Kelewele
232 Shawarma
233 Empanada
234 California Burrito
236 Bunny Chow
236 Monsoon Corn
238 Doubles
239 Patatas Bravas

LEGUMES
272 Mung Bean & Turmeric Bowl
273 Lima and Corn Succotash
275 Chole Masala
276 Rajma (North Indian Red Beans)
277 Cannellini Cassoulet

DREAMING IN SPICE - A Sinfully Vegetarian Odyssey

Page Numbers & List of Recipes - III

PASTA
284 Spaghetti Carbonara
286 Pumpkin Gnocchi Parisienne
288 Tagliatelle Bolognese
289 Spaghetti with Lemon and Rapini
291 Bucatini Fra Diavolo
292 Pasta alla Norma
294 Pappardelle with Wild and Exotic Mushrooms
297 Capellini with Creamy Lemon & Garlic
299 Roasted Fennel and Butternut Squash Lasagna
300 Penne a la Provençal

SIDES & CONDIMENTS
344 Signature Hot Sauce
346 Pickles
347 Indian Lemon Pickle
348 Ricotta Cheese
348 Yogurt
349 Balsamic Reduction
350 Creamed Collards
353 Roasted Root Vegetables with Roasted Garlic & Lemon
354 Cauliflower & Potato Gratin
355 Rum-Glazed Apples
356 Baba Ghanoush
357 Smoked Tomatoes & Roasted Grapes
359 Infused Oils
360 Colcannon

CURRIES
301 Squash & Green Bean Kerala Curry
302 Water Chestnut and Bamboo Shoots Bengali Curry
303 Jerk Spiced Taro, Plantain, and Capsicum Curry
304 Caramelized Onion and Black Chickpea Curry
305 Roasted Vegetable & Tofu Tikka Masala
306 Brassica & Chickpea Vindaloo
307 Fennel & Eggplant Thai Green
308 Jerk Spiced Lentil Kofta Curry
309 Mushroom Chettinad
310 Vegetable Xacuti
311 Vegetable Korma
312 Vegetable Kolhapuri
313 Kohlrabi and Turnip Basil Curry
314 Eggplant and Coconut Bhaji
315 Waste Not Massaman

SIDES & CONDIMENTS (...)
361 Mumbai Potatoes
363 Okra Masala
364 Zesty Chickpeas
364 Duck or Chicken Egg Salad
365 Tzatziki
365 Guacamole

LEGUMES (...)
278 Misr Wat
279 Pinto, Green Chile, and Tortilla Stew
281 Field Pea and Asparagus Purloo
282 Smoked Black-Eyed Peas and Mustard Greens
283 Dal Makhani

GLOBAL FUSION
316 Roasted Vegetable Bisteeya
317 Acorn Squash Tajine
318 Atkilt Wat
320 Duxelle Filled Quinoa Buttermilk Crepe
322 Collard Greens Gnocchi with Blistered Tomatoes and Feta
325 Kofta Etouffee 'n Grits
326 Mushroom Bourguignon
327 Shepherd's Pie
329 Umami Ramen
331 Shakshuka
332 Baby Aubergine Fesenjoon
333 Pierogi
334 Mofongo
335 Stuffed Cabbage Rolls
336 Chilaquiles
337 Hen of the Woods Moussaka
338 Sinfully Vegetarian Bread Pudding
340 Nightshade Barbecue
341 Miso & Edamame Pot Pie
342 Beet and Radish Terrine

Page Numbers & List of Recipes – IV

SINFULLY VEGAN DEGUSTATION IN 15 ACTS

1. 366 Chilled Vichyssoise, Warm Monsoon Corn, Tarragon Oil
2. 368 Tomato Terrine, Watermelon Salsa, Textured Basil
3. 369 Exotic Mushrooms Eggplant Involtini, Roasted Garbanzo, Arrabiatta
4. 370 Radish Hollow, Tiger's Milk, Roasted Garlic
5. 371 French Fennel Soup, Thyme Croutons
6. 372 Blue Corn Johnny Cake, Ackee Hash, Lily Escabeche
7. 374 Grilled Lettuce Hearts, Black Truffle Vinaigrette, Crisp Shallots
8. 375 Lentil Gumbo, Charred Okra, Scallion Rice
9. 376 Celeriac Tot, Bloody Mary Romesco, Celery Relish
10. 377 Beet Sorbet
11. 378 Jerked Sweet Potato, Coconut Thyme Velouté, Calamondin Marmalade
12. 379 Reverse-Seared Cabbage, Pine Nut and Roasted Garlic Relish, Grilled Asparagus
13. 381 Edamame Momo, Szechuan Thukpa, Doodle
14. 382 Cauliflower Manchurian, Green Peanut Hummus, Cilantro Stem Pakora
15. 383 Caramelized Onion and Raisin Bisteeya, Fava Korma, Cardamom Cashew Crumb

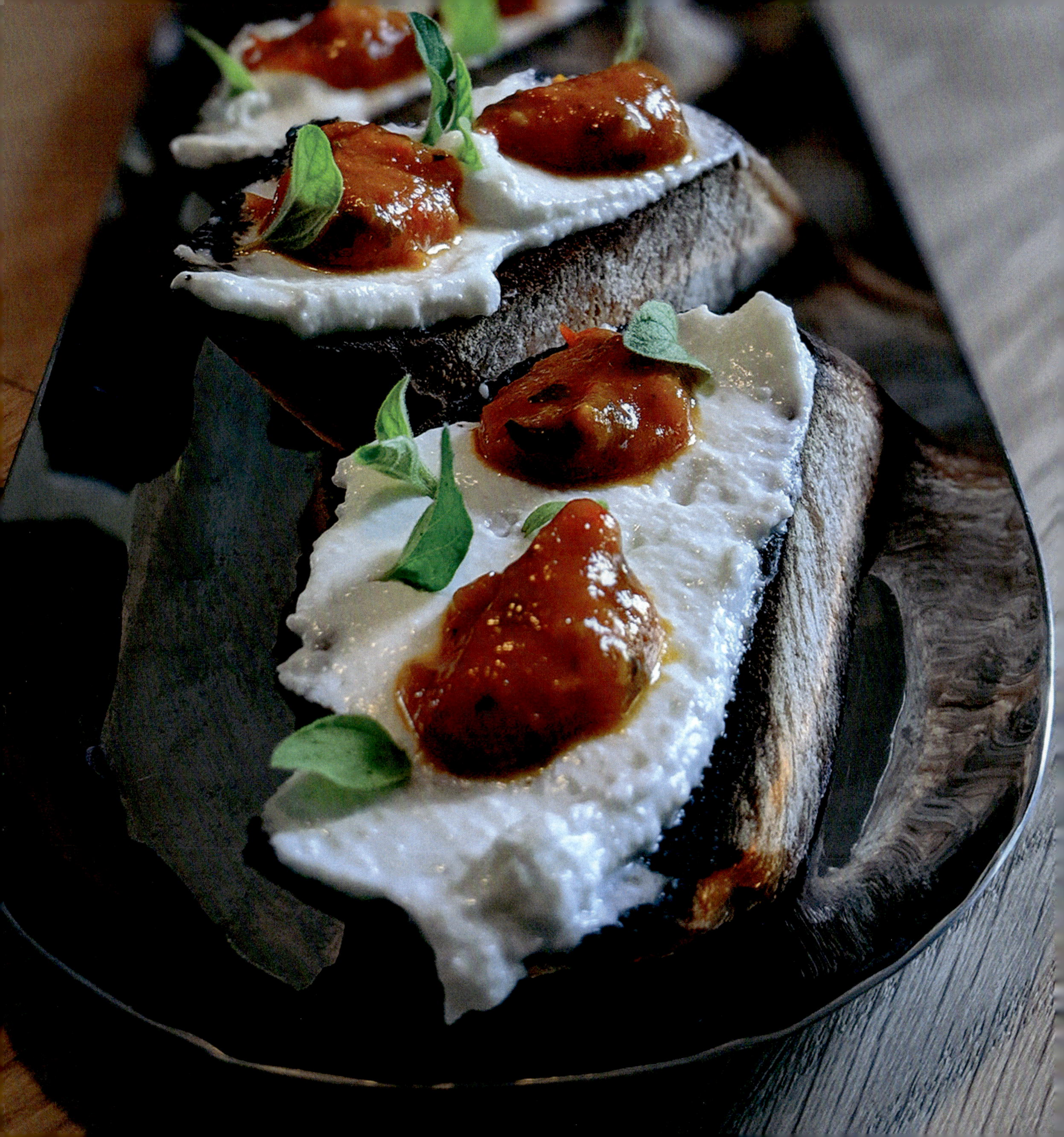

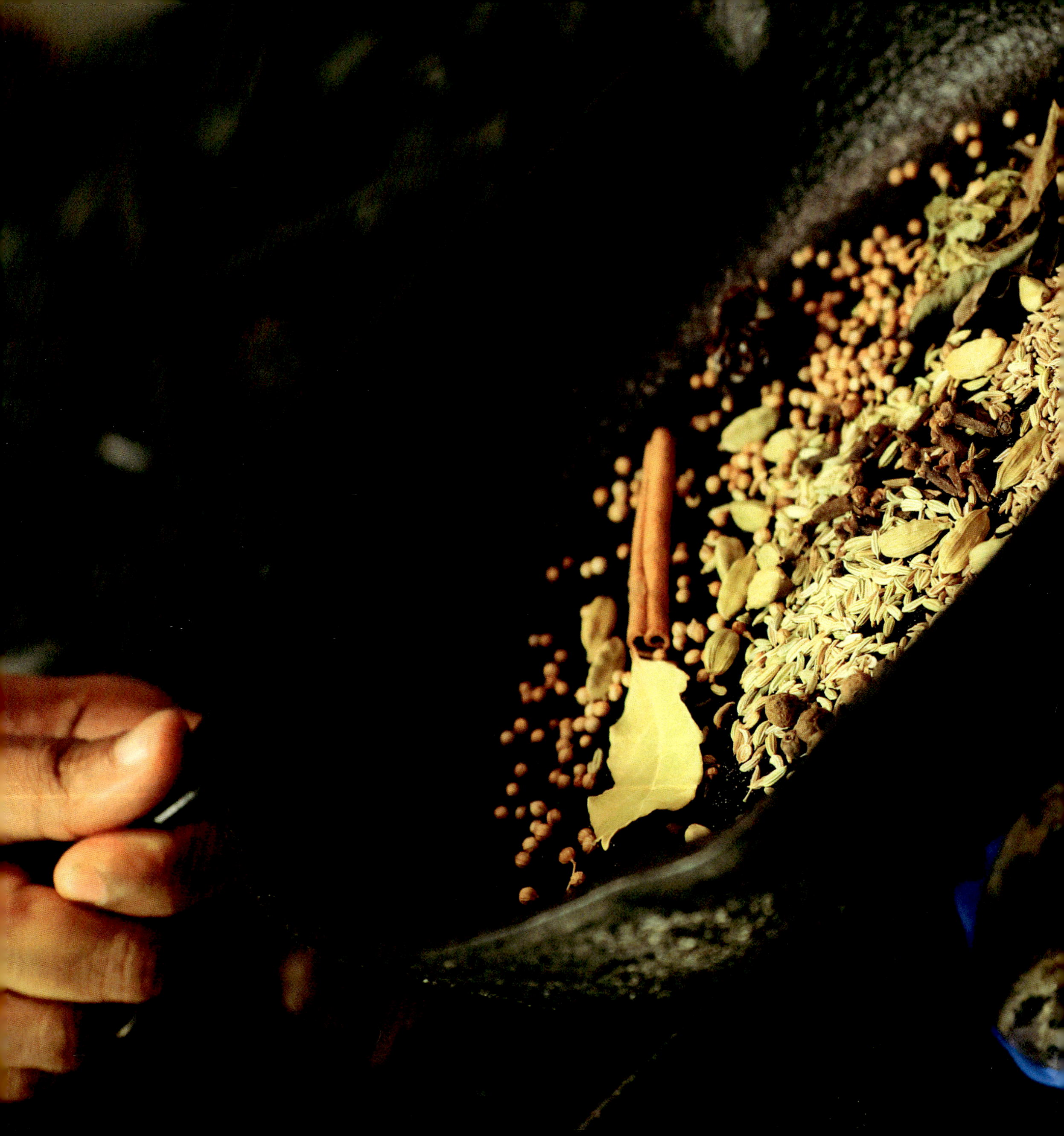

Spice Blends & Marinades

With a title like "Dreaming in Spice: A Sinfully Vegetarian Odyssey," I would be remiss if I didn't begin the recipes with an ode to spices. Here, I present world-class spice blends that are sure to fill your cooking arsenal with flavor bombs. I hope you will pardon my military metaphor. This reminds me of when the National Defense Academy of India handed me a letter stating that I did not possess sufficient officer-like qualities. They had diagnosed me well.

GARAM MASALA

This is a general-purpose blend of spices. Some have likened it to an Indian version of French herbs de Provence or Chinese five-spice powder. The word "garam" means hot or pungent, while the word "masala" simply refers to any spice or aromatic blend. This blend is not pungent, but it is simultaneously distinctive and subjective. Note: There is no "r" in masala. The fragrance and aroma can be intoxicating. Dry toast the whole spices for a few minutes on low heat before grinding in spice grinder.

LEVEL: Basic

YIELD: approximately 1/4 cup

INGREDIENTS
6 cardamom pods (green or white)
1 tablespoon coriander seed
2 teaspoons cumin seed
1 teaspoon black peppercorn
1 teaspoon whole clove
1 teaspoon fennel seed
1 cinnamon stick
1 dry bay leaf
1-piece star anise
1/2 teaspoon ground nutmeg

METHOD
Dry toast all the spices in a medium skillet over medium heat. Stir frequently. Toast for about 5 minutes or until you begin to sense the aroma. Allow the mixture to cool a bit before transferring it to a spice grinder and process to a fine blend. Store in an airtight container for up to 6 months.

TANDOORI

> The word "tandoori" suggests that the food is cooked in a traditional clay oven – a tandoor. Ideally, yes. However, these days "tandoori" is used as an adjective carrying that oven-baked suggestion. This blend is designed as a dry rub or in a marinade for grilled dishes. Slabs of firm tofu and paneer take well to this spice rub, especially when combined with yogurt and lemon juice.

LEVEL: Basic

YIELD: approximately 1 cup

INGREDIENTS
2 tablespoons coriander seed
1 tablespoon cumin seed
1 teaspoon whole black pepper (preferably Malabar)
1/2 teaspoon whole clove
1 teaspoon ginger powder
1 teaspoon garlic powder
1 teaspoon ground nutmeg
2 teaspoons fenugreek leaves
1 black cardamom pod
1 inch piece cinnamon stick
1 teaspoon ground mace
1 tablespoon Kashmiri red chili powder
1 teaspoon turmeric powder
1 teaspoon sugar
coarse salt, to taste

METHOD
Dry toast all whole spices in a thick-bottomed pan, like a cast-iron skillet, on a low to medium flame. Stir periodically to prevent burning the spices. After 10 minutes, set aside to cool. Blend all spices and seasonings in a dedicated spice grinder until you have a smooth powder. Store in an airtight container. It may be best to portion into smaller batches to preserve the integrity of the unused portions.

MALABAR

> The Malabar coast of India is best known for amazing cuisine with an emphasis on resourceful use of the bounty of the terroir - coconut many ways, spices, light and fragrant dishes bursting with freshness and intoxicating aroma are hallmarks. This spice blend tries to evoke that experience. It's best with a wide variety of tropical or coastal dishes. The distinctive Malabar peppercorns are a stand-out.

LEVEL: Basic

YIELD: approximately 1 1/2 cups

INGREDIENTS

- 1/4 cup coriander seed
- 1/4 cup dry, unsweetened coconut
- 2 tablespoons cumin seed
- 1 tablespoon fennel seed
- 1 tablespoon dried fenugreek leaves
- 4 green cardamom pod
- 4 whole clove
- 2 star anise
- 2 whole dried red chilies
- 1 inch piece cinnamon stick
- 1/2 teaspoon fenugreek seed
- 2 teaspoons Malabar black peppercorn
- 1 teaspoon black mustard seed
- 1 teaspoon turmeric powder
- 1 teaspoon dried ginger powder
- 1/4 cup curry leaf powder or 6 whole curry leaves

METHOD

Dry toast all whole spices in a thick-bottomed pan, like a cast-iron skillet, on a low to medium flame. Stir periodically to prevent burning the spices. After 10 minutes, add the remaining ingredients and toast on a slow flame for an additional 5 minutes before setting aside to cool. Blend all ingredients in a dedicated spice grinder until you have a smooth powder. Store in an airtight container. It may be best to portion into smaller batches to preserve the integrity of the unused portions.

XACUTI

> While Vindaloo may stake a claim as the iconic preparation from Goa, Xacuti best captures the complexity of what is now a stellar example of indigenous flavors gently welcoming a colonial imposition. This blend is an earthy accompaniment to coastal dishes, especially from Goa, and may also be used as part of a marinade or sauce. Blooming the blend in warm oil will give the best results.

LEVEL: Basic

YIELD: approximately 2 1/2 cups

INGREDIENTS
1/4 cup Kashmiri dry red chilies
1 teaspoon turmeric powder
1 teaspoon white poppy seed
1/2 teaspoon fenugreek seed
1/2 teaspoon black mustard seed
1 teaspoon cinnamon powder
1 teaspoon black peppercorn
1 teaspoon whole clove
4 whole green cardamom
1/2 teaspoon cumin seed
1/2 cup fennel seed
1/2 cup coriander seed
1/4 teaspoon ground mace
1 whole black cardamom
1/4 teaspoon carraway seed
1/4 teaspoon dagad phool (black stone flower, available in Indian grocery stores)
2 dried bay leaf
1 teaspoon ground nutmeg

METHOD
Dry toast all whole spices in a thick-bottomed pan, like a cast-iron skillet, on a low to medium flame. Stir periodically to prevent burning the spices. After 10 minutes, add the remaining ingredients and toast on a slow flame for an additional 5 minutes before setting aside to cool. Blend all ingredients in a dedicated spice grinder until you have a smooth powder. Store in an airtight container. It may be best to portion into smaller batches to preserve the integrity of the unused portions.

BERBERE

> The first time I tried Ethiopian food was in 1988 at *Meskerem Ethiopian Restaurant,* located in the Adams Morgan neighborhood of Washington D.C. As a graduate student at George Mason University, I routinely took a weekend foray via metro into the nation's capital. The wafting aroma of Meskerem's dining room was strangely comforting, and I vowed after the first visit to teach myself the ways of this beautiful food. Berber cuisine and berbere spice blends are the soul of Ethiopian cuisine. For cross-cultural creations, the blend may also be used in a wide swathe of North African dishes. After 30 years, Meskerem closed in 2015. Even though in its later years it fell in status and execution, when I saw the news, a silent tear may have been shed.

LEVEL: Basic

YIELD: approximately 2 cups

INGREDIENTS

1 teaspoon ground ginger
8-10 white or green cardamom pods
1/2 teaspoon fenugreek seeds
1/2 teaspoon whole coriander seeds
1/2 teaspoon whole cumin seeds
1/2 teaspoon black peppercorns
1/2 teaspoon ground cinnamon (or cinnamon stick)
6-8 teaspoons whole cloves
1/4 teaspoon allspice berries
2 teaspoons salt
1/2 cup cayenne pepper (cut back if you don't want that much spicy)
1/2 cup sweet paprika

METHOD

Heat a large heavy pan, like a cast iron skillet. Add all ingredients to the pan and toast on dry heat (no oil) for 5-10 minutes on low heat, stirring frequently. Allow cooling; blend in a spice blender, store in a sealed jar. To make the paste, mix with enough unsalted butter and set aside in a refrigerator.

BAHĀRĀT

Not to be confused with Bharat – the Hindi (via Sanskrit) word for India. Bahārāt (the Arabic word for spices) is a delicate blend that highlights dishes native to the Middle East but is equally at home in Turkish and even Greek dishes. The assertive use of warm spices is perfect for applications that demand roasting or baking. Certainly, one may combine with garlic and olive oil, creating a marinade or basting oil.

LEVEL: Basic

YIELD: approximately 1 cup

INGREDIENTS
3 tablespoons black peppercorns
2 tablespoons coriander seed
1-inch piece of cinnamon stick
1 teaspoon whole clove
2 tablespoons cumin seed
4 whole green cardamom pods
1 tablespoon ground nutmeg or 1 whole nutmeg
1/4 cup paprika

METHOD
Dry toast all whole spices in a thick-bottomed pan, like a cast-iron skillet, on a low to medium flame. Stir periodically to prevent burning the spices. After 10 minutes, add the remaining ingredients and toast on a slow flame for an additional 5 minutes before setting aside to cool. Blend all ingredients in a dedicated spice grinder until you have a smooth powder. Store in an airtight container.

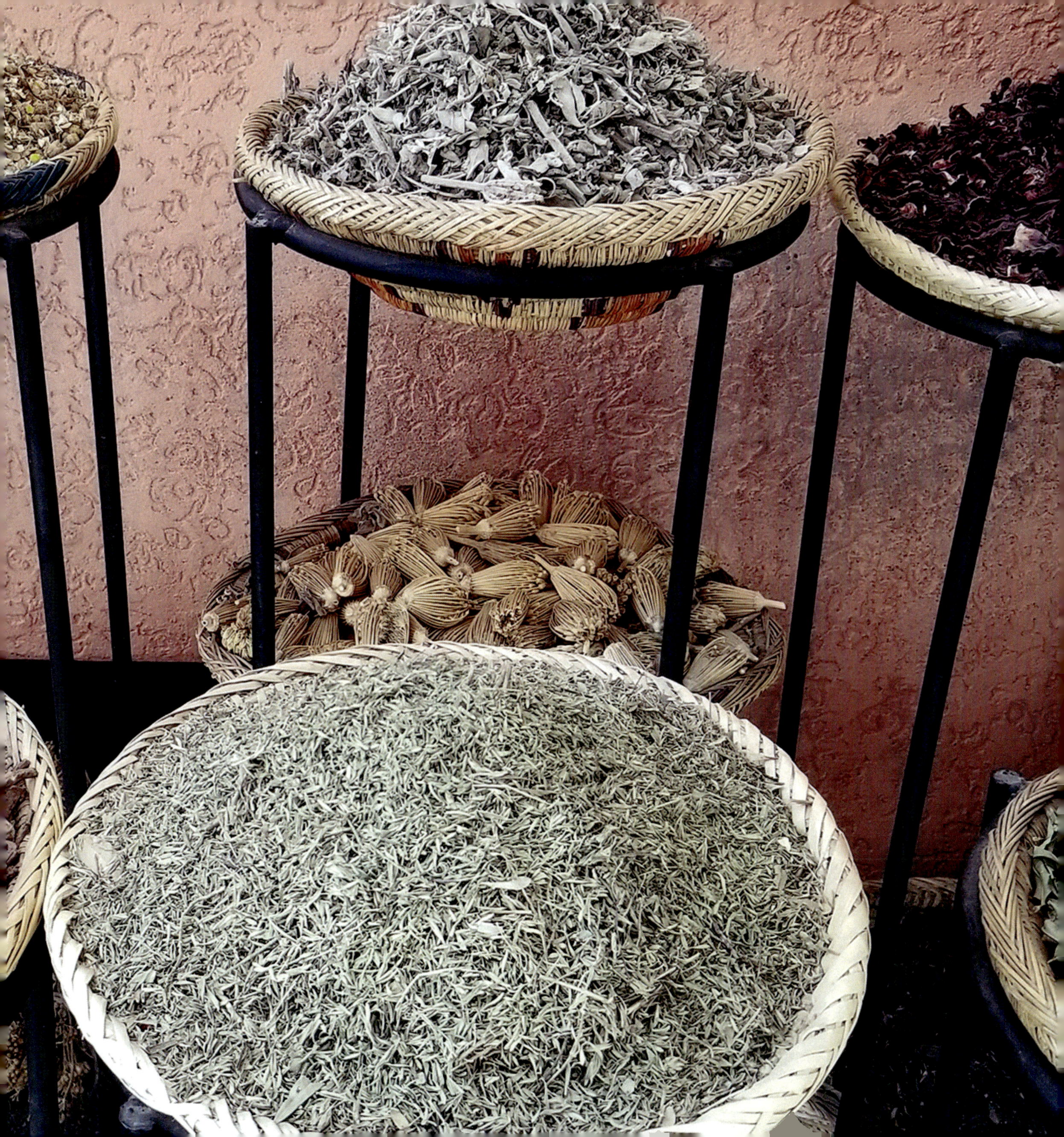

RAS EL HANOUT

> Ras El Hanout is a complex, aromatic Moroccan spice blend. Most recipes include cardamom, nutmeg, anise, mace, cinnamon, ginger, various peppers, and turmeric, but 30 or more ingredients might be used. Typically prepared by grinding together whole spices, dried roots, and leaves, this recipe keeps things simple by using mostly spices. Ras El Hanout's literal translation from Arabic is "head of the shop," implying that it's "the best (or top) of the shop." Some Moroccans use it in daily cooking; others reserve it for specialty dishes.

LEVEL: Basic

YIELD: approximately 1/2 cup

INGREDIENTS
2 teaspoons ground ginger
2 teaspoons ground cardamom
1 teaspoon turmeric
1 teaspoon smoked paprika
1 teaspoon sweet paprika
1 teaspoon cayenne or other dried chili powder
1 teaspoon whole cumin seeds
1 teaspoon whole fennel seeds
1/4 teaspoon ground cloves
1/2 teaspoon ground anise seeds
2 teaspoons ground mace
1 teaspoon ground allspice
1 teaspoon ground coriander seed
1 teaspoon ground nutmeg
1/2 teaspoon ground black pepper
1/2 teaspoon ground white pepper
1 teaspoon coarse salt

METHOD
Toast all the ingredients in a large dry pan on low-medium heat until you can detect the fragrance. Blend all the spices in a spice (I use a dedicated coffee) grinder. Transfer to a glass jar, and store in a dry, dark place. Use Ras El Hanout to season tagines, stews, meat, poultry, fish and vegetables, or even zaalouk. It keeps well for several months.

HERBS DE PROVENÇE

> Earlier this year, just before COVID-19 changed everything, Jenneffer and I visited Provençe for a week while maintaining--wait for it--Monte Carlo as home base. No, we didn't suddenly become independently wealthy, but after careful consideration, were finally able to take up Ram and Sita on their long-standing invitation to visit them in the French principality. The vineyards in Provençe are stunning enough, but the lavish fields of lavender and wild rosemary capture the beauty of the region and this spice blend almost perfectly. The blend is distinctively Provençal and ideal to use during roasting or grilling.

LEVEL: Basic

YIELD: approximately 1/2 cup

INGREDIENTS
2 tablespoons dried oregano
3 tablespoons dried thyme
2 teaspoons dried basil
1/2 teaspoon rubbed sage
2 tablespoons ground savory
2 tablespoons lavender flowers or 1 tablespoon ground lavender
1 teaspoon dried rosemary

METHOD
Mix all the ingredients well and store in an airtight container.

TUSCAN BLEND

> I haven't been to Italy (yet)--not even during a transit stopover at an airport. When it comes to food, everyone has a bit of Italian in them. How else could we explain the universal love of pizza and pasta? I feel Italian food, so you won't find me cooking pasta and topping it with dollops of sauce. Instead, a layered marriage of sauce and pasta is what I prefer. This blend is ideal for soups, stews, and roasts.

LEVEL: Basic

YIELD: approximately 1/4 cup

INGREDIENTS
4 teaspoons dried basil
2 teaspoons dried rosemary
3 teaspoons dried oregano
2 teaspoons garlic powder
2 teaspoons paprika
2 teaspoons ground fennel

METHOD
Mix all the ingredients well and store in an airtight container.

SICHUAN

> Szechuan cooking represents culinary traditions from the Sichuan Province of China. The flavors tend to be bold and sometime spicy--as in pungent. Generous amounts of garlic and Sichuan peppercorns are hallmarks. The unique, tongue-numbing tingle of these peppercorns is addictive, providing an endorphin rush like no other. This blend is ideal for quick sauté (stir-fry) in a wok for developing pan sauces. Bloom the blend early in the application.

LEVEL: Basic

YIELD: approximately 3/4 cup

INGREDIENTS
1/4 cup cumin seed
1 tablespoon dried Sichuan chile flakes
2 tablespoons black peppercorn
2 tablespoons Sichuan peppercorn
2 tablespoons ginger powder
1 tablespoon garlic powder
1 teaspoon red chili powder
coarse salt, to taste

METHOD
Dry toast all whole spices in a thick-bottomed pan, like a cast-iron skillet, on a low to medium flame. Stir periodically to prevent burning the spices. After 10 minutes, add the remaining ingredients and toast on a slow flame for an additional 5 minutes before setting aside to cool. Blend all ingredients in a dedicated spice grinder until you have a smooth powder. Store in an airtight container. It may be best to portion into smaller batches to preserve the integrity of the unused portions.

CHINESE 5-SPICE

> If one could use only five spices in a blend, what would they be? This perfectly exotic blend has been hijacked for mostly non-vegetarian proteins. I recommend challenging those stereotypical applications. The blend is very fragrant, so less can be more. Good for cast-iron cooking or grilling.

LEVEL: Basic

YIELD: approximately 1/4 cup

INGREDIENTS
2-inch piece cinnamon stick
10 whole cloves
2 teaspoons fennel seed
3 star anise
2 teaspoons Sichuan peppercorns

METHOD
Dry toast all the spices in a heavy-bottomed pan, like a cast iron skillet, for 10 minutes on low to medium heat. Let the mixture cool before grinding. Store in an airtight container.

KAMPOT PEPPER

LY CHHEANG
White pepper

200g (8 $)

Batch number:

TOGARASHI

> Without meaning to cast aspersions, one doesn't usually think of Japanese culinary traditions as employing too many dry spices or blends. However, togarashi and others like it push against that reputation. This blend exudes umami and exotic distinctiveness. It may be used as a finishing flavor for soups, stews, and noodle dishes like the ubiquitous ramen. It is also wonderful as a crust before searing or roasting. And let's not forget its place in sushi rolls.

LEVEL: Basic

YIELD: approximately 1/4 cup

INGREDIENTS
1 tablespoon Sichuan peppercorn or red chili flakes
1 tablespoon dried orange peel, chopped finely
1 tablespoon black sesame seed
1/2 sheet nori (dried and toasted seaweed)
2 teaspoons ginger powder
1 teaspoon white poppy seed
coarse salt, to taste

METHOD
Dry toast the peppercorns. Grind the nori and coarse grind the peppercorns. Mix with all the remaining ingredients and store in an airtight container.

JERK

The term *jerk* refers to a style of cooking (marinating, roasting/smoking) as well as a blend of spices as a dry rub or a wet marinade. As far as I am concerned, traditional Jamaican jerk dishes represent the perfect melding of new world and old world ingredients. I fell in love with these flavors from the very first time I experienced them in graduate school at a potluck dinner. Scotch Bonnet peppers are the pride and joy of many Caribbean islands. Recently, my friends Jim and Melissa Jackson were able to share four Scotch Bonnet peppers that purportedly trace their plant lineage back to Bob Marley himself! I don't have a green thumb, but I've saved the seeds for anyone who does. At the end of the day, this is my interpretation of the heart and soul of Jamaica. Best in a marinade followed by grilling or roasting. It is pungent...

LEVEL: Basic

YIELD: approximately 3/4 cup

INGREDIENTS
1 bunch scallions
5 cloves fresh garlic
1 tablespoon fresh ginger
3-4 Scotch Bonnet (or habanero) peppers
4 tablespoon fresh thyme
4 fresh sage leaves with stems
1 fresh orange (juice plus zest)
1/2 bunch fresh cilantro (with stems)
2 tablespoon red wine vinegar
1 teaspoon light brown sugar
1 medium onion
3 tablespoon whole allspice
1 tablespoon whole black peppercorn
1 tablespoon whole cumin seed
1 teaspoon whole coriander seed
1 teaspoon coarse salt

METHOD
Toast and coarse grind the allspice, black peppercorns, cumin seeds, coriander seeds. Add the ground spice mixture to the scallions, garlic, ginger, peppers, thyme, sage, orange juice & zest, cilantro, vinegar, brown sugar, and salt in a food processor. Blend well. This is the jerk paste.

ADOBO

Adobo, widely considered a national dish of sorts, is a specific style with origins in the Philippines. However, in many parts of Caribbean and Mexican cooking, the term *adobo* refers to a distinctive flavor profile obtained by the addition of a specific type of spice blend. The term *adobo* is a style of cooking, a specific dish, a sauce, and also a blend of spices. Here, I present a spice blend in the style of a commonly available version in Latin markets. Almost any dish shines brighter with its addition. I recommend it in one-pot rice dishes and stews.

LEVEL: Basic

YIELD: approximately 1/4 cup

INGREDIENTS
1 tablespoon paprika
2 teaspoons black peppercorn
2 teaspoons onion powder
1 teaspoon dried oregano
2 teaspoons cumin seed
1 teaspoon garlic powder
1 teaspoon chili powder
1 tablespoon coarse salt

METHOD
Dry toast all the ingredients for 10 minutes in a heavy bottomed pan, like a cast iron skillet. Let the mixture cool before grinding to desired fineness. Store in an airtight container.

CREOLE

> Is it *Creole* or *Cajun*? A common cause of confusion, but the terms should not be used interchangeably. While there are definite commonalities, one distinction is place of origin. *Creole* is considered more a product of New Orleans, the behemoth of culture and identity in the state of Louisiana. *Creole* is the formal amalgamation of Spanish, Caribbean, and certainly French, influences. *Cajun* on the other hand is influenced by the Acadiana region of the southwestern part of the state, also with a strong French influence. Some references refer to the presence of tomatoes in *Creole* and absence/omission of tomatoes in *Cajun* cuisine. Seems a bit flimsy a distinction, if you ask me. The origins notwithstanding, this blend is wonderful for sauces and in marinades prior to grilling or roasting.

LEVEL: Basic

YIELD: approximately 1 cup

INGREDIENTS
1 tablespoon paprika
2 teaspoons black peppercorn
2 teaspoons onion powder
1 teaspoon dried oregano
2 teaspoons cumin seed
1 teaspoon garlic powder
1 teaspoon chili powder
1 tablespoon coarse salt

METHOD
Dry toast all the ingredients for 10 minutes in a heavy-bottomed pan, like a cast iron skillet. Let the mixture cool before grinding to desired fineness. Store in an airtight container.

Chutneys & Relishes

India is the land of chutneys. The word "chutney" has been hijacked by colonists who seem to want to add dried fruit in every version. Here the chutneys and relishes are completed condiments, so they can used as accompaniments for just about anything.

SIGNATURE SALSA VERDE

You know how cuisines of Europe, especially the Mediterranean, have salsa verde? You know how Mexican and South American cuisines have salsa verde? Well, this is a different concoction altogether. I think you will be impressed. It tastes good with just about anything and, moreover, is a great catch-all for wilted herbs and leaves of many vegetables. Used for tacos and sandwiches or as a bright, herbaceous accent on composed dishes, the salsa stays fresh and vibrant in the refrigerator for up to a week.

LEVEL: Basic

YIELD: approximately 1 quart

INGREDIENTS
1 cup cashew nut, toasted
2 lemons, zested and juiced
2 limes, zested and juiced
4 cloves garlic, peeled
1 tablespoon extra-virgin olive oil
1/4 cup honey
1/4 cup white or golden balsamic vinegar
1 tablespoon skin-on ginger, minced
2 tablespoons Dijon mustard
1 bunch basil leaves with tender stems, washed
1 bunch cilantro with stems, washed and roughly chopped
1 bunch flat-leaf parsley with stems, washed and roughly chopped
1 jalapeño (with seeds), chopped
granulated sugar, as needed
salt & pepper, in stages and per taste

METHOD
In a food processor, grind the nuts until they are a fine crumb. Add the citrus juices and zest, garlic, olive oil, honey, vinegar, ginger, and mustard. Process well. Add remaining ingredients. Puree well. Taste the chutney and adjust the salt and sugar levels, as desired.

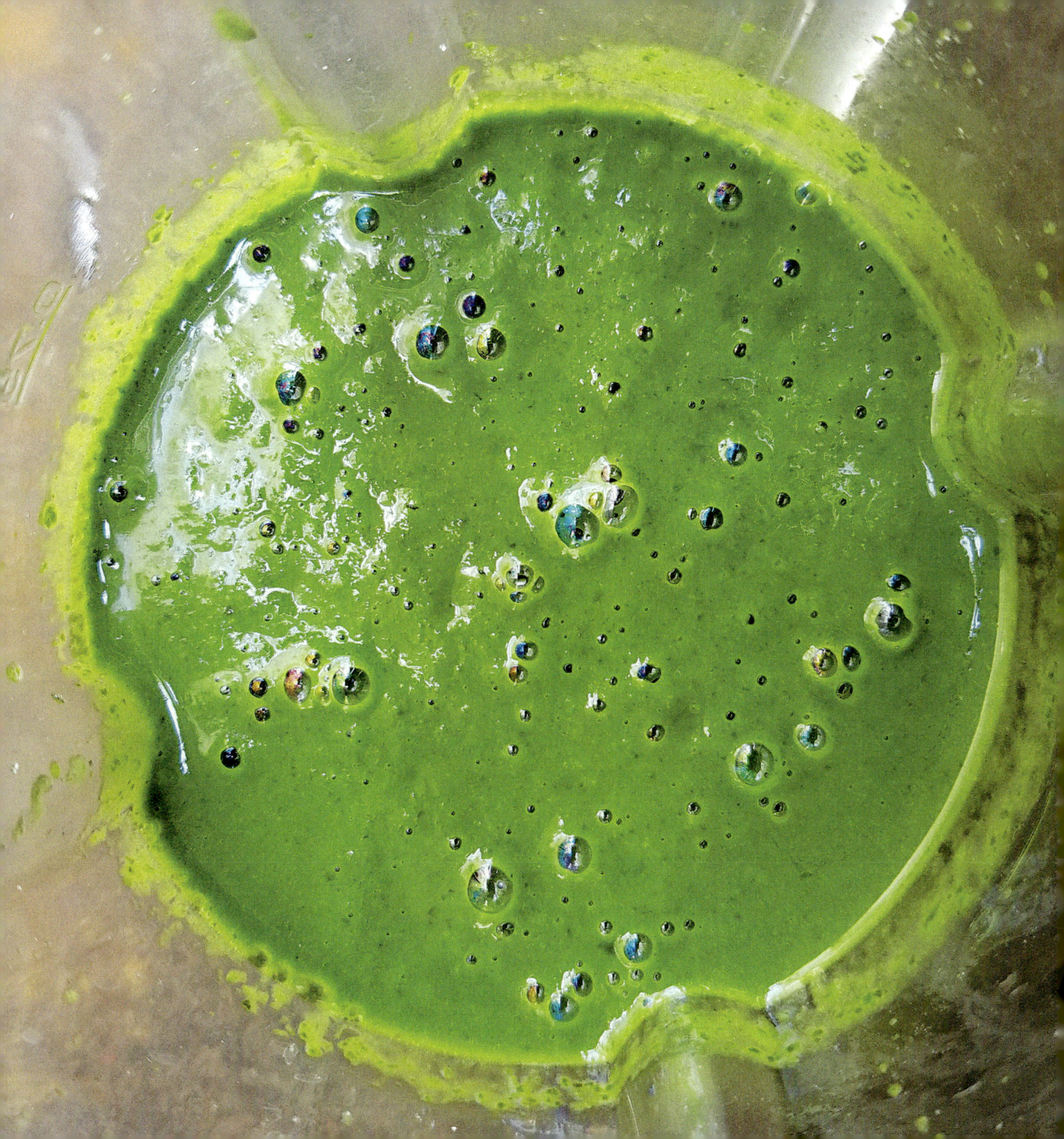

MANCHURIAN

Manchuria is a region in what is today's north-east China. Indo-Chinese cuisine is popular throughout north-eastern India and, thanks to the melting pot that is Mumbai, an extremely popular cuisine in my hometown. There is sweet and sour--and then, there is Manchurian. Gobi (cauliflower) Manchurian is a popular appetizer in many Indian restaurants, but this sauce extends that application and is wonderful for quick sautés or stir-frys or as a dipping sauce.

LEVEL: Basic

YIELD: approximately 2 quarts

INGREDIENTS
1 medium red onion, diced
1 cup scallion, chopped
1 green bell pepper, cored and diced
1 jalapeño with seeds, diced
1 tablespoon ginger, minced
1 tablespoon garlic, minced
1 bunch cilantro (chop stems and leaves separately)
1 cup ketchup
1 tablespoon cumin powder
1 tablespoon coriander powder
1 teaspoon turmeric powder
1 cup chopped tomatoes
1/2 cup low sodium soy sauce
1 cup sweet chili sauce
1 cup sambal or red chili and garlic paste
1/2 cup light brown sugar
1 cup water
1/2 cup vegetable oil
salt & pepper, in stages and per taste

METHOD
In a saucepan, heat the vegetable oil to medium heat and sauté the onions, scallions, cilantro stems, and green pepper for about 5 minutes, Next, add the ginger, garlic, and jalapeño. Stir for 30 seconds. Next add the cumin, coriander, turmeric, some salt, and pepper and stir for a minute. Now add the tomatoes and cook for about 5 minutes. Finally add the remaining ingredients including the water, and check the seasoning, adding more salt as needed. Simmer for about 20 minutes uncovered on low heat. Stir as needed. Let the sauce cool before blending with the fresh cilantro leaves. Store the sauce in an airtight container in the refrigerator. It should keep for several weeks without spoiling. This sauce is also great on Banh Mi sandwiches and tacos.

HARISSA

> Harissa has become associated with North African cuisines. When you want to spice up North African dishes covering the cuisines of Algeria, Libya, Morocco, and Tunisia, I find that harissa, more than any standard hot condiment, is the appropriate *spicer-upper*. Nowadays, it is even commonly available tableside in casual Middle-Eastern restaurants to help spice up a falafel or gyro wrap.

LEVEL: Basic

YIELD: approximately 1 cup

INGREDIENTS

3 tablespoons coriander seeds
3 tablespoons cumin seeds
1 tablespoon sumac powder
2 tablespoons dried crushed red pepper
extra-virgin olive oil, as needed
4 garlic cloves
6 tablespoons Hungarian sweet paprika (may substitute hot paprika)
1 teaspoon smoked paprika
salt & pepper, in stages and per taste

METHOD

Toast the cumin and coriander seeds in a dry pan over medium heat for 3 minutes. Add all ingredients to a food processor and whirl together until smooth. Add enough olive oil to make a smooth paste. Can be made ahead and kept (for a very long time) in the refrigerator.

MUHAMMARA

> It's just fun to say the word *Muhammara*! Now, you can repeat the name frequently as you make the mixture rather easily. The key is using pomegranate molasses and Aleppo peppers. However, a tart cherry or cranberry reduction combined with Ancho pepper powder provide reasonable substitutions. This is a fantastic dipping sauce for crudité or for hand-helds or as a dipping relish.

LEVEL: Basic

YIELD: approximately 1 1/2 quarts

INGREDIENTS
1 cup walnuts
3 large red bell peppers
2 tablespoons Aleppo pepper or red chile flakes
1 tablespoon tahini
juice and zest of 1/2 lemon
1 teaspoon paprika
2 tablespoons pomegranate molasses, plus a bit more
fresh breadcrumbs, as needed
extra-virgin olive oil, as needed
salt & pepper, in stages and per taste

METHOD
Dry toast the walnuts and set aside. In a 350F oven, coat the red bell peppers with olive oil, salt, and pepper. Roast uncovered for about 40 minutes until the peppers are well charred. Remove the seeds. Cover the peppers for 15 minutes so it is easy to peel the skin. Peel the peppers and reserve a third of the charred skin along with the flesh.

Reserve 1/2 cup of the toasted walnuts and chop coarsely. Transfer all the remaining ingredients to a food processor and grind to a smooth mixture. Transfer to a bowl and garnish with the chopped walnuts and a drizzle of pomegranate molasses.

PEPPERONATA

This is an agrodolce-style condiment made with a variety of peppers, tomatoes, fresh herbs, and bright acidity. When the vegetables are ripe and naturally sweet, the final punch of flavor is fantastically balanced. It complements any creamy flavor with the built-in vibrancy. It is also wonderful for hors d'oeuvres like crostini.

LEVEL: Basic

YIELD: approximately 1 1/2 quarts

INGREDIENTS

2 medium yellow onions, sliced 1/4 inch thick
2 each red, yellow, and orange bell peppers
1 teaspoon cayenne powder
8 cloves garlic, thinly sliced
2 medium ripe tomatoes
2 sprigs fresh oregano, leaves only
1 cup fresh basil leaves
2 tablespoons red wine vinegar
extra-virgin olive oil, as needed
salt & pepper, in stages and per taste

METHOD

Preheat an oven to 375F. On a baking sheet, coat the onions, peppers, and tomatoes in olive oil. Season lightly with salt and pepper. Roast for about 30 minutes or until the pepper skin is blistered. Peel the peppers after covering and allowing to steam. In a saucepan, brown the garlic lightly in olive oil before adding the roasted vegetables. Season lightly and cook on a medium heat until most of the moisture has evaporated. Put the cooked mixture, fresh herbs, vinegar, and cayenne in a food processor and blend to a semi-coarse consistency. Taste and adjust the seasoning as desired. Add more vinegar and spice for punch. Serve at any temperature.

CHIMICHURRI

> Traditionally, chimichurri is paired with a grilled protein. My interpretation has complementary herbs and spice, naturally. I recommend using it alongside grilled vegetables or mushrooms.

LEVEL: Basic

YIELD: approximately 1 quart

INGREDIENTS
2 cups fresh flat leaf parsley (with some stems)
1/2 cup fresh basil
2 cloves fresh garlic
1 jalapeño or serrano pepper, more if desired
1 teaspoon ground cumin
juice and zest of 1 lemon
2 tablespoons red wine vinegar
1/2 cup fruity extra virgin olive oil, or as needed
salt & pepper, in stages and per taste

METHOD
Blend all the ingredients except the olive oil. When a smooth "paste" is achieved, add the extra virgin olive oil gradually on low speed. Taste and re-season if necessary.

COCONUT CILANTRO

> A tasty accompaniment with dosas, idlis, savory crêpes, sandwiches, and fritters. One gets the idea.

LEVEL: Basic

YIELD: approximately 1 quart

INGREDIENTS
1 cup fresh unsweetened coconut (either grated freshly or available from the frozen section in some grocery stores)
1 cup plain yogurt (optional)
1 teaspoon mustard seed
1 teaspoon cumin seed
2 green chilies sliced into large pieces
1/2 inch fresh ginger, peeled, sliced thinly
4-5 curry leaves, if available
1 tablespoon vegetable oil
1 cup fresh cilantro, chopped
salt & pepper, in stages and per taste

METHOD
Grind the coconut in a food processor until it's not so coarse. Mix this with the yogurt and add some water if necessary, to thin it a bit. In a hot pan, warm the oil and add the mustard seeds and cumin seeds. They will "pop" almost instantaneously. Next, add the chilies, curry leaves, and ginger. They will also "pop." Stir for 15 seconds. Turn off the heat and pour all the ingredients of the hot pan, including the host oil into the coconut-yogurt mixture. Season with salt as needed. Mix in the fresh cilantro and stir well.

MANGO MASALA

> Finally, a chutney in the style of an English interpretation of Indian chutney: one with ripe fruit. I make an exception here because it would be a travesty to not showcase the queen of all fruit. The Alphonso mango is legendary in India. The Portuguese are said to have introduced grafting techniques, which allowed for varieties like the Alphonso to develop. Mango pulp (either Kesar or Alphonso) combined with many traditional chutney ingredients will harmonize into a spectacular condiment. One can control the natural sweetness of the fruit with complementary acidity and spice.

LEVEL: Basic

YIELD: approximately 1 1/2 quarts

INGREDIENTS
- 1 can mango puree (available at most Indian grocery stores)
- 1 medium red onion, small dice
- 1 tablespoon fresh ginger, minced
- 1 teaspoon minced garlic
- 1/2 jalapeño, minced
- 1 cup ripe tomatoes, diced
- 2 teaspoons cumin powder
- 1 teaspoon coriander powder
- 1 teaspoon turmeric powder
- 1 tablespoon light brown sugar
- 1 teaspoon red wine vinegar
- 1/2 teaspoon cayenne pepper
- 2 tablespoons vegetable or extra virgin olive oil
- salt & pepper, in stages and per taste

METHOD

In a pan, sauté the onions and ginger in the oil over medium heat until slightly caramelized. Add the garlic and jalapeno and stir for 30 seconds. Next, add the brown sugar, cumin, coriander, cayenne, and turmeric. Stir for a minute over low-medium heat. Add the tomatoes, brown sugar, and red wine vinegar. Stir for 2 minutes. Now add the mango puree and stir well. Test to see if more salt or pepper is needed. Simmer on low heat for 30 minutes, stirring frequently. Let the mixture cool. Blend to the desired consistency and store in airtight containers in the refrigerator.

MOROCCAN RATATOUILLE

This version of ratatouille may be served as a side dish or as an entree with some crusty baguette or flat bread like pita, naan, or injera. Perfect for a spring or summer spread. The first time I made this was for a national hospital cooking channel while promoting seasonal vegetables.

LEVEL: Intermediate

YIELD: approximately 3 quarts

INGREDIENTS
1 cup medium diced eggplant
1 cup medium diced summer squash
1 cup medium diced ripe tomatoes
1 cup medium diced red onions
1 cup quartered cremini mushrooms
1/2 cup pitted Kalamata or green olives (rinse in water to remove excess salt)
1/2 cup Moroccan or Spanish capers (rinse in water)
1/4 cup chopped dried prunes
1/4 cup dried cherries
1 teaspoon minced fresh ginger
1 teaspoon minced fresh garlic
1 slice orange
1 slice lemon
1/4 cup chopped flat leaf parsley
1/4 cup chopped cilantro
1/4 cup chopped mint
2 oz. red wine vinegar
1 oz. light brown sugar
1/2 teaspoon ground cardamom
1/2 teaspoon ground cinnamon
1 teaspoon smoked paprika
1 teaspoon ground cumin
1 teaspoon ground coriander
1/2 teaspoon cayenne pepper
extra virgin olive oil, as needed
salt & pepper, in stages and per taste

METHOD

In a large shallow (sauté) pan, heat some extra virgin olive oil on a medium flame. Once the oil is hot, add the onions and cook for a minute. Next, add the eggplant and cook for a couple of minutes. Next add the mushrooms and cook for a minute. Next add the squash and cook for a couple of minutes. It may be necessary to add more olive oil as needed because the eggplant and mushrooms will tend to soak up the olive oil very quickly. Also, season lightly with salt and pepper in stages to bring out the flavors. Now, add the ginger and garlic and stir for 30 seconds. Now add the citrus slices. Next, add all the dry spices and stir for about a minute. Now add the tomatoes, red wine vinegar, brown sugar, and dried fruit. Stir and cook on a low heat, ensuring that all the vegetables hold their integrity but are cooking through. Add the olives and capers and stir. Taste the mixture to make sure that the flavors are balanced. Adjust the seasoning if desired. Switch off the flame when the desired harmonious flavor is reached, and all the vegetables are properly cooked without disintegrating into nothing.

Finish with all the chopped herbs and some more high-grade extra virgin olive oil.

ZAALOUK

> Zaalouk is a delicious cooked "salad" made with eggplant (aubergine), tomatoes, garlic, olive oil and spices. It's a common side dish to many meals and is usually served as a dip with crusty bread. Use fresh, ripe tomatoes for the best results. If you like, drizzle a little extra olive oil on the salad when serving. It is a wonderful celebration of eggplant. One may also use in burgers, wraps, pasta, and pizza.

LEVEL: Basic

YIELD: approximately 1 1/2 quart

INGREDIENTS
2-3 medium sized eggplant (aubergine), diced
4 large tomatoes, diced
3 cloves of garlic, finely chopped or minced
1/3 cup chopped fresh cilantro and parsley, mixed
1 tablespoon paprika
1 teaspoon cumin
1/8 teaspoon cayenne pepper (optional)
1/4 cup olive oil
1/3 cup water or as much is needed
salt & pepper, in stages and per taste

METHOD
Mix all ingredients in a large, deep skillet or pot. Cover and simmer over medium to medium-high heat for 30 minutes, stirring occasionally. Adjust the heat if necessary, to avoid burning the zaalouk. Use a spoon or potato masher to crush and blend the tomatoes and eggplant. Continue simmering, uncovered, for 10 minutes or until the liquids are reduced and the zaalouk can be stirred into a heap in the center of the pan.

Serve warm or cold with crusty bread.

ROMESCO

> Traditionally, romesco is a Catalonian tomato-pepper-nut sauce. Roasting and peeling ripe bell peppers is preferred to the pre-peeled products available from a jar because I find those products often carry a bitter note which lingers. Also, I think leaving some of the roasted pepper skin on provides a depth of flavor which is quite satisfying. Use it in a number of ways, but for sure as an accompaniment for roasted or grilled dishes.

LEVEL: Basic

YIELD: approximately 1 1/2 quarts

INGREDIENTS

2 slices of white bread
1 teaspoon Spanish paprika
1/2 tablespoon hot red pepper flakes
4 garlic cloves
4 each peeled ripe tomatoes
2 tablespoons red wine vinegar
2 tablespoons fruity olive oil plus a bit more for shallow frying
1 cup whole or blanched almonds, lightly toasted
3 each roasted whole red peppers, remove skin and seeds
2 tablespoons freshly chopped flat leaf parsley
salt & pepper, in stages and per taste

METHOD

Fry the bread in olive oil until golden brown. Do not over brown. Let cool. In a food processor, blend all the ingredients including the bread and any remaining oil that it did not absorb. Blend and process until very smooth. Adjust seasoning to find the balance between the acidity and sweetness. Serve at room temperature with grilled marinated vegetables or breads.

ARUGULA & TOMATO PESTO

> Pesto is one of the classic condiments of the world. A traditional pesto with Genovese basil is a study in beautiful simplicity. I will often use pistou to finish sauces. Essentially, this is a Provençal variant of pesto, but without the nuts. But to me, pesto is a canvas one could think of as being a mostly uncooked chutney. So, for a more pungent and acidic version, roasted tomato and arugula are great options.

LEVEL: Basic

YIELD: approximately 3 cups

INGREDIENTS
2 cups fresh arugula, washed and dried
1/2 cup fresh basil leaves, washed and dried
2 large ripe tomatoes
1 tablespoon freshly minced garlic
1/2 cup dry toasted pine nuts
1/4 cup grated pecorino Romano cheese (optional)
1/4 cup extra virgin olive oil
salt & pepper, in stages and per taste

METHOD
Preheat an oven to 350 F. Toast the pine nuts on low heat in a dry pan until lightly browned, set aside. Cut the tomatoes into large chunks, season with salt and pepper, drizzle some extra-virgin olive oil, and roast for about 30 minutes. Remove the skins. In a food processor, add all the ingredients except the olive oil. Blend to assimilate. Slowly drizzle in the extra-virgin olive oil on low speed until the desired consistency is reached.

TOMATILLO SALSA FRESCA

> This is a bright and versatile condiment that can be used as a garnish or sauce for just about anything - tacos, enchiladas, tamales, burgers, grilled or roasted vegetables, stews, etc.

LEVEL: Basic

YIELD: approximately 1 1/2 cups

INGREDIENTS
4 medium tomatillos, quartered
3 cloves garlic
1 tablespoon fresh ginger
1 cup cilantro stem, washed
1 teaspoon extra virgin olive oil
1 hot or medium chili pepper (I use serrano)
1 teaspoon Dijon mustard
1 teaspoon honey
2 tablespoons apple cider vinegar
salt & pepper, in stages and per taste

METHOD
Are you ready for this? Put all ingredients in a food processor or blender and process to the texture you want. I went about 1 minute.

ROASTED RED PEPPER COULIS

> Think of this as the pistou version of a romesco. It provides a contrast of color and flavor for dishes.

LEVEL: Basic

YIELD: approximately 1 cup

INGREDIENTS
1 large red pepper
1 shallot, minced
1 teaspoon fresh ginger, minced
1 tablespoon crème fraîche, sour cream, or plain yogurt (optional)
1/4 cup flat leaf parsley
extra virgin olive oil, as needed
salt & pepper, in stages and per taste

METHOD
Toss the red pepper with extra virgin olive oil, salt, and pepper. Roast in the oven at 350 F for about 45 minutes. Place in a bowl and cover it for a few minutes, so it peels easily. Sauté the shallot and ginger in some extra virgin olive oil for about 30 seconds. Puree the roasted red pepper, cooked shallots, ginger, salt, pepper, and parsley to a smooth consistency. Add the crème fraîche and pulse a few times. Adjust the seasoning as desired. This is the red pepper coulis. Keep it in the refrigerator until needed.

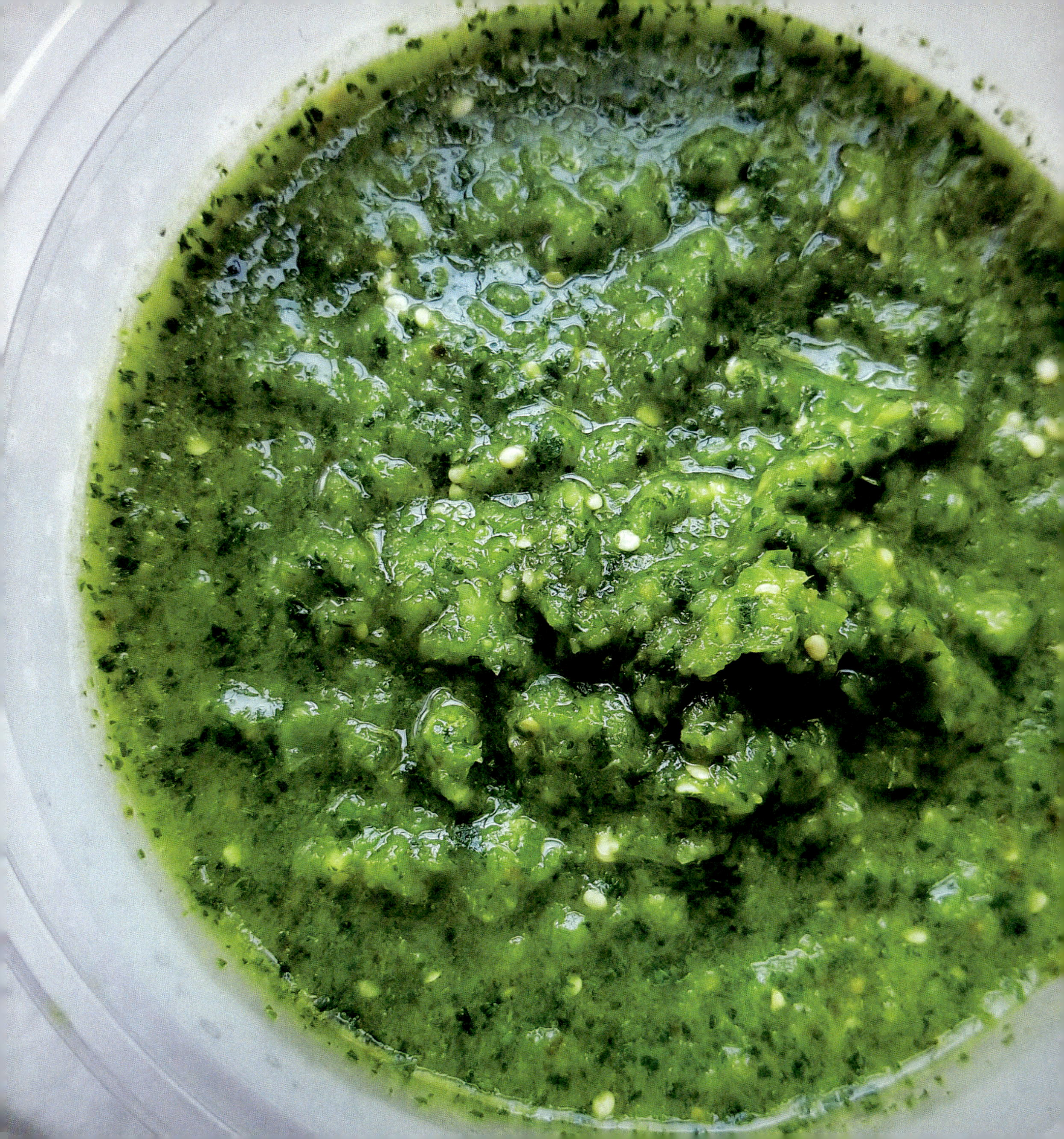

GRILLED EGGPLANT & FAVA BEAN HUMMUS

The most luxurious hummus Jenneffer and I have had was at Naya Mezze and Grill in New York City. It was a green garbanzo hummus, where the skin was meticulously peeled to provide the silkiest texture imaginable – the generous amounts of fine Lebanese olive oil didn't hurt the case. This version provides more texture and more complexity. Scoop away or use in in wraps and sandwiches.

LEVEL: Basic

YIELD: approximately 3 cups

INGREDIENTS
2 Japanese eggplant, cleaned sliced into 1/4 inch slices
2 cups fresh fava beans
1 tablespoon tahini
3 cloves fresh garlic
juice and zest of 1 lemon
1/4 cup chopped flat leaf parsley
1/4 cup extra virgin olive oil
1 teaspoon smoked paprika, optional
salt & pepper, in stages and per taste

METHOD
Cook the fava beans in salted water. The outer skin should come off easily. Drain well. Brush the eggplant with extra virgin olive oil, season with salt and pepper and grill on both sides until cooked through and soft. Meanwhile, steep the minced garlic in the lemon juice for 10 minutes. Transfer to a food processor. Add the grilled eggplant, tahini, and cooked and peeled fava beans. Blend to a smooth mixture. Add some salt and pepper and with the motor running, slowly drizzle in the extra virgin olive oil until smooth. Sprinkle some smoked paprika, if desired. Serve with pita bread or naan.

PEANUT CORIANDER

> Here coriander refers to cilantro. Use it as a scoop-worthy sauce for rolls and fritters.

LEVEL: Basic

YIELD: approximately 3 cups

INGREDIENTS
- 1 cup creamy peanut butter
- 1/4 cup low sodium soy sauce
- 1 tablespoon chili paste
- 1 teaspoon freshly grated ginger
- 1/4 cup orange juice
- 1 tablespoon granulated sugar
- 2 stalks scallions, sliced thinly on a bias
- 1 cup chopped fresh cilantro
- 1 teaspoon honey
- salt & pepper, in stages and per taste

METHOD

To make the sauce, simply whisk all the ingredients in a bowl except the scallions and cilantro. Test for balance of salty, sweet, spicy, and acidic flavors. Adjust as preferred. Finish with the scallions and cilantro.

BEET & CARDAMOM

> This chutney more closely resembles the types of chutneys I grew up with - a stand-out chutney, unique in flavor and application. Experiment for yourself.

LEVEL: Basic

YIELD: approximately 2 cups

INGREDIENTS
- 1 cup grated yellow beets
- 1 cup grated red beets
- 2 green chilies or 1 small jalapeño pepper
- 1/4 cup chopped cilantro with stems
- 1/2 teaspoon whole cumin seed
- 1 teaspoon ground cardamom
- 1/2 inch piece of fresh ginger, minced
- 2 cloves garlic, minced
- 2 tablespoons toasted and ground almonds
- juice and zest of 1/2 lemon
- 2 tablespoons extra-virgin olive oil
- salt & pepper, in stages and per taste

METHOD

In a shallow pan, heat the oil and add the cumin seed for 10 seconds. Next add the ginger and garlic and fry a couple of minutes. Now add the cardamom powder and stir for a few seconds before adding the grated beets and chili pepper. Stir fry for about 15 minutes before adding almonds. Be sure to season with salt and pepper in stages. Finish with the lemon juice, lemon zest, and chopped cilantro. Re-season as desired, adjusting for salt and spice. Transfer all ingredients to a food processor and pulse a few times. Store in the refrigerator.

SOFRITO

Sofrito is a flavor starter, flavor enhancer, or finished condiment. The heart and soul of many dishes from Central and South America, and specifically, the beautiful island of Puerto Rico. Our times strolling around Old San Juan during two separate trips evoke fond memories of sofrito frying in olive oil.

LEVEL: Basic

YIELD: approximately 3 cups

INGREDIENTS
1 medium white onion, diced
2 cubanelle peppers, stemmed, cut into large chunks
3 ajices dulces (a sweet perennial pepper found in Latin markets, or substitute 1 yellow bell pepper)
1 small jalapeño pepper
1 teaspoon cumin powder
1 teaspoon coriander powder
1 tablespoon white balsamic vinegar
12 medium cloves garlic, peeled
1/2 large bunch cilantro, washed and roughly chopped
2 leaves of cilantro with stems
1/4 bunch flatleaf parsley
2 ripe plum tomatoes, diced
1 small red bell pepper, cored, seeded, and roughly chopped
1/4 cup extra-virgin olive oil
salt & pepper, in stages and per taste

METHOD
In a strong food processor, break down all the ingredients except the olive oil to a coarse mixture. With the motor running, slowly drizzle the olive oil in until you have a smooth mixture. Store in an airtight container in a refrigerator.

TAMARIND DATE

> This is a ubiquitous accompaniment to Indian fried food or chaats. Tangy, sweet, fruity, and spiced.

LEVEL: Basic

YIELD: approximately 2 1/2 cups

INGREDIENTS
- 1/4 cup tamarind paste
- 1 cup chopped dates
- 3 cups water
- 1 teaspoon Kashmiri red chili powder
- 1/2 teaspoon cumin powder
- 1/2 teaspoon ginger powder
- 1 teaspoon lemon juice
- 1/4 cup brown sugar
- salt & pepper, in stages and per taste

METHOD

Simmer all ingredients in a heavy-bottomed saucepan on low for about 45 minutes, stirring periodically to prevent burning on the bottom. When the sauce is thick enough to coat the back of a spoon, taste it and adjust salt, sugar, and spice level. Transfer everything to a blender and process into a smooth sauce. Store in the refrigerator.

CHERMOULA

> A garlicky marinade for North African and Mediterranean dishes. Great as a basting sauce for the grill.

LEVEL: Basic

YIELD: approximately 2 cups

INGREDIENTS
- 1 teaspoon cumin seed
- 1 teaspoon coriander seed
- 1/2 teaspoon black peppercorns
- 1 1/2 cups coarsely chopped cilantro
- 1 cup coarsely chopped parsley
- 1/2 teaspoon Dijon mustard
- 2 tablespoons coarsely chopped mint
- 1/4 preserved lemon, deseeded
- 4 garlic cloves
- 1 teaspoon sweet paprika
- juice and zest of 1/2 lemon
- 1/2 teaspoon crushed red pepper
- 1/3 cup extra-virgin olive oil
- salt & pepper, in stages and per taste

METHOD

Dry toast the whole spices in a heavy-bottomed skillet for 5 minutes before grinding finely in a spice grinder. Combine all the ingredients, including the ground spices but not the olive oil, in a food processor. Pulse the mixture to a coarse consistency. With the processor running on low, drizzle in the olive oil. Taste and re-season with salt, as preferred.

Sauces

Jenneffer will be the first to tell you that my greatest strength is my sauce-making ability. And I don't just mean the French mother and secondary sauces. I mean the sauces that complete dishes. My secret to making sauces? Tasting and adjusting obsessively. And, sometimes, a good blender.

LECHE DE TIGRE

APPLICATION: I was first introduced to ceviche about 15 years ago just out of culinary school. It was a punchy and vibrant experience. Often seeking balance, I leaned on my Indian heritage to create this version of what is usually the best part of a ceviche – the tiger's milk. Drink it or use it to cure fresh ingredients but avoid cooking it.

LEVEL: Basic

YIELD: approximately 3 1/2 cups

1/2 cup freshly squeezed orange juice
1/2 cup freshly squeezed lemon juice
1/4 cup freshly squeezed lime juice
1 cup coconut milk
1 medium red onion, peeled and sliced very thinly
1/2 bunch fresh cilantro, chopped finely including stems
1/4 cup fresh basil leaves
2 fresh jalapeño or serrano peppers, chopped finely including seeds
1/4 cup first cold press extra virgin olive oil
1/2 tablespoon freshly grated ginger root
1 teaspoon freshly minced garlic
orange blossom or other citrus honey, as needed
granulated sugar, as needed
salt & pepper, in stages and per taste

METHOD

Steep the ginger and garlic in the combined citrus juices in a nonreactive bowl (stainless or plastic) for 10 minutes. Add all the remaining ingredients to the bowl. Find a balance in the flavors so that the acidity is not overpowering by adding more sugar or honey, if necessary. Mix well so that the onions are completely submerged in the juices. Set aside for 20 minutes. Blend to a smooth consistency.

Refrigerate. Note that the sauce may separate a bit over time; whisking it or shaking it will re-emulsify.

CREOLE

> APPLICATION: Over the years, any dish labeled *creole* seemed to instantly draw curious diners at the restaurant. And why not?! Alongside deep-flavored sauces from India, China, Thailand, and many countries in North Africa, to name only a few, the food from Louisiana promises big and bold flavors. It is completely reasonable and possible to make creole and cajun inspired dishes while sticking to only vegetarian ingredients. This sauce is a good starting place for that journey.

LEVEL: Basic

YIELD: approximately 2 quarts

INGREDIENTS
2 cup medium onion, diced
1 cup celery, diced
1 cup green and red bell peppers, diced
3 cloves fresh garlic, minced
3 sprigs fresh thyme, leaves picked
1 sprig fresh rosemary, leaves picked, chopped
2 tablespoons creole seasoning (page 87) or store-bought creole blend
1 teaspoon freshly ground black pepper
2 bay leaves, fresh if available
1 quart water
1/2 cup flat leaf parsley, chopped finely
2 cup ripe tomatoes, diced
1/2 cup heavy cream (as preferred)
1/4 cup extra-virgin olive oil
salt & pepper, in stages and per taste

METHOD
Over medium heat, start with the olive oil and sauté the onions, celery, and bell peppers until they are soft and slightly caramelized. Next, add the remaining fresh thyme, rosemary, and minced garlic. Stir briefly for about a minute being careful that the garlic doesn't burn. Next add the creole blend of spices, salt as needed, and bay leaves. Stir for a few seconds. Add the tomatoes and water. Let the sauce simmer for about 30 minutes, stirring periodically.

Finish with chopped, fresh flat leaf parsley and heavy cream. Re-season at the end as desired.

TIKKA MASALA

> APPLICATION: The quintessential "Indian" curry--*not*. An invention resulting from the British Raj, chicken tikka masala is a wonderfully balanced dish. For a while during culinary school, I lived in Altamonte Springs, FL, and would stage at a nearby Indian restaurant. That is where I first saw it being made in a restaurant space. I noted the key elements of fenugreek leaves and the low and slow simmering for a couple of hours, so the spices develop and bloom. At home, most of us would make the complete dish from start to finish, but in restaurants, we make mother sauces and use them to finish dishes. That is one of the reasons foods at home do not taste like food in restaurants. It is a starter "Indian" curry base. Familiar and satisfying to anyone who enjoys North Indian-style red gravies.

LEVEL: Intermediate

YIELD: approximately 3 quarts

INGREDIENTS

2 large red onions, peeled, diced
1 large green bell pepper, cored, diced
1 tablespoon each minced fresh ginger
4 cloves garlic, minced
6 fresh curry leaves (if available)
1 cinnamon stick
5 whole cloves
4 whole cardamom pods
1 teaspoon cumin seed
1 teaspoon coriander seed
2 bay leaves, crushed
1 teaspoon dried fenugreek leaves, crushed
1 tablespoon ground cumin
1 tablespoon ground turmeric
1 teaspoon ground coriander
1 teaspoon cayenne pepper (more if preferred)
32 oz. high quality crushed tomatoes (avoid anything with citric acid)
8 oz. water or vegetable stock
1/2 cup clarified butter or vegetable oil
granulated sugar, to taste
salt & pepper, in stages and per taste

METHOD

In a heavy-bottomed pot, heat the butter or oil on medium heat. Add the cinnamon sticks, cloves, cardamom, cumin seeds, and coriander seeds and stir for a minute. Add the curry leaves, diced bell pepper, and onions. Cook on low to medium low heat until the onions are lightly caramelized. This will take about 25 minutes. Now add the fresh ginger and garlic as well as all the remaining spices. Stir well. Add salt and sugar for taste and balance. Next add the crushed tomatoes and water/stock. Test the seasoning for balance. Simmer on low for one hour, stirring periodically. Allow the sauce to cool a bit.

If your blender is not powerful, remove the cinnamon sticks and discard. Otherwise, simply blend the entire mixture to a very smooth consistency.

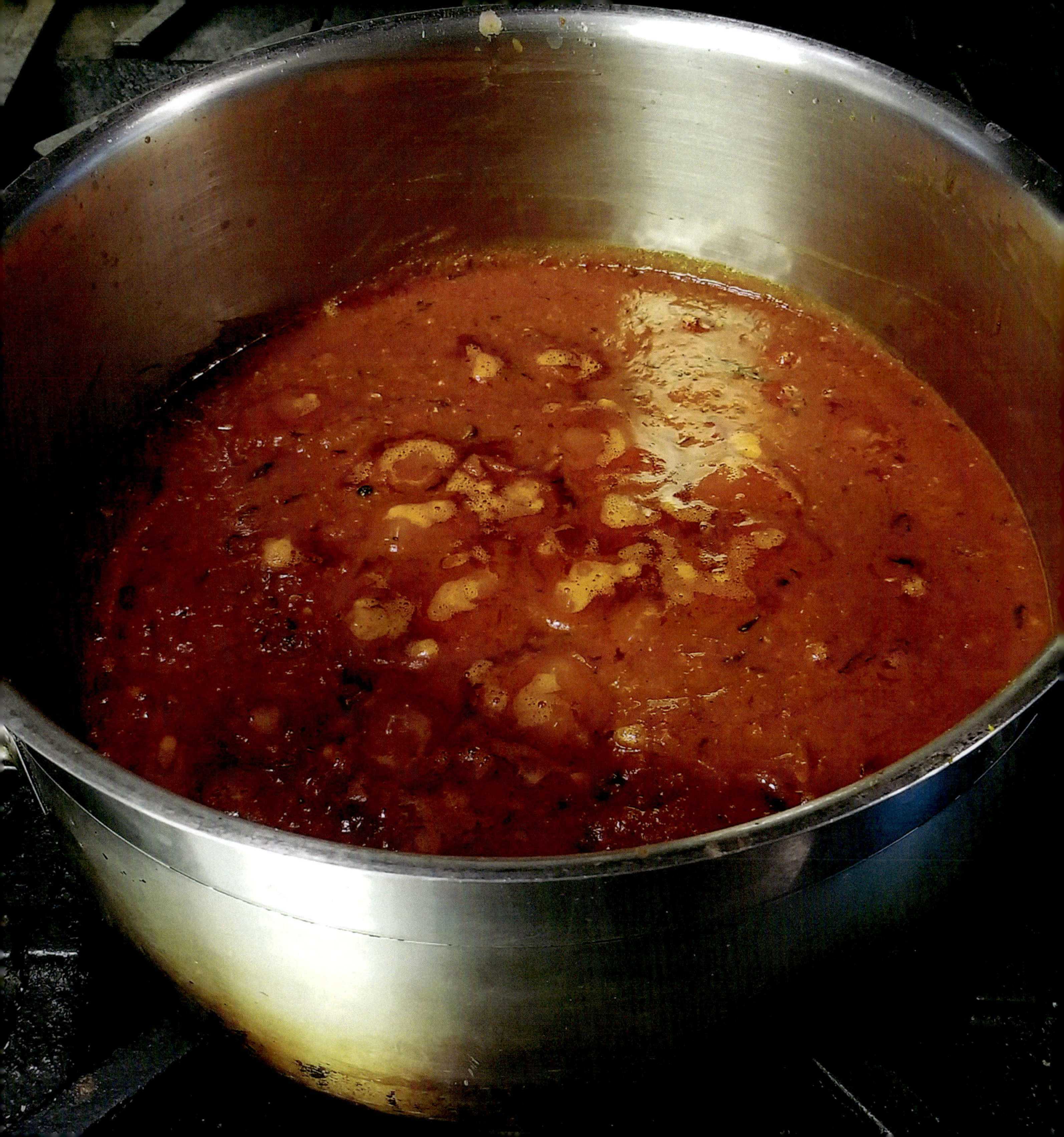

SAAG MASALA

> APPLICATION: *Saag* can refer to a wide variety of delicate or assertive greens. *Saag Paneer* in many Indian restaurants restrict themselves to only spinach. In this version, I've expanded that option to include Swiss Chard and mustard greens for a more pronounced vegetal flavor. Certainly, one may stick to only spinach, but I recommend including other greens. Collards may be too much. Overall, this sauce shows the versatility of combining abundant greens and spices.

LEVEL: Basic

YIELD: approximately 2 quarts

INGREDIENTS
- 2 lbs. spinach leaves and stems
- 1 lb. Swiss Chard leaves
- 1 lb. mustard greens
- 1 bunch fresh cilantro with stems
- 1/4 bunch fresh mint
- 1 tablespoon garlic paste
- 1 tablespoon ginger paste
- 1 jalapeño or serrano pepper, minced
- 3 medium onions, sliced
- 1 teaspoon cumin powder
- 1 teaspoon coriander powder
- 1 teaspoon turmeric powder
- 1 cup plain yogurt or heavy cream (optional)
- 1/4 cup vegetable oil or clarified butter
- water, as needed
- salt & pepper, in stages and per taste

METHOD

In a medium saucepan, heat the oil and sauté the onions until just translucent. Next add the ginger and garlic paste. Stir for about 15 seconds. Add the spices and chilies. Stir for about 1 minute. Next add the yogurt. Stir and cook for about 2 minutes. Add salt as needed. Next add the spinach and cook until just wilted. Remove the saucepan from the stove and blend the mixture to a smooth consistency in a blender. Add the fresh coriander and mint and blend them in.

The sauce can be used immediately or stored for up to a week in the refrigerator.

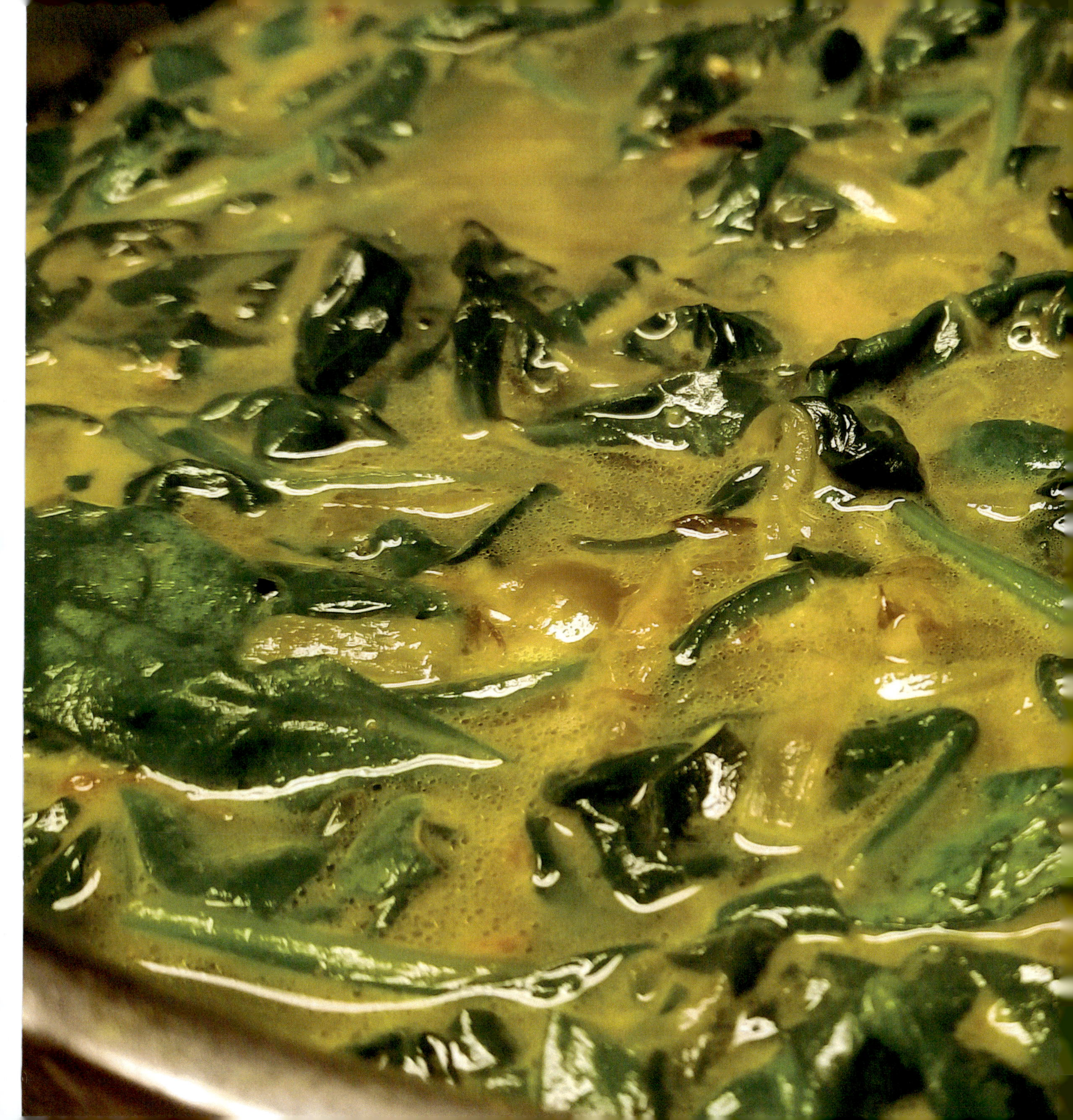

VINDALOO

> APPLICATION: A *vindaloo* is what happened when the foodies of colonial Portugal interacted with the locals in Goa and surrounding regions. During the Portuguese rule of parts of India, peppers, tomatoes, and wine (vinegar, even) were introduced to the region. Combining those with indigenous ingredients like seafood, meats, coconut, kokum, and of course spices, resulted in the birth of this beloved curry for those who like pungent food. Chef Emeril Lagasse requested I make this sauce for his tasting. I did and used local prawns. I believe his exact words were "Some of the best I've ever had." Use this sauce when you want a zippy "Indian" red curry.

LEVEL: Intermediate

YIELD: approximately 2 1/2 quarts

INGREDIENTS
2 large onions, diced
10 cloves garlic, minced
2 tablespoons fresh ginger, minced
1 tablespoon turmeric powder
2 tablespoons whole cumin seeds
2 tablespoons whole coriander seeds
2 whole dried bay leaves
5-6 dried red chilies
1 teaspoon ground cayenne pepper
1 teaspoon ground cumin
1 teaspoon ground coriander
1 tablespoon dried fenugreek leaves
1 teaspoon smoked paprika
12 oz. can San Marzano tomatoes
1 teaspoon freshly ground black pepper
1/4 cup red wine vinegar
2-3 cups water, more or less
1 tablespoon light brown sugar
1/2 cup clarified butter (ghee) or vegetable oil
salt & pepper, in stages and per taste

METHOD
The method is very similar to that of Tikka Masala. The difference is in the timing of the blooming of ingredients. Heat the oil or ghee in a heavy bottomed pot and bloom the whole spices. Stir continuously to not burn the spices. After a few minutes, add the ginger and garlic and fry the combination for a bit until the garlic browns a bit. Next add the onions, mix well, and cook on a low heat for 20 minutes, stirring periodically. Now add the remaining spices, mix well and cook for a few minutes. Now add the tomatoes, vinegar, brown sugar, enough salt, and some water. The sauce must be deeply spiced, spicy, tangy with a balanced background of sweetness. Cook this sauce low and slow for about 45 minutes before blending smoothly.

The sauce can be used immediately or stored. It has a long shelf-life in the refrigerator if stored properly.

SINFULLY VEGETARIAN
SV
POWERED BY CHEF HARI PULAPAKA
SINFULLY VEGETARIAN
SV
POWERED BY CHEF HARI PULAPAKA

MOJO

> APPLICATION: Typically, *mojo* is most commonly used as a marinade rather than a sauce. It is undoubtedly a deliciously vibrant marinade for ingredients prior to grilling. But when cooked on a low heat and balanced with seasonings or dairy, it may be used as a delicious sauce.

LEVEL: Basic

YIELD: approximately

INGREDIENTS

10 cloves garlic, minced
1 cup fresh sour orange juice (substitute a combination of 1/2 cup of fresh orange juice and 1/2 cup of fresh lime juice)
1/2 teaspoon Dijon mustard
1/3 cup olive oil
1/2 teaspoon dried oregano
1/2 teaspoon fresh oregano
1/2 cup cilantro stems
3/4 teaspoon cumin powder
1 teaspoon adobo seasoning (page 86)
salt & pepper, in stages and per taste

METHOD

Blend all ingredients except the olive oil in a blender. Taste and re-season as desired. With the motor running, slowly drizzle in the olive oil. Refrigerate, until needed.

MARCELA HAZAN INSPIRED MARINARA

> APPLICATION: This is the easiest and best Italian-inspired tomato sauce. The butter amount is flexible.

LEVEL: Basic

YIELD: approximately 1 1/2 quarts

INGREDIENTS

2 cans San Marzano Tomatoes (invest in a true and high quality product from Italy. One without any additives.)
2 sticks unsalted butter
1 onion, peeled and quartered
1 tablespoon coarse salt
1 teaspoon granulated sugar

METHOD

Cook all the ingredients in a heavy bottomed saucepan on medium to medium low heat for about an hour. Stir occasionally, mashing any large pieces of tomato with a spoon. Add the salt and sugar. After the sauce cools, blend to a smooth consistency.

MOLE

> APPLICATION: Not authentic anything, but this confident use of spices offers a deep balance.

LEVEL: Pro

YIELD: approximately 2 quarts

INGREDIENTS
3 dried pasilla chile
1 chile de arbol
4 dried ancho chile
4 dried guajillo chile
1 New Mexico chile
2 tablespoons sesame seed
1/2 teaspoon fennel seed
1/2 teaspoon cumin seed
1/2 teaspoon coriander seed
1/2 teaspoon black peppercorns
1/2 teaspoon whole cloves
1 dried avocado leaf
1 teaspoon dried thyme
1/2 teaspoon dried Mexican oregano
2 dried bay leaves, crumbled
1/2 inch stick cinnamon, broken into pieces
1 tablespoon skin-on almonds
1 tablespoon raw shelled peanuts
1 tablespoon pumpkin seeds
1 tablespoon raisins
1/4 cup ripe banana or plantain, sliced
1 corn tortilla
1 small onion, sliced
6 medium cloves garlic, sliced
1 tomatillo, husked, rinsed, and quartered
1 small ripe tomato, quartered
1/3 cup finely chopped Mexican chocolate
granulated sugar, as needed
water, as needed
vegetable oil, as needed
salt & pepper, in stages and per taste

METHOD

Deseed the chiles. Roast the seeds and whole spices in a heavy-bottomed skillet, on medium heat; dry toast the deseeded chiles separately from the whole spices, each for about 10 minutes, until you can smell the aroma. Grind the spices and chile seeds finely in a spice grinder and set aside.

In the same skillet, fry the deseeded chiles in some vegetable oil and drain on a paper towel. Next, sauté the onions, garlic, pumpkin seeds, peanuts, and almonds until golden brown. Set aside. Add more oil, if needed, to the same pan and increase the heat to medium high. Sear the tomato, tomatillo, and plantain in the same pan until they are a dark color. Add water or stock to deglaze the pan. Scrape off all the flavor bits. In batches, using a strong blender, and adding enough water to allow blending, blend all the ingredients into a smooth sauce. Strain the sauce, using a fine strainer to catch any coarse bits. Transfer the smooth, strained sauce to a heavy-bottomed pan or pot. Simmer on low-medium for 45 minutes. Halfway through this step, add the chocolate and whisk to make sure it is melted. Taste at the end of 45 minutes; adjust the salt and sugar. Strain the sauce again. Use immediately or store in an airtight container and refrigerate.

MUSHROOM DEMI

APPLICATION: Classically, a *demi-glace* is an intensely reduced and fortified stock – and a very specific kind at that. On contemporary restaurant menus, the used of the word *demi* implies a reduction of sorts usually by at least half. Here, I offer a fairly simple sauce in the style of a reduction. Use in pasta dishes and as a base for an earthy gravy.

LEVEL: Intermediate

YIELD: approximately 2 quarts

INGREDIENTS
1 cup dried porcini mushrooms
1 cup dried shiitake mushrooms (available in Asian markets)
3 cups cremini mushrooms, sliced
3 cloves garlic, minced
2 sprigs fresh thyme
1 sprig fresh rosemary
1 shallot, minced
2 bay leaves (preferably fresh)
2 teaspoons tomato paste
2 cups dry red wine
1/4 cup all-purpose flour
1/4 cup vegetable oil
4 cups warm water
salt & pepper, in stages and per taste

METHOD
Wash the dried mushrooms well in cold water. Typically, porcini mushrooms tend to have sand and dirt. Rehydrate the dried porcini and shiitake in the warm water for about 30 minutes. Squeeze the mushrooms and carefully strain the water taking care that any sediment and sand is discarded. Keep the mushroom-infused water and chop the rehydrated mushrooms.

In a heavy-bottomed pot, sauté the shallots and garlic in the oil for about 5 minutes on medium heat. Add the flour and cook mixture, stirring frequently for about 10 minutes until the flour turns light brown. Add the fresh herbs and tomato paste. Fry for about a minute. Add all the mushrooms and sauté for 15 minutes. Add the wine, bay leaves, and mushroom water and bring to a simmer. Season with salt and pepper. Reduce the sauce by about half the volume. Discard the herb stems and bay leaves.

Allow the sauce to cool down before blending to a smooth consistency. Store in the refrigerator.

BEURRE BLANC

> APPLICATION: I'm amazed at how infrequently a beurre blanc is offered to vegetarians as a sauce option. It is a fickle and delicate sauce, but the versatility of a compound beurre blanc is vastly underutilized. Classically, a beurre blanc is a barely stable, white butter sauce - not exactly a rousing recommendation. Here, I stabilize and balance the classic version. This is now a finished accompaniment that is rich yet vibrant.

LEVEL: Intermediate

YIELD: approximately 2 cups

INGREDIENTS
- 1/2 cup fresh lemon juice
- 1/2 cup fresh orange juice
- 1/4 cup fresh lime juice
- 2 tablespoons granulated sugar
- 1/2 stick cold unsalted butter, cubed
- 1/4 cup heavy cream
- salt & pepper, in stages and per taste

METHOD
Combine the lemon juice, orange juice and lime juice in a non-reactive pan (such as stainless steel). Simmer over medium heat until reduced by half, about 10 minutes. Add enough sugar and salt for an intense yet balanced flavor. Turn the heat to low and whisk in the butter one cube at a time. Once all the butter is incorporated, whisk in the heavy cream and heat through. Taste and season with salt. Cover the sauce to keep it warm.

PINEAPPLE HABANERO

APPLICATION: One may substitute any juicy, fresh fruit for the pineapple. I've used blackberry commonly as a substitute for pineapple. The finesse lies in reducing the sauce enough, balancing the sauce with enough sugar and salt. The sauce which is punchy and fruity with versatile but focused flavors, is best with any tropically-influenced dish.

LEVEL: Basic

YIELD: approximately 1 quart

INGREDIENTS
1 whole fresh pineapple cut in pieces
2 bay leaves (fresh, if available)
2 sprigs fresh rosemary
3 sprigs fresh thyme
3 whole cloves garlic
2 habanero pepper, cut in half
4 quarts water
1/4 cup heavy cream
2 oz. unsalted butter (optional)
1 cup sugar
salt & pepper, in stages and per taste

METHOD
Simmer all the ingredients in a heavy-bottomed stainless pot for 1 hour. Blend with a hand blender. Strain through a fine strainer. Simmer slowly until the liquid reduces by half. To finish the sauce, test the seasoning to find a balance between sweet and salty. Add more sugar or salt if necessary. Add the heavy cream and continue reducing until the sauce coats the back of a spoon. Turn off the flame and mount (whisk quickly) the sauce with the butter in stages for a glossy finish and smooth mouth feel.

TRUFFLED GORGONZOLA CREAM

APPLICATION: Pasta dishes, croquettes, with roasted vegetables, especially roasted tubers.

LEVEL: Basic

YIELD: approximately

INGREDIENTS
2 cups heavy cream (may substitute with half and half)
6 oz. gorgonzola
1 teaspoon chopped fresh sage
1 tablespoon fresh thyme, leaves only
1 teaspoon chopped fresh rosemary leaves
1 teaspoon white truffle oil
salt & pepper, in stages and per taste

METHOD
In a heavy bottomed pan, add all the sauce ingredients and simmer on low until the cheese melts and sauce thickens. Be sure to whisk periodically. Serve warm or at room temperature.

SMOKED ONION CREAM

> APPLICATION: Smoking the onions layers a complexity of flavor giving the perception of a sauce cooked for hours. It is possibly to over smoke the onions so try to be restrained. In this case, less is more. But apply just enough smoke and the sauce is sure to satisfy non-vegetarians and vegetarians, alike.

LEVEL: Basic

YIELD: approximately 1 1/2 cups

INGREDIENTS
1 large yellow or white onion
1 tablespoon horseradish
2 tablespoons blue Stilton cheese
1 cup heavy cream
extra-virgin olive oil, as needed
salt & pepper, in stages and per taste

METHOD
Toss the onions lightly in extra virgin olive oil, salt, and pepper and place in a traditional, electric, or a stove top smoker setup (with soaked wood chips in a perforated pan and a smoking insert). I use a combination of apple and cherry for the wood. Smoke the onions on "medium" for about 45 minutes, until the desired smokiness is reached. In a food processor, blend smoked onions, horseradish, cream, and cheese. Season as desired. This is the smoked onion cream.

Hors d'Oeuvres

Small bites of food packed with style, depth, and vegetarian sensibility can titillate one's taste buds. At the restaurant, every guest receives an amuse bouche, something creative and full flavored. And over 99% of them have been vegetarian.

JUMBO LUMP CAULIFLOWER CAKE

> The title rose at an event with my friend Chef William Dissen of Asheville. During prep for a significant fundraising dinner featuring a veritable who's who of chefs of the American southeast, I conceived this as a component of my vegetarian option. I kept referring to it as "Jumbo Lump Cauliflower Cake" – evoking chuckles from some chefs. One had to be there…

LEVEL: Basic

YIELD: approximately 8

INGREDIENTS

2 cups cooked cauliflower florets (preferably roasted)
1/2 green bell pepper, small dice
1/2 red bell pepper, small dice
1/2 large yellow onion, small dice
2 sticks celery, small dice
1 teaspoon minced fresh garlic
2 tablespoon freshly chopped flat leaf parsley
1 tablespoon mayonnaise (homemade or Duke's)
1 teaspoon Dijon mustard
1/4 cup chopped fresh tarragon
1 whole egg
2 tablespoon Old Bay seasoning
1/2 stick unsalted butter, extra for cooking cakes
unseasoned panko breadcrumbs
salt & pepper, in stages and per taste

METHOD

Sauté the onions, peppers, and celery in a little more than half the butter, until translucent. Season with salt and pepper. Add the garlic and creole spice blend. Stir for 30 seconds. Empty contents in a large bowl and let them cool. Add the remaining ingredients, including the Old Bay, and fold in the cooked cauliflower carefully, leaving some larger chunks. Slowly add just enough breadcrumbs to be able to form into disks. Do not add too much breadcrumbs and do not pack the disks too tightly. Make six to eight cakes.

Preheat an oven to 350 F.

Lightly dredge the top and bottom in breadcrumbs mixed with the chopped fresh tarragon. Melt some unsalted butter in a pan and sauté on medium heat until golden brown on both sides. Finish in a 350F oven for about 10 minutes.

Serve with a classic remoulade or red pepper coulis and a wedge of lemon.

EXOTIC MUSHROOM & GOAT CHEESE CRÈME BRÛLÉE

When one hears the phrase "crème brûlée," it usually conjures up the image of the much-revered dessert, brilliantly conceived by burning a coating of sugar on custard. However, for me, this custard is simply a canvas, and with the correct proportions of eggs to cream and baking temperature, one can create a great variety of savory custards which can be served as appetizers or as side dishes during the holidays. This is an example of a savory custard that combines the tangy notes of fresh goat cheese with the earthy notes of wild and exotic mushrooms. The addition of fresh thyme ties it all together.

LEVEL: Intermediate

YIELD: approximately 12

INGREDIENTS
4 cups wild and exotic mushrooms, chopped (if you cannot get these, use cremini and shiitake)
2 shallots, minced
1 tbs. minced garlic
2 tbs. fresh thyme leaves, chopped
1 quart heavy cream
6 oz. fresh goat cheese
2 bay leaves (fresh, if you can get them)
2 oz. unsalted butter
8 egg yolks
1 cup dry white wine
salt & pepper, in stages and per taste

METHOD
Preheat oven to 280F. Sauté the mushrooms and shallots in butter. Add the fresh garlic, and thyme. Deglaze with a cup of dry white wine. Simmer until "au sec." Season with salt and pepper. In a heavy bottomed pan, bring the heavy cream and bay leaves, seasoned with salt and pepper, to a scald (just before boiling). In a stainless bowl, whisk the egg yolks until pale. Temper the yolks with the hot cream. Take out the bay leaves. In 8 ramekins, distribute the sautéed mushrooms equally, after draining off any excess liquid. Add about ½ ounce of goat cheese to each ramekin. Pour the yolks and heavy cream into each ramekin. Torch-off any bubbles. Place ramekins in hot water bath and baking dish or large pan. Place on a rack in the middle of the oven. Bake for 2 hours. The custards should be set. If not, continue to bake until they are set. After they cool a bit, add a touch a sugar and torch the tops evenly.

Serve with a salad of fresh greens and herbs dressed lightly and some warm crusty bread for a great lunch or even dinner

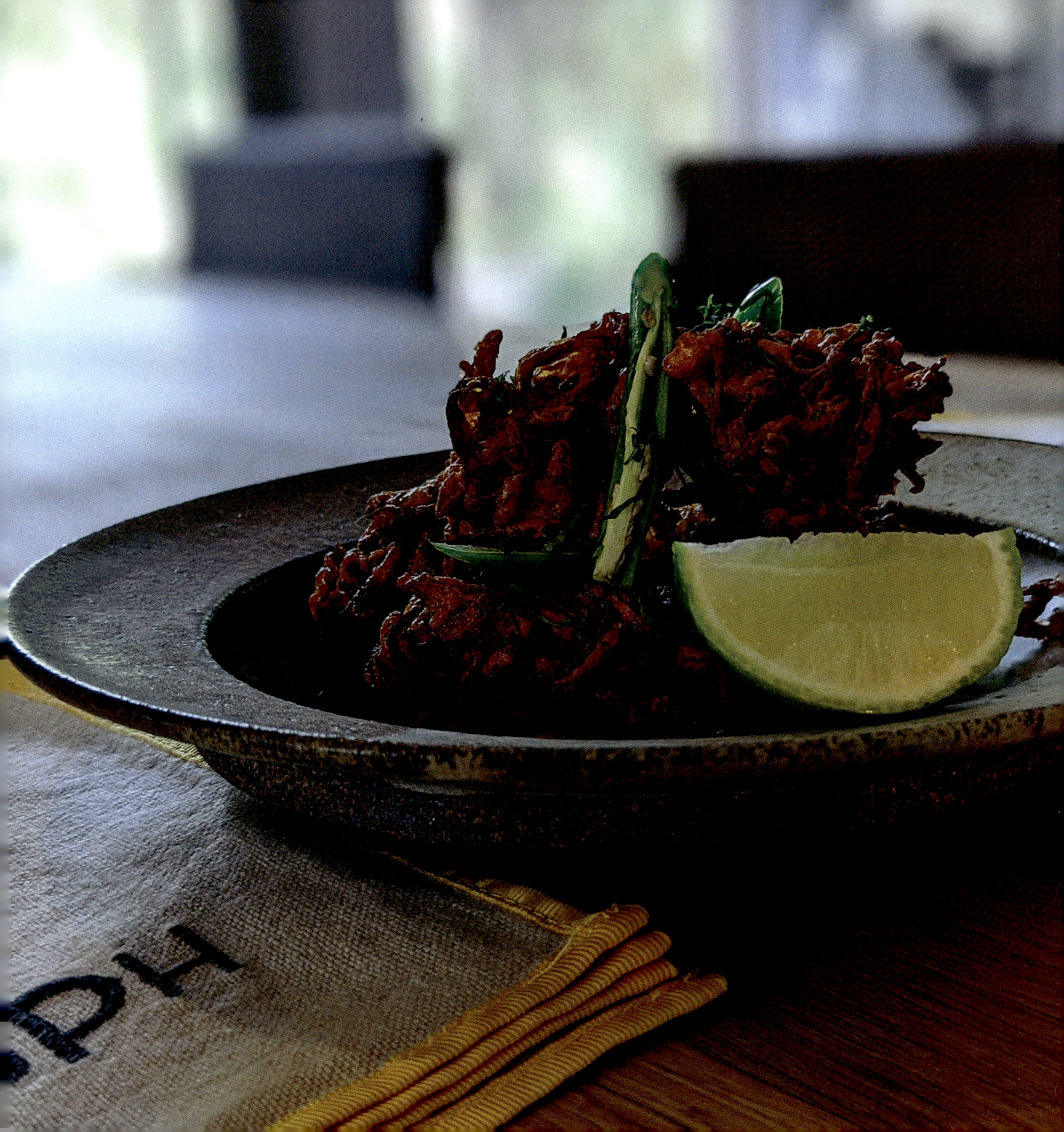

ONION & CARROT TOP PAKORA

> Afternoon pakoras and *kadak* chai during the Indian monsoons accent some of my early food memories. Here, I include prolific carrot tops for a earthy accent and a prime opportunity to reduce food waste. The fresh ginger elevates an average pakora to new heights.

LEVEL: Basic

YIELD: approximately 16

INGREDIENTS
2 large red onions, sliced thinly
2 tablespoons peeled and grated fresh ginger
2 cups picked carrot tops
1 teaspoon turmeric powder
1 teaspoon ground cumin
1 teaspoon ground coriander
1 teaspoon cayenne pepper
1 cup garbanzo flour, more or less
1/2 bunch, fresh cilantro, chopped
vegetable or peanut oil, for frying
salt & pepper, in stages and per taste

METHOD
In a large bowl, mix all the spices and salt into the onions, ginger, and carrot tops and set aside for 10 minutes. Meanwhile, preheat the frying oil to 350F. Add the garbanzo flour into the onions a bit at a time until it is possible to form a loose medium sized "ball". Do not pack the portions too tightly but just enough so they hold together. Drop them gently into the heated oil, move around, and fry until uniformly golden brown. Drain in the fry basket (if using one) for a bit before transferring to a sheet tray lined with paper towels.

Sprinkle with the chopped fresh cilantro and enjoy by themselves or with a chutney (see section on Chutneys).

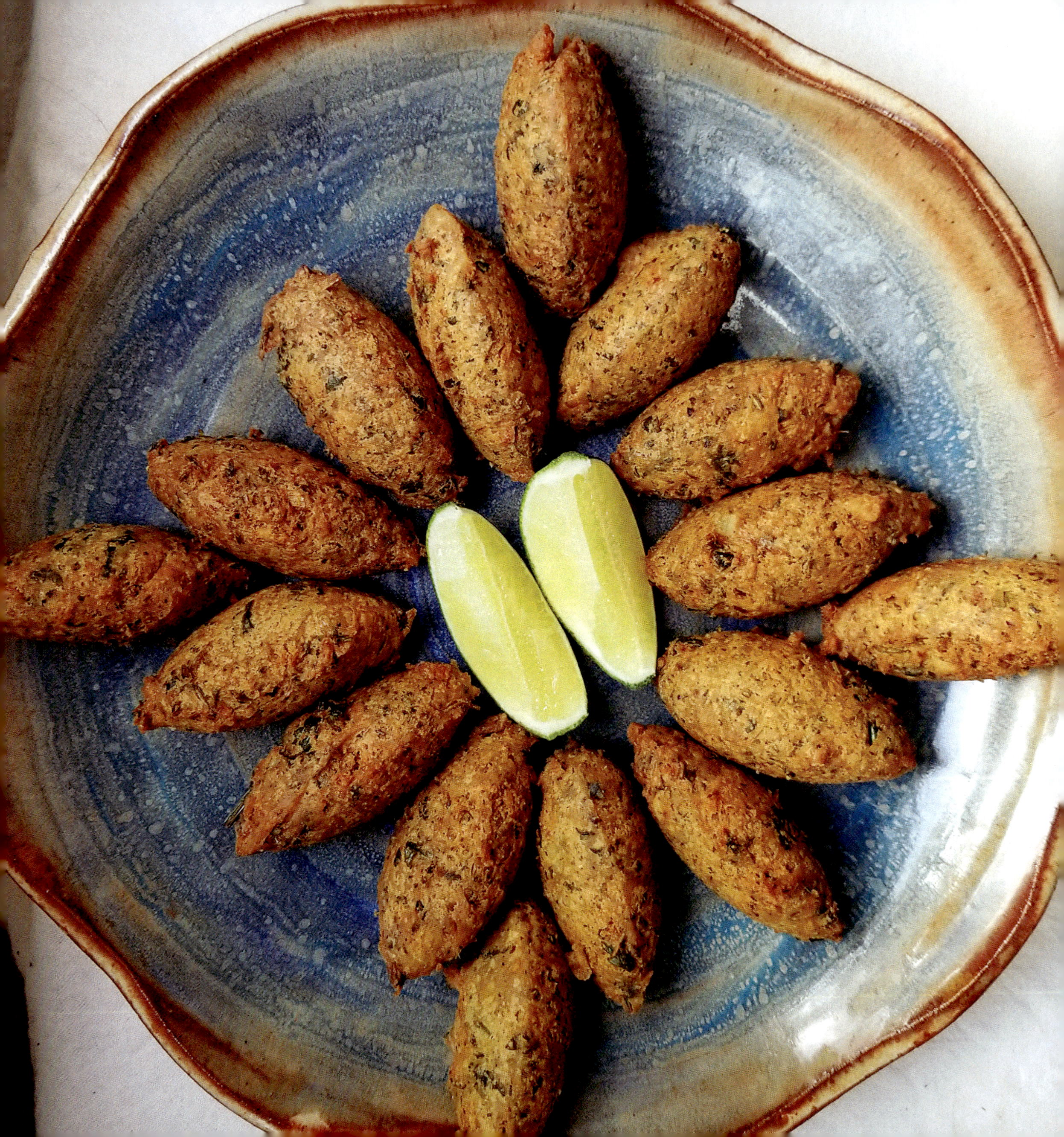

NOT YOUR AVERAGE FALAFEL

> I have a weakness for falafel in pita with hummus, pickles, tomato, and harissa. If you are able to procure fresh, green garbanzo beans, your standard for falafels will be altered forever. However, by using enough fresh herbs and citrus, it is possible to achieve a reasonable approximation. The key is to dry the garbanzo beans and herbs so that the mixture requires only a minimal amount of flour as a binder.

LEVEL: Basic

YIELD: approximately 16

INGREDIENTS
- 1 small can of garbanzo beans (15.5 oz), rinsed and drained well
- 3 cloves garlic
- 1/2 small jalapeno, chopped
- 1/4 cup fresh parsley with stems
- 1/4 cup fresh cilantro with stems
- 1 small shallot or spring onion or regular onion
- 1 teaspoon sumac powder
- 1 teaspoon cumin powder
- 1 teaspoon coriander powder
- 1 tablespoon paprika
- 1/2 to 3/4 cup garbanzo flour, just enough to make sure batter is not too wet
- juice of half a lemon or lime
- 1 tablespoon extra-virgin olive oil
- few drops of water, as needed to process
- salt & pepper, in stages and per taste

METHOD

Blend all the ingredients except the flour to a somewhat coarse consistency in a food processor, scraping sides and bottom periodically. Adjust the seasoning as desired. It must be well seasoned. Transfer the mixture to a bowl and incorporate all the garbanzo flour well with a spatula or mixing spoon.

Preheat vegetable or peanut oil to 350F. Form quenelles (or use a 1 oz ice-cream scoop). Fry until golden brown. Drain on a paper towel or rack. Bake in a 325F oven for 15 minutes to ensure cooking through. Serve as desired with dipping sauces, in sandwiches, etc.

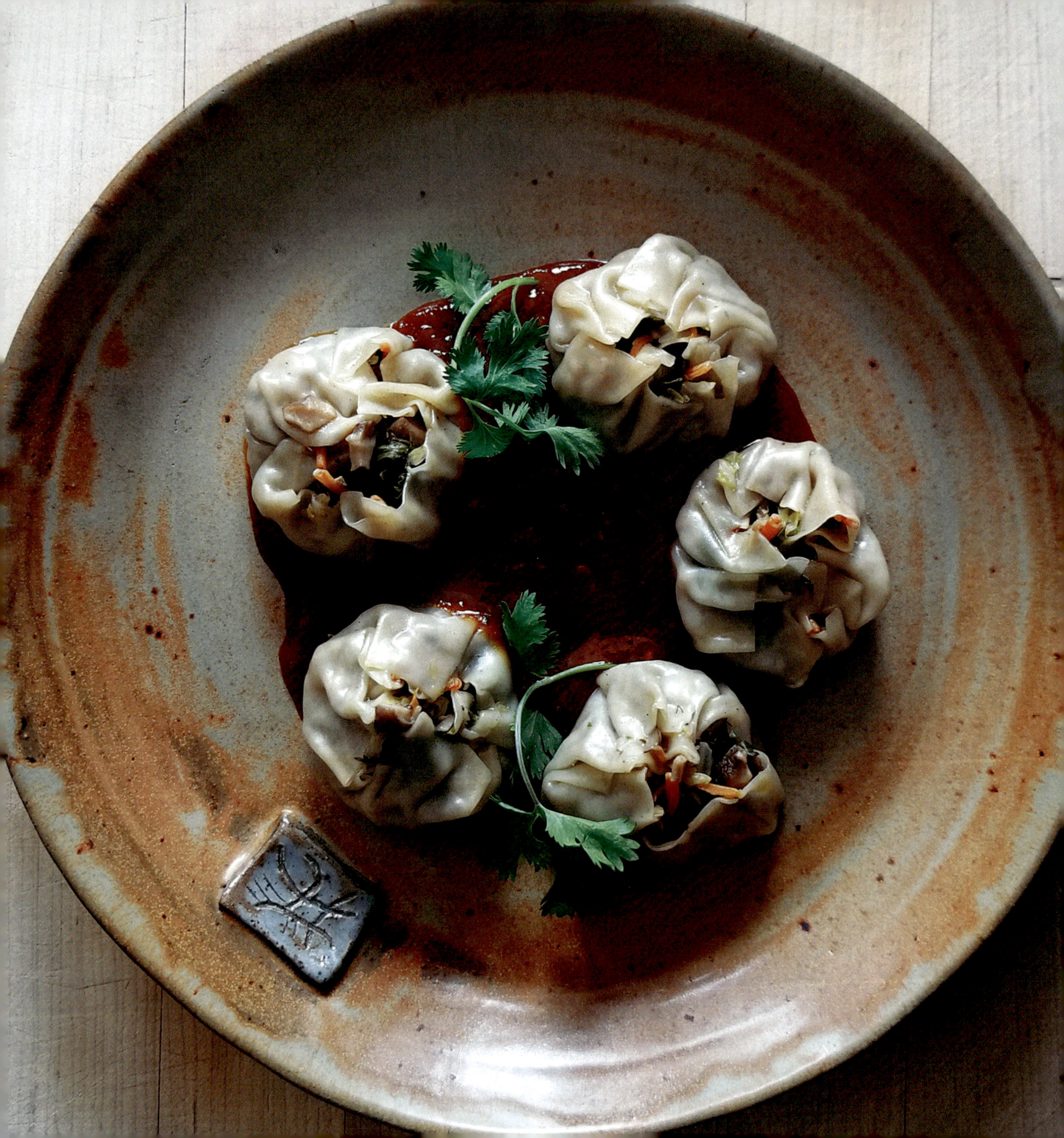

ROASTED CABBAGE MOMO

> Momos at 7 am after seeing 4 of the 5 highest peaks in the world from Tiger Hill make me miss Sikkim.

LEVEL: Intermediate

YIELD: approximately 12

INGREDIENTS
1/4 green cabbage, chopped into large pieces
1/4 cup finely chopped Napa or savoy cabbage
1 small onion, finely chopped
1/4 cup scallions, finely chopped
1/4 cup fresh cilantro, finely chopped
1 tablespoon garlic, minced
1 tablespoon ginger, grated
1 teaspoon turmeric
1/2 teaspoon red chili powder
2 tablespoons olive oil, more or less
2 cups unbleached all-purpose flour
3/4 cup warm water, more or less
salt & pepper, in stages and per taste

METHOD

Dough

In a bowl, add some salt to the flour and mix well. Make a well in the flour and add 1/2 the water and bring the dough together gently, without kneading too much. Add more water if it is too dry. Once the flour and water come together, knead the dough for a couple of minutes to a smooth texture. Place the dough in an airtight container (a Ziplock bag making sure to press out any air). Let the dough rest at room temperature for about an hour.

Filling & Make-Up

Coat the cabbage well, season with salt and pepper and roast in a 375F oven until the cabbage is soft and browed around the edges. This should take about 45 minutes. Roasting the cabbage intensifies its flavor. While the cabbage is roasting in the oven, in a pan, sauté the onion, ginger, garlic, and green chilies over medium heat for about 5 minutes. Season with salt and pepper. Cool it down in a bowl and add the chopped Napa, turmeric, red chile powder, cilantro, and roasted cabbage. Either by hand or in a food processor, pulse the mixture a few times to both mix and break down the mixture to a uniform consistency. Taste and re-season as desired. Form 1 inch balls of the dough and roll out to a 4 inch diameter disks using just enough water to prevent sticking. Place a tablespoon of filling in the center of the disk, moisten the edges of the disk with water and either bring them in to a point or crimp them to a decorative, fanned look not unlike pie dough.

Bring water to a boil and using either a traditional bamboo steamer or a perforated pan, steam the momos for 30 minutes or until the dough is completely opaque and glistens. Some like to then lightly sauté the steamed momos in a pan like pot stickers. But this step is optional. Serve with your favorite chutney or sauce--perhaps the Manchurian sauce.

ZUCCHINI ROCKEFELLER

How could I not concoct a scooped out vegetable that is stuffed and baked? It was a toss-up between a stuffed pepper, tomato, or zucchini squash. The zucchini won, easily, not because I prefer squash to peppers or tomatoes, but because the neutral flavor of zucchini provides the appropriate vehicle for assertive and complementary fillings. Contrast is a powerful trait in cooking.

LEVEL: Basic

YIELD: approximately 16

INGREDIENTS
- 3 medium zucchini, washed and dried
- 2 cups Swiss Chard leaves, chopped
- 1 cup beet greens or fresh spinach, chopped
- 3 cloves garlic, minced
- 1/2 cup freshly grated Parmigiana Reggiano
- 1 teaspoon red chile flakes
- 1/4 cup dry white wine
- 1 shallot, minced
- zest and juice of 1 lemon
- toasted bread crumbs, as needed
- 2 tablespoons extra virgin olive oil
- salt & pepper, in stages and per taste

METHOD

Trim the ends of the zucchini (keep) and cut the zucchini lengthwise. With a spoon, scoop out the zucchini to form boats. Chop the scooped-out zucchini and ends. Brush the zucchini boats with 1 teaspoon olive oil, season lightly with salt and pepper and roast in a 350F oven for 25 minutes. Remove and cool a bit.

While the zucchini boats are roasting, in a sauté pan, heat the remaining oil and cook the shallots and garlic until the garlic browns a bit. Add the chile flakes, chopped zucchini, and greens. Cook for 3 minutes or just until the greens wilt. Add the wine and lemon juice. Once the mixture in pan is dry, transfer to a bowl and cool. Some moisture will extrude. Add the lemon zest, salt, pepper, and half the breadcrumbs to form the filling. Mix the other half of the breadcrumbs with the cheese in a separate bowl and hold.

Cut the roasted zucchini boats into approximately one-inch pieces. Stuff them with the greens mixture and top off with the breadcrumbs and cheese mixture. Bake at 350F for another 10-15 minutes or until the tops become golden brown. Let them cool a bit before enjoying.

SAMOSA SPRING ROLL

> Samosa is the quintessential Indian appetizer, known world-wide. Its roots lie in the northern Indian state of Uttar Pradesh, but it's variants across the globe go by a variety of names in other countries: sambusa, samsa, sambosa to name a few. The version of samosa depends on where you are from. Essentially, it's a hand-made pastry filled with a savory filling consisting of potatoes, green peas, chilies, onions, sometimes cauliflower. This version is basic, but chock full of savory and spicy goodness.

LEVEL: Intermediate

YIELD: approximately 12

INGREDIENTS
- 4 medium sized russet potatoes
- 1 medium yellow onion
- 3/4 inch fresh ginger, minced
- 2 cloves garlic, minced
- 1 serrano pepper, minced
- 1 teaspoon turmeric powder
- 1 teaspoon cumin powder
- 1 teaspoon coriander powder
- 1/2 teaspoon cayenne pepper
- 1 teaspoon whole cumin seeds
- 1/2 teaspoon whole coriander seeds
- 1 teaspoon garam masala (page 73) OR chat masala (available in Indian grocery stores)
- juice of 1 lemon
- 1 bunch cilantro, chopped finely
- egg roll wrappers, as many as needed based on filling volume.
- 1 whole egg
- salt & pepper, in stages and per taste

METHOD

Boil the potatoes in salted water and a pinch of turmeric. After they drain and cool completely, put then in a stainless bowl. Sauté the onions, ginger, garlic, and serrano chili in vegetable oil or clarified butter, until translucent. Add all the dry spices including the masala and the whole spices. Season with salt and pepper. Stir for about 3-4 minutes until the spices "cook out." Add this mixture to the cooked potatoes. Next add the lemon juice and chopped cilantro. Using a potato masher, smash down all the ingredients until uniformly mixed and smashed. Taste this filling for desired flavor and re-season if necessary.

Form two-inch-long cylindrical "croquettes." Wrap in the egg roll wrappers following the instructions on the package. Seal with egg wash. Fry at 350 F until golden brown. Cut on a bias and serve warm with your favorite chutney.

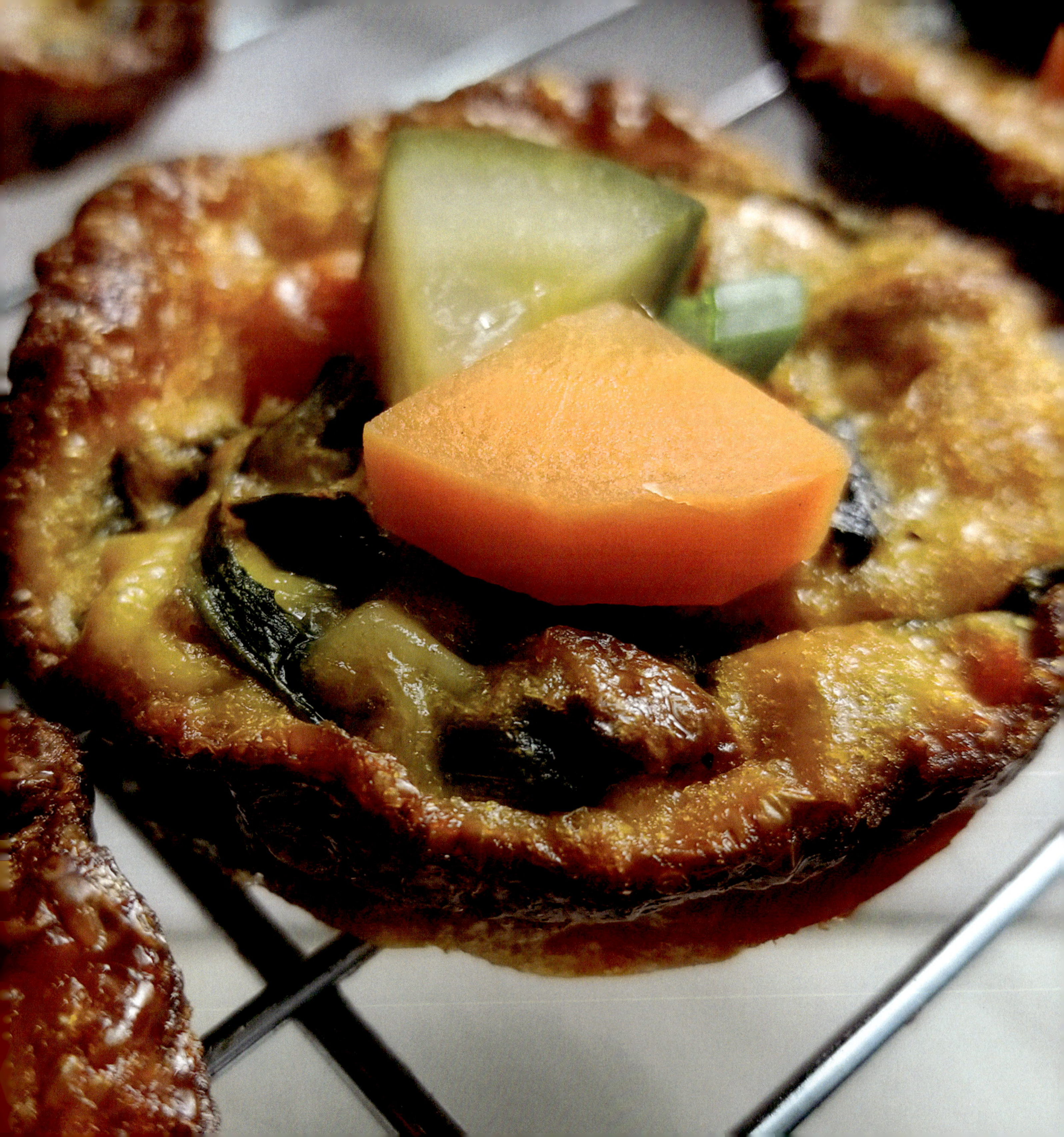

ROASTED TOMATO, SPINACH, LEEK QUICHLET

> On a whim, this was a breakfast snack before heading to nearby Lake Woodruff National Wildlife Refuge. Many households have muffin molds. At the end of the day, this is simply a mini frittata. And for that reason, the possibilities for flavorings are as numerous as one's imagination.

LEVEL: Basic

YIELD: approximately 12

INGREDIENTS
2 cups leeks, shaved thinly
12 cherry tomatoes, halved
2 cups fresh spinach
2 cloves garlic, minced
1/4 cup medium spicy green pepper, minced
1/4 cup all-purpose flour
1 teaspoon smoked paprika
1/4 cup grated gruyere cheese
2 eggs, beaten
1 teaspoons baking powder
2 tablespoons extra virgin olive oil
salt & pepper, in stages and per taste

PROCEDURE
Slow roast the onions, garlic, tomatoes, and pepper in the olive oil for 15 minutes. Season with salt and pepper, in stages. Add the spinach and stir gently until barely wilted. Remove the mixture from the heat and let cool for 5 minutes. Mix all the ingredients in a bowl.

Preheat an oven to 360F and lightly coat a muffin pan with release (I used one that makes a dozen). Evenly distribute the mixture into 12 portions. Make sure all the portions get a uniform amount of tomato and spinach.

Note: It helps to first portion the solids and then the egg mixture for consistency. Bake for 25 minutes until they are golden brown. Let cool before gently unmolding with a spoon. Garnish with diced pickles and fresh herbs like basil or parsley.

With this template, you are now ready to make a zillion different quichelets. Keep it seasonal and fun.

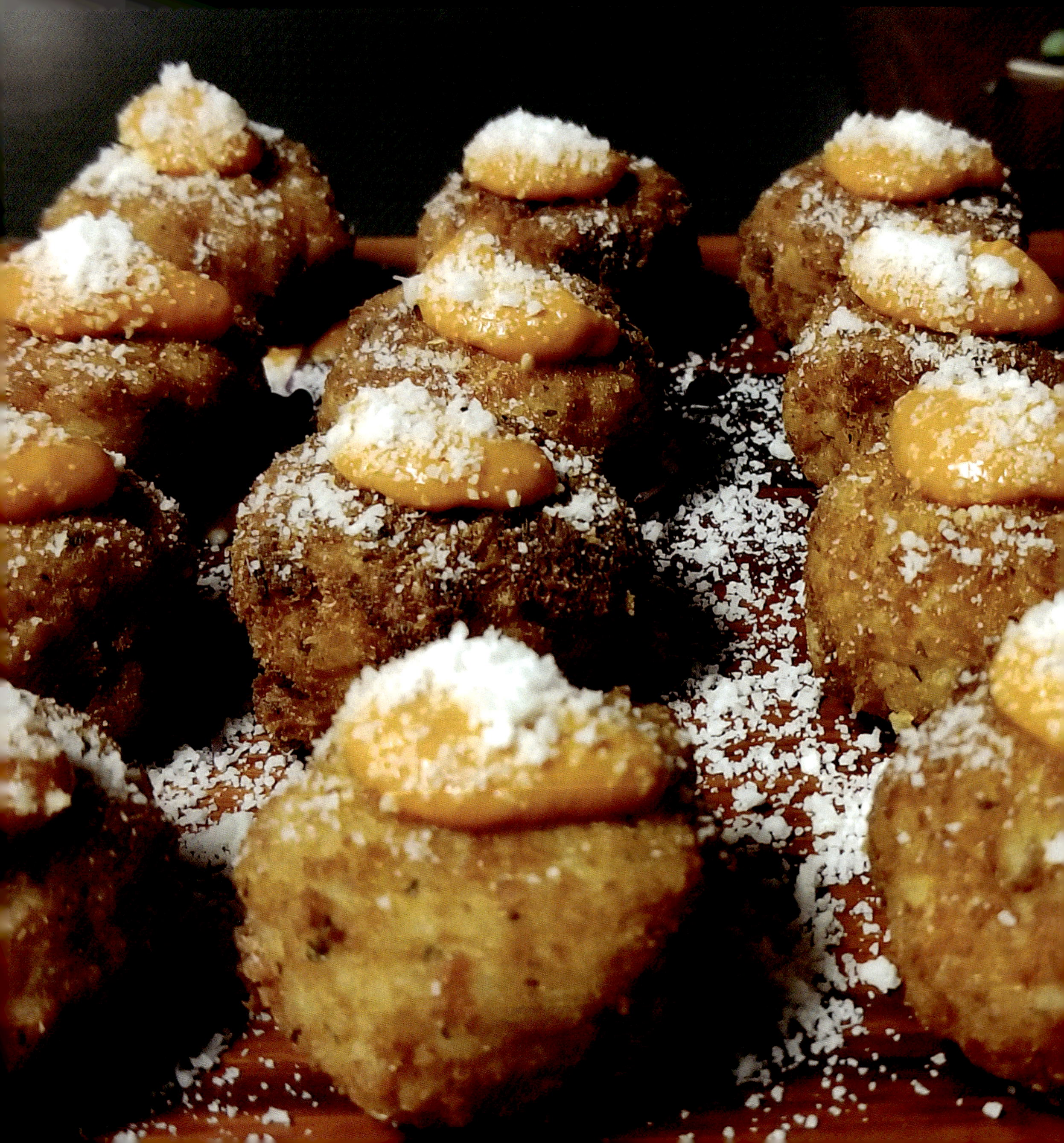

OREGANO & FONTINA ARANCINI

This is an easy and wonderful use of leftover cooked rice or grits. Classically, it must be Arborio rice, perhaps some leftover risotto (how can that be possible?). The infusion of fresh oregano makes it distinctly Italian or Greek. Fontina is a nutty melting cheese.

LEVEL: Intermediate

YIELD: approximately 16

INGREDIENTS

1 cup Arborio or other short grain rice
2 shallots or 1 red onion, minced
2 cloves garlic, sliced very thinly
seasoned vegetable stock, as needed
1 cup dry white wine
2 cups grated Fontina cheese
extra virgin olive oil, as needed
1/2 cup chopped fresh oregano
seasoned breadcrumbs, as needed
eggs, as needed
seasoned all-purpose flour, as needed
salt & pepper, in stages and per taste

METHOD

In a shallow wide pan, sauté the shallots in extra virgin olive oil until just translucent. Add the garlic and stir for a few seconds. Add the rice and coat well with everything in the pan. Add the white wine and stir well. After about 30 seconds begin cooking the rice by adding enough stock a little at a time. After about 20 minutes or so, the risotto should be cooked. Check the seasoning and finish with the chopped oregano. Spread on a sheet tray and let it cool in the refrigerator. Take 2 ounces of rice, spread in the palm of your hand and stuff it with a small amount of Fontina cheese. Make a ball with cheese inside. Bread each ball using seasoned flour, egg, and breadcrumbs and deep fry to a golden brown.

Serve immediately with a marinara or other tomato-based sauce.

BASIL & BRIE WONTONS

When we opened the restaurant, I wanted a simple appetizer, which would fire quickly and could be used a sharing plate. What we didn't realize is that it would quickly become one of our most beloved creations. I was inspired by the idea of combining mainly European flavors with Indian flavors. So, the filling has brie cheese, shallots, lots of fresh basil and fresh ginger while the sauce I served it with was a mango chutney.

LEVEL: Basic

YIELD: approximately 24

INGREDIENTS

square wonton wrappers, as needed
1 shallot, minced
1 tablespoon fresh ginger, minced
4 oz. Brie cheese, rind removed
1 cup fresh basil
1 tablespoon extra-virgin olive oil
salt & pepper, in stages and per taste
oil, for frying
mango masala chutney, as desired (page 95)

METHOD

Sauté the shallots and ginger in the olive oil until translucent. In a food processor, combine the brie, basil, warm sautéed shallots and ginger salt, and pepper and blend until smooth. Make sure the filling is well seasoned. Place a bit more than half teaspoon of filling in the middle of each wonton wrapper, brush with an egg wash (or plain water around the edge and make a "beggar's purse" by pulling up the sides and "pinching" the middle. Make as many as desired. Flash fry at 350 F making sure the wontons don't get too crispy.

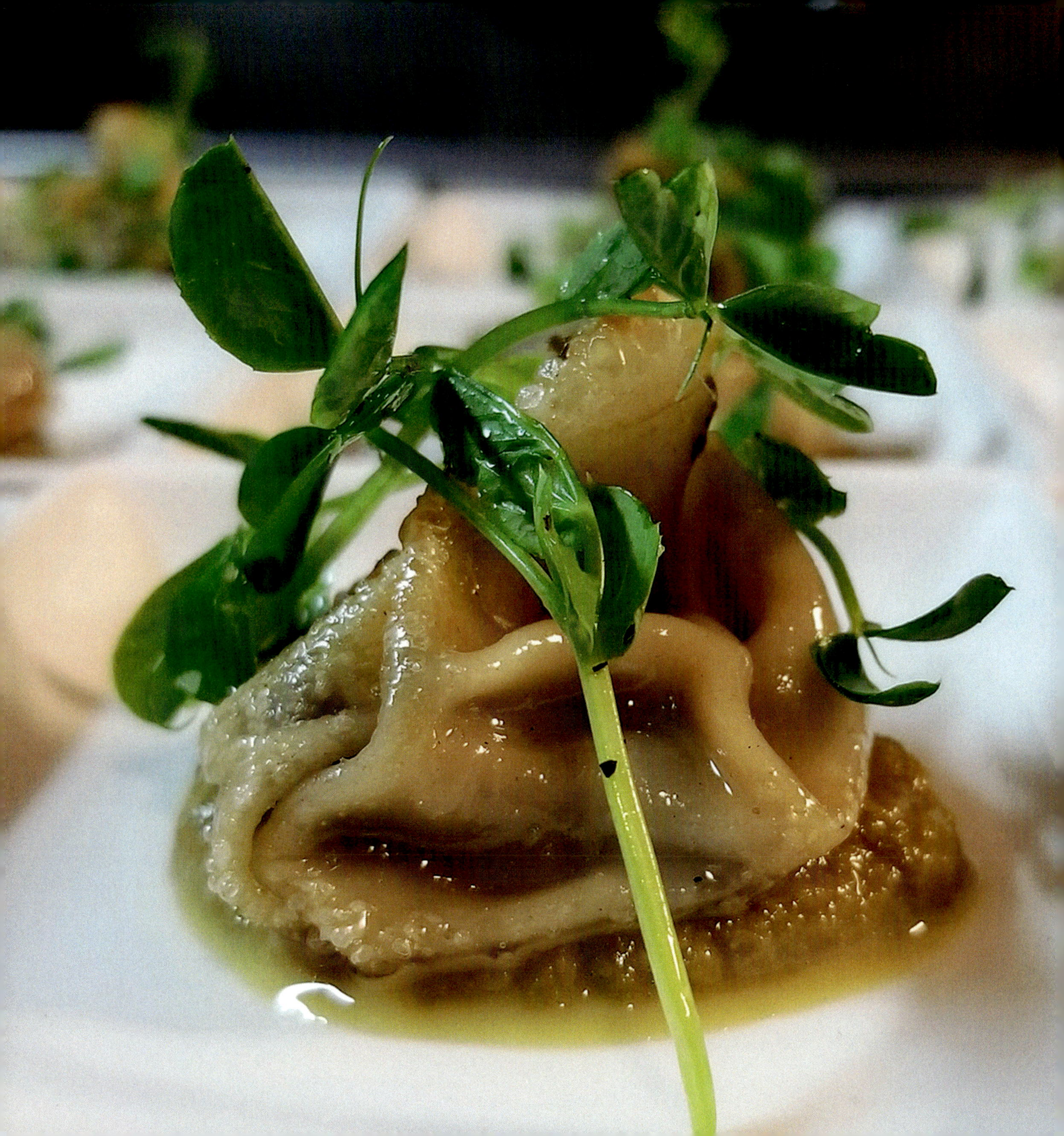

RAPINI & CANNELLINI CROSTINI

Crostini as an hors d'oeuvre is tricky for folks who don't like to eat their food with their hands. The flavor profile for this crostini is versatile enough to be the focus of a pasta dish, soup, or on pizza.

LEVEL: Basic

YIELD: approximately 12

INGREDIENTS

1 can cannellini beans, drained and rinsed
2 cups rapini leaves and tender stems, washed & dried
juice and zest of 1 lemon
1 shallot or small red onion, minced
1 clove garlic, sliced thinly
2 cloves garlic, halved
1 sprig fresh rosemary
1 sprig fresh thyme
1/2 teaspoon red chili flakes
1 bay leaf (fresh, if available)
baguette-style bread, sliced on a bias into 1/2 inch slices
extra-virgin olive oil, as needed
balsamic reduction, as needed (page 349)
water, as needed
salt & pepper, in stages and per taste

METHOD

Beans

In a saucepan, cook the beans in water, rosemary, thyme, bay leaf, three halved cloves of garlic (reserve one half for the crostini), salt and pepper. This should take about 30 minutes. Drain the cooked bean and smash it coarsely. Make sure it is seasoned to your liking.

Rapini

In a sauté pan, on medium heat, brown the sliced garlic in a small amount of olive oil. Next add the minced shallot and chili flakes. Cook for 5 minutes. Next add the rapini and sauté for 10 minutes. Finish with the lemon juice and zest. Season with salt and pepper, as desired.

Crostini

Preheat an oven to 350F. Brush the sliced bread with extra-virgin olive oil on both sides and rub one side with a halved garlic clove, once. Arrange on a baking sheet and bake for 10 minutes or until lightly golden brown, turned once halfway through the baking process.

Assembly

Spread each slice of toasted bread with a tablespoon of white beans. Next, top with a teaspoon of the cooked rapini. Drizzle with some balsamic reduction.

CURED HEARTS

The title of this creation seems straight out of a Halloween menu for a vegan restaurant. The key to a satisfying execution of this dish is in the perfect blanching of the vegetables. They must be cooked, but not under or over cooked. I had to use the Tiger's Milk somewhere. And for this book, this is the exact spot.

LEVEL: Intermediate

YIELD: approximately 8 servings

INGREDIENTS

1 cup Leche de Tigre (page 106)
1 cup hearts of palm, either fresh cooked or from a can, rinsed, drained, cut into 1/2 inch disks
1/2 cup tender broccoli stem, cooked, cut into rings, cooled
1/2 cup tender cauliflower core, cooked, diced, cooled
1 shallot, sliced
1/2 cup cooked fingerling potatoes, cut into 1/4 inch disks, cooled
1/4 cooked fresh corn, cooled
1 avocado, diced
1/2 cup ripe cherry or grape tomatoes, halved
2 sprigs fresh cilantro, picked
high-quality finishing extra-virgin olive oil, as desired
salt & pepper, in stages and per taste

METHOD

In a glass bowl, mix the hearts of palm, broccoli stem, cauliflower core, and shallot. Pour enough Leche de Tigre to coat everything well. Refrigerate for 30 minutes. Season the corn, potatoes, tomatoes, and avocado with salt and pepper. Plate each portion of the dish by including a dollop of the refrigerated ingredients, the potatoes, tomatoes, corn, extra-drizzle of the Leche de Tigre, fresh cilantro, and a few drops of a fruity extra-virgin olive oil.

ASPARAGUS & TOFU EGG ROLL WITH PEANUT SAUCE

What is the difference between an egg roll and spring roll? It's all in the wrapper. An egg roll wrapper has egg and flour while a spring roll wrapper is usually made with rice paper and is hence, noticeably thinner. They are both fried, but an egg roll is more substantial and can take more hearty fillings. The filling here is earthy and so, the peanut sauce complements it very well.

LEVEL: Basic

YIELD: approximately 12

INGREDIENTS
- 2 cups blanched asparagus cut into small pieces
- 1 cup firm tofu, small diced
- 1 medium sized yellow onion, small dice
- 1 tablespoon minced garlic
- 1 teaspoon thyme leaves
- 1 tablespoon fresh ginger, minced
- extra-virgin olive oil, as needed
- 1/2 cup creamy peanut butter
- 1/4 cup low sodium soy sauce
- 1 teaspoon chili paste
- 1 teaspoon freshly grated ginger
- 1/4 cup orange juice
- 1 tablespoon granulated sugar
- 2 stalks scallions, sliced thinly on a bias
- 1 tablespoon chopped fresh cilantro
- 1 teaspoon honey
- peanut or vegetable oil for frying
- egg roll wrappers, as needed
- 1 egg
- salt & pepper, in stages and per taste

METHOD

Egg Roll

Sweat the onions in olive oil. Add the minced ginger and garlic. Season with salt and pepper. Add to a food processor along with the tofu. Add the thyme leaves and season with salt and pepper. Pulse a few times and empty into a bowl. Fold in the blanched asparagus pieces. Mix well to form the filling for the rolls. Following the directions on the packaging, make the egg rolls. Be sure not to over fill and seal well with the egg wash. Store the rolls seam side down until ready to fry. Fry at 350F until golden brown. Drain, let cool a bit before slicing with a sharp knife at an angle in half.

Sauce

To make the sauce, simply whisk all the remaining ingredients in a bowl except the scallions and cilantro. Test for balance of salty, sweet, spicy, and acidic flavors. Adjust as preferred. Finish with the scallions and cilantro.

CHAR SIU TURNIP

Char Siu is a popular Cantonese technique or style of slow roasting non-vegetarian proteins over an open fire or in an oven. Here, I create a char siu preparation of one of my favorite root vegetables to roast – the humble turnip. The outcome is a deeply flavored, glazed and gooey root vegetable snack.

LEVEL: Basic

YIELD: approximately 8 servings

INGREDIENTS
1/4 cup hoisin sauce
1 tablespoon honey
1 tablespoon fresh ginger, minced
2-3 drops of liquid smoke
2 cloves fresh garlic, minced
1/4 cup low sodium soy sauce
1/4 cup Chinese cooking wine or dry sherry
2 tablespoons Chinese five spice (page 82)
6 medium turnips, washed well and quartered
1 scallion, sliced thinly on bias
extra-virgin oil, as needed
salt & pepper, in stages and per taste

METHOD
Preheat an oven to 350F. Coat the turnips in extra-virgin oil and lightly in salt and pepper. Place on a baking sheet and roast until just soft. Remove from the oven and cool a bit. While the turnips are cooling, mix the remaining ingredients in a glass bowl. Taste and re-season, as preferred. In a sauté pan, mix the Char Siu sauce and roasted and stew down on a medium-low heat until the sauce begins to caramelize over the turnips, forming a rich glaze. Serve hot, warm, room temperature, or cold.

Sprinkle the sliced scallions on the glazed turnips prior to serving.

CASHEW CUTLET

> Cutlets are a revered appetizer in the repertoire of Indian cuisine. The range of possibilities run the gamut. From the modest potato and pea cutlets to decadent paneer versions, the combinations can be excitingly diverse. In fact, like croquettes, the flavor-profiles can be as globally-inspired as food can be. This version is royal with the focus on cashew nuts.

LEVEL: Intermediate

YIELD: approximately 12 cutlets

INGREDIENTS
- 1 medium onion, diced
- 1/2 cup carrot, small diced
- 1/2 cup green pepper, small diced
- 1 teaspoon jalapeno or serrano pepper, minced
- 2 cloves garlic, minced
- 1 teaspoon fresh ginger, minced
- 1 teaspoon garam masala (page 73)
- 1/2 teaspoon turmeric powder
- 2 small potatoes, quartered, leave the skin on
- 2 sprigs cilantro leaves and stems, chopped finely
- 1 cup cashews, dry toasted and chopped coarsely
- 1/4 cup green peas
- white poppy seeds, as needed
- garbanzo or corn flour, as needed
- 1 quart water
- vegetable oil, as needed
- salt & pepper, in stages and per taste

METHOD

Add the turmeric and some salt to the water and boil the potatoes. Let them drain in a colander while preparing the rest of the dish. Grate the boiled potatoes to a crumb.

Sauté the onion, carrot, peppers in just enough oil for 5 minutes. Next add the ginger and garlic. Season lightly with salt and pepper. Add the garam masala and stir well. Next add the green peas and cashews. Cook for a couple of minutes before adding the grated potato. Mix all the ingredients well and taste the mixture. Re-season, if needed. Transfer all the ingredients to a bowl and let it cool. Add enough garbanzo or corn flour to be able to form 1/2 inch circular disks.

Preheat an oven to 350F. To finish the cutlets, lightly dredge the disks in a mixture of flour and poppy seeds. Brown on both sides in a skillet with some oil and finish in the oven for 10 minutes. Serve with your favorite chutney or relish. I would recommend the coconut cilantro chutney.

Soups

I believe that the ability to make a good soup fortifies the foundation for flavor development. This skill extends to several other dishes. Even if it is an uncooked soup, like a Gazpacho, the ability to have the ingredients combine harmoniously to produce a satisfying taste requires sound habits, like seasoning in layers and balancing flavors so they contrast as well as assist. Many of the world's great soups have a few elements in common.

- Aromatics (onions, celery, carrots, peppers, fennel, leeks, shallots, garlic, ginger, etc.)
- Spices or herbs
- Often a good stock (I think non-vegetarian stocks and cured meats are used as unnecessary crutches by many cooks.)
- A layered development of flavor (season in stages and add ingredients in order or cook times and their effects on the overall flavor. Usually, one begins with aromatics in a fat medium.)

GUMBO

I made my first gumbo during my final year at the University of Florida because like many in America, I was addicted to Chef Emeril Lagasse's cooking show on TV. This recipe is inspired by that memory. Since then, I've had the honor of meeting Chef Emeril and feeding him some of my creations, including gumbo.

LEVEL: Intermediate

YIELD: approximately 3 quarts

INGREDIENTS
1 large white or yellow onion, small dice
3 stalks celery, small dice
1 large green bell pepper, small dice
1 poblano pepper, small diced
1 cup eggplant, diced
1/2 cup carrots, diced
1/2 cup fennel, diced
2 cups fresh okra, sliced
1 tablespoon tomato paste
1 cup canned crushed tomatoes
1 cup vegetable oil
1 cup all-purpose flour
6 cloves garlic, minced
2 quarts vegetable stock
2 bay leaves
1 tablespoon fresh thyme leaves
2 teaspoon cayenne pepper, more if desired
1 tablespoon ground gumbo file (sassafras)
2 tablespoons creole spice blend
1 tablespoon oregano leaves, chopped
1 tablespoon rosemary leaves, chopped
1/2 cup flat leaf parsley, chopped
salt & pepper, in stages and per taste

METHOD
In a heavy bottomed pot, add the garlic to half the oil over medium heat and cook until it browns slightly. Remove the garlic and set aside. Add the remaining vegetable oil and whisk in the flour. On low heat, periodically stir the flour and oil mixture to form a dark roux. While the roux is working, it would be a good idea to prepare the rest of the ingredients. Obtaining a dark roux should take at least 45 minutes. Don't rush the roux making process.

Sweat the onions, fennel, carrots, bell peppers, and celery in the completed dark roux. Add the browned garlic, bay leaves, okra, thyme, oregano, rosemary, cayenne, and creole blend. Stir and season lightly with salt and pepper. Add the tomato paste. Mix well. Add the eggplant next. Finally, add the crushed tomatoes and stock. Stir well and test the seasoning. Simmer the ingredients in the pot for about 2 hours on low heat. Stir occasionally. About ten minutes from the end, add the ground sassafras and continue simmering. When the desired thickness is reached, switch off the stove and finish with the chopped parsley. Like all low and slow stews, gumbo tastes better the next day! Serve with some white rice and sliced scallions or substitute the rice with crusty baguette.

Celery Core Values

YOUNG YELLOW LEAVES
Delicate, Nuanced Celery Flavor - salads, purees, sauces

LIGHT GREEN LEAVES
Focused Celery Flavor - salads, torn on pizzas, finish pastas

DARK GREEN LEAVES
Strong Celery Flavor - crisp in fryer or oven and garnish for dishes

PEEL/SKIN OF CELERY STEMS
Dehydrated, fried, or in fritters

TENDER HEARTS
Raw applications

TOP OF CELERY STEM
Versatile

HEART OF CELERY
Soups, mirepoix, sticks, etc.

FIBROUS LOWER TIPS OF STEMS
Stocks or cooked and blended for folding into mashed potatoes, breads, etc.

BASE
re-hydrate, re-root, re-grow, re-harvest

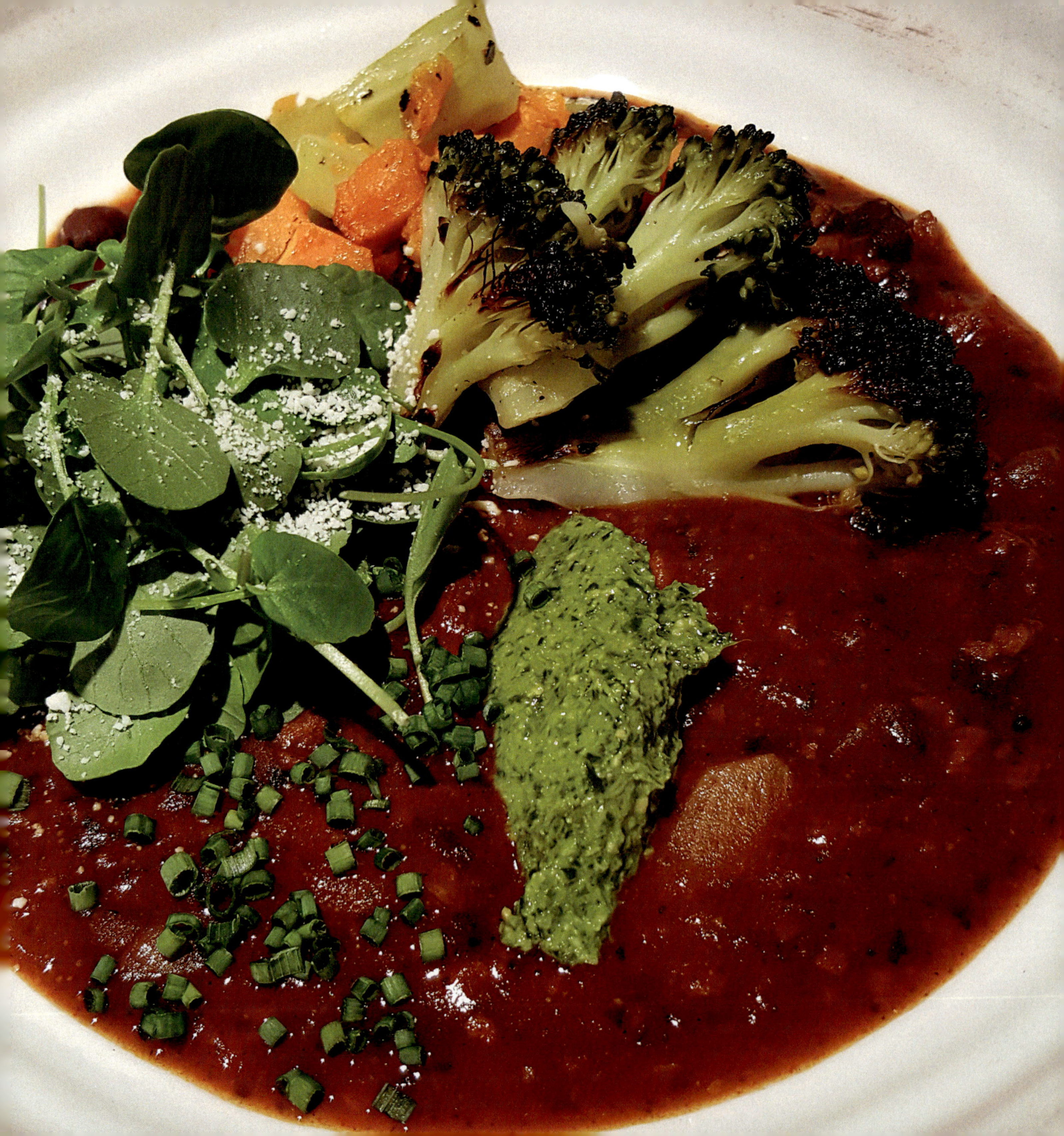

CHILI

> Every cuisine I know has a low and slow stew. Chili isn't exactly a stew, but one does stew it down. This version is packed with flavor, comfort, nutrition, and decadence.

LEVEL: Basic

YIELD: approximately 4 quarts

INGREDIENTS

2 cups firm tofu, crumbled
1 cup chopped tempeh
1 cup chopped cremini mushrooms
1 small can red beans, drained and rinsed
1 small can white beans, drained and rinsed
2 large Spanish onions, small diced
2 stalks celery, small diced
2 carrots, peeled, small dice
10 cloves of garlic, minced
1 jalapeños, minced
2 cups chopped tomatoes
1 bunch scallions, sliced
1 tablespoon chipotle in adobo
1/2 teaspoon smoked paprika
1/4 cup Worcestershire (make sure it doesn't contain anchovies)
2 tablespoons preferred hot sauce
1 teaspoon cayenne pepper
1 tablespoon ground cumin
1 tablespoon onion powder
1 tablespoon paprika
1 teaspoon dried oregano
1 teaspoon garlic powder
2 bay leaves
1 teaspoon mustard powder
1 tablespoon preferred chili powder
1 quart low sodium vegetable stock, more or less
vegetable oil, as needed
salt & pepper, in stages and per taste

METHOD

In a heavy-bottomed pot, brown the tofu and tempeh in some vegetable oil. Remove and set aside. Add some more vegetable oil if needed. Add the onions, celery, carrots, jalapeno and sweat for about 10 minutes. Add the fresh garlic and cook for about a minute. Add all the dried spices and cook for about a minute. Add the mushrooms and cook for 5 minutes. Add the browned ingredients back in and stir well. Next, add all the remaining ingredients except the fresh parsley. Stir well. Add enough salt and pepper to achieve a good balance. Adjust seasonings as desired by adding more spices or salt. Bring to a simmer, cover, and cook on low for 1 hour. For the last 15 minutes, remove the lid and simmer uncovered.

Blend a cup of the chili in a food processor and add it back to the pot. Mix well.

Finish with fresh parsley and add hot sauce if desired. Of course, like most stews, this will taste better the next day.

SOPA DE MANI

I taught myself to make this delicious Bolivian soup when we partnered with one of my favorite local musicians, *Beartoe* (Roberto Aguilar), during an event titled *Pachamama* (Mother Earth). The soulful and honest music of my friend pairs beautifully with the purity of this dish. Beartoe told me that growing up, he was rather fond of this soup. I can clearly see why and only hope that my recipe does justice to his memory, spirit, and craft.

LEVEL: Basic

YIELD: approximately 3 quarts

INGREDIENTS
- 1 large yellow onion, medium diced
- 3 sticks celery, medium diced
- 1 large green bell pepper, cored, medium diced
- 3 medium carrots, medium diced
- 1 habanero pepper, diced with seeds
- 6 cloves peeled garlic, minced
- 4 ripe plum tomatoes, medium diced (or 1 cup of canned San Marzano tomatoes)
- 2 tablespoons ground cumin powder
- 2 tablespoons ground paprika powder
- 1 teaspoon ground cayenne powder (less or more)
- 1 tablespoon onion powder
- 1 teaspoon garlic powder
- 1 tablespoon dried oregano
- 2 tablespoons chopped fresh thyme
- 1 whole bay leaf
- 1 cup roasted peanuts, ground up
- 2 cups blanched peanuts
- 3/4 cup red quinoa, washed well under cold water
- 1 cup green peas
- 1 quart milk (optional)
- 1 quart water (double, if not using milk), more if needed
- 1/4 cup extra virgin olive oil
- finely chopped cilantro, for garnish
- salt & pepper, in stages and per taste

PROCEDURE

In a heavy-bottomed pot, over medium heat, sauté the onions, peppers, celery, and carrots in the olive oil for about 10 minutes. Season lightly. Next add the garlic and ground peanuts and cook for about a minute. Add the bay leaf, cumin, paprika, cayenne, onion powder, garlic powder, oregano, and thyme. Cook for about 5 minutes, stirring periodically, and adding more olive oil, if needed. This step blooms the spices. Season lightly. Add the tomatoes and blanched peanuts. Cook for about 5 minutes, stirring periodically. Next add the milk and/or water. Stir well. Season lightly. Turn down the heat to medium-low, cover the pot, and simmer for 20 minutes.

Add the quinoa, making sure there's enough liquid in the pot. This is not a quinoa dish, so you need more liquid than if are simply cooking quinoa. Season lightly. Cover and simmer for 30 minutes.

Uncover, add the green peas, and simmer for another 10 minutes, stirring periodically. This is the time to adjust all seasonings, including the amount of salt. Serve with chopped cilantro and a drizzle of extra virgin olive oil (optional).

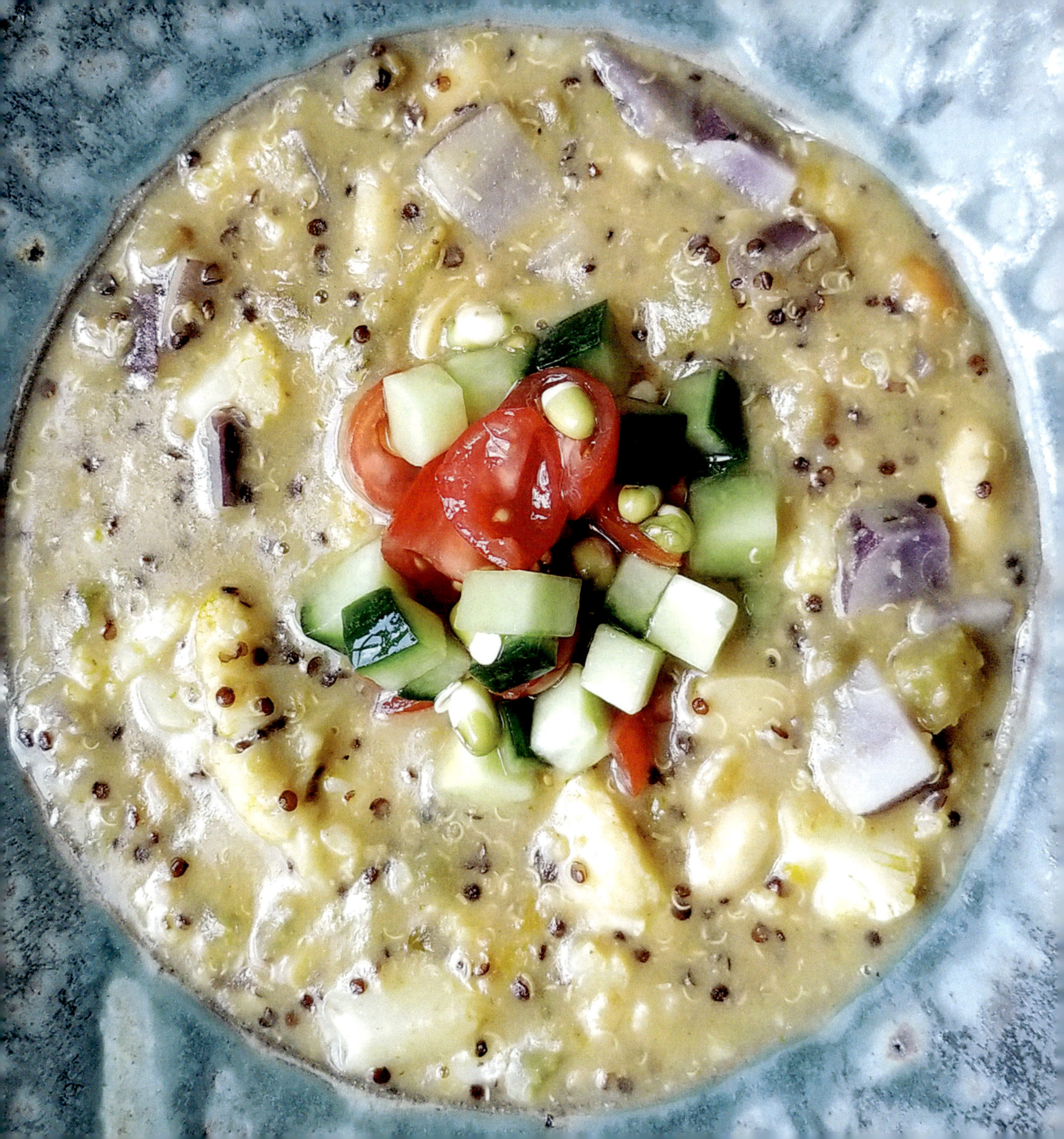

GREEN CHILE & COCONUT

Most chutneys can be extended to soups. India has a vast coastline, and coconut is extremely popular and prolific. While the basic idea behind this soup came from its cousin--the chutney--I think as a soup, it packs a glorious sense of the exotic. The addition of Hatch green chilies (when available) rounds out the fusion perfectly.

LEVEL: Basic

YIELD: approximately 2 quarts

INGREDIENTS
2 poblano peppers, small dice
2 serrano peppers, small dice
2 green bell peppers, small dice
2 medium hot Hatch green chiles (if available), small dice
2 cups coconut milk or coconut cream
1 teaspoon whole cumin seeds
1 teaspoon whole mustard seeds
1 teaspoon turmeric powder
1 teaspoon cumin powder
1 teaspoon coriander powder
8 fresh whole curry leaves (optional)
1 medium sized red onion, peeled, minced
2 whole bay leaves, preferably fresh
1 tablespoon fresh ginger, minced
4 cloves fresh garlic, minced
1 ripe tomato, diced
4 medium fresh basil leaves, chopped
1/4 bunch fresh cilantro, chopped
4 fresh mint leaves, chopped
vegetable stock (made from vegetable trims), as needed
vegetable or extra virgin olive oil, as needed
salt & pepper, in stages and per taste

METHOD
Simmer the vegetable and herb trims in some water for 45 minutes to make a stock. Strain the stock and keep warm.

As the stock is being made, in a heavy bottomed pot, heat some vegetable or extra virgin olive oil. Add the whole cumin and mustard seeds. When the mustard seeds start popping, add the curry leaves (if available). Next, add the ginger and garlic and stir for a few seconds. Next add the onion and all the peppers. Sauté until translucent. Season with salt and pepper in stages, rather than all at once, to develop a greater depth of flavour. Add the bay leaves, cumin, coriander, and turmeric. Stir for a minute or so on medium heat. Next add the tomatoes and shrimp stock and simmer for 20 minutes or so.

Test the seasoning. Stir in the coconut milk, mint, cilantro, and basil. Turn off the heat and let the flavors marry for 10 minutes before serving.

ASSORTED GREENS STEW

> Greens are prolific in the fall where we live. Every community supported agriculture (CSA) ration is filled with a wide variety of them. Each green is unique. However, when combined together in this simple way, the end result is a beautiful marriage of earth and chlorophyll. One may add cooked grains like farro or quinoa to really make this is a meal in a bowl.

LEVEL: Basic

YIELD: approximately 4 quarts

INGREDIENTS
- 2 bunches kale, cleaned, chopped
- 1 bunch broccoli rabe (rapini), cleaned, chopped
- 1 bunch escarole, cleaned, chopped
- 1 bunch collard greens, cleaned, chopped
- 1 bunch mustard greens, cleaned, chopped
- 1 tablespoon fresh ginger root, minced
- 4 cloves fresh garlic, minced
- 1 large yellow onion, diced
- 1 teaspoon cumin powder
- 1 teaspoon coriander powder
- 2 quarts greens stock (see method)
- 1/4 cup extra virgin olive oil
- 1 cup heavy cream (optional)
- salt & pepper, in stages and per taste

METHOD

Greens Stock

Wash the greens several times in cold water to make sure there is no dirt or sand whatsoever. Take the leaves off the stems. Put all the stems of the greens, onion, garlic, and ginger in a pot of water and bring to a boil. Let simmer for 45 minutes. Strain.

In a good-sized heavy-bottomed pot, sauté the onions in extra virgin olive oil until translucent. Add the fresh ginger and garlic, and sauté for 30 seconds. Add the cumin, coriander, and some salt and pepper. Stir for a minute. Add the greens. Toss in the pot until they start to wilt. Cover the pot if necessary. Add the stock and simmer for 1 hour (uncovered, adding more stock as needed).

Test the seasoning, adding more salt or pepper if needed. Finish with heavy cream (optional). Blend with a hand blender. Serve with some wild or brown rice or good bread.

PROVENÇAL WHITE BEAN

> Cannellini beans are luxuriously creamy. This is a simple soup but a great example of flavor through simplicity. The recipe doesn't call for it, but some freshly grated lemon zest will waft the diner through the fields of Provençe.

LEVEL: Basic

YIELD: approximately 2 quarts

INGREDIENTS

1 small onion, finely chopped
1 small carrot, diced
1 celery, stalk finely chopped
2 garlic cloves, minced
1 tablespoon herbs de Provençe (page 81)
1 sprig fresh basil, chopped, for garnish
1 small can cannellini beans, drained and rinsed
1 small tomato, diced
1 bay leaf
2 cups vegetable stock or water
2 tablespoon, extra-virgin olive oil
salt & pepper, in stages and per taste

METHOD

This soup illustrates Soup-Making 101. Start by sautéing the mirepoix (onions, carrots, and celery) in the olive oil for about 5 minutes over medium heat. Next add the garlic, herbs de Provençe, and bay leaf. Season with salt and pepper. After 2 minutes, add the tomatoes and beans, and stew for 5 minutes. Now add the stock, season the broth as desired, and simmer for 30 minutes. Discard the bay leaf. Transfer a cup of the beans and some broth to a blender and puree before adding back to the soup or use an immersion blender to break down some of the beans and vegetables a bit. This provides body and deeper flavor to the soup.

Finish with the fresh basil and serve warm with some crusty bread on the side.

CREAM OF ROOT VEGETABLES

> There is no sugar-coating the fact that this is decadent soup. A small portion goes a long way. At the restaurant, this creation also serves as a root vegetable puree alongside bright and contrasting flavors and textures. I would recommend a bright and acidic texture with a crisp texture – say a pickled relish and herb croutons.

LEVEL: Basic

YIELD: approximately 3 quarts

INGREDIENTS

1 cup medium parsnips, peeled and diced
1 cup medium carrots, peeled and diced
1 cup medium Yukon gold potatoes, peeled and diced
1/2 cup peeled and small diced turnips
3 whole garlic cloves, sliced
1 stick unsalted butter
1 quart heavy cream
1 quart water or vegetable stock, more if needed
4 sprigs fresh thyme
1 sprig fresh rosemary
1 tablespoon thinly "sliced" fresh chives
1 tablespoon finely minced fresh tarragon
3 bay leaves
2 teaspoon white truffle oil (optional)
salt & pepper, in stages and per taste

METHOD

In a heavy-bottomed pot, combine all the ingredients and simmer on low for 45 minutes or until all the vegetables are soft. Check the seasoning and add more liquid as desired. Remove the bay leaves and the herb sprigs. Blend in a food processor (adding more liquid or heavy cream as desired) to a smooth consistency. Finish with the fresh chives and tarragon. Serve with warm crusty bread or garnish with fresh croutons.

TURNIP & PARSNIP VICHYSSOISE

On the surface, this is a very similar creation to the previous recipe for *Cream of Root Vegetables*. However, I can assure you that the leeks make all the difference in the world. Additionally, it's a lighter outcome, exuding the deceptive simplicity of classic French cooking. One may serve this soup chilled (during the hot months) or warm. Simple and fresh garnishes complement the complex flavor of the vichyssoise.

LEVEL: Basic

YIELD: approximately 4 quarts

INGREDIENTS
4 small turnips, washed well, diced
3 parsnips, peeled, cut into small pieces
3 sprigs fresh thyme, chop leaves
1 sprig rosemary, chop leaves
4 cloves garlic
2 cups halved and sliced leeks
2 tablespoon unsalted butter
1 cup heavy cream or half and half
1 bay leaf
2 quarts stock made from the thyme & rosemary stems, parsnip skin, and leek trims
salt & pepper, in stages and per taste

METHOD
As the stock is simmering, in a heavy bottomed pot, melt the butter and sauté the leeks on medium-low heat until the leaves are very soft and translucent. Next add the garlic and cook for a couple of minutes. This should take about 20 minutes. Next add the turnips, parsnips, and some salt and pepper. Now add the remaining ingredients including the stock and dairy.

Re-season the liquid to make sure it is to your liking. Simmer on low for about 45 minutes. Let the soup cool a bit before blending it to a very smooth and velvety consistency.

WATERMELON & TOMATO GAZPACHO

I sneak in some smooth mustard anytime I want a stable emulsion. There is a lot of water content in the ingredients of a typical gazpacho and why wouldn't there be? After all, it is fresh ingredient puree. Ultimately, I am providing a template for an amalgamation between a classic gazpacho, salsa fresca, and my interpretation of balanced flavor. This is a punchy composition at first but does mellow out after refrigeration. Be sure to stir it well before consuming to ensure essential flavor hasn't settled due to that pesky and necessary force which guarantees that what goes up must come down.

LEVEL: Basic

YIELD: approximately 4 quarts

INGREDIENTS
4 large heirloom tomatoes (or any other ripe, flavorful tomatoes)
2 cups ripe seedless watermelon, diced
1 stalk celery, peeled, chopped
1 red bell pepper, seeded, chopped
1 small red onion, peeled, chopped
1 seedless cucumber, peeled, diced
2 cloves garlic, minced
1 teaspoon smoked paprika
1 jalapeño or serrano pepper
1/4 cup sherry vinegar
1 teaspoon honey
1 teaspoon Dijon mustard
1 slice white bread, lightly fried in olive oil
1 cup chopped basil
1 cup chopped flat leaf parsley
1/2 cup fruity extra virgin olive oil
water, as needed to allow for blending
salt & pepper, in stages and per taste

METHOD
Steep the minced garlic in the vinegar for 15 minutes. In a blender, combine all the ingredients except the olive oil. Blend well. Test the seasoning to find the balance between the acidity, brightness, spiciness, and herbaceous notes. Now, slowly add the extra virgin olive oil with the blender running at medium speed. Add as much as needed for a reasonably emulsified consistency. Chill for at least 2 hours before serving.

ROASTED POBLANO & CORN CHOWDER

The American Southwest has cornered the flavor market when it involves creations involving corn, beans, and capsicum. The influence of Mexican culinary traditions coupled with the grounded history of indigenous foods has helped shape the food of the region as being destination-worthy.

LEVEL: Basic

YIELD: approximately 3 quarts

INGREDIENTS
4 ears of corn with husk, shave kernels off cob
4 poblano peppers
2 small potatoes, medium diced
1 large onion, cut into large pieces
1 stalk celery, diced
1/2 bunch cilantro, chop stems and leaves separately
juice and zest of 1 lime
4 cloves garlic
2 bay leaves (preferably fresh)
1 medium tomato, diced
1 teaspoon cumin powder
1 teaspoon coriander powder
1/2 teaspoon cayenne powder
corn/vegetable stock, made from the corn & vegetable trims, as needed
extra-virgin olive oil, as needed
salt & pepper, in stages and per taste

METHOD
Preheat an oven to 360F. Coat the poblano, onions, corn kernels, cilantro stems, and garlic with some olive oil, salt, and pepper. Bake on a sheet tray for about 30 minutes. Remove from the oven and core out the poblano peppers. Separate half the roasted corn and set aside. Coarsely chop all the roasted vegetables and transfer to a medium stock pot. Add the celery and spices. Cook for 5 minutes before adding the potatoes, tomatoes, the zest of the lime, and lime juice. Add enough stock to barely cover the ingredients. Cook on low until the potatoes are soft.

Taste the broth and adjust the seasoning as desired. Puree the soup to a smooth consistency. Fold in the reserved roasted corn kernels and garnish with chopped fresh cilantro.

LENTIL VERACRUZ

> Spanish settlers have influenced the cuisine of the Mexican port city of Veracruz on the Gulf of Mexico. A common denominator includes bright, briny flavors emanating from a deft use of olives, capers, tomatoes, fresh herbs, and peppers. Here, I harness that brightness with lentils, which take on other flavors harmoniously while adding their own personality.

LEVEL: Basic

YIELD: approximately 3 quarts

INGREDIENTS

- 2 cups assorted lentils
- 1 medium-size onion, sliced thinly
- 1 cup green pepper, diced
- 4 cloves garlic, minced
- 6 cups diced tomatoes
- 1 teaspoon cumin powder
- 1/2 teaspoon smoked paprika
- 1 cup dry white wine
- 3 tablespoons chopped fresh thyme
- 1 tablespoon chopped fresh oregano
- 2 tablespoons chopped flatleaf parsley
- juice and zest from 1 lemon
- 1/2 cup pitted, sliced green olives
- 1/4 cup capers, drained and rinsed
- 2 pickled jalapeño peppers, thinly sliced
- 6 cups water
- extra-virgin olive oil, as needed
- salt & pepper, in stages and per taste

METHOD

In a pot, heat some olive oil and sauté the onions, green pepper, and garlic for 5 minutes. Add the cumin and paprika next and cook for 1 couple of minutes. Now add the lentils. Season with some salt and pepper. Cook the lentils for about 4 minutes. Add the white wine and deglaze for about 30 seconds. Now add the tomatoes and cook for 5 minutes. Next, add all the remaining ingredients except the olives and parsley. Simmer for about 30 minutes or until the lentils are soft. Remove 1 cup of the soup and blend before adding it back to the pot.

Taste for proper level of seasoning before finishing with the chopped olives and parsley.

GINGER & BUTTERNUT SQUASH

This is a well-known combination but leading with ginger takes the soup to another place. Furthermore, roasting the butternut squash first intensifies not only its natural sugars, but also its tannins. Yes, tannins. Many roasted hard squashes have this quality. To round off the warm and comforting flavors, I've used a wide variety of aromatics.

LEVEL: Basic

YIELD: approximately 2 quarts

INGREDIENTS
2 ripe medium (or 1 large) butternut squash
2 tablespoons minced fresh ginger
1 teaspoon fresh garlic, minced
3 whole cloves of garlic
1 medium red onion, small dice
1 tablespoon fresh thyme
2 fresh thyme sprigs
1/2 teaspoon freshly grated nutmeg
2 bay leaves (fresh, if available)
1 tablespoon fresh tarragon, chopped
vegetable stock (low/no sodium, preferably homemade), as needed
1 cup heavy cream (optional)
extra virgin olive oil (for roasting)
salt & pepper, in stages and per taste

METHOD
Preheat an oven to 350F. Peel the butternut squash, scoop out the core, and cut into medium-sized pieces. Toss the squash in extra virgin olive oil, salt, pepper, the thyme sprigs, and garlic cloves. Place on a baking sheet and roast at for 30-45 minutes until the squash is soft. You may have to turn the squash once during the process, so it doesn't scorch on one side. Discard the whole thyme sprigs but retain the garlic cloves. In a heavy-bottomed pot, heat some extra virgin olive oil and sauté the onion and fresh ginger for a couple of minutes. Add the garlic and stir briefly. Next, add the remaining ingredients except the heavy cream. Stir and check to make sure it's well-seasoned. Simmer on low-medium heat for 20 minutes. Blend to a smooth puree and finish with the heavy cream (optional) and tarragon.

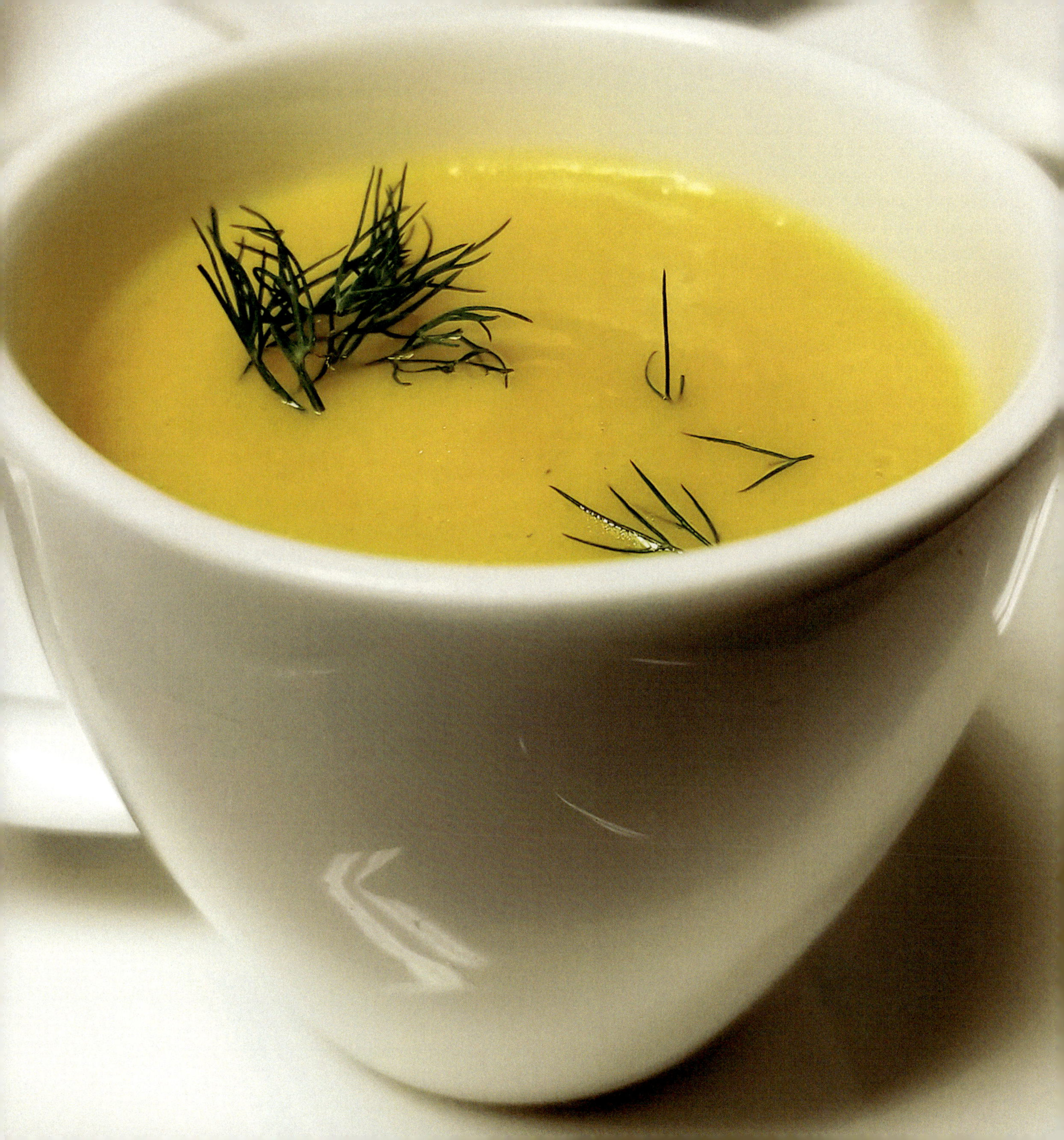

TUNISIAN LENTIL STEW

I'm not done illustrating the versatility of lentils as an ingredient in soups. Here, I am slowly inching my way towards my origins. But first, a thoughtful pause in North Africa reveals a completely fulfilling and exotic preparation. When Jenneffer and I visited Morocco recently, the cuisine in the city of Marrakech offered up the vast repertoire of dishes featuring legumes. Crossing over local giant Algeria, one arrives in Tunisia and her spectacular port towns. This soup could be just as easily be claimed by Morocco, based on flavor profile alone.

LEVEL: Basic

YIELD: approximately 2 1/2 quarts

INGREDIENTS
2 tablespoons olive oil
1 red onion, finely chopped
2 garlic cloves, finely chopped
1/2 teaspoon ground cumin
1/2 teaspoon ground cinnamon
1/2 teaspoon cayenne pepper
1.5 cups green lentils
3 cups vegetable stock (preferably homemade)
water, as needed
3 medium carrots, diced
2 celery sticks, chopped
2 potatoes, peeled and diced
half a bunch of coriander, chopped
juice and zest of 1 lemon
salt & pepper, in stages and per taste

METHOD
Add the lentils to a pan of lightly salted water. Cook until they are half done and set aside. Add the oil to a pan and use to fry the onions, carrots and celery until translucent. Then add garlic, stirring for few seconds. Add the spices and potatoes and continue frying, stirring constantly, until they become fragrant (about 2 minutes); then add the lentils and stock. Bring to a boil and skim any fat from the surface. Reduce to a simmer and partly cover the pot. Continue cooking for about an hour. Pulse slightly with a hand blender to thicken the soup. Adjust the seasoning, then stir in the coriander, lemon zest, and lemon juice.

SORREL & DAIKON RADISH

> In India, sorrel goes by *gongura* and is a favorite perennial green for many dishes native to the state of Andhra Pradesh. I grew up eating this dish in the style of a sambhar, although we called it *pulsu*. It can be brothy, so I've made some adjustments like including a legume to give the soup some body. This soup has South Indian flavors, but the addition of sorrel brings it closer to home for me.

LEVEL: Basic

YIELD: approximately 2 quarts

INGREDIENTS

1 cup urad dal (shelled and split black gram)
3 ripe tomatoes, medium dice
1 small onion, small dice
4 cups, medium diced daikon radish
4 cups chopped sorrel leaves
2 tablespoons black mustard seeds
1 inch fresh ginger, peeled, cut into long thin strips
1 tablespoon cumin seeds
1 teaspoon asafoetida powder
1 teaspoon cayenne pepper
1 tablespoon turmeric powder
2 tablespoons Malabar spice blend (page 75)
1 teaspoon tamarind concentrate (or 1 cup tamarind water)
4 green chilies, split lengthwise
10 each fresh curry leaves
1 bunch fresh cilantro, chopped
water, as needed
2 tablespoons vegetable oil or ghee, as preferred
salt & pepper, in stages and per taste

METHOD

Wash and rinse the urad dal well. In a stainless pot, cook the dal in a broth made of water, tamarind, turmeric, salt, and pepper. You will have to skim the foam off the top as it accumulates. This will take about 35 minutes or so. Coarsely puree the dal and some its broth. Meanwhile, in a heavy-bottomed pot, sauté the onions for a couple of minutes. Add the ginger, green chilies, and radish, and stir for a minute or two. Add the sorrel leaves and tomatoes and sweat for a few seconds. Add enough water or dal broth, Malabar blend, turmeric, and cayenne, and more tamarind; cover and cook on a low simmer until the radish is almost cooked. Now add the pureed dal and simmer until the desired consistency is reached.

To finish the soup, heat some oil/ghee in a hot pan until it just smokes. Add the cumin seeds, mustard seeds, curry leaves, and asafoetida, and stir for 10 seconds. The seeds will crackle and pop. Pour this infused hot oil and all its ingredients into the sambhar. Watch to ensure you don't get splattered. This is the "Tadka" stage, a common procedure in Indian cooking. Finish with lots of fresh cilantro.

MASALA LENTILS (DAL)

> I could have given this dish many fitting titles. At the end of the day, this is a hearty *Dal* – a ubiquitous Hindi name for a wide variety of legumes. There are many traditional dal dishes in India, with Dal Makhani being perhaps the most well-known and revered. The best versions of a Dal-style dish are kissed by the aroma and smoke of a tandoor. If one has the ability to finish this dish in a smoker, by all means, one should.

LEVEL: Basic

YIELD: approximately 3 quarts

INGREDIENTS
- 1/2 cup red lentils
- 1/2 cup yellow lentils
- 1/2 cup green lentils
- 1 medium red onion, minced
- 1 cup ripe tomatoes, chopped
- 1 green bell pepper, diced
- 10 each fresh curry leaves (if available)
- 1 tablespoon freshly grated ginger
- 1 jalapeño pepper, minced
- 1 tablespoon freshly minced garlic
- 2 medium potatoes, peeled, small dice
- 1 teaspoon mustard seeds
- 1 teaspoon cumin seeds
- 1 tablespoon ground cumin
- 1 teaspoon coriander powder
- 1 teaspoon turmeric powder
- 1 teaspoon cayenne pepper powder
- juice of one lemon
- 1 bunch fresh cilantro, chopped without bruising
- 3 tablespoons extra-virgin olive oil or vegetable oil
- water or vegetable stock, as needed (at least 4 cups)
- salt & pepper, in stages and per taste

METHOD

Wash the lentils well in cold water. In a small stock pot, heat the oil over medium heat. Add the mustard seeds, cumin seeds and curry leaves (if available). When the mustard seeds start popping, add the onions, green pepper, ginger, jalapeno, and sauté for a minute. Note: Season with salt and pepper in stages until the very end. Next, add the garlic and stir for 30 seconds. Now add the drained and washed lentils and stir. Now, add all the ground spices and stir well. Add the potatoes. Cover with water, stir well, and simmer on low for about an hour. Periodically, foam will form at the top which may be spooned off. Add more water (and re-season) if necessary.

Finish with the fresh tomatoes, cilantro, and lemon juice. Test for the proper seasoning and balance.

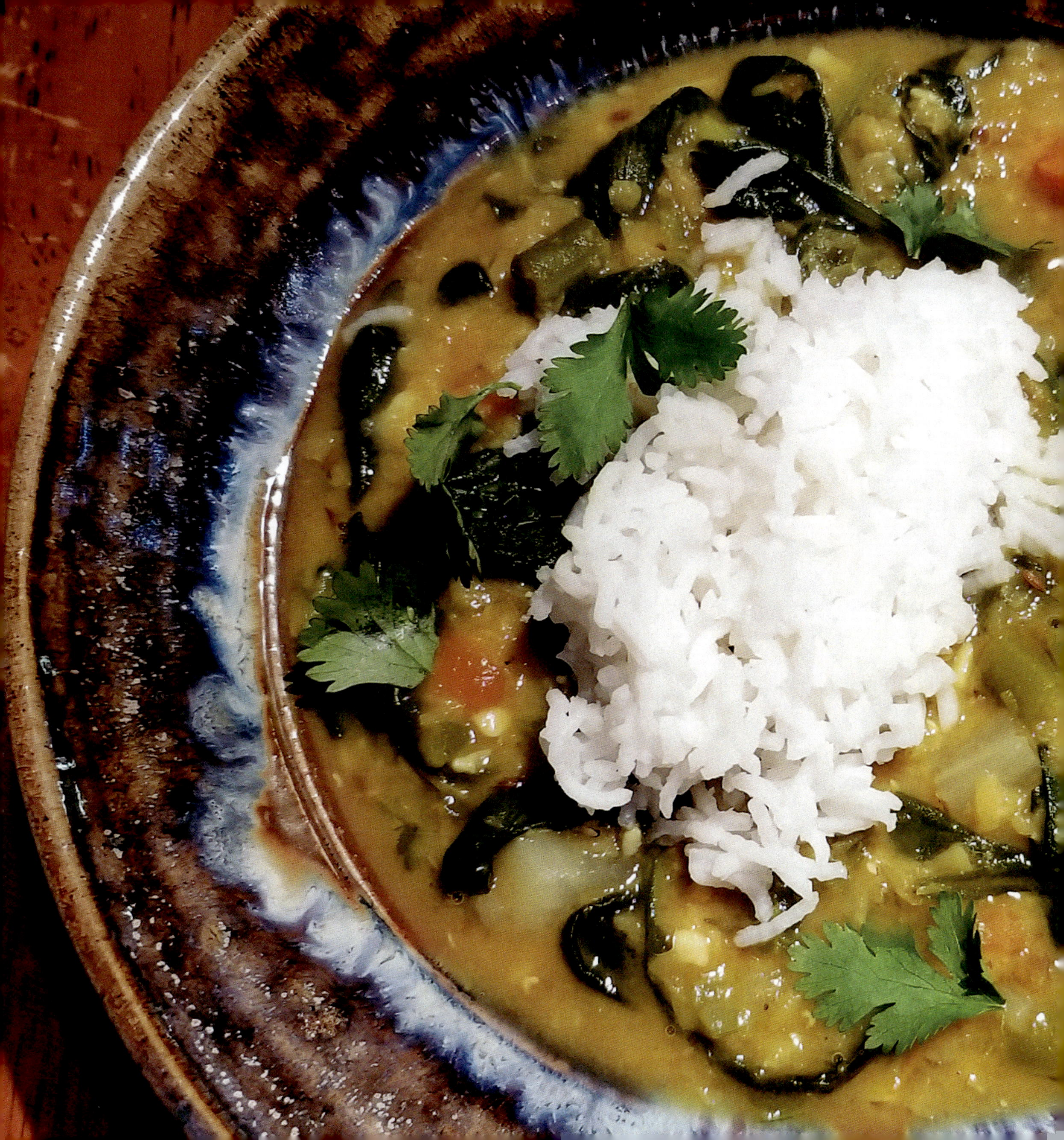

Salad Dressings

Salad dressings may be used beyond dressing salads. They can be accents on dishes for unexpected pops of flavor that offer contrast and brightness. Classically, a vinaigrette contains a prescribed ratio of 3 parts oil to 1 part vinegar (acidity). I haven't used that high a proportion of oil in a salad dressing since culinary school because I think it's excessive and damaging to the integrity of fresh greens.

SESAME SHERRY

LEVEL: Basic

YIELD: approximately 2 1/2 cups

INGREDIENTS
1 cup sherry vinegar
1 tablespoon dark sesame oil
1 tablespoon Dijon mustard
1/4 cup honey
2 tablespoons light brown sugar
granulated white sugar, as needed
3/4 cup grapeseed or canola oil
salt & pepper, in stages and per taste

METHOD
In a food processor, mix the mustard, sherry vinegar, honey, brown sugar, some salt, some pepper, some granulated white sugar and the sesame oil. Once the desired balance of acidity and sweet flavors is reached, with the motor running, add the grapeseed oil slowly at first and then completely. This is an assertive dressing so use sparingly.

PASSION FRUIT & LEMON BALM

LEVEL: Basic

YIELD: approximately 3/4 quart

INGREDIENTS
1 cup passion fruit concentrate or fresh pulp
1 vanilla bean
1/4 cup fresh lemon balm leaves (substitute tarragon, if necessary), chopped finely
1 cup granulated sugar
1 cup water
confectioner's sugar, as desired for balance
1 cup grape seed or canola oil
coarse salt, to taste
freshly ground black pepper, to taste

METHOD
Split the vanilla bean in half and scrape the pods out into a pot with the water and sugar. Heat the water, stirring until the sugar dissolves completely. This is the vanilla bean simple syrup. Let the syrup cool. In the bowl of a food processor, add the vanilla-infused simple syrup to the passion fruit puree. Mix. Add some salt, pepper, and confectioner's sugar. Find that balance in flavor. With the motor running, very slowly add the grape seed oil to the sweetened passion fruit until completely done. Adjust seasoning as desired. Finish by adding the fresh lemon balm and mix.

CRANBERRY

LEVEL: Basic

YIELD: approximately 3 cups

INGREDIENTS
1 cup fresh cranberries, washed
1/4 cup dried cranberries, rehydrated in warm water
1/2 cup white balsamic vinegar
1/4 cup Dijon mustard
1/2 cup grape seed oil
granulated sugar, as needed
pure honey, as needed
salt & pepper, in stages and per taste

PROCEDURE
Cook the fresh cranberries and sugar in some water and the white balsamic until they break down. Be sure to season them with salt and pepper. Puree them to a smooth pulp. Check the seasoning to make sure that the puree is balanced and add more sugar or honey, if it is too acidic. Combine the mustard and cranberry puree together and whisk in the oil slowly to form a vinaigrette. Note that classically, a vinaigrette is 1-part acid, 3 parts oil. But this, certainly, is a much healthier version.

ORANGE GINGER

LEVEL: Basic

YIELD: approximately

INGREDIENTS
1 cup fresh orange juice
zest of 1/2 orange
1 teaspoon soy sauce
1/2 teaspoon Dijon mustard
1/2 inch piece of fresh ginger, peeled
1/3 cup grapeseed oil
2 fresh basil leaves
salt & pepper, in stages and per taste

METHOD
This can be completed either in blender or bowl. Grate (using a micro plane) the fresh ginger into the orange juice. Mix all the ingredients well. With the motor running, slowly drizzle the oil into the mixture. Taste and adjust the salt and pepper. Store refrigerated in an airtight container.

HERB TRUFFLE

LEVEL: Basic

YIELD: approximately 2 cups

INGREDIENTS
1/2 cup black truffle puree or shavings
1 tablespoon Dijon mustard
1 teaspoon fresh thyme
2 tablespoons champagne vinegar
4 leaves fresh basil, chopped
1 tablespoon fresh flat leaf parsley, chopped
1/2 cup grape seed oil
1/4 cup extra virgin olive oil
3 drops, white truffle oil
salt & pepper, in stages and per taste

METHOD
Combine the extra virgin olive oil and grape seed oil. Mix all the remaining ingredients in the bowl of a food processor. Test the blend for the desired balance of flavors. Emulsify slowly with the oil blend.

CARAMELIZED SHALLOT & CIDER

LEVEL: Basic

YIELD: approximately 2 cups

INGREDIENTS
4 shallots, peeled and sliced thinly
1/2 cup apple cider vinegar
1 tablespoon Dijon mustard
2 tablespoons granulated sugar
1/4 cup extra-virgin olive oil
1/2 cup grape seed oil
salt & pepper, in stages and per taste

METHOD
Sauté the shallots in the extra-virgin olive oil on medium heat, until caramelized. Remove and cool. Add the vinegar, Dijon mustard, sugar, salt and pepper to taste. Whisk in the grape seed oil, slowly. Taste and adjust the seasoning as desired.

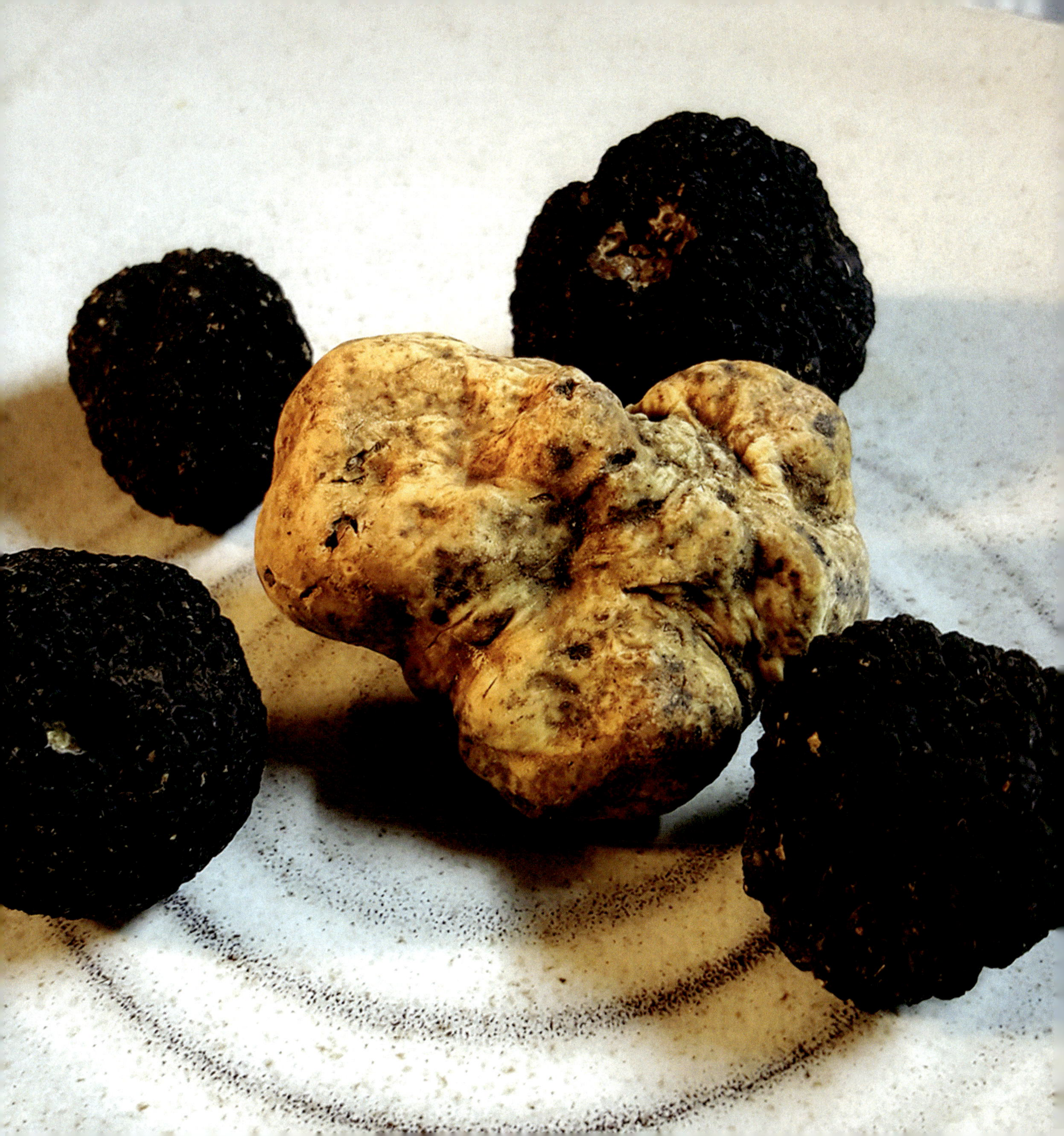

GREEN GODDESS

LEVEL: Basic

YIELD: approximately 3 cups

INGREDIENTS
1/2 cup yogurt or mayonnaise or sour cream or aqua faba
1 teaspoon Dijon mustard
1 cup flat-leaf parsley leaves
1 cup watercress
1/4 cup arugula
¼ cup fresh tarragon
2 tablespoon fresh chives, chopped
1 clove garlic, chopped
zest and juice of 1/2 lemon
1 tablespoon champagne or white balsamic vinegar
salt & pepper, in stages and per taste

METHOD
Mix all ingredients in a blender and puree. Season to find the balance you prefer.

POMEGRANATE, MINT & WALNUT

LEVEL: Basic

YIELD: approximately 1 1/2 cup

INGREDIENTS
1/4 cup pomegranate molasses
1/2 cup almond or cashew milk
1 shallot, minced
2 tablespoons fresh mint, chopped
1 teaspoon fresh ginger, minced
1 tablespoon grapeseed oil
2 tablespoons toasted walnut oil
salt & pepper, in stages and per taste

METHOD
Combine the walnut and grapeseed oil. In a blender, mix all the ingredients except the oil and tarragon. Season it as needed with salt and pepper. With the motor running, slowly drizzle in the oil combination. Fold in the fresh mint and refrigerate until needed in an airtight container.

TURMERIC MISO

LEVEL: Basic

YIELD: approximately 1 cup

INGREDIENTS
1/4 cup white miso paste
1 tablespoon low sodium soy sauce
1 teaspoon turmeric powder
1 teaspoon fresh ginger root, grated (if available)
1/2 teaspoon fresh ginger, minced
1/2 teaspoon honey
water, as needed
salt & pepper, in stages and per taste

METHOD
In a bowl, simply whisk all the ingredients well. If it is too thick, add some water to thin it out. Taste before storing or using.

CREAMY CAESAR

LEVEL: Basic

YIELD: approximately 3 cups

INGREDIENTS
1 cup plain yogurt
1 cup crème frâiche or sour cream
1/2 cup grated or prepared horseradish
1 tablespoon Worcestershire (optional and make sure it is vegetarian)
1 tablespoon Dijon mustard
1/4 cup mayonnaise
1 cup grated Parmigiana Reggiano
salt & pepper, in stages and per taste

METHOD
Mix all the ingredients except the cheese in a food processor until smooth. Finish by mixing in the cheese. Test the seasoning making sure there is plenty of black pepper.

Composed Salads

A salad without a complementary dressing is like pasta without any sauce. Mind you, I consider garlic and olive oil to be a sauce.

SIGNATURE WITH PASSION FRUIT

Nowadays, at least in North America, hydroponic versions of lettuce are widely available in standard grocery stores. But the best versions come when we can get juicy lettuces grown in the ground during their season. I learned a version of this dressing on my culinary externship at *Canoe Restaurant and Bar* in downtown Toronto. One evening, Garde Manger chef taught me this "loose" emulsion. The recipe does not include a natural emulsifier like, say, mustard or egg yolks to stabilize the forced emulsion of the grape seed oil and passion fruit puree, but the natural viscosity of the puree is what keeps the emulsion stable.

LEVEL: Basic
YIELD: approximately 6 servings

INGREDIENTS
2 heads of Boston lettuce, washed
1 cup coarsely chopped walnuts
1 cup smoked tomatoes (page 357)
1 cup roasted grapes (page 357)
1/2 cup dried cranberries
1/4 cup crumbles of blue Stilton cheese
1/4 cup fresh blueberries or strawberries
1/4 cup passion fruit emulsion, more or less (page 164)
salt & pepper, in stages and per taste

METHOD
To assemble the salad, wash and dry the Boston lettuce. Toss the remaining ingredients (including the lettuce), except the Blue cheese, in the passion fruit emulsion as desired. Be sure to season with salt and freshly ground pepper. Layer as needed, being sure not to overdress the salad. Finish by sprinkling some of the blue Stilton around the salad.

KALE WITH APPLE CIDER

> Some people might say that kale has been over-used to its slow demise. But to that view I say, pish tosh. There are of course a number or varieties of kale that are appropriate for salad, but for me, Lacinato or Red Russian are the best and most easily available options. The apple cider vinaigrette pairs well with the earthy heartiness of the kale. Ben Walter of Hermitage Farms grows a killer Lacinato kale. It doesn't hurt that he composts, in his flower garden, scraps from our restaurant.

LEVEL: Basic

YIELD: approximately 4 servings

INGREDIENTS
4 cups kale, washed, de-stemmed, crushed a bit to soften, and sliced into strips
1/2 cup toasted almonds tossed in rosemary oil
1/2 cup heirloom grape tomatoes
2 oz. young goat cheese
1/2 cup dried cranberries, re-hydrated
cider vinaigrette, as needed (page 166)
salt & pepper, in stages and per taste

METHOD
Toss in the kale and all the remaining ingredients except the goat cheese. Serve the salad with dollops of the goat cheese on the side.

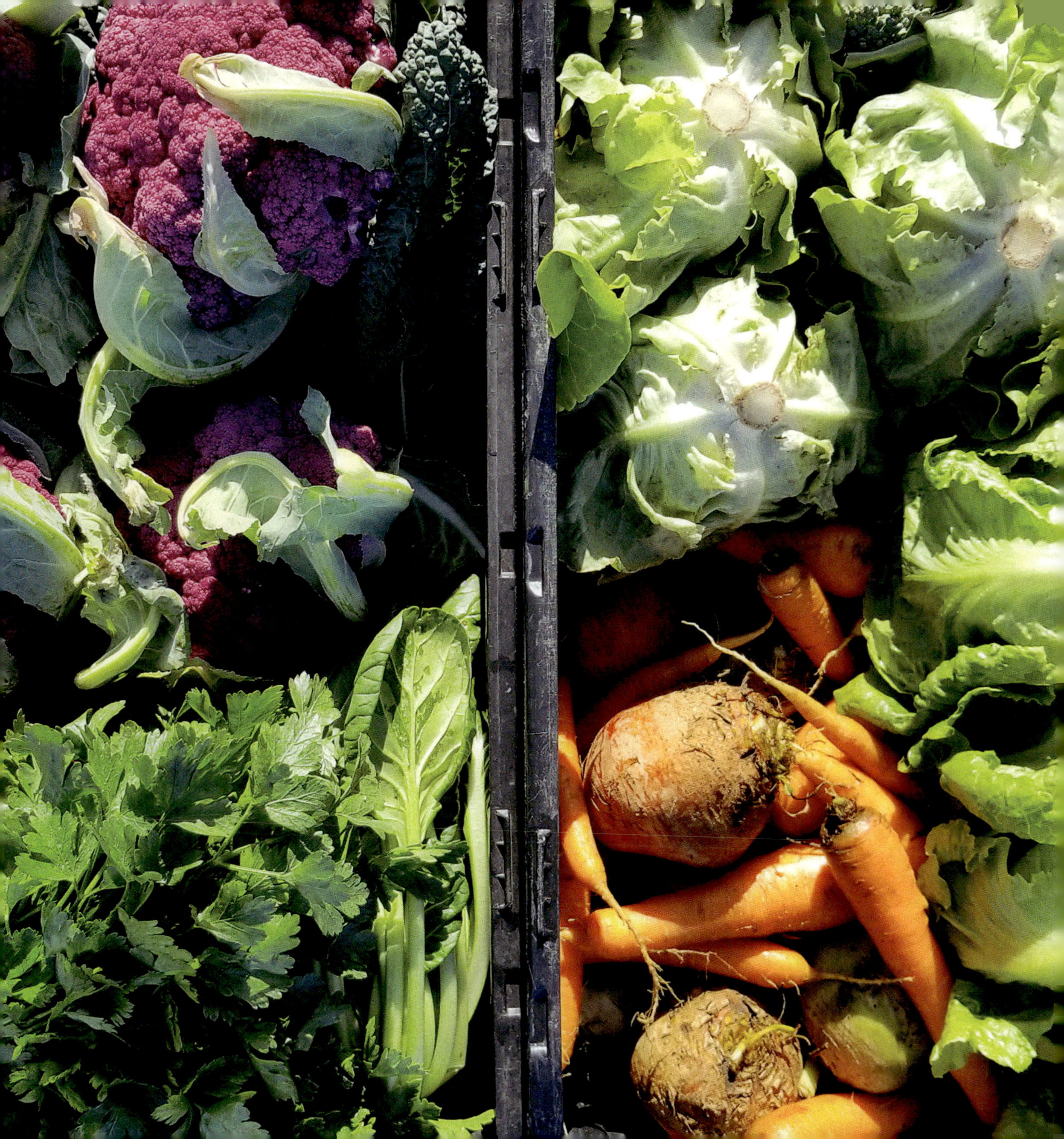

CAPRESE WITH BASIL PISTOU

This is going to sound like a broken record, but the addition of watermelon to the caprese is a stroke of genius, which I must credit to my time at Canoe Restaurant and Bar in Toronto. One evening, when I was in the back with Chef Frank, we were plating during a meal for a private party. The first course was a caprese with heirloom tomatoes, buffalo mozzarella, and watermelon! I've re-interpreted it with the addition of the pistou and reduced balsamic. A touch of finishing sea salt and coarsely ground fresh black pepper, and a fruity Sicilian olive oil, makes this a fantastic composition. Ingredients in the peak of their quality make this salad all that is.

LEVEL: Basic

YIELD: approximately 6 servings

INGREDIENTS

4 cups heirloom or other in season ripe tomatoes, bite sized pieces or wedges
12 oz. buffalo mozzarella, large diced
4 cups fresh basil leaves, cleaned & dried
1 clove garlic, minced
juice of 2 lemons
pure honey, as needed
balsamic reduction or aged balsamic as needed (page 349)
1/2 cup ripe watermelon, large dice
extra virgin olive oil, as needed
salt & pepper, in stages and per taste

METHOD

Steep the garlic in the lemon juice for 5 minutes. Then, blend this with the basil, extra virgin olive oil, salt, and pepper. Taste the pistou. It should be bright, but not overpoweringly acidic. If it is, simply add some honey and mix. Set aside. Toss the tomatoes, mozzarella, and watermelon in the pistou. Plate the salad and finish with more extra virgin olive oil, some sea salt, and coarsely ground black pepper.

GRILLED ASPARAGUS WITH PINE NUT

The inspiration for this salad came from the pine nut relish I once made for a gathering at home with friends. Roasted garlic, fresh thyme, toasted pine nuts, extra-virgin olive oil, salt, and pepper form the basis of a delicious relish, which can be enjoyed with fresh vegetables or a baguette. Often, one might find a blanched asparagus salad with shaved cheese, but I think the nutty notes of the relish pairs well with in-season asparagus, which is blanched in salted water, or better yet, grilled.

LEVEL: Basic

YIELD: approximately 4 servings

INGREDIENTS
1 lb. medium-sized asparagus, trimmed
4 oz. pine nuts, toasted
1 bulb garlic
1/4 cup parmigiana Reggiano, grated
1 tablespoon fresh thyme leaves
1/4 cup extra-virgin olive oil
salt & pepper, in stages and per taste

METHOD
Drizzle half the extra-virgin olive oil on the garlic, cover with aluminum foil and roast in the oven at 325 F. After an hour, you should have roasted garlic. Store the oil in the pouch for grilling the asparagus. Squeeze out the roasted garlic cloves and combine with the pine nuts, remaining extra-virgin olive oil, light amount of salt, pepper, the cheese, and the thyme leaves. Set aside.

Lightly season the asparagus with salt and pepper and coat with some of the roasted garlic oil. Grill until just done. Spoon the pine nut relish over the grilled asparagus and serve warm or at room temperature.

ARUGULA WITH CRANBERRY

LEVEL: Basic

YIELD: approximately 4 servings

INGREDIENTS
4 cups baby arugula, washed and dried
1 cup fresh cranberry, washed
1/4 cup dried cranberries, rehydrated
1/2 cup shelled pumpkin seeds, toasted
4 oz. young goat cheese
1/4 cup assorted pickled peppers and carrots
cranberry dressing, as needed (page 165)
salt & pepper, in stages and per taste

METHOD
Toss the arugula lightly with the cranberry dressing. Season with salt and pepper. Assemble the salad with the dressed arugula, pumpkin seeds, goat cheese, rehydrated cranberries, and pickled vegetables.

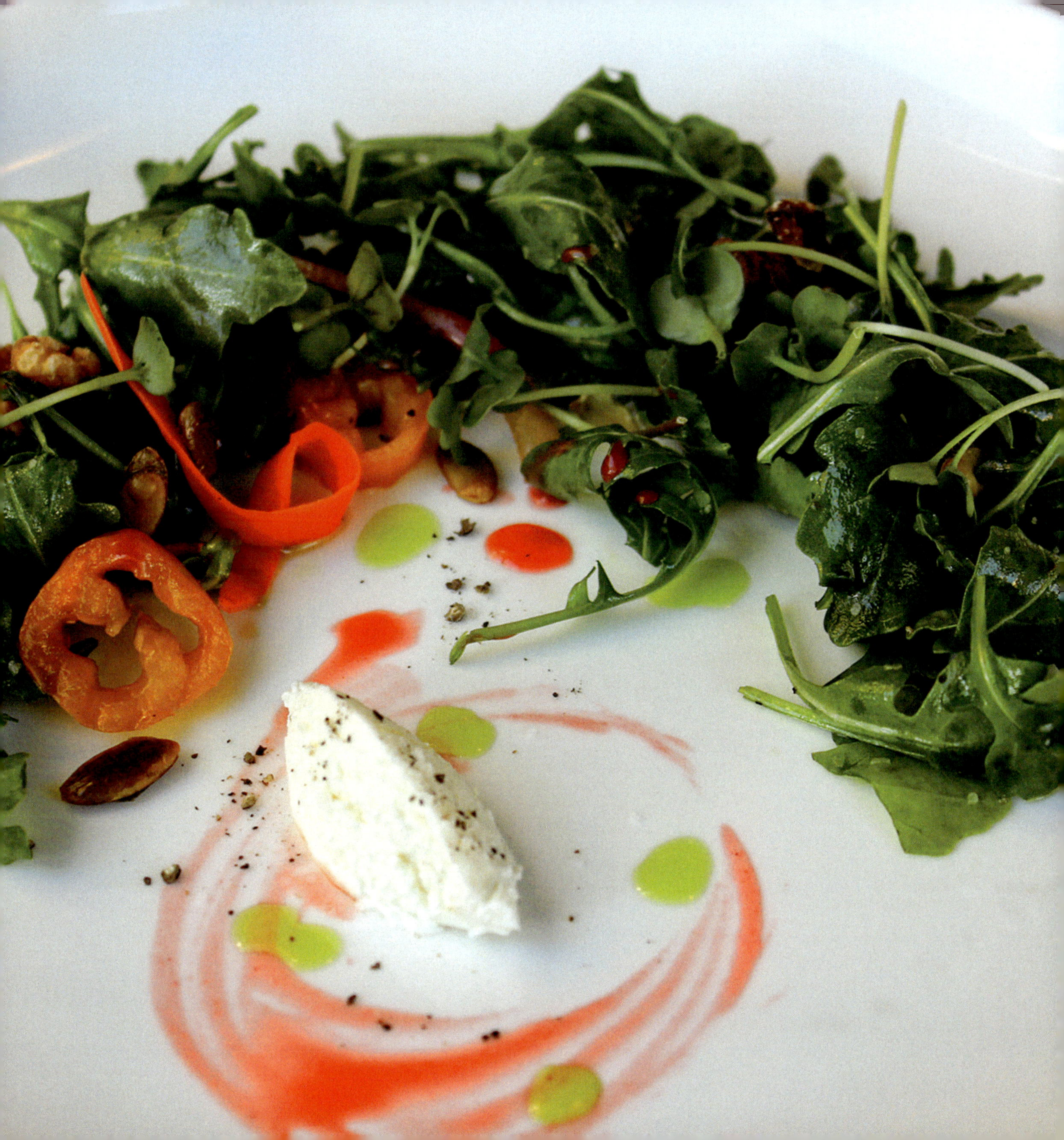

HEIRLOOM GRAINS WITH SESAME SHERRY

This salad has been called the "Heirloom Grain Salad" on our menus. When we include it on the menu, it has a cult following, and guests swear that it is the best thing they have eaten in a long time. Not just best *salad*, but the best thing, period. Accurately, the couscous isn't a grain, nor is the wild rice. So, certainly some replacements, like quinoa or barley would make sense. But, when made correctly, this salad will blow your mind and is a meal. It is best when served over a bed of fresh, juicy lettuce also dressed in the sesame and sherry vinaigrette.

LEVEL: Basic

YIELD: approximately 4 servings

INGREDIENTS
1/2 cup dry toasted farro
1/2 cup calico wild rice
1/2 cup quinoa
1/2 cup dried cranberries or dried cherries
1/4 cup toasted walnuts or almonds
1 cup red seedless grapes, sliced in half
4 oz. young goat cheese
1 teaspoon aged or reduced balsamic (page 349)
1 gallon water (to cook the grains & rice)
1 head Boston lettuce
2 tablespoons fresh basil, chopped
1/4 cup sesame sherry vinaigrette, more or less (page 164)
salt & pepper, in stages and per taste

METHOD
Bring the water to a boil, add salt and pepper and then, add the toasted farro. On medium heat, cook the farro for 20 minutes. Next add the wild rice and cook for an additional 25 minutes. Finally add the quinoa and cook for about 20 minutes. Drain the grains and toss lightly in extra virgin olive oil so they don't stick. Toss the lettuce separately and lightly in the vinaigrette. While the grains are still slightly warm, toss all the remaining ingredients, including the goat cheese in a stainless bowl. Serve the warmed grains mixture over the lettuce for a hearty and fulfilling salad.

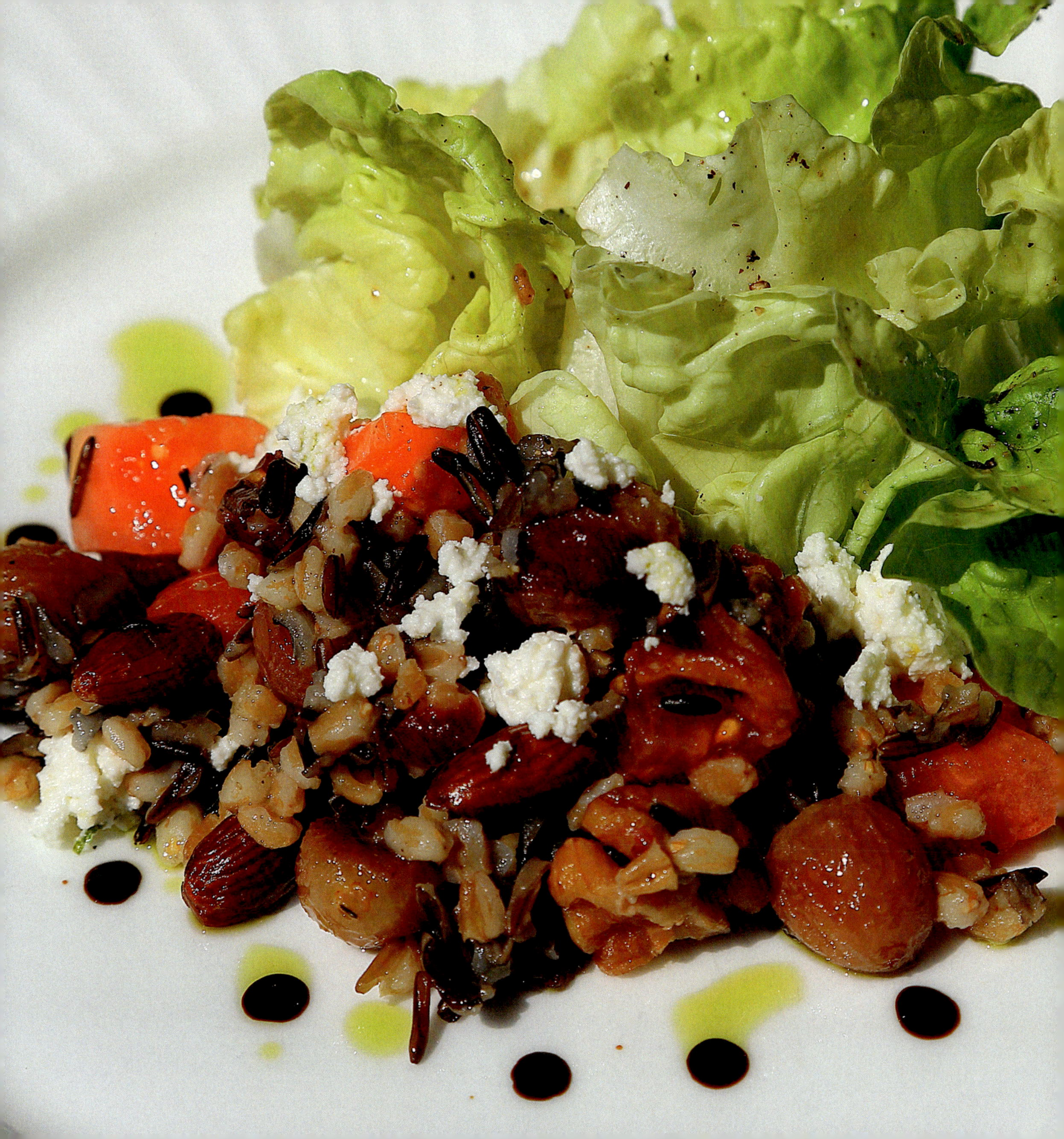

FENNEL WITH ORANGE GINGER

> People often ask us about the origin of the name of the restaurant. Well, the word refers to, among other things, the young leaves of cruciferous plants like watercress. Watercress can be extremely assertive, so this is a salad which can of course be a salad, but it can also be garnish atop a juicy burger. The cooling aspects of the shaved fennel bulb and pungency of the watercress (I recommend the baby variety) marry well with the brightness of an in-season orange. The segments of orange when bitten into are almost all the dressing you need because of the orange juice that results.

LEVEL: Basic

YIELD: approximately 4 servings

INGREDIENTS
2 cups baby watercress, cleaned, dried
1 bulb fennel, cored, shaved thinly on a mandoline. Save the fennel tops (fronds)
1 large sweet navel orange, segments
1 teaspoon orange zest
extra-virgin olive oil, as needed
salt & pepper, in stages and per taste

METHOD
Save the orange juice which results from the process of segmenting the orange. Whisk it with some-extra virgin olive oil, salt, and pepper for a quick orange dressing. Toss all the ingredients, except the orange segments with this quick dressing. Gently fold in the orange segments and fennel fronds. Re-season with salt and pepper as needed. Drizzle a bit of extra virgin olive oil at the end.

SPINACH WITH ROASTED CHERRIES

> This may sound like a ho-hum salad, but when you are able to get tat-soi (an Asian variety of spinach) and in season (pitted) Rainier cherries, the combination is simple, elegant, and wholesome. As you might guess by now, I am big fan of roasting fruit (or just about anything). About the other ingredients of the salad: the possibilities are nearly endless, but I would recommend a lemon-infused freshly made ricotta and sugar snap peas.

LEVEL: Basic

YIELD: approximately 4 servings

INGREDIENTS

2 cups, pitted fresh cherries
1/4 cup pecans, toasted
1 lb. spinach, washed, cleaned
1/4 cup fresh lemon ricotta
1 cup sugar snap peas, cleaned, cut into strips
balsamic reduction, as needed (page 349)
extra-virgin olive oil, as needed
1 tablespoon wildflower honey
grape seed oil, as needed
salt & pepper, in stages and per taste

METHOD

Toss the cherries with enough grape seed oil to coat them and roast them on a baking sheet in a 350F oven for about 30 minutes. They should blister. Retain the natural juices. Whisk the natural juices with a bit more extra-virgin olive oil and the honey. This is the dressing. Gently toss the spinach, pecans, and sugar snap peas with the dressing and salt and pepper, as desired. Compose the salad with the lemon ricotta, roasted cherries, and a drizzle of balsamic reduction.

ROASTED BEETS & CARROTS

I remember growing up with boiled beets as a snack, so I've been eating beets for a very long time. My parents even made a dry bhaji with beets and fresh coconut, which is delicious with chapatis. I love the tops of most root vegetables. When washed well and sautéed simply with olive oil and garlic, beet greens--probably more so than any other root vegetable greens--taste like the root itself. The sesame sherry vinaigrette and some toasted walnuts add just the right amount of acidity and nutty texture for a beautifully composed, unconventional salad.

LEVEL: Intermediate

YIELD: approximately 8 servings

INGREDIENTS

4 medium sized golden beets, cleaned well
4 baby carrots, cleaned well, trimmed
3 cups beet greens, de-stemmed, cleaned
4 oz. young goat cheese
1/2 cup walnuts, dry toasted
1/4 cup sesame sherry vinaigrette (page 164)
coarse salt, to taste
fresh coarsely ground black pepper, to taste

The Brine
2 quarts water + more for cooking greens
1 cinnamon stick
1/2 tablespoon whole black peppercorns
1/2 tablespoon fennel seeds
1/2 tablespoon coriander seeds
1/2 tablespoon whole spice berries
2 dried bay leaves
1/2 cup light brown sugar
1/4 cup honey
1/2 cup red wine vinegar
salt & pepper, in stages and per taste

METHOD

Roots: Preheat an oven to 350F. Toss the beets and carrots in extra virgin olive oil, salt, and pepper. Cover with aluminum foil and bake for about 45 minutes to an hour or until "fork tender." Meanwhile, add all the remaining ingredients to the water in a stainless pot and bring to a boil. Add enough salt so that the brine has almost the salinity of the ocean. Peel the roasted beets & carrots, cut in half, and drop into the brine. After approximately 48 hours, the beets & carrots should be ready to eat. If one doesn't have that much time, then certainly a few hours of pickling will provide a quick and perfectly good version. In fact, since the sesame sherry vinaigrette has plenty of acidity, the beets and carrots may be roasted only.

Greens: Cut the beet greens into thick strips. Sauté them in some extra virgin olive oil, salt, and pepper, for about 2 minutes. Add 2 cups water and simmer on low for about 15 minutes. Let the greens cool.
Salad: Use a young goat cheese as a bottom spread and assemble the salad as desired. Lightly toss the roots in the vinaigrette

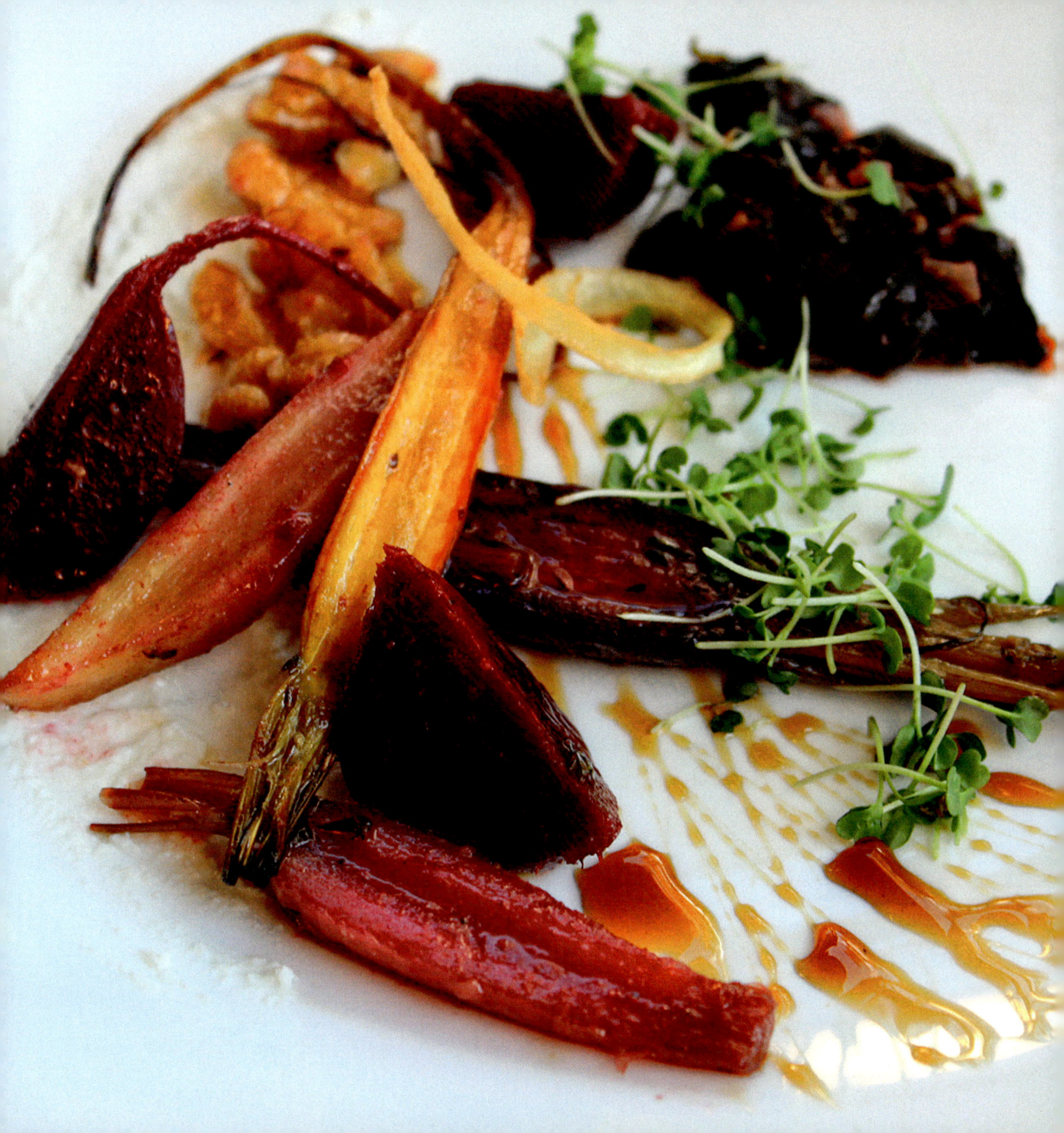

SEASONAL BERRRIES AND GENTLE HERBS

The term "fruit salad" may evoke memories of an "ambrosia salad" in the South, but this is no ambrosia salad. Here, my inspiration is to showcase fresh fruits and berries harmoniously mixed with complementary fresh herbs and a very light dressing to be served in a bed of wild rice or simply dressed, nutritious lettuce greens. In general, bush berries and basil pair well together. The goal is to treat the fresh in-season fruit not just as a snack, but rather as a first course during a festive meal. Cheese is optional.

LEVEL: Basic

YIELD: approximately 6 servings

INGREDIENTS
2 large heads of Boston lettuce
1 lb. assorted seasonal bush berries
1/4 cup fresh tarragon, chopped finely
1/4 cup fresh basil, leaves torn
1 tablespoon fresh mint, chopped finely
grape seed oil, as needed
Blue Stilton or Gorgonzola Dolce cheese crumbles, as desired
balsamic reduction or aged balsamic, as desired (page 349)
wildflower honey, as desired
salt & pepper, in stages and per taste

METHOD
Wash and dry the berries well. Toss them gently with the fresh herbs, honey, salt, and pepper. Let them sit for about 30 minutes in the refrigerator. Reserve the juices. Combine the juices with some grape seed oil. This is the dressing. Dress the lettuce with this dressing. Compose the salad with the lettuce, berries and herbs, some blue Stilton cheese; drizzle some aged balsamic or balsamic reduction.

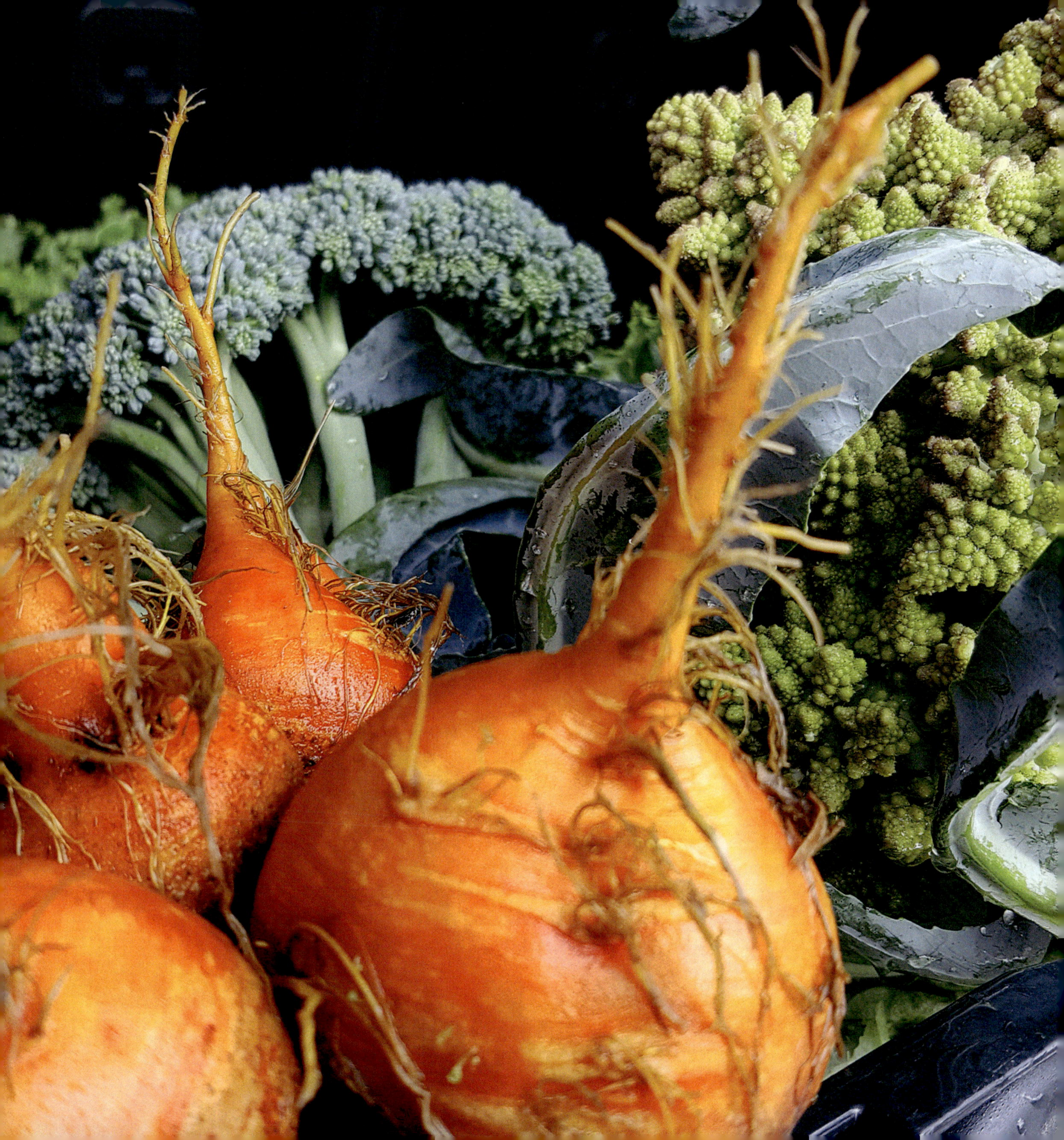

Flour-Based

Naturally, one could write the entire volume on baking. Mind you, it wouldn't be I who would write that. Yet, growing up in Mumbai, I was used to handling dough at home when making chapatis, but I had never worked with a leavening agent and especially not fresh yeast. So, when I baked my first loaf of bread (a baguette, I believe), in culinary school, my mind was officially blown. The idea that flour, water, salt, maybe sugar, and yeast could be transformed so significantly and deliciously re-affirmed my faith that I was doing the right thing by learning this new craft.

NO-KNEAD COVID-19 TABLE BREAD

During the COVID-19 global pandemic of 2020, bread flour quickly became a scarcity in grocery stores. So, I concocted this no-knead with easily available generic flour. Because minimal gluten is developed, it is a soft-texture bread ideal for dipping into oils, vinegars, and such. Also, I found another great use for my tajine!

LEVEL: Basic

YIELD: 1 loaf

INGREDIENTS
4 cups all-purpose flour (use bread flour, if available), plus more for the bench
1 tablespoon active dry yeast
1 tablespoon fresh thyme, chopped
1/2 teaspoon sugar or honey
1 tablespoon coarse salt
1/4 teaspoon freshly ground pepper (optional)
2 tablespoons capers, drained (optional)
14 oz warm water (95F)

METHOD
Whisk the sugar, yeast, and water in a large bowl and bloom the yeast for 20 minutes. With a wooden spoon, mix in the remaining ingredients until the flour is incorporated. Cover the bowl with a tight fitting lid or plastic wrap. Store in a warm place, in the kitchen or elsewhere.

After the dough doubles (about an hour), pull the 4 sides (NESW) as shown in the image and allow to rest for 30 minutes, covered. Repeat this process 3 more times. Now tuck in to smooth out the surface and form onto a ball (boule) or oval (bâtard). Pull the surface tight to allow the formation of a good crust. Transfer to a baking sheet, cover, and proof one last time until the dough doubles. Preheat an oven to 500F. Use a sharp blade to score the risen dough. Transfer to a pre-heated cast-iron skillet (I used my trusted tajine.).

Bake covered with, say, a large oven-proof bowl for the first 30 minutes. Reduce the temperature to 450F and bake uncovered for an additional 20 minutes. Allow to cool on a rack before slicing. Enjoy as a dip-ping bread or just for the table.

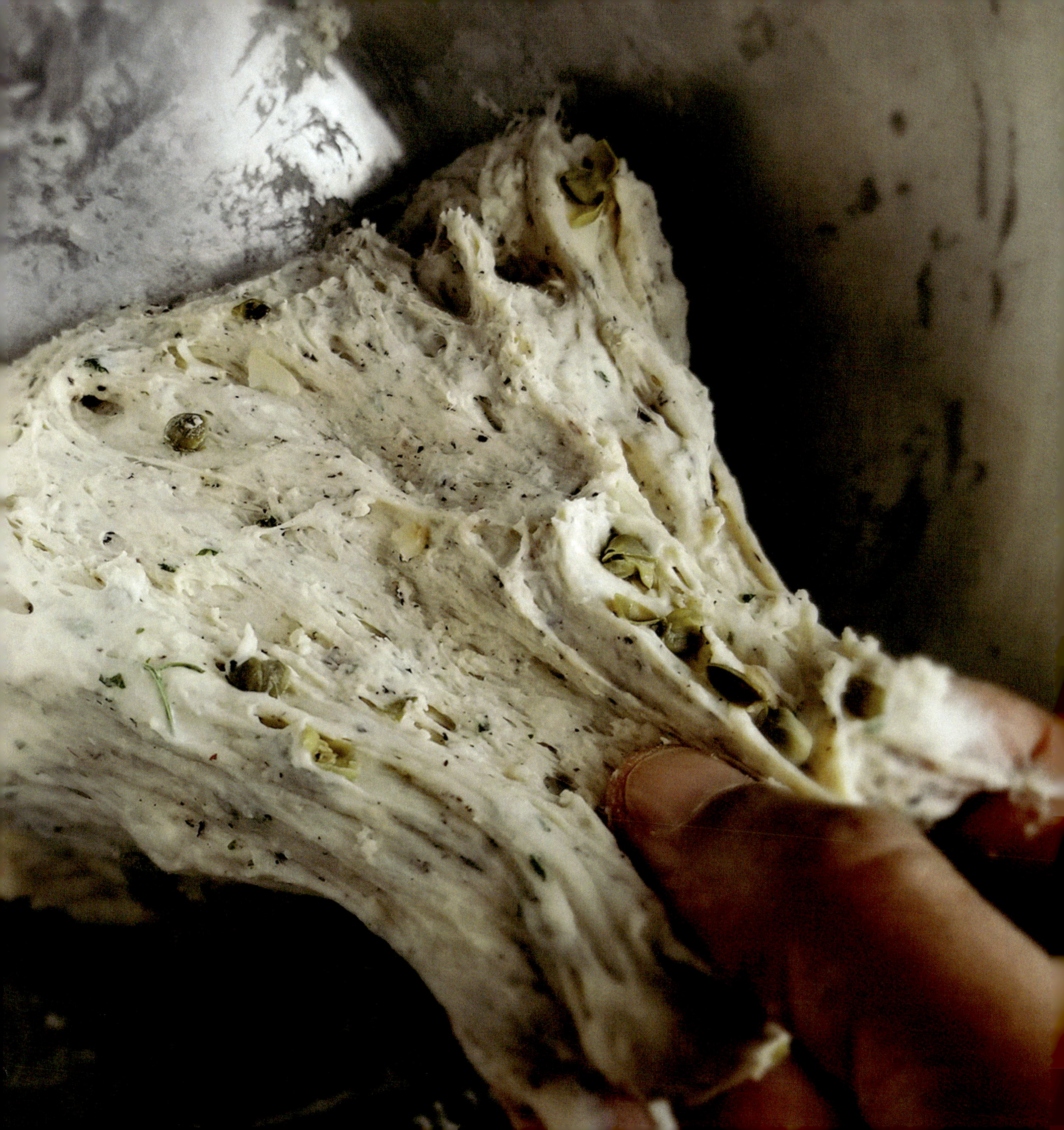

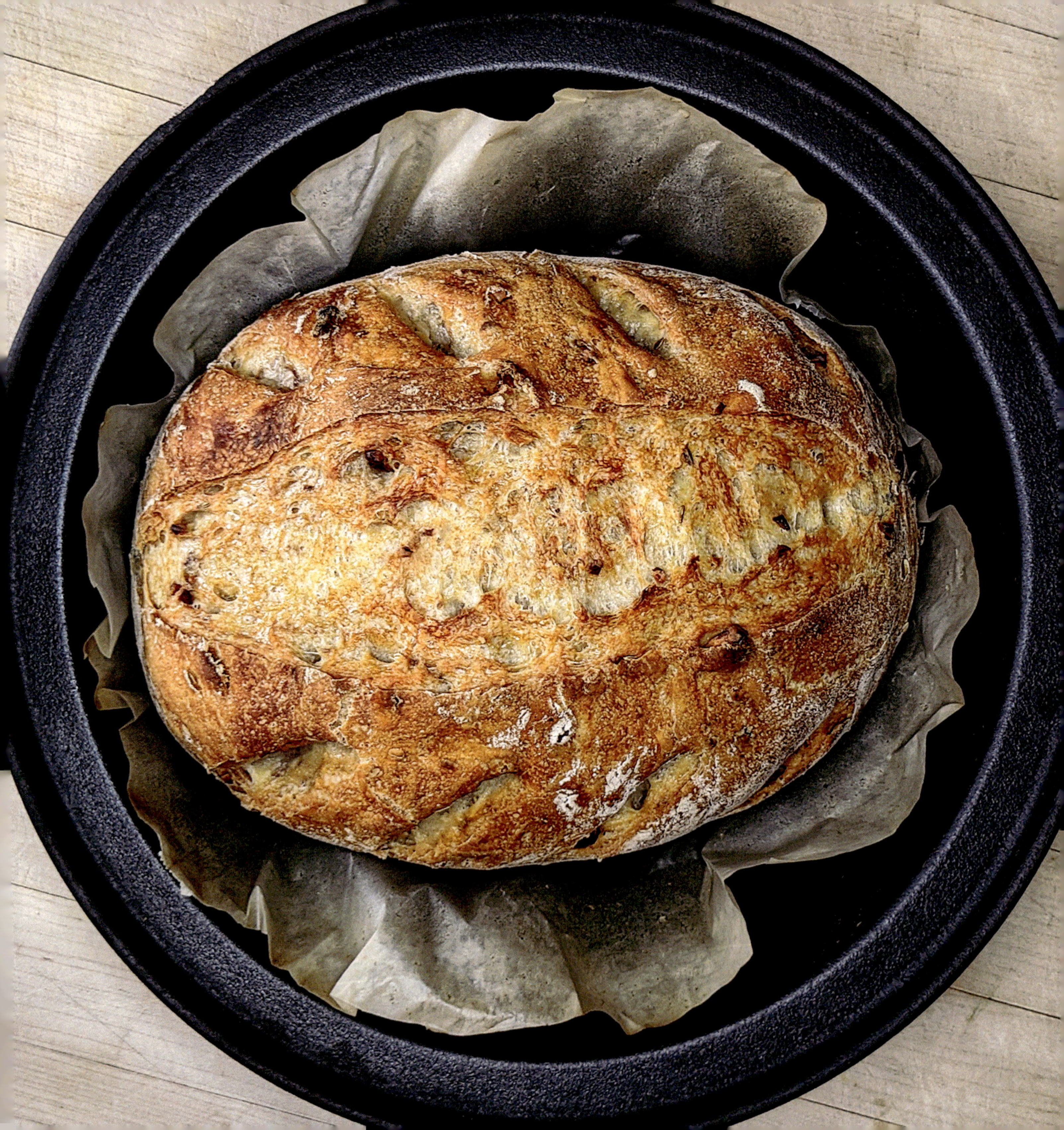

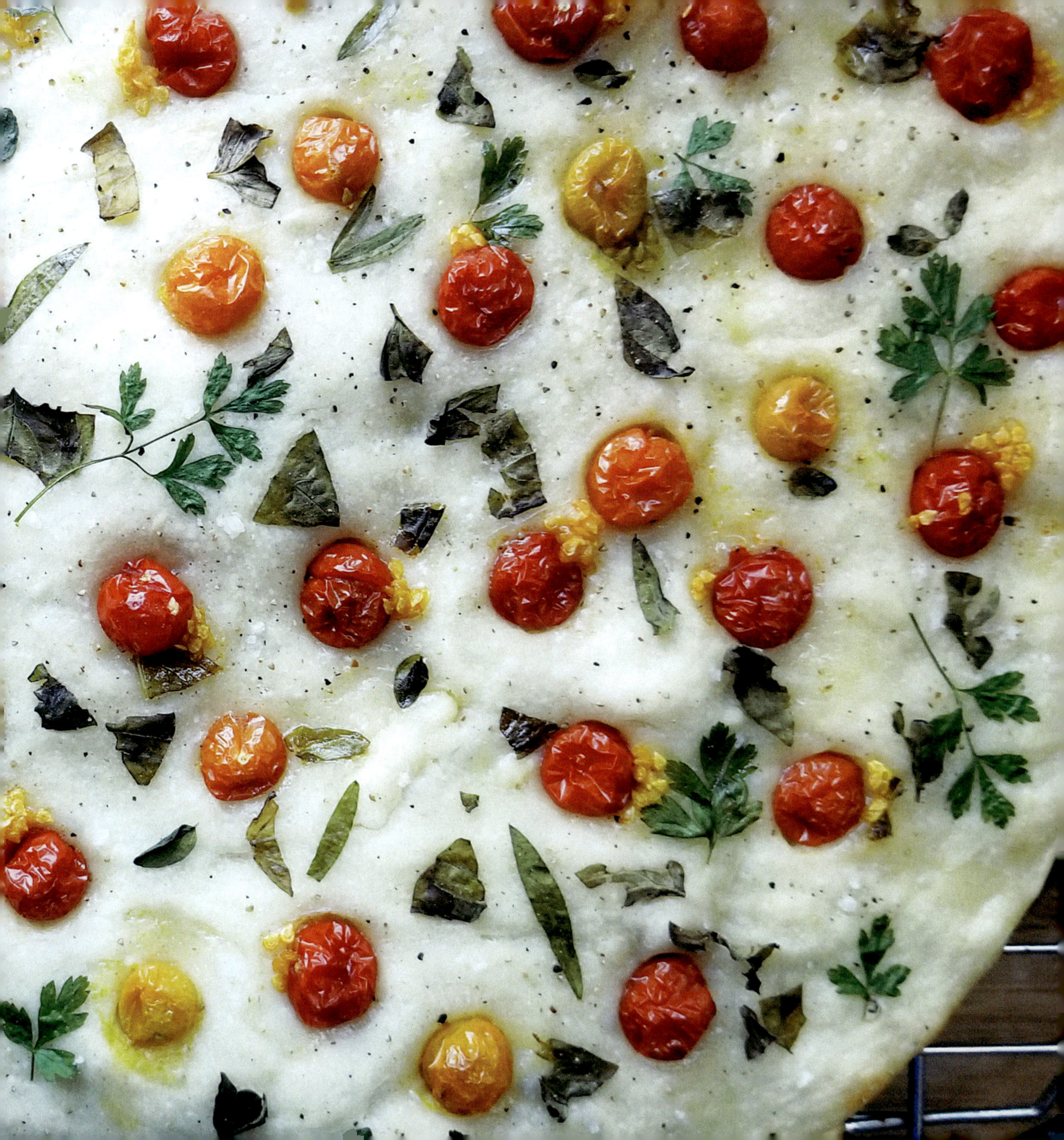

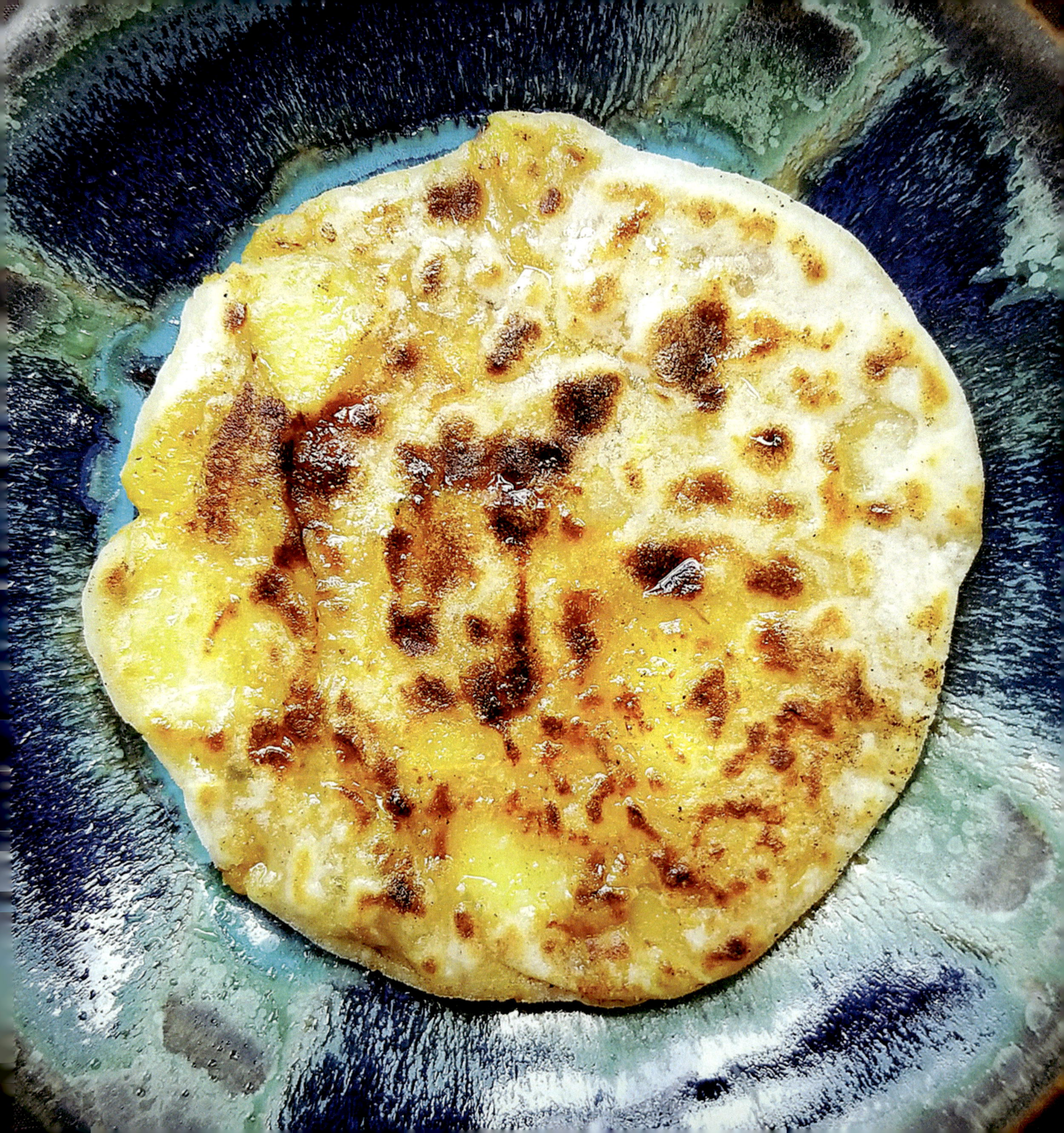

ALOO PARATHA

LEVEL: Intermediate
YIELD: approximately 8

INGREDIENTS

The Dough
1.5 cups all-purpose flour
1/2 cup whole wheat flour
warm water, as needed
1 teaspoon coarse salt
vegetable oil for cooking

The Filling
3 medium potatoes boiled in salted water with a pinch of turmeric powder
2 medium onions, minced
1 inch fresh ginger, finely minced
2 green chilies or 1 jalapeño, finely chopped
1/2 teaspoon turmeric powder
1 teaspoon coriander powder
1 teaspoon cumin powder
1 teaspoon red chili powder or cayenne
1/2 teaspoon garam masala
1 teaspoon dry mango powder (if available)
2 sprigs fresh cilantro, chopped
salt & pepper, in stages and per taste

METHOD

In a large bowl, mix the flours, salt and a small amount of oil. Rub the oil into the flour with your fingertips. Add the warm water a little at a time and knead to make a soft dough. Knead for 2-3 minutes. Next, add a small amount of oil and continue kneading the dough into a smooth and silky texture. Divide the dough into 8 equal portions. Cover the dough and allow it to rest. Mash the boiled potatoes with a fork. Add the onions, ginger, chilies, spices, salt, and cilantro to the mashed potatoes. Divide the filling into 8 equal portions. Dust the dough in dry wheat flour, flatten it with your finger, and place it on a flat surface. Roll out to an approximately 3-inch diameter circle. Take a portion of filling and place it in the center. Next, gather the sides of the paratha dough and bring them together. Remove the little excess dough which pops out when you bring the edges together. Press the filled aloo paratha dough down. Dust the filled aloo paratha dough in some flour and roll it gently, applying very little pressure. Roll it to desired thickness and proceed the similar way with the remaining portions of paratha dough and filling.

Preheat a skillet on medium heat and place the filled aloo paratha on the skillet. Cook on medium heat for about 1 minute on each side and flip over. Brush each side with a bit of oil and continue browning on both sides until the dough is opaque and browned evenly on both sides. Serve each with Indian lime pickle and a dollop of yogurt.

NAAN

While naan may have become the standard for what to use to pick up bhajis and even gravies, there are hundreds of varieties of flatbread, and most of them are unleavened. The key to a soft and fluffy naan is minimizing kneading, being comfortable with a sticky dough, and cooking on a high heat.

LEVEL: Basic

YIELD: approximately 6

INGREDIENTS

2 cups all-purpose flour, more as needed
1/4 cup plain yogurt
1/3 cup milk or water, more as needed
1 teaspoon active dry yeast
1/2 teaspoon baking powder
2 tablespoons melted butter or vegetable oil
1 teaspoon coarse salt
pinch of granulated sugar
water, for steaming the naan in the oven

METHOD

Sift the flour into a bowl. Add the salt and baking powder. Warm milk to about 95F, add the sugar and yeast. Whisk and set aside for 5 minutes. In a bowl, whisk the yogurt to a smooth consistency. Make a well in the dry ingredients. Pour the yogurt mixture into the well. Also add the milk mixture to the well. Using your fingertips work the flour into the liquid until you form a smooth and sticky dough. Do not knead the dough. It should be somewhat sticky. Oil a large bowl. Pour in the dough. Coat the dough with vegetable oil. Cover lightly with a damp towel. Set aside for 2 hours.

After the dough has roughly doubled, punch it down (do not work it too much). Form 3-inch diameter balls. Let rest for 10 minutes. On a well-floured surface, roll out the dough without exerting too much pressure into round or oblong "disks" (about 1/8 in thickness).

Heat oven to 500F with a pizza or other type of baking stone. With fingertips, add water to tops of disks. Bake in oven for approximately 2 minutes per side. Brush with melted butter or ghee.

GNOCCHI

When I was in culinary school, we were taught how to make seemingly traditional potato-based gnocchi. I thought I followed the recipe to a tee, but the outcome was uninspired, to say the least. Mind you, from an early age, I was used to handling dough while making chapatti and puri in our family kitchen in Mumbai; naturally, at the time, I wasn't particularly impressed with the dumpling. Fast forward about 15 years and, after making numerous versions of gnocchi (or is it gnudi?), I'm a believer. So, what's the difference?

Here's how I think of them:

Gnocchi: A pasta-like dumpling, containing potato, eggs, flour, olive oil, sometimes cheese

Gnocchi Parisienne: A softer dumpling, containing ricotta or other soft cheese, flour, eggs, butter, water, sometimes cheese, sometimes Dijon mustard, sometimes fresh herbs

Gnudi: This is the Italian counterpart of Gnocchi Parisienne inspired by the filling in a ravioli without the wrapper. A nude ravioli, as it were. Gnudi is a pillow-like dumpling, containing ricotta, egg yolks (optional), cheese, just enough (semolina) flour to hold the dumpling together when poached.

Gnudi Tips:
- Drain the ricotta well, for at least two hours, and pat it dry with paper towels to soak up any excess moisture. This will ensure that you don't have to use excess semolina flour to make the gnudi. An excess of flour inhibits the characteristic and desired "light as a cloud" texture.
- Roll (or scoop with a small ice-cream scoop) the formed gnudi and roll lightly in semolina flour.
- Refrigerate the formed gnudi for at least 30 minutes before poaching in seasoned simmering water.
- When ready to eat, consume an entire gnudi at a time, without cutting it.

INJERA

My first experience with injera was at the legendary (now closed) Ethiopian restaurant Meskerem in Washington D.C. When I was instructed to eat with my hands, it was love at first bite. After I tasted the perfectly fermented flavor of injera, I remember closing my eyes with deep satisfaction.

LEVEL: Basic

YIELD: approximately 8

INGREDIENTS
3 cups teff flour
1 cup all-purpose flour
5 cups lukewarm water (or as needed for a semi-loose batter)
1.5 teaspoon active dry yeast
1/2 teaspoon honey
salt & pepper, in stages and per taste

METHOD
In a large mixing bowl, combine the flours and salt until well mixed. Bloom the yeast in warm water, adding some honey to help activate the yeast. Add the water and yeast, stirring until combined. Cover loosely with a towel and let stand undisturbed overnight. Gently agitate the mixture with a wooden spoon in the morning (there should be bubbles already forming on the surface, and the fermenting water should have risen to the top), cover again and let stand at room temperature, undisturbed overnight. Repeat this cycle once more. After 3-4 days, your injera should smell sour and be very bubbly, which means that it's ready.

Stir the mixture until combined. Heat a large, lightly oiled heavy-bottomed skillet over medium-high heat. Add about 1/3 cup of the batter to the skillet, forming a thin layer of batter over the pan. Cook until bubbles form across the entire surface of the flatbread (do not flip; only cook one side like a crepe), and, using a metal spatula, remove the injera and transfer to a plate.

Repeat until all the batter is used, adding oil to the skillet as necessary. Serve with spicy vegetables, lentils, or stew dishes of your choice.

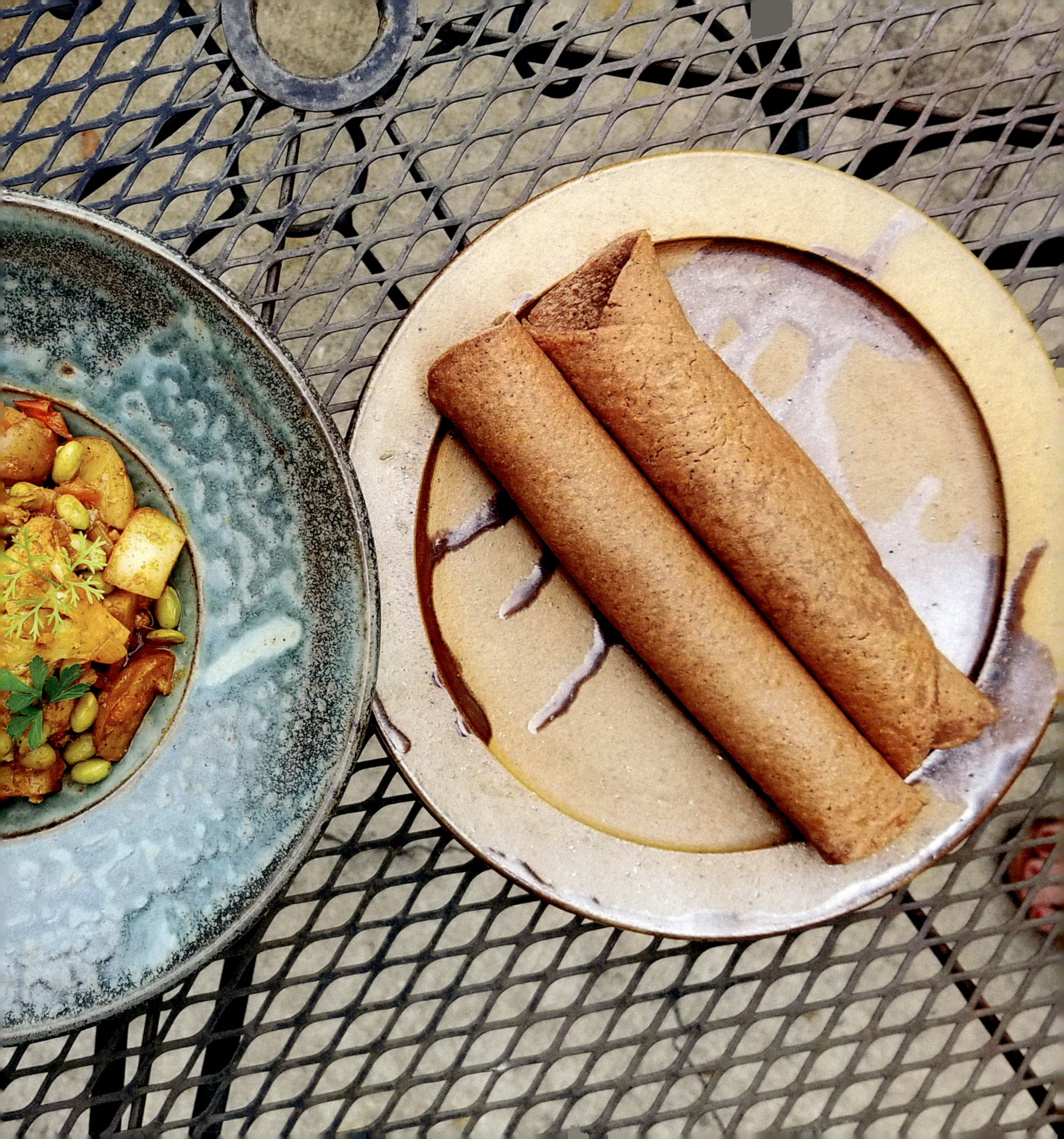

GORGONZOLA GNUDI WITH SAGE INFUSED BROWN BUTTER & WALNUTS

Comforting fall flavors give us an opportunity to perfect the technique of making *a la minute* brown butter. Unless you must, avoid being heavy handed with the gorgonzola, because it can overpower the dish and make it too salty.

LEVEL: Intermediate

YIELD: approximately 6 servings

INGREDIENTS
10 oz. ricotta cheese, completely drained (page 348)
6 ounces gorgonzola cheese, drained
2 egg yolks
semolina flour, as needed
1/2 cup toasted and chopped walnuts
10 sage leaves with stems
1/2 stick unsalted butter
extra virgin olive oil, as needed
water, for poaching
salt & pepper, in stages and per taste

METHOD
Toast the walnuts in a dry pan and set aside. Drain the ricotta for at least two hours until it is devoid of perceived moisture. Whip the drained ricotta and gorgonzola in a bowl or food processor. Add the egg yolks and mix. Season the mixture lightly with salt and pepper, as needed. Spread the mixture on a baking sheet and refrigerate uncovered for an hour. Using an ice-cream scoop (1 oz. size), drop chilled scoops into a bowl of semolina flour and roll lightly into balls using the palm of your hand. Place them on a baking sheet and refrigerate for 30 minutes. Carefully drop the chilled gnudi into a pot of salted simmering water. Wait 1 minute after the gnudi have floated to the top before scooping them out and draining on a sheet tray coated with extra virgin olive oil.

Melt the butter in a non-stick pan until it starts to brown, add the sage leaves, and fry for a minute on medium heat. Lightly brown the poached gnudi uniformly. Season lightly with salt and pepper. Pour the brown better and sage leaves on the lightly crisp gnudi. Garnish with the toasted and chopped walnuts.

PIZZA DOUGH

> I learned to make a version of pizza dough in baking class in culinary school. That night, we made pizzas but used a canned tomato product for a sauce. I was horrified that we wouldn't take the time to make a quick marinara from fresh tomatoes and herbs. But that didn't detract from my fascination at how a few ingredients could be turned into something so versatile and delicious.

LEVEL: Basic

YIELD: approximately 2 large pizzas

INGREDIENTS
- 28 oz. bread flour
- 16 oz. warm (95F) water
- 1/2 oz. active dry yeast
- 1/2 tsp. honey
- 1 tablespoon coarse salt
- 1/4 cup extra-virgin olive oil

METHOD

Mix honey and extra virgin olive oil into the warm water and add the yeast. Stir well. You should see small bubbles within minutes. If you don't, then the yeast is inactive, and you will need a fresh batch. Add the salt to the flour in a large bowl and mix well. Make a well in the flour and pour half of the liquid into it. Bring in the flour from the sides a bit at a time. Once all the liquid has been absorbed, add the remaining liquid and mix well. Transfer to a clean, cool surface and knead using a rhythmic motion. This will take about 10 minutes. Tear off a small piece, roll it in the middle of the palm of one hand and stretch it. View it against the backdrop of light and you should see some "strands." This is proof that gluten has been developed and the dough is ready to rest. Put the dough back into the mixing bowl and brush liberally with some extra-virgin olive oil. Leave at room temperature, covered, until it doubles in size. Punch it down and portion the dough into 3 equal parts and roll into smooth balls. The dough is best the next day, but if you must, you may make pizza in about 3-4 hours.

Note: This dough can easily be formed into a delicious loaf of bread. Be sure to form loaves and allow a second proofing.

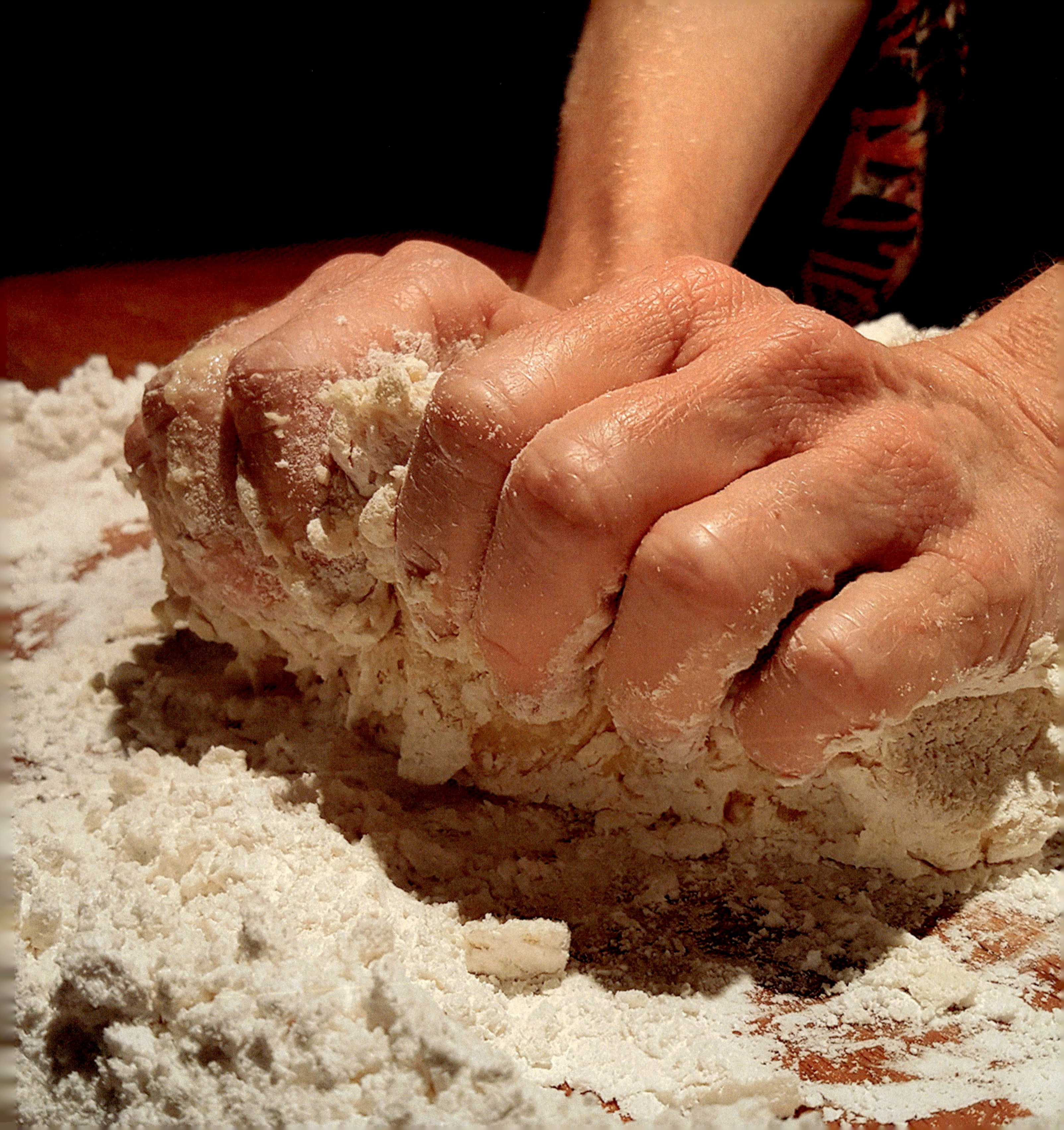

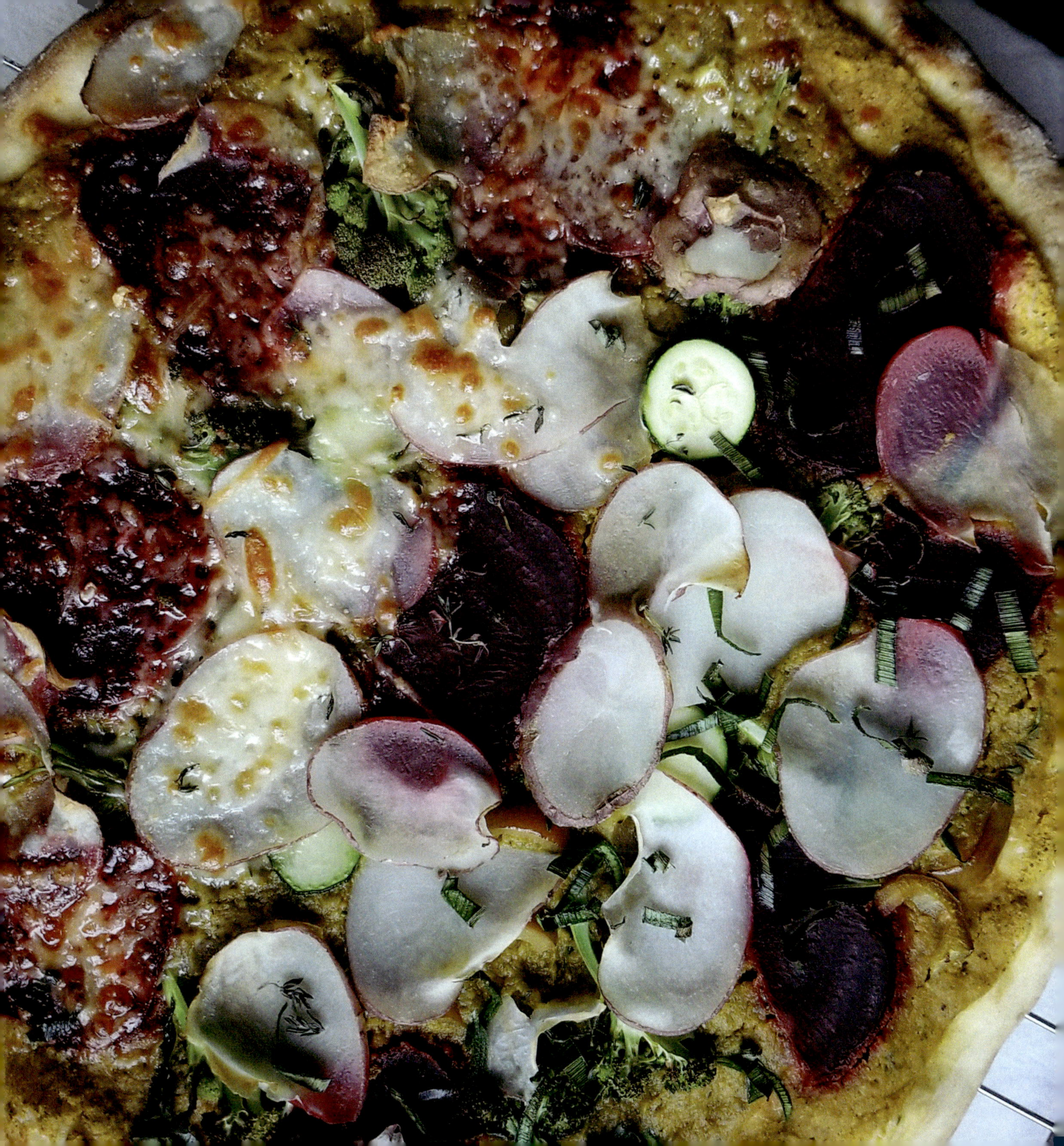

BLUE CORN TORTILLA

Learning how to make fresh tortillas was thrilling enough, but once I discovered blue corn masa harina, I realized that I prefer the hearty and nutty flavor and texture of blue corn masa. Jenneffer shares this belief. I believe a famous celebrity chef on television whose last name rhymes with *okay* also shares this preference.

LEVEL: Basic

YIELD: approximately 12

INGREDIENTS
2 cups blue corn masa harina
1/2 teaspoon baking powder (optional)
1/4 cup all-purpose flour (optional)
1.25 cup warm water or vegetable stock
1 tablespoon extra-virgin or vegetable oil
1 teaspoon coarse salt, more or less

METHOD
Mix all the dry ingredients in a bowl. Add the oil and rub it in with your fingertips to coat the flour. Make a well in the flour as one would for pasta. Add 1 cup of warm water or stock and fold in the flour mixing well. It will still be dry. Next, slowly add in more warm water until you obtain a soft and pliable dough. Cover with a damp cloth and let it rest at room temperature for at least 30 minutes before pressing out the tortillas using your preferred size tortilla press. Cook the tortillas on a flat cast iron or non-stick pan for at least a minute on both sides until the dough appears opaque and lightly browned in spots. Serve immediately or store covered to steam and keep soft.

QUINOA & BUTTERMILK CRÊPE

> Here, I was inspired by the wide variety of fortified, batter-based crêpes found in South India. Often, dinner at home consisted of a *dibba rotti* (thick lentil pancake), *pesarattu* (page xxx), or standard *dosa* with a chutney. I've always had thoughtful vegetarian options on the restaurant menu. One Sunday brunch, I served this crêpe filled with mushroom duxelle, roasted corn, and my signature salsa verde. To this day, Jenneffer swears it's the best thing I've made. She may be on to something.

LEVEL: Basic

YIELD: approximately 8

INGREDIENTS
1 cup buttermilk
1 cup cooked quinoa (follow the directions on the packaging)
1 cup all-purpose flour
1 tablespoon melted unsalted butter, more for cooking
1 tablespoon chopped fresh parsley
1 tablespoon chopped fresh chives
1 large egg
salt & pepper, in stages and per taste

METHOD
Combine all the ingredients except the fresh herbs in a blender and mix well for about 15 seconds until you have a smooth batter. Fold in the fresh herbs. Grease a non-stick pan with unsalted butter, and, over medium heat, drop just enough batter to be able to swirl it to the shape of the pan with a uniform thickness. Cook on one side for about 1 minute before flipping. Cook for about 15 seconds on the other side.

Serve as is, or let them cool before filling them with your favorite fillings. Mushroom duxelle is a wonderfully decadent option.

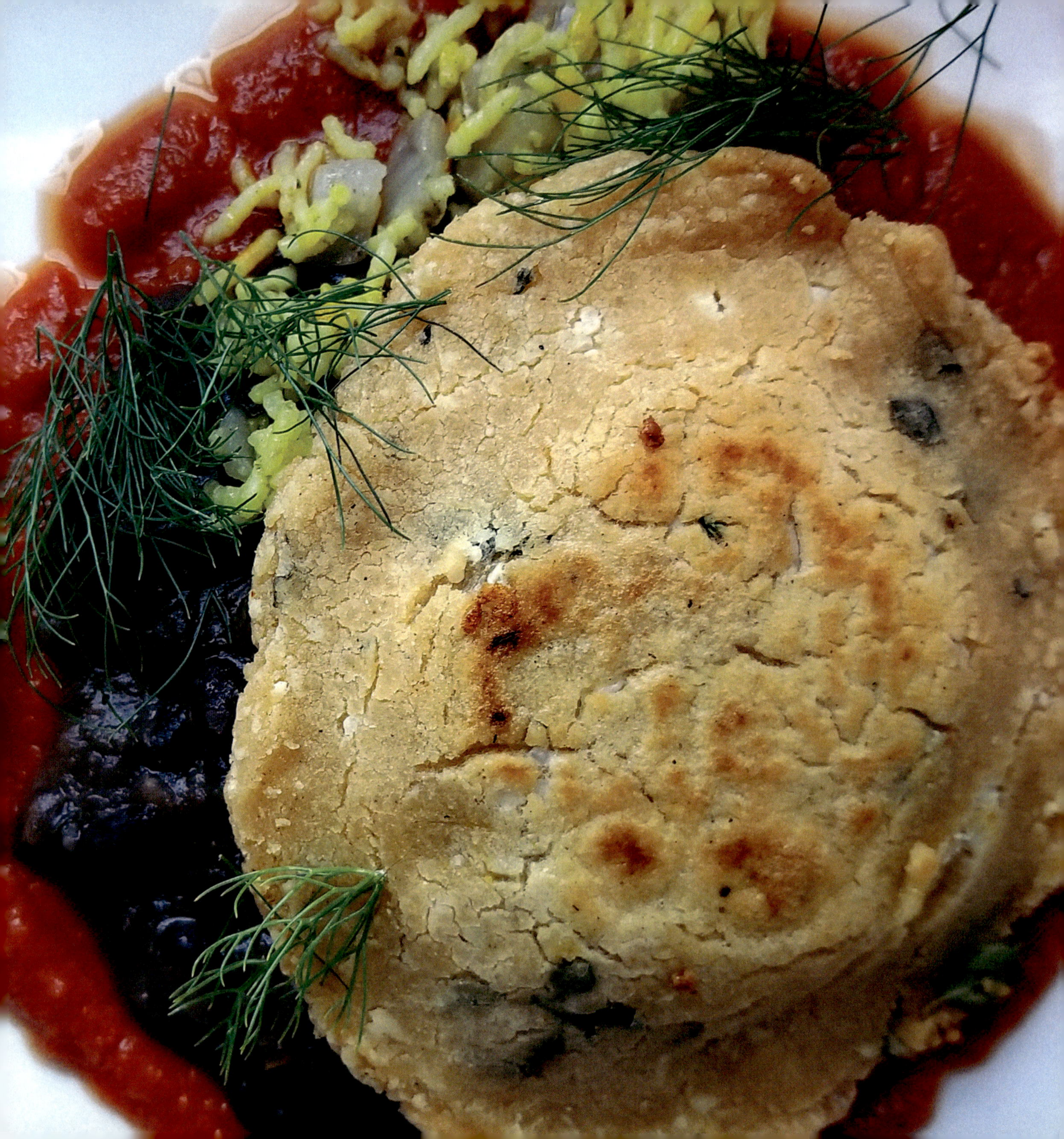

PUPUSA

> It was only a matter of time before a civilization would think to fill corn-based dough with delicious possibilities to essentially make hand pies. This is an extremely popular snack in El Salvador, and we are so glad that the concept leaked out of the country. Here I propose a vegetarian version with simply cooked beans, melty cheese, and my punchy salsa verde.

LEVEL: Basic

YIELD: approximately 6

INGREDIENTS

2 cups corn masa
1.25 cup warm water, more or less
1 cup cooked and seasoned beans, smashed almost to a puree
salsa verde, as needed
grated Oaxaca cheese, as needed
extra virgin or vegetable oil, as needed
salt & pepper, in stages and per taste

METHOD

Form basically a tortilla dough. Take a one-inch round ball of dough and press it in the center to form a well. Take 1 teaspoon of cooked beans and one teaspoon of cheese and place it in the center. Put a dollop of salsa verde on top of the cheese bean mixture. Carefully fold the dough so that you have a stuffed ball. Pressing with your fingers, flatten the ball to a disk just thick enough to hold the filling. Continue forming these stuffed discs until you run out of dough or out of filling.

In either a cast iron skillet or a thick-bottomed pan, cook the pupusas over medium heat so that they brown evenly on both sides. Transfer them all to a baking sheet. Bake for 15 minutes in a 375F oven.

Remove and let cool a bit before serving with a fresh slaw or more salsa verde.

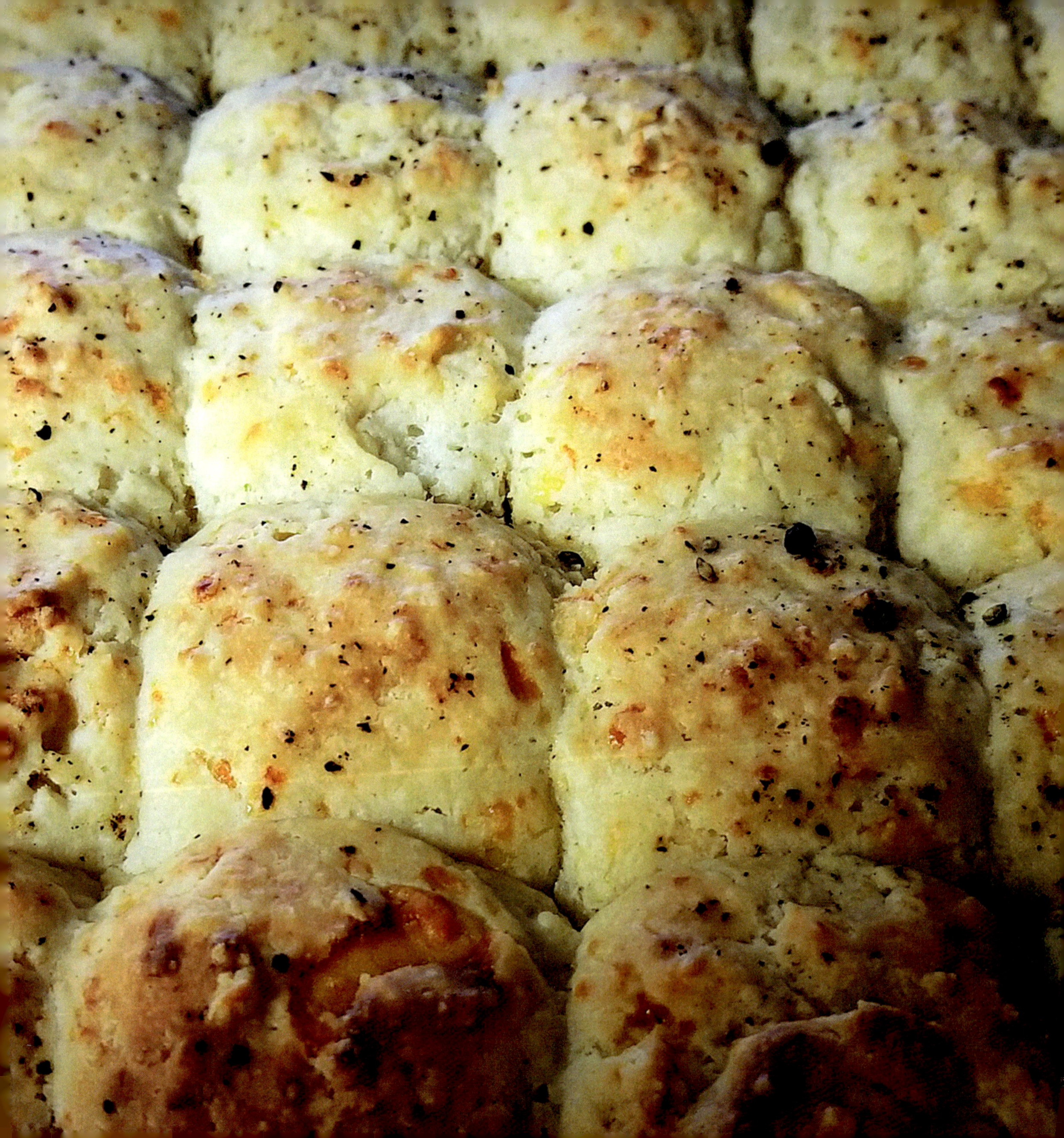

TARRAGON BUTTERMILK BISCUIT

> This innocuous-sounding recipe may very well be one of the most sinfully vegetarian recipes in this book. The key is to cut the cold butter swiftly into the flour before it begins melting and to barely mix the ingredients without kneading. Also, only use as much flour as absolutely necessary.

LEVEL: Basic

YIELD: approximately 8

INGREDIENTS
2 cups self-rising all-purpose flour
1 tbsp. dried tarragon
1 tbsp. freshly chopped tarragon
6 oz. unsalted butter, cold, cubed or grated
buttermilk, as needed
melted unsalted butter, as needed

METHOD
Preheat and oven to 425F. Sift the flour into a stainless bowl. Add the dried tarragon and season. Cut the cold butter into the flour mixture making sure there are still large pieces of butter left. Use the tips of your fingers to do this.

Dump the mixture onto a work surface, preferably a cold stone or marble. Make a well and add some buttermilk. Start incorporating the flour and butter mixture into the buttermilk. It is very important to not use any pressure or knead the forming dough in any way. Add as much buttermilk as will allow for the formation of a moist and workable dough.

Flour another area of the surface lightly and roll out the dough to an even 1-inch thickness. Lift and fold the dough onto itself using a spatula or bench scraper. Repeat in the opposite direction. This creates the "layers" of the biscuit. Eight to 12 layers are enough.

Use a round metal cutter punching out disks. Place on a baking sheet lined with a silicone or baking mat. Be sure to pack the disks tightly against each other to allow for proper rising in the oven.

Brush with melted butter and bake in the oven for about 25 minutes or until risen and lightly golden brown. After the biscuits come out, brush again lightly with melted butter and sprinkle with the fresh tarragon.

PESARATTU (SOUTH INDIAN MUNG BEAN CRÊPE)

My mother loves pesarattu, a green mung bean savory crêpe similar to a dosa. However, a traditional version is not as fermented, nor does it contain urad dal. It's extremely nutritious and widely consumed as breakfast in the State of Andhra Pradesh (my parents' home state) in South-Central India. It is extremely versatile, given its texture and structural integrity. The recipe here provides a canvas for a wide variety of variations.

LEVEL: Basic

YIELD: approximately 6

INGREDIENTS
1 cup green mung bean, soaked overnight in turmeric water
1 green chile, chopped
1 tablespoon fresh ginger, minced
water, as needed
1/4 cup rice flour
pinch of asafoetida
1 small onion, minced (optional)
vegetable oil, as needed
salt & pepper, in stages and per taste

METHOD
Drain the soaked beans well, and, using a powerful blender, blend all the ingredients except the rice flour, adding just enough water to form a crepe batter consistency. Pour the batter into a bowl and whisk in the rice flour.

Making of a pesarattu is like making a crepe, except you may need a bit more oil in the skillet. One may add minced onion to the batter before making the pesarattu. Serve with your favorite chutney and sides. I would recommend a coconut cilantro chutney and an eggplant potato bhaji for a complete meal.

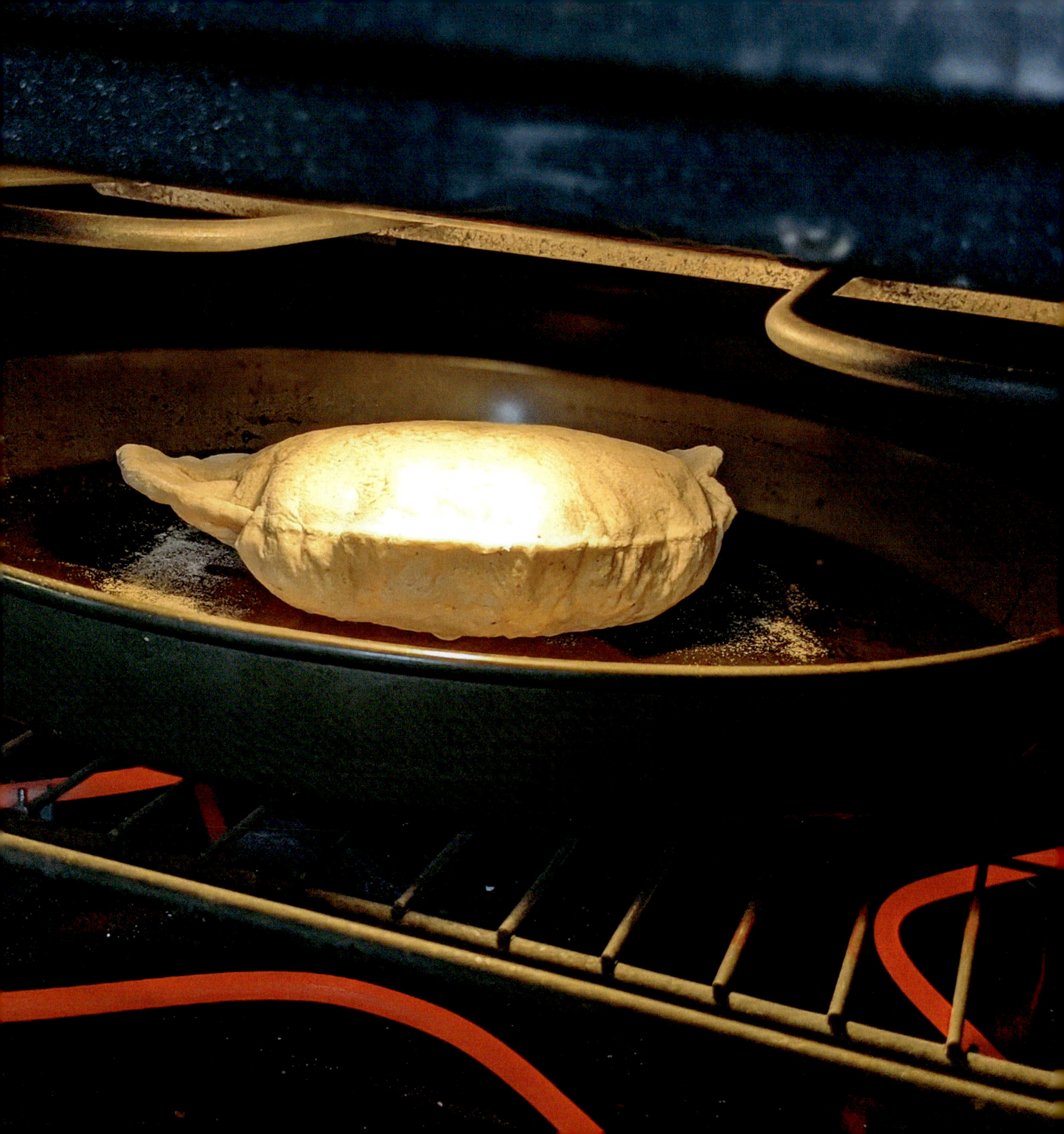

TURNBULL
SAUVIGNON BLANC
ESTATE GROWN
OAKVILLE, NAPA VALLEY
2018

Hand-Helds

Stuff in between two slices of bread, stuff inside a roll, stuff inside a dough that's baked. You get the idea. As one might imagine, these compositions offer a lot of comfort and glee.

ULTIMATE BURGER

> There are a multitude of premade veggie burgers on the market, but this version will leave both vegetarians as well as non-vegetarians satisfied. There is no mistaking the titillating and moistly delicious flavors of this burger when one accompanies it with the recommended condiments.

LEVEL: Basic

YIELD: approximately 8

INGREDIENTS
1 large red onion, small diced
1 medium carrots, peeled, small dice
2 tablespoons fresh garlic, minced
12 oz. can black beans, drained well
12 oz. can red beans, drained well
6 oz. tempeh, cubed
1/4 cup toasted cashew nuts
1 cup cooked farro or barley
2 poblano peppers, small dice
2 tablespoons creole spice blend (page 87)
2 tablespoons fresh flat leaf parsley, chopped
2 tablespoons fresh cilantro, chopped
1 tablespoon fresh garlic, minced
1 teaspoon cumin powder
1 teaspoon coriander powder
1 teaspoon smoked paprika
1/4 cup flax seed soaked in warm water
panko breadcrumbs, as needed
extra virgin olive oil, as needed
salt & pepper, in stages and per taste

METHOD
Preheat oven to 325F and, on a baking sheet, roast the beans and tempeh, seasoned a bit with olive oil, salt, and pepper. In a heavy-bottomed pan on medium heat, sauté the onions, carrots, and poblano peppers in the olive oil, until softened. Season with some salt and pepper to bring out the flavors. Add the garlic and sauté for 30 seconds.

After all ingredients have cooled, mix all the ingredients, including the roasted bean-tempeh mixture, in a large bowl. Add the remaining ingredients except the breadcrumbs and the fresh herbs. Stir to coat evenly. Now add all the spices and stir to coat evenly. Taste and re-season, if necessary. Add the fresh herbs and enough breadcrumbs to be able to form 1/2-inch-thick patties.

To finish, sauté the patties in extra virgin oil until golden brown on both sides. Top with your favorite cheese if preferred and finish in a preheated 350F oven for about 10 minutes until the cheese has melted and the burgers have warmed through.

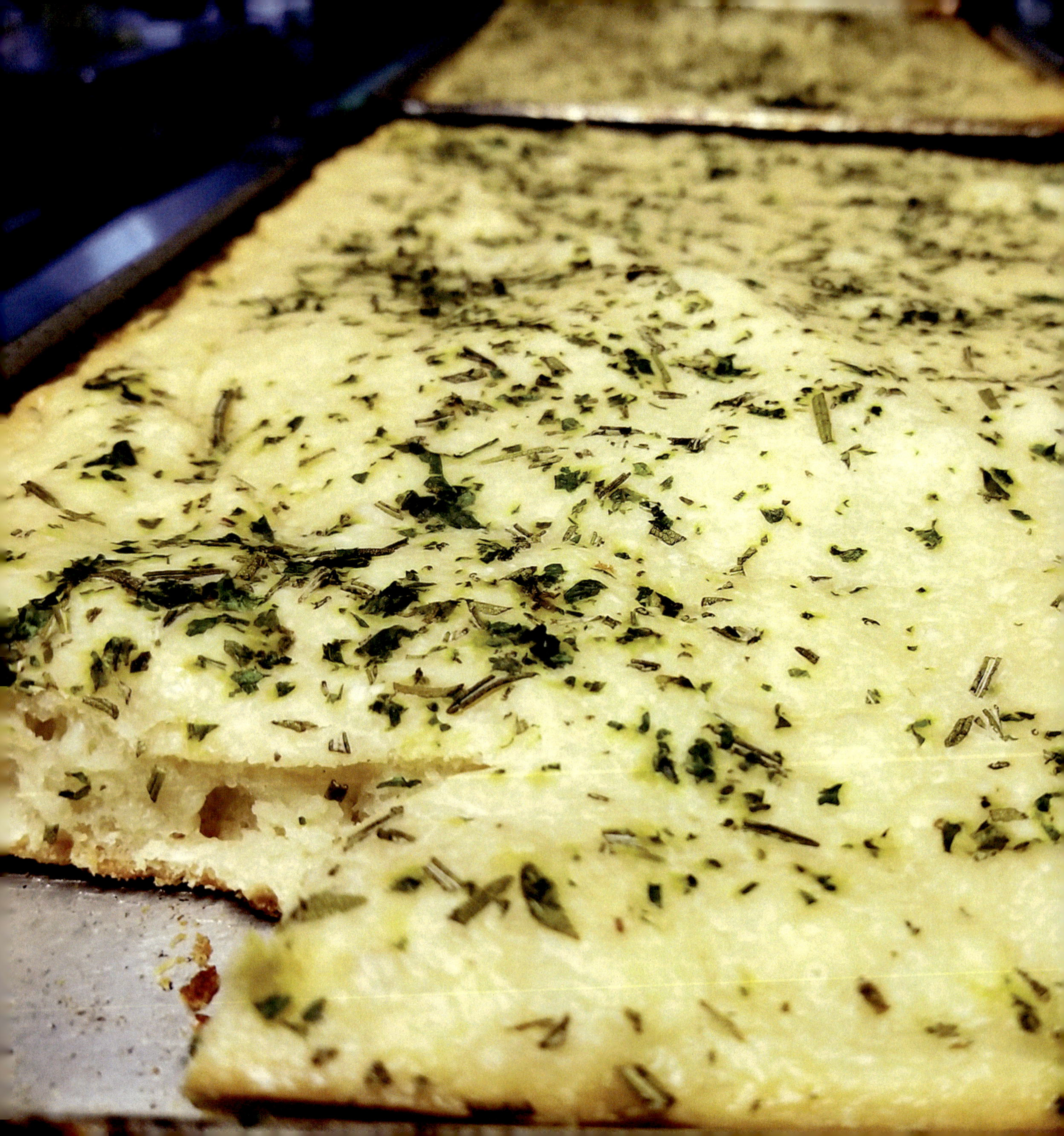

SLOPPY JOE

> I'm not sure who Joe is in this case, but *sloppy* is a desired experience. Admittedly, Indians would eat such a dish a bit differently by sopping up the filling with the bread. Certain spices like allspice and clove make the experience comforting. However, I urge you to consider other possibilities that offer substance and flavor.

LEVEL: Basic

YIELD: approximately 4

INGREDIENTS
- 1 medium onion, finely chopped
- 4 cloves garlic, minced
- 2 pickled or fresh jalapeños (more or less), chopped
- 1/2 cup brown lentils
- 1 tablespoon chili powder or creole blend (page 87)
- 8 oz. tempeh, chopped up
- 1 cup canned San Marzano tomatoes
- 1/4 cup fresh parsley, chopped
- 1 tablespoon Dijon mustard
- 1/2 cup thinly sliced Napa or savoy cabbage
- 1/2 cup thinly sliced carrots
- 1/2 cup thinly sliced red onion, previously soaked in water
- 1 tablespoon caramelized shallot cider vinaigrette (page 166)
- water, as needed
- 4 hamburger buns
- extra-virgin olive oil, as needed
- salt & pepper, in stages and per taste

METHOD

In a skillet on medium heat, brown the onions in some extra-virgin olive oil for 5 minutes before adding the garlic. Cook for a minute before adding the spices. Cook for 30 seconds and add the lentils. Stir well and coat the lentils in the oil. Next add the jalapeno, tempeh, tomato, and just enough water to barely cover the lentils. Season with salt and pepper. Cover the pan and maintain a medium-low heat. The lentils should be cooked in 25 minutes. If the mixture is too wet, strain it and return it to the pan to semi-dry roast for another 10 minutes. Fold in the mustard and parsley. Hold warm.

Next, make a slaw with the cabbage, carrots, onions, and vinaigrette. Toast the buns in a skillet or in the oven brushed with a small amount of extra-virgin olive oil. Mound the lentil-tempeh mixture and top with the slaw to complete the assembly.

TORTA

> One of the finest tortas I've had was at *Tortas Frontera* by Rick Bayless at Chicago's O'Hare International Airport. It made such an impression on me that as fast as I could scarf it down, the seed had already been planted to include my interpretation in a future book. That was two years ago while I was returning from the annual James Beard Awards at Lyric Opera House. As an invited chef for the after-party, I created a sustainable seafood Bhel accented with my takes on leche de tigre, date-tamarind chutney, and salsa verde. Pipes...so many pipes in the narrative of one's life.

LEVEL: Basic

YIELD: approximately 4

INGREDIENTS
1 large can black beans, pre-cooked, drained, and rinsed
1/2 cup assorted pickles (page 346)
1 cup queso Oaxaca, thinly sliced or grated Manchego
2 fresh or pickled jalapeños, sliced thinly
1/2 cup watercress greens
2 ripe avocados, thinly sliced
1/4 cup picked fresh cilantro leaves and tender stems
1/2 cup sofrito (page 104)
2 tablespoons adobo blend (page 86)
3 tablespoons mayonnaise or aquafaba
4 torta (bolillo) rolls (available at any Mexican bakery) or a demi-baguette
1 lime
extra-virgin olive oil, as needed
salt & pepper, in stages and per taste

METHOD
In a bowl, combine the black beans and sofrito. Make a compound mayonnaise by mixing the adobo seasoning and the standard mayonnaise. Make a salad with the watercress, cilantro, some salt, pepper, olive oil, and juice of half a lime.

Toast the bread by first brushing lightly with some extra-virgin olive oil. Next, assemble each torta by spreading the adobo mayonnaise on both sides, adding a layer of sofrito enhanced black beans, and then adding the cheese. Use the oven's broil feature to melt the cheese.

Continue assembling the torta by layering jalapeño slices, avocado slices, and the watercress-cilantro salad. Squeeze a bit more lime juice on top of the filling and serve immediately.

MUMBAI SANDWICH

This omnipresent sandwich is available all over Mumbai: at street carts, in sit-down cafes, and in many homes. My parents worked full-time and took turns cooking for the family. On the rare occasion when they just weren't up to it and felt uninspired, we were treated to a modest version of this sandwich and it was "chutney sandwich night" at home. Hari loved chutney sandwich night. I would often be tasked with procuring the provisions for said sandwiches. They included Wibbs or Britannia brand white bread (I was adept at picking the freshest possible loaves), salted Amul brand butter, cucumber, tomato, kotmir (cilantro), mirchi (green chiles), and pudina (mint). The version below is more representative of ones found on the street.

LEVEL: Basic

YIELD: approximately 4

INGREDIENTS
8 slices of a sturdy but soft white bread
1 cup coconut cilantro chutney (page 94)
1 red onion, sliced into thin rings and soaked in water
1 red beet, roasted, peeled, and sliced into thin slices
1 Yukon gold potato, boiled in salted water, sliced thinly after cooling
1 large ripe but firm tomato, sliced thinly
1 seedless cucumber, peeled, sliced thinly
1 teaspoon chaat masala (available in Indian stores)
unsalted butter at room temperature, as needed
salt & pepper, in stages and per taste

METHOD
Once you have assembled all the ingredients, the making of the sandwich is a simple matter. Toast the bread in a toaster or oven to a golden brown. For each sandwich, spread a generous amount of butter on two slices. Next spread the chutney on both sides. Assemble the sandwich with layers of potato, beet, tomato, cucumber, onion, and a uniform sprinkle of chaat masala.

One word: delicious.

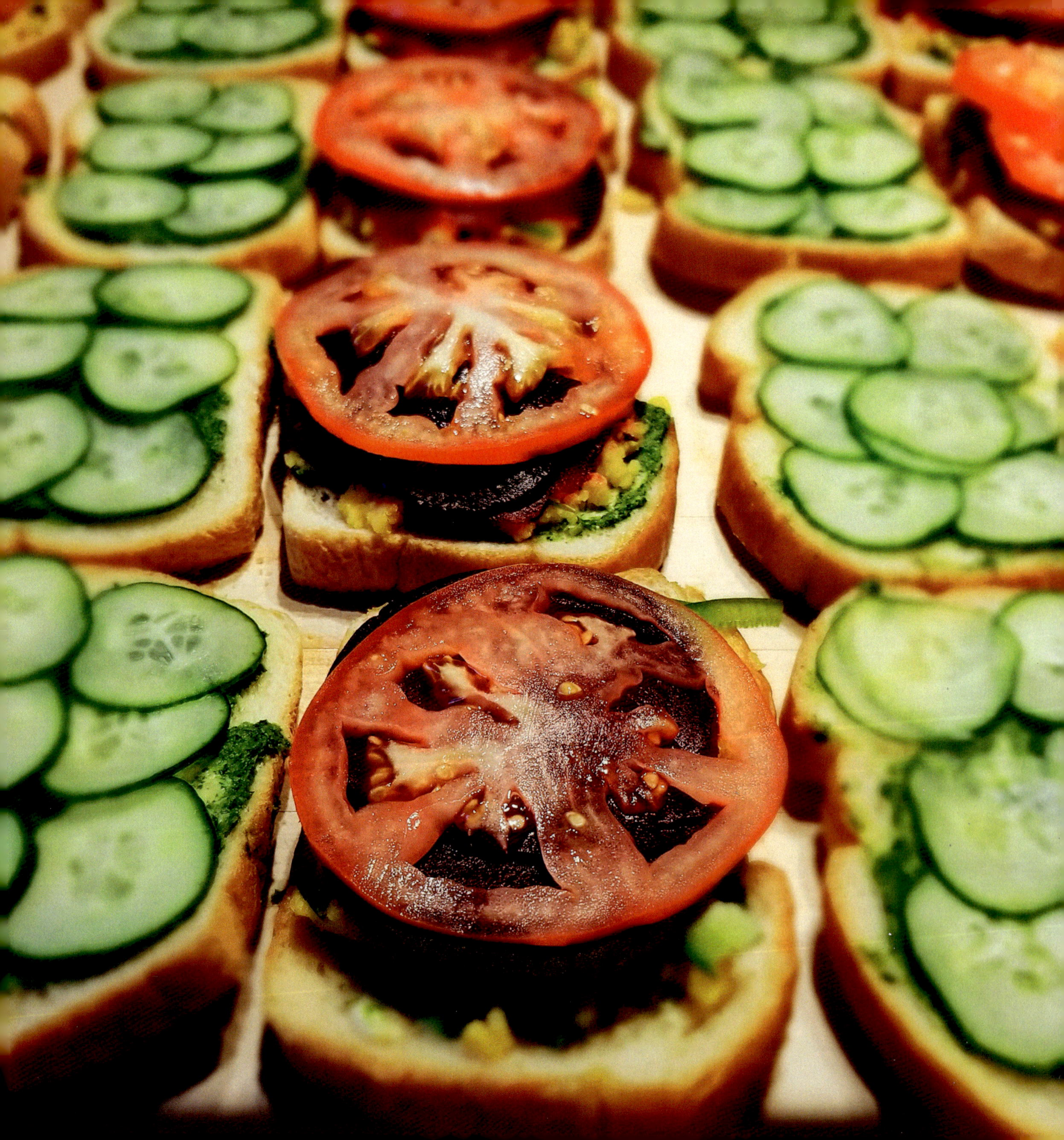

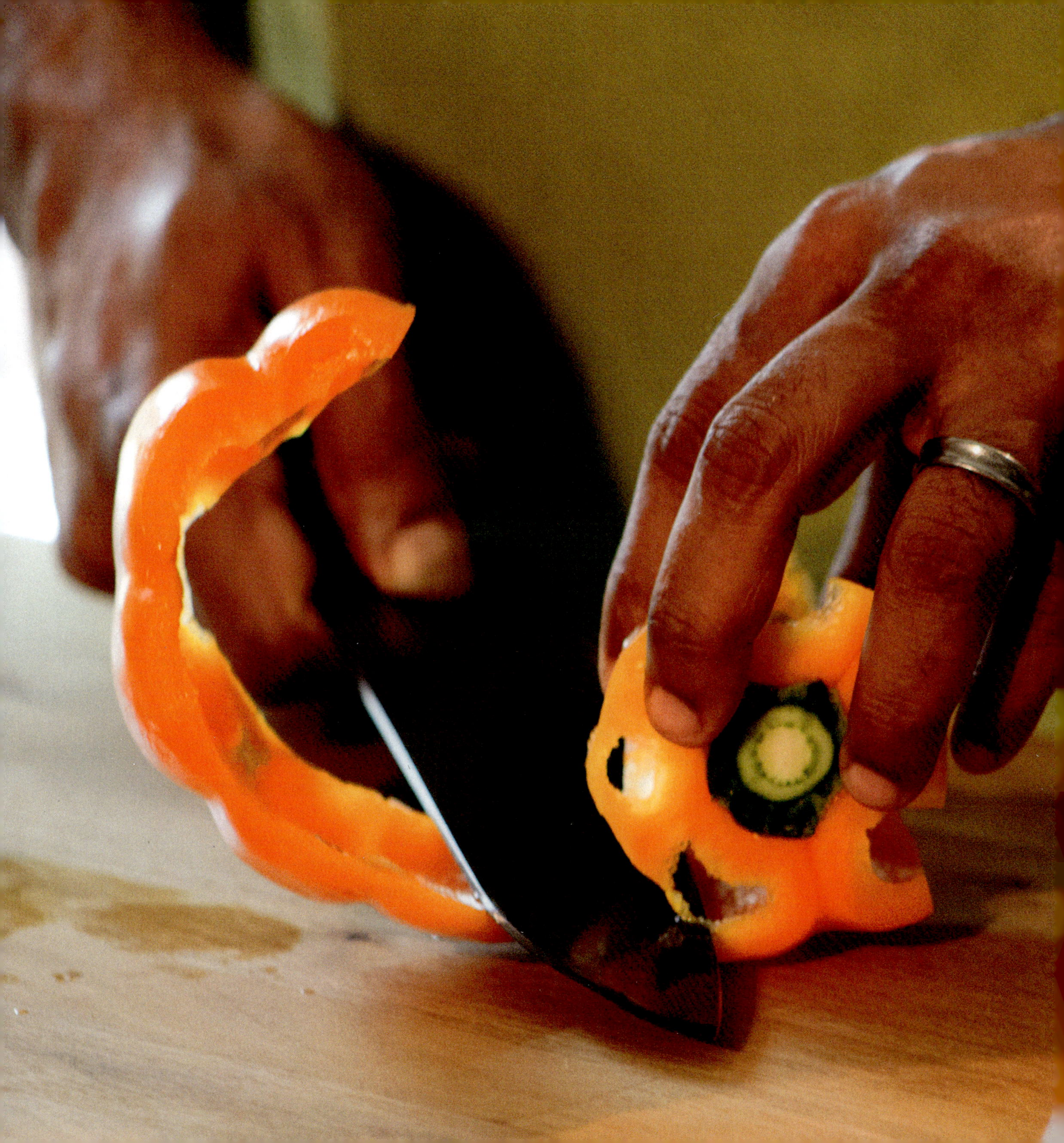

REUBEN

Tempeh is already fermented, so it is ideal for an application. This vegetarian version is legitimized even more if one is able to slice the tempeh thinly. Pastrami spices are optional but add a level of comfort.

LEVEL: Basic

YIELD: approximately 4

INGREDIENTS
8 slices pumpernickel bread
8 slices Swiss cheese
4 slices tempeh, 1/4 inch thick
1/2 head red cabbage, sliced thinly
2 sprigs fresh thyme
1 bay leaf
1/4 cup apple cider vinegar
1 shallot, minced
1/2 teaspoon caraway seeds
4 cloves garlic, minced
2 tablespoons Dijon mustard
1 teaspoon capers, minced
2 tablespoons assorted pickles (page 346), minced
1 cup mayonnaise
1/4 cup ketchup
2 tablespoons prepared horseradish
softened unsalted butter, as preferred
3 tablespoons extra-virgin olive oil
salt & pepper, in stages and per taste

METHOD

In a bowl, combine the mayonnaise, ketchup, horseradish, capers, and assorted pickles. Mix well and taste it. If needed, add salt and pepper to highlight the flavors. This is the dressing for this sandwich.

In a skillet, brush the tempeh with olive oil, salt, and pepper. Roast the slices well to a golden brown on both sides. Set aside. In the same skillet, heat a half and half mixture of olive oil and butter and brown the shallot and garlic. Add the red cabbage and cook on a medium high heat to brown the cabbage a bit. After about 10 minutes, add fresh thyme, bay leaf, caraway seeds, and apple cider vinegar. Cover the skillet and reduce the heat to medium. There is enough water in cabbage to allow for it to steam and cook through after 20 minutes. Let the cabbage cool down.

The sandwich is assembled as follows. Start by spreading a thin layer of dressing on both slices, then a slice of cheese on both sides, then the slice of roasted tempeh, then the cabbage, followed by a bit more dressing. Press the two sides to form the sandwich and cook it in a skillet with melted butter or olive oil on both sides as you would a pressed sandwich or grilled cheese sandwich. Slice the pressed sandwich in half and serve immediately.

BANH MI

> There is no mistaking the perfectly harmonious blend of French and Vietnamese culinary traditions in a well-executed banh mi. Now imagine if the great sandwiches of the world cross-pollinated with the great filling-style flavors from around the world! It is how I think about food. One world, one species, millions of possibilities. For this hand-held, be sure to invest in a good baguette or learn to make one yourself (four ingredients – good bread flour, water, yeast, and salt).

LEVEL: Basic

YIELD: approximately 4

INGREDIENTS

- 2 slabs tempeh
- 1 lemongrass stalk, chopped
- 2 Thai chiles, slit in half
- 1/4 cup low sodium soy sauce
- 1 teaspoon toasted sesame oil
- 1/2 inch piece fresh ginger, sliced thinly
- 2 cloves garlic, smashed
- 4 demi baguettes
- 1/2 cup mayonnaise or aquafaba
- 1 medium carrot, thinly shaved
- 1 small daikon radish, thinly shaved
- 1/4 cup rice wine vinegar
- honey, as needed
- 1-2 jalapeños, shaved thinly
- 8 cilantro sprigs with tender stems
- 1/4 cup fresh mint leaves, cut thinly
- 1/4 cup peanuts, roasted and salted, chopped coarsely
- extra-virgin olive oil, as needed
- salt & pepper, in stages and per taste

METHOD

Marinate the tempeh in the lemongrass, chiles, soy sauce, sesame oil, garlic, and ginger for at least an hour. Shake off all the marinade and conserve for another day. In a heavy-bottomed skillet like cast-iron, over low-medium heat, cook the tempeh for about 10 minutes on each side to develop a deep crust and flavor. After it cools a bit, slice the cooked tempeh thinly and hold. In a glass bowl, mix then vinegar, honey, some salt, and pepper to make a quick dressing. Toss the carrots and daikon in it and let sit for at least minutes.

The sandwich assembly is straightforward. Spread mayonnaise in both sides. Lay out the sliced tempeh the length of the bread and top with the dressed carrot-daikon slaw, two whole sprigs of cilantro, chopped mint, and as much sliced jalapeno as you desire.

FALAFEL DÖNER

> The first time I ate a döner was during my visiting professor stint in Freiburg, Germany. Admittedly, it was at 2 am, so one can infer as to why I was eating on the street at that time--and one wouldn't be far off. The freshness of the cabbage slaw was a memorable touch. The fresh taste of the bread is still memorable. It is no wonder that döner kebabs and döner sandwiches are so beloved in Europe and beyond.

LEVEL: Intermediate

YIELD: approximately 4

INGREDIENTS
8 falafel (page 127)
1/2 cup muhammara (page 92)
2 cups assorted lettuce
1 cup seedless cucumber, sliced thinly
1 cup red cabbage, shaved very thinly
1 cup yogurt or aquafaba
1/4 cup fresh dill, chopped
pinch or two of teaspoon smoked paprika
1 medium red onion, sliced thinly and soaked in cold water
2 cloves garlic, grated
zest and juice of 1 lemon
4 partially slit pita or naan (page 192)
salt & pepper, in stages and per taste

METHOD
In a glass bowl, steep the garlic in the lemon juice with the zest for 10 minutes. Add the yogurt, dill, smoked paprika, shaved cabbage, shaved onion, some salt, and pepper. Let this slaw stand for at least 10 minutes. The döner is assembled easily once all the ingredients are ready. Spread muhammara on the inside of the flatbread, next two falafel flattened gently, followed by cucumber, some lettuce, and the cabbage slaw. Fold the hand-held as a cone and be sure to wrap some sort of wax paper on the bottom end to prevent lower ingredients from falling out.

CROQUE MADAME

> Between a *croque madame* and a *croque monsieur*, the madame is definitely more decadent. Given the premise of this book, it was only appropriate that I opt for decadence. The execution is as important as the quality of ingredients. It may or may not be possible to pick this hand-held with one's hands, so it is completely acceptable to use dining utensils.

LEVEL: Basic

YIELD: approximately 4

INGREDIENTS
- 8 slices hearty, crusty French bread
- 8 slices Swiss or Comté cheese
- 1 cup truffled Gorgonzola cream (page 120), thick and cool
- 8 thin slices ripe tomato
- 1 teaspoon light brown sugar
- 1/2 teaspoon smoked paprika
- 4 eggs
- unsalted butter, softened, as needed
- salt & pepper, in stages and per taste

METHOD

Place the tomato slices on a baking sheet and sprinkle some brown sugar and smoked paprika on each. Bake in a 300F oven for 30 minutes or until the sugar is caramelized. Remove and hold.

To make each sandwich, toast the bread in an oven or toaster until golden brown. Next, spread unsalted butter on both toasted slices, one slice of cheese on each side, two slices of the roasted tomato, salt, and pepper. Press down the sandwich and spread the gorgonzola cream on both sides of the pressed sandwich. Bake in a 375F oven until you see that the cream has started to bubble and develop some brown spots.

Serve each sandwich whole with a seasoned fried egg on top for a showstopping, decadent sandwich.

PO'BOY

> The style of sandwich and its name are said to have originated in the French Quarter district in New Orleans when the Martin Brothers Coffee Stand and Restaurant opened. When the striking Streetcar men came for a sandwich, one might have overheard "here comes another poor boy."

LEVEL: Basic

YIELD: approximately 4

INGREDIENTS

12 oyster mushrooms
1/2 cup garbanzo flour
1/4 cup rice flour or corn starch
1 tablespoon fresh thyme leaves
1 cup mayonnaise
1/2 teaspoon honey
a few drops of hot sauce (page 344)
1 teaspoon Dijon mustard
2 cloves garlic, grated
2 tablespoons creole blend (page 87), more or less
juice and zest of 1 lemon
2 tablespoons fresh tarragon, chopped
1 large ripe tomato, halved and sliced thinly
2 cups crisp mild lettuce, shredded or sliced thinly
1/2 cup assorted pickles, chopped (page 346)
oil, for frying the mushrooms
4 soft Italian style sub rolls
salt & pepper, in stages and per taste

METHOD

Essentially, we will fill this sandwich with an assertive oyster mushroom pakora. Dust off any dirt off the mushrooms. Transfer them to a bowl and coat them in one tablespoon of creole spice and the fresh thyme. Dust half the garbanzo flour and the rice flour onto the mushrooms and some salt and pepper. Move the mushrooms around to obtain an even coating. Fry them at 350F until golden brown and allow to dry out on a metal rack. Season with more creole blend, salt, pepper, as desired.

In a bowl, steep the garlic in the lemon juice and zest for 5 minutes. This takes the raw edge off the garlic and may be used immediately. Add the mayonnaise, honey, mustard, remaining creole blend, chopped pickles, and tarragon. Mix well and taste this sauce (remoulade). If desired, add some hot sauce for an extra kick.

The sandwich is assembled easily. Slice the bread lengthwise without separating it. Spread the remoulade generously on both sides. Next, place the lettuce, followed by slices of tomato, salt and pepper, and top with the fried mushrooms. Dust with more seasoning of hot sauce, as preferred.

ULTIMATE GRILLED CHEESE SANDWICH

Most grilled cheese sandwiches aren't even grilled, but that's another matter. This version is on one end of the spectrum because of the overabundance of different cheeses, each providing a different character and flavor profile to the end result. I don't think one needs a tomato-basil soup to dip this in, but if you must, go for it. Resting the finished sandwich for a bit before cutting will help settle the melt.

LEVEL: Basic

YIELD: approximately 4

INGREDIENTS
8 slices of a sturdy white bread
4 slices extra sharp cheddar
1 cup red onion, sliced thinly and caramelized slowly until almost melted in butter
1/2 cup grated jalapeno jack cheese
1/4 cup cream cheese, softened
1/2 cup grated gruyere cheese
2 tablespoons fresh thyme leaves, chopped
unsalted butter, at room temperature
salt & pepper, in stages and per taste

METHOD
Toast the bread lightly in a toasted or oven. Mix the cream cheese, thyme, and some butter to form a spread. For each sandwich, start by spreading both slices with the spread. Place one slice of cheddar, follow with caramelized onions, jalapeno jack, and gruyere, then another slice. Press down and in a large cast-iron skillet, griddle the sandwiches on both sides until most of the cheese is melted. Let it rest a bit before cutting each sandwich in half. Plan to not eat for a bit after eating one.

Street-Inspired

What came first? Street Food or Restaurant Food? I'm no anthropologist or food historian, but using common sense intuition, I would say, a version of food on a street. Nevertheless, there is no denying the influence of what may be termed street food even in the finest restaurants in the world. Here, I try not to muck them up with fuss, but I do incorporate my spin, as should you.

POMEGRANATE & PAKORA CHAAT

Chaats are found all over the Indian Subcontinent offered by street-side vendors. Despite some core fundamentals, their creativity and composition vary as widely as the regions. Be prepared for a huge burst of flavor in a small bite of food.

LEVEL: Intermediate

YIELD: approximately 4 servings

INGREDIENTS
12 small onion and ginger pakoras (page 125)
1 cup fresh pomegranate seeds
2 tablespoons pomegranate molasses
1/4 cup tamarind and date chutney (page 105)
1/4 cup salsa verde (page 88)
1 large white potato, boiled in salted water and small diced
1 cup canned garbanzo, drained (keep juices) and boiled for 30 minutes
1 medium ripe tomato, small diced
1 teaspoon chaat masala (available in Indian stores)
juice of 1 lime
1/4 cup sev (fried garbanzo crisps, available in Indian stores)
2 tablespoons confectioner's sugar
1/4 teaspoon cream of tartar
1 teaspoon dry roasted cumin powder
1/4 cup fresh cilantro, chopped
1/4 cup chopped mint
water, as needed
salt & pepper, as needed

METHOD
Make the pakoras and hold. Mix the pomegranate molasses and tamarind date chutney in a saucepan. Loosen with some water and warm. It should coat the back of a spoon. Whip the drained juices from the canned garbanzo with the confectioner's sugar and cream of tartar for about 5 minutes in a stand or with a hand mixer. This is a sweetened aquafaba, a substitute for the more traditional yogurt.

The chaat is a layered composition bursting with flavor and contrast. Start with potatoes, garbanzo, roasted cumin powder, tomatoes, lime juice, pakora, salsa verde, sweetened aquafaba or yogurt, pomegranate tamarind date sauce, sev, chaat masala dusting, fresh mint, fresh cilantro, and pomegranate seeds.

After this dish, you will be left searching for flavor in most other dishes.

PAV BHAJI

> The dish is owned by Mumbai. Pav bhaji represents a study in colonial history and is said to have originated in the 1850s as a fast lunch-time snack for mill workers. The pav (soft savory rolls) is definitely a Portuguese influence, as are the tomatoes and peppers in the bhaji. During 1985-86 while in my final year of undergraduate education at St. Xavier's College, I would relish in the pav bhaji at Cannon, an institution that is still going strong. Gobs of melted butter, chasing each bite with a chomp of the accompanying spring onion, nodding one's head ever so slightly for additional orders of the warm buttered pav, and scarfing it down while standing and hunched over makes this an unforgettable experience.

LEVEL: Intermediate

YIELD: approximately 4 servings

INGREDIENTS

2 medium sized potatoes, peeled, small diced
1 cup grated cauliflower
1/2 cup green peas, fresh or frozen
1/2 teaspoon cumin seeds
1 large onion, minced
1 inch fresh ginger, minced
6 cloves garlic, minced
2-3 Thai or Indian green chiles, minced
1 poblano pepper, cored, small diced
4 ripe medium tomatoes, chopped finely
1 teaspoon turmeric powder
1 teaspoon Kashmiri red chili powder
2 tablespoons pav bhaji masala (available in Indian stores) or Berbere (page 77) for a delicious fusion
1/2 teaspoon garam masala (page 73)
1/4 cup roasted cashews, chopped coarsely
water, as needed
1/2 stick unsalted butter, plus more for the rolls
8 split pavs (unsweetened, yeasty dinner rolls)
salt & pepper, in stages and per taste

Garnishes: chiles, spring onion, cilantro, lime

METHOD

The process is basically the same as any bhaji in Indian cuisine. Make a paste of the ginger and garlic using a mortar and pestle or food processor. Use a shallow pan or skillet to make the bhaji. Maintain a medium heat throughout most of this dish and cook it uncovered to intensify the flavors. Start by melting the butter and frying the cumin seed. Next fry the ginger-garlic paste and minced green chiles for two minutes. Add the onion and poblano and cook for 5 minutes. Next, add the potato and cauliflower, and brown for 5 minutes. Add the turmeric and Kashmiri powder. Stir well and season with some salt. Stir this dish well on a regular basis. When the potato and cauliflower are cooked, add the tomato and break it down with a spatula. Keep the dish on a low simmer, continually mixing and harmonizing the flavors. Once you have a thick sauce-like consistency, add the garam masala and pav bhaji masala. Season with enough salt for a full-flavored outcome. Mix well and add the peas. After about 5 minutes or so, the bhaji is ready. Garnish with the cashews and cilantro. Serve with a pat of butter and the bread (pav), split in half and browned in more butter.

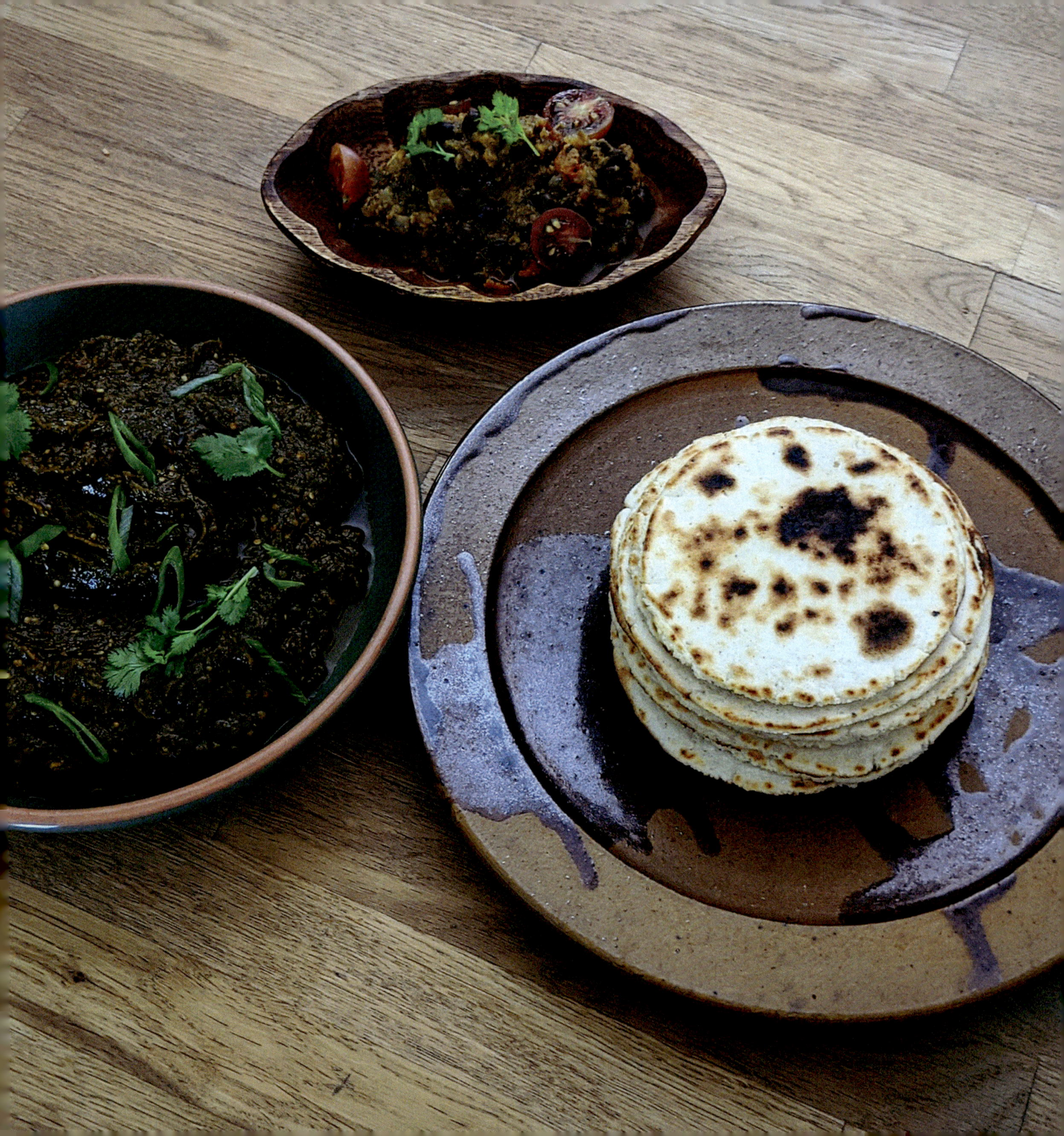

BHEL

> Indulging in bhelpuri on Chowpatty Beach (Mr. John Clark refers to it as Cow-Patty) in Mumbai is as iconic as gorging on hot dogs at Coney Island. Traditionally presented in a funnel cup made *a la minute* with newspaper, the best ones have the correct amount of potato, tamarind chutney, coriander chutney, puffed rice and chickpea crisps, and a finishing chaat masala.

LEVEL: Basic

YIELD: approximately 4 servings

INGREDIENTS

1 large potato, boiled in salted water, sliced into small pieces
1/4 cup tamarind date sauce (page 105)
1/2 cup salsa verde (page 88)
2 cups puffed rice (murmura, available in Indian stores)
1/4 cup sev (fried garbanzo flour, available in Indian stores)
4 puri or papdi (fried dough, available in Indian stores)
1 tablespoon spiced roasted garbanzo or chana dal
1/4 cup tablespoons roasted peanuts
1 teaspoon chaat masala
1/4 teaspoon cumin powder, dry roasted for 2 minutes on low heat
juice of 1 lime
1 small onion, small diced, soaked in cold water
1/4 cup fresh cilantro, chopped
salt & pepper, in stages and per taste

METHOD

Essentially, this is a mix and serve dish. But the order of mixing matters a bit and the dish must be served immediately to maintain some crisp textures. In a large bowl, mix half the salsa verde and tamarind date sauce together with the lime juice. Toss in the cooked potato, puffed rice, sev, peanuts, garbanzo, cumin powder, chaat masala, and onion. Take care to mix the ingredients with a light touch to maintain their integrity. Finish and serve the dish by topping with the cilantro, drops of tamarind date and salsa verde, and the puri or papdi. The desired outcome is an ethereal balance of tangy, spicy, herbaceous, sweet, crisp, and salt. It is typically served on the street in a newspaper cone, so you can catch outdated news, often in a script you won't be able to read, as you devour the dish.

RAGDA PATTICE

Typically, ragda is a spiced stew made with rehydrated white peas, but any pea will do. The dish is a traditional Maharashtrian dish and I ate my fair share of ragda pattice at Guru Kripa Restaurant near SIES College during my four years of "hanging out" after high school. Just enough spice, tamarind chutney, and sometimes plain yogurt (which would make it dahi ragda pattice) make for a delicious bite of dancing flavor.

LEVEL: Intermediate

YIELD: approximately 4 servings

INGREDIENTS
2 medium Yukon gold potatoes, boiled in salted water
2 tablespoons corn flour
1/2 teaspoon Kashmiri chile powder
1 teaspoon garam masala (page 73)
1/2 cup sev (fried garbanzo crisps, available in Indian stores)
2 cups chole masala (page 275)
2 tablespoons tamarind date chutney (page 105)
1 medium onion, small diced and soaked in water
1 cup cilantro leaves
1/2 cup mint leaves
1 green chile, chopped
1 teaspoon fresh ginger, minced
juice of half a lemon
vegetable oil, as needed for the potato pattice
salt & pepper, in stages and per taste

METHOD
Pattice
Combine the cooked potatoes, corn flour, Kashmiri powder, and garam masala in bowl and mix well. Add salt if needed. Form 8 round cakes, not unlike the cauliflower cakes. Fry these cakes until golden brown on both sides. Hold warm.

Combine the cilantro, mint, green chile, fresh ginger, lemon juice, and some salt in a blender to make the green chutney.

The dish is a tiered assembly of pattice on the bottom, ragda (we are using chole masala), tamarind date chutney, green chutney, sev, and soaked onions.

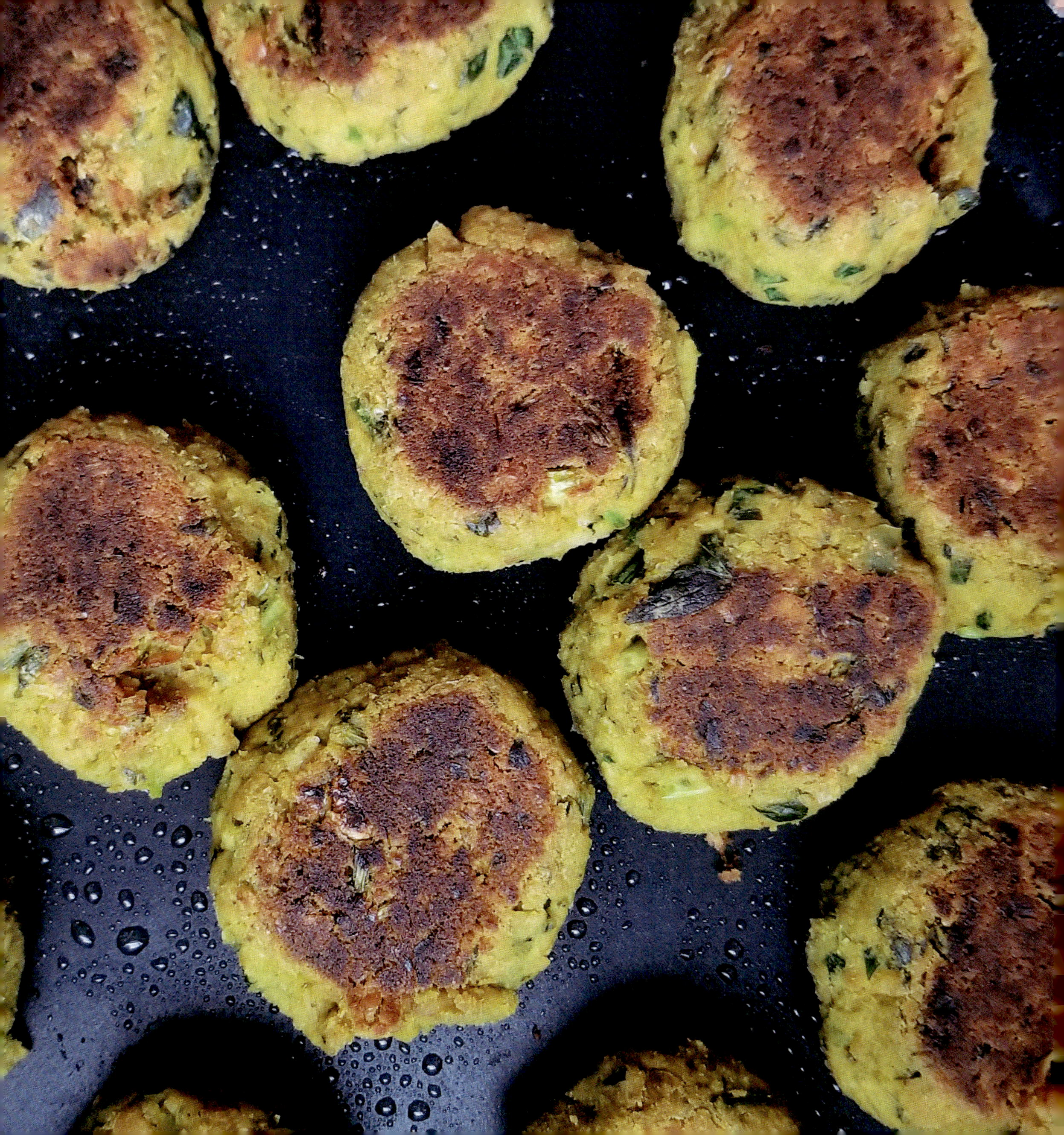

VADA PAV

> The names of so many dishes the world over are literal--as long as one knows the meanings of the word(s). Vada is essentially a battered fritter. Here the fritter is more of a battered (always in chickpea flour) and fried samosa-style filling with some subtleties. More precisely, it is a *batata vada* (fried spiced potato ball). Stuck inside a warm pav lathered with garlic chutney and fresh *hari mirch* (green chile), the humble vada pav may be the most beloved Mumbai street-food. I've been known to enjoy many at one sitting or, rather, one standing.

LEVEL: Intermediate

YIELD: approximately 4

INGREDIENTS

- 2 medium russet potatoes, peeled, quartered, and boiled in salted water
- 3 green chiles, minced
- 3 cloves garlic, sliced thinly
- 1/2 inch piece fresh ginger, minced
- 1/2 teaspoon mustard seeds
- 8 curry leaves
- 1/2 teaspoon cumin seeds
- 1/4 cup fresh cilantro, chopped
- 1 teaspoon turmeric powder
- 1 teaspoon garam masala (page 73)
- 1 cup garbanzo flour
- 1/4 teaspoon baking soda
- pinch of asafoetida (optional)
- 1/4 teaspoon Kashmiri red chile powder
- 1/2 cup water, more or less
- 4 soft medium slider buns, sliced but not separated
- 2 tablespoons harissa (optional, page 91)
- 1/2 cup coconut cilantro chutney (page 94)
- 1/4 cup tamarind date chutney (page 105)
- vegetable oil, as needed, for sautéing and frying
- salt & pepper, in stages and per taste

METHOD

Heat some oil in a pan and add the mustard seeds, cumin seeds, and curry leaves. After 15 seconds or as soon as the mustard seeds begin popping, add the garlic, ginger, and green chilies. Fry for 2 minutes and pour contents over the boiled potatoes. With a fork or potato masher, smash the potatoes and season with salt. Set aside and allow to cool. Form 4 equal-sized balls.

In a bowl, mix the garbanzo flour, garam masala, red chile powder, asafoetida, and salt. Make a thick batter by slowly mixing in water until it just comes together and easily coats the back of a spoon.

Preheat the fryer oil to 350F. Coat the potato balls in a uniform coating in the garbanzo batter and fry until golden brown, making sure you turn them around in the oil as one would for donuts or dumplings. Drain and allow to cool a bit.

Each vada pav is assembled easily. Spread the harissa (if using) on both sides of the bread roll. Place a fried potato inside, top with the coconut cilantro chutney and tamarind date chutney. Press down the sandwich a bit before serving.

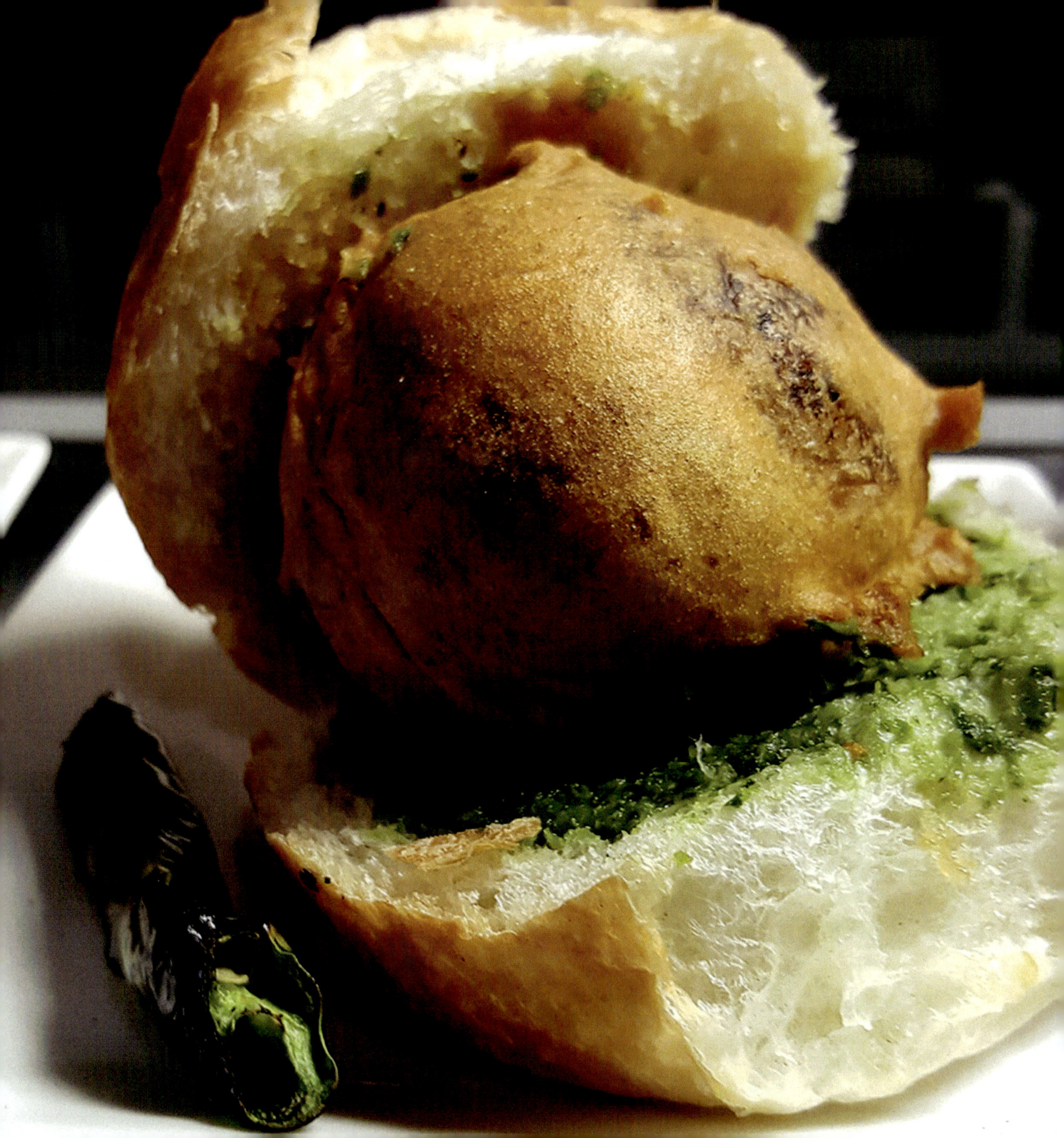

AREPA

Similar to a pupusa, arepas are extremely popular in Colombia and Venezuela. I present a basic arepa here, but clearly, one can fill an arepa with a wide variety of possibilities. In a way, this reminds me of a paratha (page xxx), but these are typically smaller and with more filling. It goes to show us that good food knows no boundaries and deserves the embrace and celebration of all.

LEVEL: Basic

YIELD: approximately 4

INGREDIENTS
2 masarepa flour (available in most Latin markets)
1 1/2 cups warm water, maybe a bit more
1 teaspoon adobo seasoning (page 86)
1/4 cup queso fresco (optional)
1 teaspoon extra-virgin olive oil
unsalted butter, as needed
1/2 cup cooked beans without gravy, of your liking (page 276 or page 275)
4 slices queso Oaxaca (optional)
salt & pepper, in stages and per taste

METHOD
Mix the adobo seasoning, masarepa flour, some salt, and queso fresco (if using) in a bowl. Add warm water, slowly, to start forming a dough not unlike tortilla dough. Mix well and knead to a soft and pliable consistency. Portion the dough into four balls and using both hands, flatten each ball to a 5-inch disk. Place a small amount of cooked beans in the center and a piece of queso Oaxaca on top of the beans. Carefully, pull in the sides and pinch to seal the beans and cheese as a filling. Turn the stuffed disk over so the pinched side is on the bottom. Again, carefully flatten out the stuffed arepa to a 4-inch diameter and round off the edges. Heat a cast iron skillet and melt some butter. Cook the arepas on low for about 10 minutes per side to ensure a crisp exterior and steamed and cheesy inside. Serve immediately as is or accompanied with your favorite chutney or salsa.

POUTINE

> In 2016, I was invited to compete in the inaugural Central Florida Poutine Challenge hosted by some fine folks, including the inimitable Faiyaz Kara of the Orlando Weekly. The event was in recognition of Victoria Day and I was fortunate that my creation, the M & M (Mumbai to Montreal) Poutine, was deemed Best of Show by the judges. The version here is much simpler but doesn't lack in flavor or comfort.

LEVEL: Basic

YIELD: approximately 4 servings

INGREDIENTS

3 medium russet potatoes, washed well and cut as fries
2 cups mushroom demi (page 118)
1 cup roasted wild and exotic mushrooms (optional)
1 shallot, minced
3 cloves garlic, minced
1 sprig fresh thyme
1 tablespoon all-purpose flour
8 ounces cheese curds
2 tablespoons fresh chives, cut thinly
1 tablespoon unsalted butter
oil for frying
salt & pepper, in stages and per taste

METHOD

Soak the cut potatoes in cold water for at least 15 minutes, strain rinse, and dry. Double fry the potatoes. First, for 5 minutes at 300F, draining well; then, at 375F until golden brown. After the first fry, make the gravy. Melt the butter and add the flour. Cook this mixture to a light brown roux (about 15 minutes). Now add the minced shallot, garlic, and thyme sprigs. Cook these ingredients in the roux until the shallots get soft. Add the mushroom demi and cook until the sauce is the consistency of a thick gravy. Season with salt, if necessary and discard the thyme sprigs. As soon as the fries are golden brown after the second frying, assemble the poutine by spreading about 2 ounces of cheese curds pieces amongst a portion of fries and ladling enough warm gravy to begin melting the curds. Finish with roasted mushrooms (if using) and chives.

KELEWELE

> Before *Solidarity Sunday*, my friend Holly Kapherr Alejos spent many hours in our modest restaurant kitchen, peeling hordes of plantains prior to helping prepare a large amount of Kelewele. This popular and tasty Ghanaian street-food is best when the natural pan-kiss between the ingredients does all the talking.

LEVEL: Basic

YIELD: approximately 4 servings

INGREDIENTS
- 4 plantains, just ripe, peeled and medium cubed
- 1/2 teaspoon cayenne pepper
- 1/2 Habanero pepper (optional), chopped
- 1 teaspoon fresh ginger, grated
- vegetable oil, as needed
- small amount of water
- salt & pepper, in stages and per taste

METHOD
Grind together grated ginger root, pepper, and salt, then mix with water. In a bowl, toss together the plantain and spice mixture. Shallow fry the spiced plantains in a skillet with vegetable oil until the plantain is golden brown and slightly soft. Drain and serve immediately. Garnish with cilantro or mint, as desired.

SHAWARMA

LEVEL: Basic

YIELD: approximately 4 servings

INGREDIENTS
- 1 cup fava beans (if unavailable, substitute garbanzo), rehydrated, cooked, and peeled
- 1 small eggplant, sliced into 1/4 inch slices
- 1 red onion, cut into wedges
- 2 cups seitan or tempeh, cut into strips
- zest and juice of 2 lemons
- 4 cloves garlic, smashed
- 1 tablespoon bāhārat spice blend (page 78)
- 1/2 teaspoon cinnamon powder
- 1/2 teaspoon Kashmiri red chile powder
- 1/2 cup tzatziki (page 365)
- 1/4 cup fresh parsley, chopped
- 1/4 cup extra-virgin olive oil, more or less
- coarse salt and black pepper, to taste
- cooked saffron rice (optional)
- cucumber and tomato salad (optional)
- salt & pepper, in stages and per taste
- 4 pita

METHOD
Whisk the spices, olive oil, lemon juice and zest, garlic, parsley, onions, salt, and pepper to essentially make a spiced lemon vinaigrette. Marinate the fava beans, eggplant, and plant protein in the vinaigrette for at least 2 hours. If possible, roast the plant protein and fava beans in a 350F oven for 30 minutes, and grill the eggplant and onions. Season all ingredients well with salt and pepper and toss them in the roasting juices and remaining vinaigrette. Serve the grilled and roasted ingredients that fill a hand-held in pita, with tzatziki, or as a plate with the rice, salad, and tzatziki.

EMPANADA

> Empanadas are extremely popular and found all across Portugal, Spain, Latin America, and even the Philippines. There are as many versions as there are culinary traditions. Here, I decided to impart my own style and tendency to cross-pollinate many cuisines. It's time-consuming, but I hope you find it enjoyable. Certainly, I would urge you to make it your own.

LEVEL: Basic

YIELD: approximately 4

INGREDIENTS
1 cup all-purpose flour
1/2 cup masa harina
2 tablespoon unsalted butter
1/4 cup cold water, more or less
2 boiled eggs, chopped up
1 cup Mumbai potatoes (page 361)
1 cup sauerkraut or braised cabbage like colcannon (page 360)
1/4 cup melting cheese like gruyere or queso Oaxaca, grated
2 tablespoons assorted fresh herbs like basil, parsley, mint, and cilantro, chopped
melted unsalted butter for brushing the empanadas
salt & pepper, in stages and per taste

METHOD

In a food processor, crumb the flours, some salt, and cold butter. Transfer the ingredients to a bowl and make a well. Slowly begin adding cold water to bring the dough together. Do not over knead. Wrap the dough in plastic and refrigerate until ready to use.

For the filling, the possibilities are as extensive as there are fillings in the world. Here, I present one such possibility. Mix the spiced cooked potatoes, boiled eggs, cabbage, and fresh herbs in a bowl. Portion the dough into 4 equal portions. Round each ball and roll out each round on a lightly floured surface to an approximately 6-inch round. Place approximately one-fourth of the filling in the center of each round. Sprinkle some grated cheese on top. Moisten the edges of the dough and carefully fold over one half onto the other to form a semicircle. Avoid trapping air pockets inside. Using a fork or by folding in a pattern, crimp the edges.

Place the empanadas on a baking sheet lined with parchment paper sprayed with a release product, or simply brush it with some oil. Brush both sides of each empanada with melted butter and bake at 400F until golden brown. This may be approximately 25 minutes. Allow the baked empanadas to cool before serving with your favorite chutney like, say, romesco (see recipe on page xxx).

CALIFORNIA BURRITO

Leave it to a health-conscious state to purportedly fill a burrito with hot French fries, salsa, guacamole, etc... A burrito in this style is typically a carbohydrate-loaded meal. It makes sense if one can then slip into an afternoon siesta under the warm Southern California sun, listening to the crashing waves of the mighty Pacific Ocean and dreaming California dreams. One may double-wrap and steam the tortillas, so it allows for a stable and temporarily sealed burrito.

LEVEL: Basic

YIELD: approximately 4

INGREDIENTS

4 large flour tortillas, either store bought or homemade
1 cup tomatillo salsa (page 100)
2 large russet potatoes, washed and cut up to be French fries
1 cup jack cheese, shredded
1/4 cup pickled jalapenos (page 346)
1 portobello mushroom, de-bearded, grilled, and cut into thin strips
1 cup cooked black beans
1 cup seitan or tempeh, seasoned and roasted, cut into strips (optional)
1 cup roasted corn salsa (page 268)
peanut or vegetable oil for French fries
1/2 cup smoked onion cream (page 121)
salt & pepper, in stages and per taste

METHOD

Once you have gathered all the ingredients, it is a straightforward assembly. Just ensure that the burrito is sealed well by tucking in the filling and folding in the sides and tucking before rolling it shut. Soak the cut potatoes in water for at least 10 minutes before drying them well and frying them to a golden brown. In this instance, the fries are not expected to be crisp because they will begin getting soggy in the burrito. It is more about the decadent gall of filling a burrito with French fries.

Layer the filling made of French fries, black beans, grilled portobello, tomatillo salsa, jalapeno, cheese, roasted corn salsa, drizzle of smoked onion cream, and plant protein (optional). Once the burrito is tightly wrapped, either grill it lightly or pan roast it in the skillet. Serve the burrito wet (napped with warm tomatillo salsa) or dry. Just don't expect to eat a wet burrito with your bare hands and look respectful.

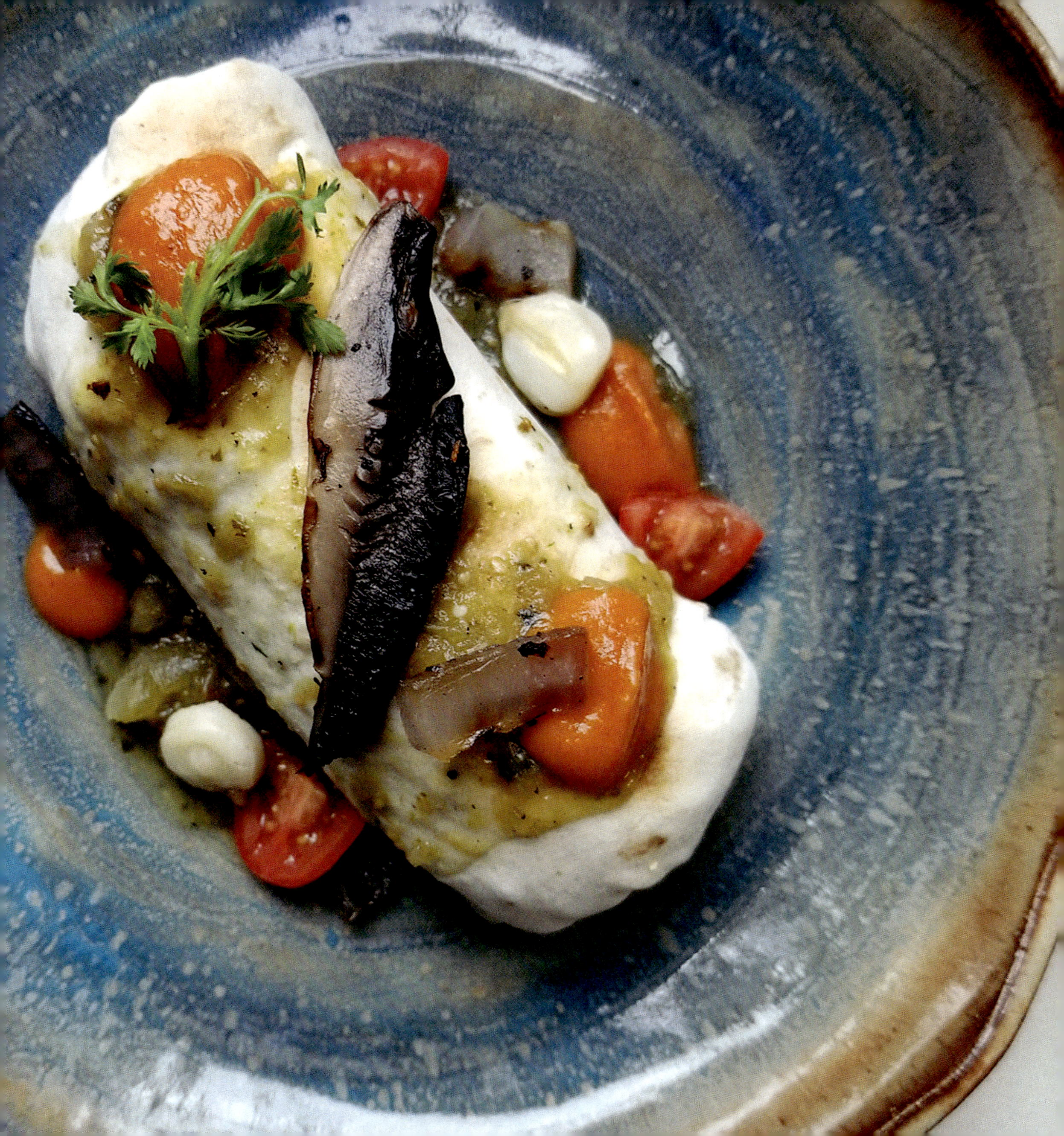

BUNNY CHOW

> No bunnies or other animals were harmed in the making of this chow. One day, we hope to visit South Africa with our dear friends Bram & Geraldine to see how it's done in the birthplace of bunny chow.

LEVEL: Basic

YIELD: approximately 4

INGREDIENTS
4 ciabatta rolls, sliced in half and hollowed out
1 cup of your favorite dry-style curry (page 275)
1/4-inch piece fresh ginger, peeled, thin strips
2 tablespoons fresh cilantro, chopped
1 shallot, sliced thinly
extra-virgin olive oil, as needed
salt & pepper, in stages and per taste

METHOD
In a pan, fry the shallot to a golden-brown stage. Drain on a paper towel and season with salt. Assemble each portion by filling each hollowed bread half with warm curry. Garnish with fresh ginger, fried shallot, and fresh cilantro.

MONSOON CORN

> I was eating street corn long before I came to the United States and heard about eloté (Mexican street corn). This way of eating corn on the cob has ruined me for all other preparations.

LEVEL: Basic

YIELD: approximately 4

INGREDIENTS
4 ears of corn, unsweet if you can get it.
1/2 juice Persian lime
1/2 teaspoon cayenne or Kashmiri red chili powder
1/2 teaspoon iodized salt (a deviation!)

METHOD
In a small bowl, mix the salt and chili powder, and set aside. This preparation is best when one can grill the corn slowly over hot charcoal or wood. Use a mild, sweet flavored wood like peach. Wash and dry the corn as you await the grill's readiness. Grill the corn on consistent and medium heat taking care to move the cobs around on the grill to ensure uniform charring. Once all the cobs are uniformly charred, press the lime half into the pepper and salt mixture. While the corn is still warm, applying uniform pressure, rub the spiced lime half up and down each cob while squeezing the lime gently. This method spreads the spicy fresh lime juice all over the corn. Enjoy.

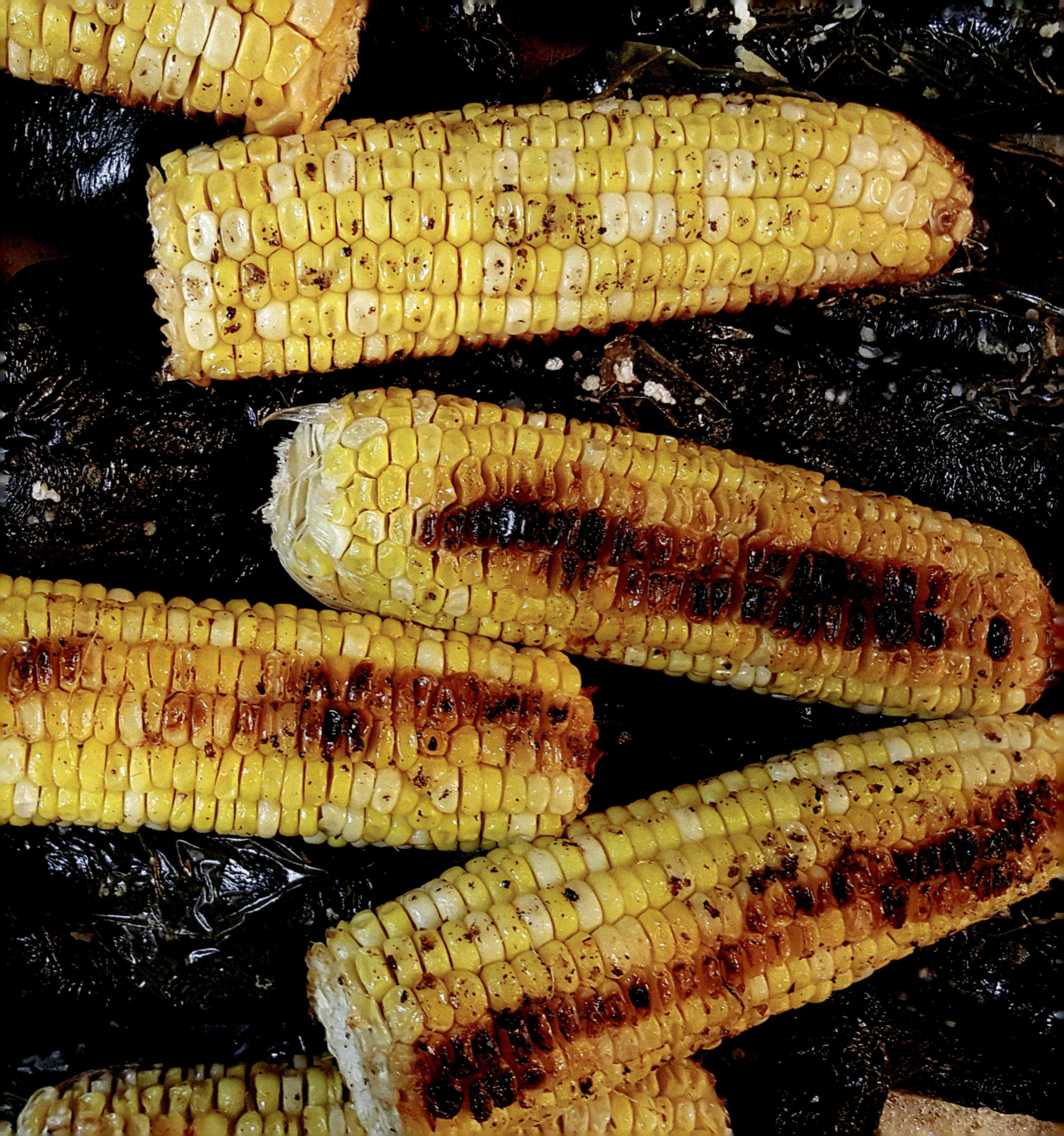

DOUBLES

> Carnival in Trinidad is legendary. Doubles on the streets of Trinidad and Tobago may be more quintessential. At its core, it is modest food just like its cousin found in *dhabas* (truck stop diners) all over North India. Legend has it that doubles originated in Trinidad in the 1930s when a single version of *bara* (fried bread) and *channa* (spiced chickpeas) were asked to be "doubled." And a legend was born. Nowadays, the toppings on doubles are what distinguish one vendor's doubles from another's.

LEVEL: Intermediate

YIELD: approximately servings

INGREDIENTS
1 cup all-purpose flour
1 teaspoon Trinidadian or similar curry powder
3/4 teaspoon active dry yeast
3 tablespoons warm water, more or less
pinch of sugar, food for the yeast
1 cup vegetable oil, for frying, more or less
1/4 cup tamarind date chutney (page 105)
2 sprigs fresh cilantro, chopped
1.5 cups chana masala, more or less (page 275)
salt & pepper, in stages and per taste

METHOD
Make the chana masala.

In a bowl, mix the flour, curry powder, and some salt. Add a teaspoon of oil to the spiced flour and rub it with your fingers. Combine the warm water, yeast, and sugar and whisk well. Let the yeast bloom for about 5 minutes or until you see it get bubbly. Add this bloomed liquid in stages to a well-made in the dry ingredients until the dough comes together. Cover and store in a warm area.

Once the dough doubles (pun intended), punch it down and hold covered for 15 minutes. Portion into 4 pieces. Make each piece a round and roll into 5-inch rounds. Fry each round in a skillet or deep fryer until they puff up and get golden brown. Drain each fried bread well.

Serve each double with chana masala inside a wedged bread with dots of tamarind date sauce and fresh cilantro. Fold and enjoy.

PATATAS BRAVAS

> This is a healthier take on a classic. Instead of deep frying the potatoes, I recommended roasting a creamy variety of potato. Lately, I've been almost dry roasting medium-sized red potatoes with garlic and diced peppers. No matter how one executes the dish, this popular tapa from Madrid have found a grip amongst aficionados of street food.

LEVEL: Basic

YIELD: approximately 4 servings

INGREDIENTS
- 1 lb. baby Yukon gold potatoes, cut in half
- 2 sprigs fresh thyme
- 1 teaspoon Dijon mustard
- 1 tablespoon balsamic vinegar
- 1 teaspoon smoked paprika
- 1/2 teaspoon cayenne pepper
- 1/4 cup flatleaf parsley, chopped
- 2 cloves garlic, grated
- juice and zest of half a lemon
- 1/4 cup tablespoons good quality mayonnaise
- extra-virgin olive oil, as needed
- salt & pepper, in stages and per taste

METHOD

Preheat an oven to 360F. Coat the potatoes in olive oil, salt, and pepper. Mix in the thyme sprigs and roast the potatoes in the oven for about 30 minutes or until golden brown. While the potatoes are roasting, in a large bowl, steep the garlic in the vinegar and lemon juice for 5 minutes before adding the remaining ingredients, making a compound aioli. Once the potatoes are properly roasted, add the roasted thyme leaves from the sprigs to the aioli. Once the potatoes have cooled a bit, add them to the bowl with the aioli and mix well. Serve immediately.

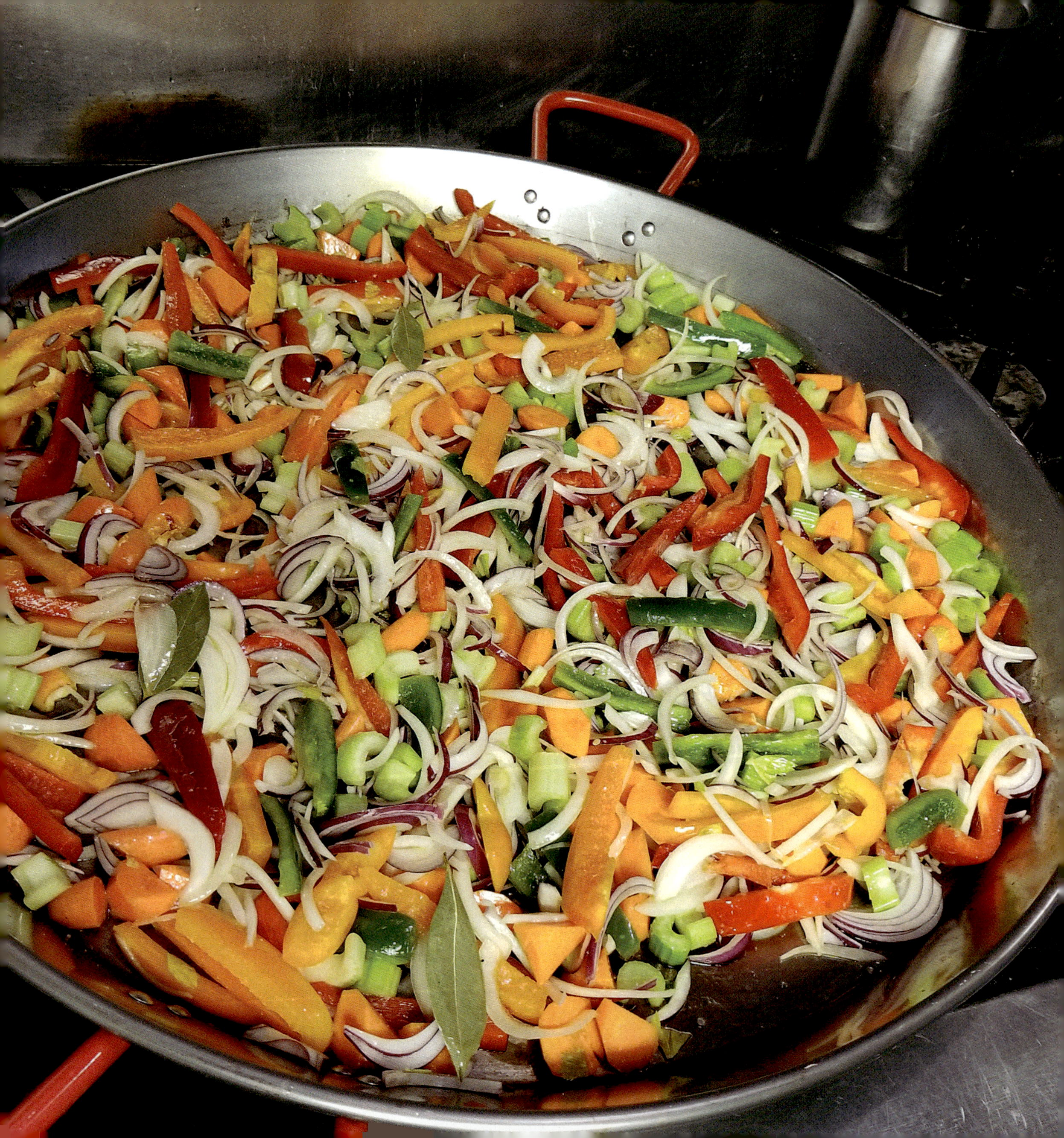

Rice Dishes

Rice is one of the most widely consumed grains in the world. It was a staple for me in India and we had rice at almost every table. It's no surprise then that some of the rice dishes I present in this section are inspired by childhood memories. Others are my interpretations of classics.

PAELLA

> They tell me it's about the *socarrat* (the crisp and caramelized bottom layer). But there's so much more. The timing of adding ingredients has a lot to do with the outcome. Be sure to have enough warm seasoned broth on hand should the rate of evaporation be faster than expected. Also, allow the finished dish to rest and absorb every last bit of the broth for the perfect paella.

LEVEL: Intermediate

YIELD: approximately 4 servings

- 2 bell peppers, cored and sliced (I'm using red bell peppers)
- 2 red onion, sliced
- 2 cups sliced cremini mushrooms
- 5 cloves garlic, sliced
- 1/2 cup Spanish olives, rinsed and halved
- 2 cups fresh greens like mustard greens or kale
- 2 tablespoons tomato paste
- 2 cups arborio or sushi rice
- ½ cup white wine
- 3 cups or more of warm, seasoned vegetable stock
- chopped flatleaf parsley, as needed for garnish
- extra-virgin olive oil
- salt & pepper, in stages and per taste

METHOD

Use a flat sauté pan or a proper paella pan for this dish. Over medium-high heat, sauté mushrooms in the olive oil until golden brown. Next add the garlic, peppers, and onions and cook on medium heat for 5 minutes. Next add the tomato paste and fry for 2 minutes before adding the rice and greens. Stir well and even out the rice and other ingredients in the pan. Add the white wine and let it sizzle for about a minute. Now add the warm stock one ladle at a time, but do not disturb the rice. Cook for at least 25 minutes or until the rice is cooked and a crust (socarrat) has formed on the bottom. Let the rice rest for at least 10 minutes to absorb all the broth. Finish by sprinkling the olives and parsley on the cooked rice. Be sure to serve the socarrat with every portion.

Note: You may serve a fried egg on top of each portion for added protein and decadence.

PULAO

The origins of pulao are a bid muddled, but there are numerous interpretations of this style of rice. Alternate names include *pilau*, *pilaf*, and *polow*. Mughlai cuisine does a fantastic job of incorporating Indian spices into the Persian classic. The key is to ensure that all the vegetables are perfectly cooked, and the rice absorbs the flavors of the broth.

LEVEL: Basic

YIELD: approximately 4 servings

INGREDIENTS

2 cups Basmati rice
1 medium red onion, sliced thinly
1 cinnamon stick
4 whole green or white cardamom pods
4 whole cloves
2 bay leaves (fresh, if available)
1/2 teaspoon whole black peppercorns
pinch of saffron
3.5 cups seasoned vegetable stock or water
1 cup cauliflower florets, blanched in salted water
1 cup Yukon gold potatoes, halved, blanched in salted water
1/2 cup shelled green peas
1 cup sliced carrots, blanched in salted water
1/2 cup 1-inch long pieces green beans, blanched in salted water
1 tablespoon golden raisins plumped up in ghee or vegetable oil
1 tablespoon cashews, toasted
1/4 cup fresh cilantro, chopped
1 tablespoon fresh mint, chopped
2 tablespoons vegetable oil or ghee
salt & pepper, in stages and per taste

METHOD

Wash and rinse the rice three times. Let soak in water for 30 minutes. Heat ghee or vegetable oil in a heavy bottomed pot. Sauté cinnamon, bay, cloves, and cardamom for 15 seconds. Add onions and sauté to a light golden brown. Season with salt. Add cauliflower and stir periodically for 10 minutes. Add washed and drained rice. Stir well. Add remaining vegetables. Stir well. Add warm stock (1 part rice, 1 ¾ part stock). Stir well. Add saffron. Bring to a simmer. Check that the liquid is well-seasoned. Cover pot with a tight-fitting lid. Lower flame to low. Check in about 20 minutes. Switch off the flame in 10 minutes. Let the pot stay covered for 15 minutes so that any excess water is absorbed. Fluff rice gently with a fork. Add the raisins and cashews and finish by sprinkling with cilantro and mint.

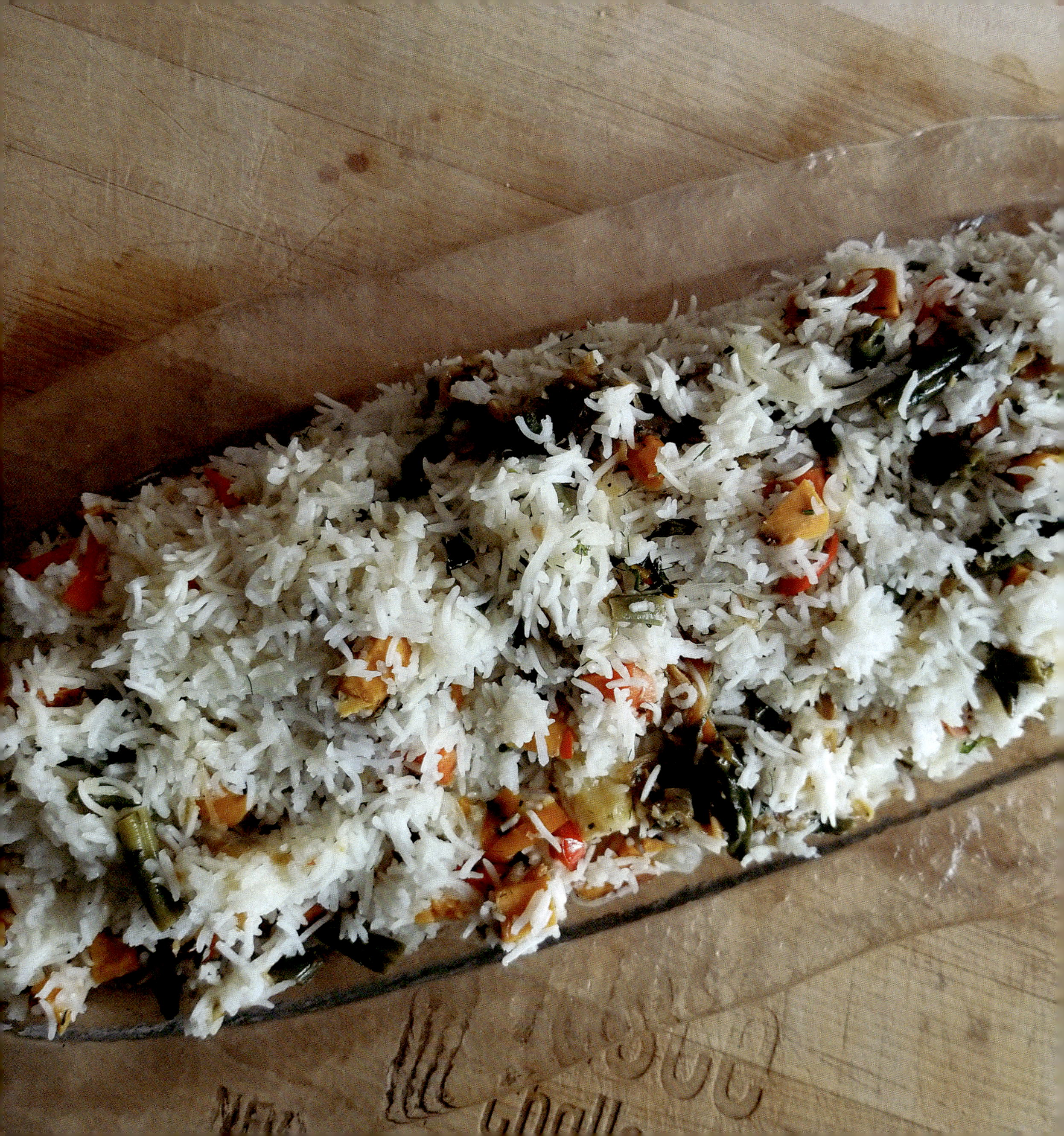

JAMBALAYA

I was reprimanded on one occasion by a guest for serving a jambalaya that wasn't authentic. Bless their heart. I stand by my interpretation of it. Traditionally, jambalaya is a creole dish with Spanish and French influences. Every time I visit New Orleans, I make it a point to seek out a good gumbo and jambalaya. And while I've had mixed success with getting what I like, there is no denying the soul of this dish. The mark of a great jambalaya is the balance of spices and the degree to which the rice absorbs the flavor of the broth and aromatics.

LEVEL: Intermediate

YIELD: approximately 4 servings

INGREDIENTS
2 cups Louisiana long to medium grain rice, washed and soaked in water
2 cups leeks, cut into 1/4 inch rings
2 cups carrots, medium dice
1 cup onion, medium dice
1 cup green bell pepper, medium dice
1 cup celery, small dice
2 quarts vegetable stock, made from all the trims
1 cup eggplant, medium dice
1 cup tempeh, medium dice
2 bay leaves
2 jalapeños, minced
5 cloves garlic, minced
1 bunch flat leaf parsley, chopped finely
1 cup tomatoes, diced
2 tablespoons smoked or plain paprika
1 tablespoon cayenne pepper
1 tablespoon onion powder
1 tablespoon garlic powder
1/4 cup Louisiana hot sauce
extra virgin olive oil, as needed
salt & pepper, in stages and per taste

METHOD
In a wide, heavy-bottomed pot, sauté the tempeh in some extra-virgin olive oil. Next, add the eggplant and brown. Remove the tempeh and eggplant from the pot and add the leeks, onions, peppers, celery, and jalapeños to the pot. Sauté for a few minutes before adding the garlic, paprika, cayenne, bay leaves, onion powder, and garlic powder. Stir well. Add the rice and stir to coat each grain well. Return the tempeh and eggplant to the pot, add the tomatoes, and sauté for a couple of minutes. Add the hot sauce and all the stock. Stir well and re-season the stock just the way you like it. Cover the pot and cook the rice starting on medium and returning to low, once it starts simmering. In general, adding hot stock will expedite this transition.

Once the rice is cooked, uncover it and let some of the steam escape. Finish with lots of fresh parsley and a wedge of lemon.

BIRYANI

> A true Hyderabadi biryani is art in a pot. The care with which the layers are imagined and seasoned is like that of a perfect paella. Except, in this case, great care is taken to layer the spices and aromatics interspersed with the vegetables. In a perfect world, each serving of biryani would be individually cooked as a perfect parcel of spices, fluffy basmati rice, and a variety of fresh vegetables, each cooked to perfection.

LEVEL: Intermediate

YIELD: approximately 4 servings

INGREDIENTS

- 2 cups high-grade basmati rice, washed multiple times and soaked in water
- 2 cups cauliflower florets
- 1 cup, green beans, cleaned, cut into 1 inch segments
- 6 baby Yukon Gold potatoes, skin on, cleaned, halved
- 1 medium red onion, sliced thinly
- 2 inch piece of ginger, sliced thinly
- 4 cloves garlic, minced
- 1 tablespoon cumin powder
- 1 tablespoon coriander powder
- 1 teaspoon turmeric powder
- 1 teaspoon cayenne pepper (optional)
- 1 cup milk a pinch of saffron
- 1/2 cup toasted cashews
- 1/2 cup golden raisins plumped up in a small amount of butter
- 1 cup chopped tomatoes
- 1 tablespoon each cilantro and mint
- 2 green chilies (1 jalapeño will do), minced
- salt & pepper, in stages and per taste

METHOD

Soak the rice in water for at least an hour while you prepare the vegetables. In a shallow pot (sort of like a rondeau), start by sautéing the onions in ghee or unsalted butter. Add the cauliflower and potatoes. Season with salt and pepper. Next, add the green beans. Add the garlic, green chilies, and all the spices. Stir well. Next, add the tomatoes and stew down until all the vegetables are cooked. Taste and re-season as desired. When a mostly dry consistency is reached, store what is basically a bhaji and set it aside.

Drain the rice well. In the same pot, toast the rice in some more butter or ghee and add enough water and all the milk and saffron. Generally, basmati rice cooks perfectly with a ratio of 1 parts rice to 1.5+ parts water. Make sure the liquid cooking the rice is properly seasoned. Cover the rice, bring to a simmer and turn the heat to low. The rice should be cooked in about 15 minutes. Let the rice cool a bit before fluffing it. One may either stir in the vegetarian bhaji or make a dome with the vegetables as a stuffing. Garnish with the nuts, cilantro, and mint.

BENGALI PORRIDGE

For millions, this savory dish provides great comfort and nutrition. If that wasn't reason enough, it is absolutely delicious and simply to execute. I see this as a template and base to which one may add a wide variety of garnishes, including salsa frescas.

LEVEL: Basic

YIELD: approximately 4 servings

INGREDIENTS

1 cup Jasmine rice, washed several times and soaked in cold water for 15 minutes
1 teaspoon turmeric powder (or a 1 inch piece of fresh turmeric, if available)
1 inch fresh ginger, minced
3 cloves garlic, sliced thinly
2 tablespoons unsalted butter or vegetable oil
1/2 teaspoon Kashmiri red chili powder
1/2 cup red lentils, sorted and rinsed
6 cups vegetable stock or water
2 small Yukon gold potatoes, medium diced
1 portobello mushroom, cleaned well, medium diced
1 bunch cilantro, finely chopped
2 green chilies, finely chopped
zest and juice of 1 lime
2 tablespoons mustard oil
fried shallot or red onion, for garnish
salt & pepper, in stages and per taste

METHOD

In a saucepan over medium heat, melt butter or oil. Add turmeric, ginger, garlic, and red chili powder, and cook for about 1 minute. Add the rice, lentils, and stock. Season with salt and freshly ground black pepper. Bring to a boil, then reduce to a bare simmer. Simmer porridge, uncovered, until rice and lentils are tender, about 30 minutes. Stir periodically to prevent burning the bottom of the pan.

While the rice and lentils are cooking, in a separate shallow pan, heat the mustard oil and sauté the mushrooms, potato, and green chile. Be sure to season with salt and pepper. After the potatoes are cooked, transfer the mixture to the porridge. Re-season as needed. Simmer on low for 5 more minutes before finishing each serving with the chopped cilantro, lime zest and juice, and fried shallot.

SOUTH OF THE BORDER RISOTTO

> Not long after culinary school, while still being enamored with food on television, I tried seriously to be a contestant on a TV food show. The year was 2006 (well before the restaurant) and for my cooking segment, I prepared a version of this dish. I never made the show (that may have been for the best), but I've always thought that this dish was a nice use of flavors from Mexico while still maintaining the integrity of the Italian staple.

LEVEL: Basic

YIELD: approximately 4 servings

INGREDIENTS
- 2 cups arborio rice
- 1/2 cup diced tomatillos
- 1/4 cup roasted or grilled corn, off the cob
- 1/2 cup diced fuji or similar apple
- 1 jalapeño, diced
- 1/2 cup tequila
- 1 tablespoon garlic, minced
- 1 small onion, minced
- 1 bay leaf
- warm seasoned vegetable or corn stock, as needed
- 1/2 cup chopped cilantro
- salt & pepper, in stages and per taste

METHOD

In a large sauté pan, start with some extra-virgin olive oil and sauté the onions and apples. Season with salt and pepper. Add the garlic, corn, jalapeno, and bay leaf and stir for a few seconds over medium heat. Next add the rice and tomatillos, stirring well, and sauté for two minutes. Deglaze with the tequila. Now add the warm stock and finish the risotto by adding more warm stock, in stages, stirring frequently to extract the starch in the rice. It is very important that the stock is well seasoned. Finish by stirring in the cilantro. Serve immediately.

BASIL & EDAMAME FRIED RICE

I once saw a comic make fun of a celebrity chef for not cooking fried rice in a wok. That was the least of the ridicule. So, I would recommend wok-cooking, if available. The quick and high-heat cooking does result in a wonderfully smoky outcome. Beyond that, it's important to have all the ingredients ready to go before beginning this journey.

LEVEL: Basic

YIELD: approximately 4 servings

INGREDIENTS

2 cups cooked white rice, make sure the grains are mostly separate
1 cup fresh basil, chopped
1 cup fresh shelled edamame, blanched in salted water
1/4 cup low sodium soy sauce
1 teaspoon sesame oil
1 teaspoon yellow mustard
1 tablespoon fresh ginger, minced
3 cloves fresh garlic, minced
1 shallot, sliced thinly
1 teaspoon chili garlic paste or sambal olek
2 tablespoons vegetable oil
2 eggs, beaten (optional)
salt & pepper, in stages and per taste

METHOD

In a bowl, mix the soy sauce, mustard, sesame oil, and chili garlic paste. Heat the vegetable oil in a shallow pan or wok. When medium hot, add the shallots, ginger, and garlic. Cook for a minute, stirring frequently. Next add the blanched edamame and cook for 2 minutes. If using eggs, add them now and cook the eggs almost to the scrambled stage. Next add the cooked rice and mix all the ingredients well on a medium high heat so that the rice is frying a bit and even browning a bit. Finally, adding the soy mixture from the bowl and mix well. Maintain a good heat for at least 3 minutes. Taste and re-season as desired. Finish with the fresh basil and stir well with the heat on for 2 more minutes before turning off the heat. Serve hot or warm.

PULIHARA

> One of my favorite and most comforting rice dishes. I would plead with my mother to make this dish because it ate so well even days later. I love peanuts in rice.

LEVEL: Basic

YIELD: approximately 4 servings

INGREDIENTS

2 cups cooked long-grained rice like Basmati, preferably cooled, fluffed, and separate
1/2 cup tamarind water (dissolve fresh tamarind in warm water for several minutes, squeeze)
1 tablespoon Jaggery or dark brown sugar
1/4 cup skin on peanuts, roasted
1 teaspoon black mustard seed
1 teaspoon cumin seed
1 tablespoon chana dal
2 dry red chili like chili de arbol
3 small Indian green chilies, deseeded and slit length-wise
1 teaspoon turmeric powder
1/4 teaspoon asafoetida
1 sprig fresh curry leaves
2 tablespoon vegetable oil
1 tablespoon sesame oil
salt & pepper, in stages and per taste

METHOD

Heat vegetable oil in a heavy bottomed pan and when the oil is hot, add the mustard seeds, cumin seeds, dry red chilis, green chilis, curry leaves and sauté for 15 seconds. The seeds will start crackling. Next, add the turmeric powder, asafoetida powder, jaggery, the tamarind pulp, some salt, and some pepper. Cook the tamarind pulp in the seasoning for about 5 minutes over medium heat, stirring frequently. Once the pulp is thick, add the cooked rice and peanuts and stir to combine all the ingredients well. Cover the pan and allow the rice to absorb all the flavors from the tangy masala. Finish with the sesame oil for added aroma and flavor.

KHICHIDI

A humble one pot meal like few others - similar in composition to the Bengali porridge.

LEVEL: Basic

YIELD: approximately 4 servings

INGREDIENTS

1 small onion, diced
1/2 cup carrots, diced
1/4 cup edamame or green peas
1 teaspoon whole black peppercorns
1 teaspoon cumin seed
1 bay leaf
1 inch piece ginger, minced
2 green chilies or 1 jalapeño, minced
pinch of ground asafoetida
1 cup green, red or brown lentils, washed and drained
1/2 cup cremini mushrooms
1 cup rice, washed several times and soaked
1 teaspoon turmeric powder
1/2 teaspoon cayenne or red chili powder
4 cups vegetable stock or water
vegetable or olive oil, as needed
salt & pepper, in stages and per taste

METHOD

In a shallow pot with a proper lid, heat some oil and sauté the onions, carrots, ginger, bay leaf, mushrooms, and chilies on medium heat for about 10 minutes. Season with some salt. Next add the lentil and turmeric powder. Cook for about 15 minutes, stirring frequently. Now add the rice and edamame, stir well, season with some salt, and add the liquid. Stir well and taste the broth to make sure it is seasoned to your liking. Cover the pot, reduce the heat to low-medium and cook for 20 minutes. Open the lid one time at the end to make sure the lentils are cooked.

In a small pan, heat some oil on medium-hot setting. When the oil is hot, add the cumin seeds, peppercorns, asafoetida, and curry leaves and fry for 15 seconds. Immediately pour everything including the infused oil onto the rice and lentil dish. This step is referred to the "tadka" stage. Gently mix the dish together and serve with a wedge of lime and some yogurt.

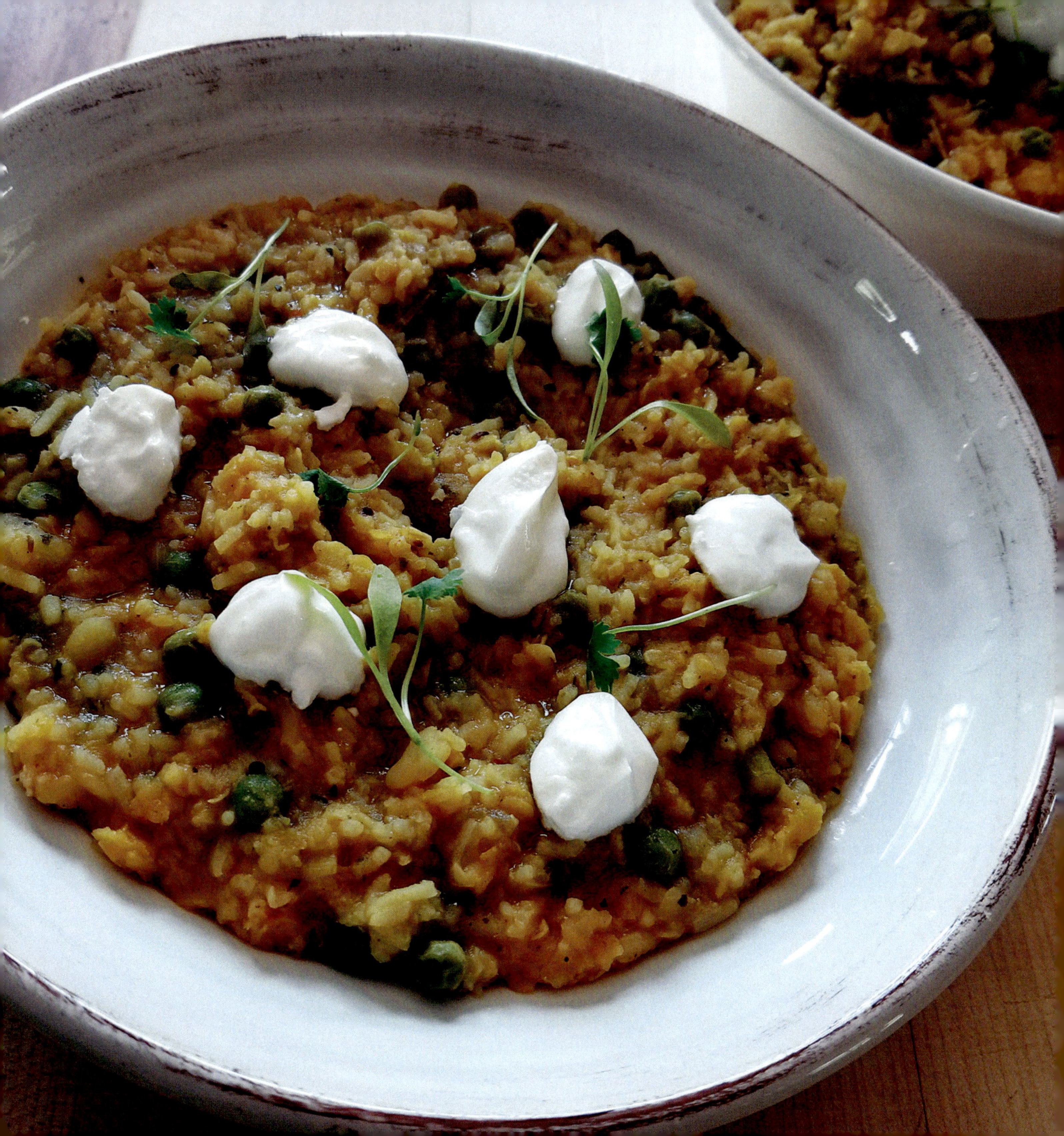

COCONUT HABANERO

> Coconut milk provides a wonderful richness to rice dishes, and since one cooks the rice on a low temperature, the coconut milk doesn't separate. This dish eats like a truly tropical dish. In a way, addition of coconut milk to the cooking liquid is consistent with my addition of coconut milk to a ceviche marinade – *Tiger's Milk*.

LEVEL: Basic

YIELD: approximately 4 servings

INGREDIENTS
- 2 cups medium grained Puerto Rican rice
- 1 large red onion, sliced thinly
- 1 tbs fresh ginger, minced
- 2 habanero or scotch bonnet peppers, minced
- 1.5 cups coconut milk
- 1 tablespoon fresh thyme leaves
- 2 bay leaves
- 1 cup canned (or rehydrated) pigeon peas, drained and rinsed
- 1/2 cup fire-roasted canned tomatoes
- 2 cups vegetable stock or water
- vegetable or olive oil, as needed
- salt & pepper, in stages and per taste

METHOD
Sauté the onions, ginger, peppers in vegetable or olive oil in a heavy bottomed pot. Add the rice and sauté for a minute. Add the remaining ingredients (Note: The proportion of total liquid to rice should be slightly more than the rice requires to cook properly). Bring to a simmer and cover tightly. Reduce heat to a low setting. Stir only once or twice during the cooking.

RED BEANS & RICE

> Jenneffer and I used to religiously camp twice a year at the Spirit of the Suwanee Blue Grass Festival near Live Oak, FL. At night on the way back to our primitive tent, we would stop by the happy guy who served vegetarian red beans and rice with hot sauce, sour cream, and scallions. Cold nights, beautiful music, love in the air, free spirits, and spicy red beans and rice.

LEVEL: Intermediate

YIELD: approximately 4 servings

INGREDIENTS

2 cups Louisiana long to medium grain rice, washed and soaked in water
2 cups dried kidney beans, soaked 24 hours in 8 cups of initially warm water
2 cups onion, small diced
1 cup celery, small diced
1 cup green bell pepper, small diced
1 poblano pepper, small diced
2 bay leaves
2 jalapeños, minced
4 cloves garlic, minced
1 bunch flat leaf parsley, chopped finely
1 cup tomatoes, diced
2 tablespoon plain paprika
1 tablespoon cayenne pepper
1 tablespoon onion powder
2 tablespoon dried thyme
1 teaspoon cumin powder
2 tablespoon dried oregano
1/4 cup Louisiana hot sauce
extra virgin olive oil, as needed
vegetable stock, as needed
salt & pepper, in stages and per taste

METHOD

There are two ways to execute this dish. One could either cook the rice and beans together or one could cook them separately and mix together. For ease of execution, one may choose the latter, but we will go with the former.

Drain the beans. In a heavy bottomed, wide pan, heat the oil and cook the trinity (onions, all peppers, celery) for 5 minutes. Add the garlic and cook for 5 minutes. Next add the remaining spices and cook for 2 minutes. Now add the beans, tomatoes, and enough vegetable stock to cover the beans. Season well with salt and cover the pan. Cook on medium heat for about an hour, stirring frequently. Taste the beans and make sure they are almost cooked. Now add the rice, hot sauce, enough stock to help cook the rice, more salt, as needed and stir well. Cover the pan and reduce the heat to low-medium. Do not open the lid until the recommended cook time for the rice. Turn the rice over once so the top layer has a chance to cook. Cover and cook for another 10 minutes. Turn off the heat and serve after 15 minutes.

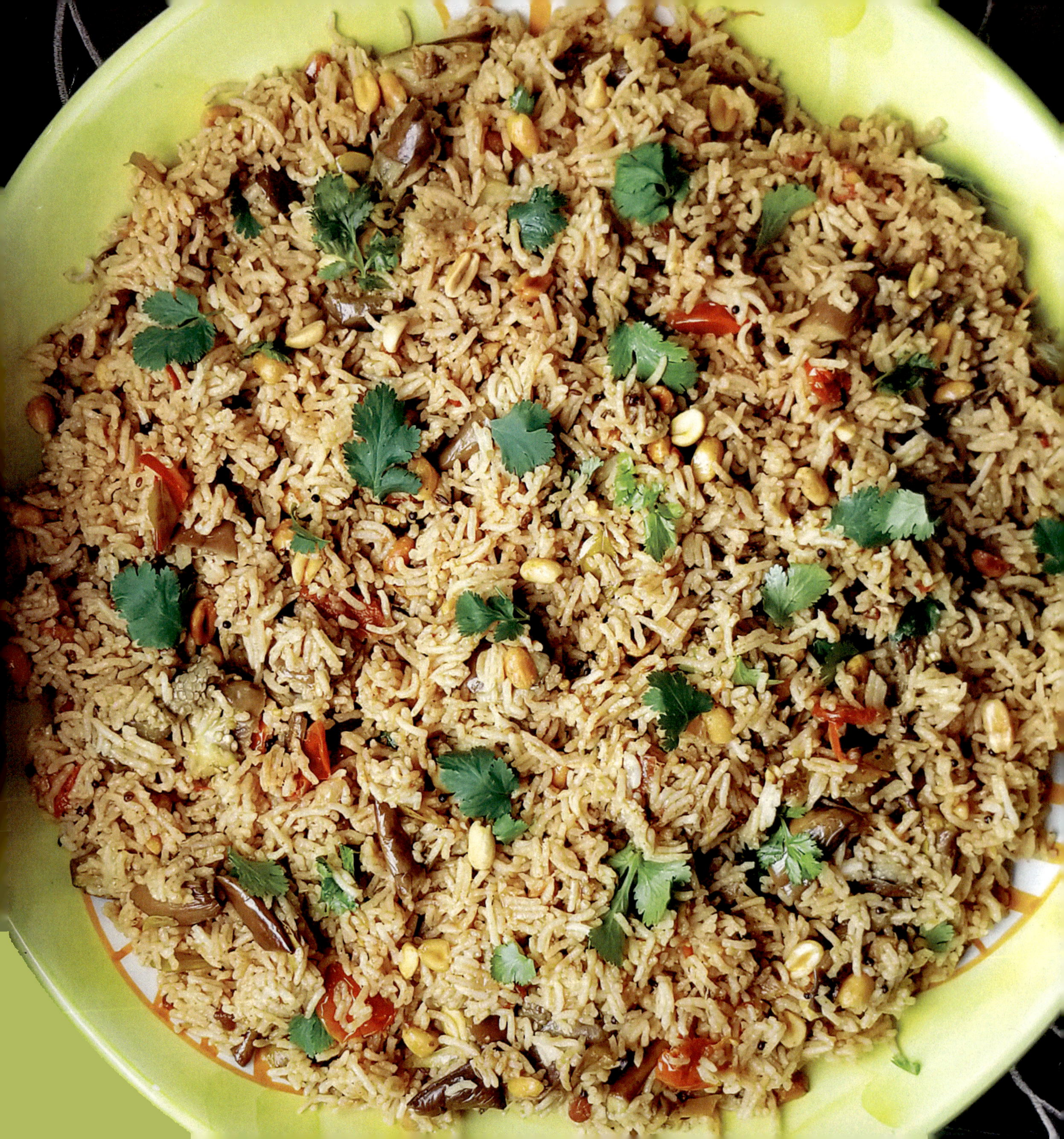

EGGPLANT & TAMARIND

> Tomato and eggplant are well-suited for a variety of dishes. Of course, we all know about combinations in Italian dishes. This dish can be made in two different ways. In graduate school, during my period of "death by rice," I would make a one pot version of this, in which I cooked the whole dish by building layers in one pot. Now, I would do this separately. The rice can be cooked separately and the eggplant and tomato compote separately, and then we simply and carefully mix the two for a more perfectly cooked rice. The only disadvantage is that the rice doesn't absorb the flavors of the dish. But that's how the basmati gets to shine.

LEVEL: Basic

YIELD: approximately 4 servings

INGREDIENTS
- 2 cups basmati rice, washed a few times
- 2 cups diced eggplant
- 2 tablespoon tamarind paste dissolved in warm water
- 1 teaspoon cumin seeds
- 1 teaspoon mustard seeds
- 5 curry leaves
- 1/2 cup peanuts, toasted
- 4 Indian green chilies or 2 jalapeños, minced
- vegetable oil as needed
- 2 cups tomatoes, diced
- 1 tablespoon ginger, grated or minced
- 1/4 cup cilantro, chopped
- 1 tsp. turmeric powder
- 4 cups of water
- salt & pepper, in stages and per taste

METHOD
Cook the rice in a little more than 3 cups of water and hold it. In a saucepan, sauté the cumin seeds, mustard seeds, curry leaves, green chilies, ginger, and eggplant in some vegetable oil for about 15 minutes until the eggplant is soft. Next add the tamarind water, turmeric, and tomatoes. Season with salt and pepper as needed. Stew down this mixture and when the eggplant is fully cooked, fold this mixture uniformly into the rice. Garnish the rice with the peanuts and cilantro.

PONGAL

This is a traditional rice and mung bean preparation during Hindu festivals. It is simply savory. By most standards, it would be considered a dry dish. So, it could benefit from a side of chutney or simply mango pickle, plain yogurt, and pappadam (roasted or fried lentil crisp).

LEVEL: Basic

YIELD: approximately 4 servings

INGREDIENTS
1/2 cup white rice, washed and rinsed
1/2 cup split mung beans
3 cups water
1.5 tablespoon vegetable oil
1/4 cup cashews, halved
1/2 teaspoon cumin seed
1/2 teaspoon black pepper corn, coarsely crushed
1 inch ginger, sliced thinly
1 sprig curry leaves
1 pinch asafoetida
1 pinch turmeric
1 green chili, sliced in half
salt & pepper, in stages and per taste

METHOD
Cook the rice separately in water and a small amount of salt. Do the same with mung beans. (They have different cooking times.) Mix the cooked mung beans and rice. Check the seasoning to make sure the salt is adequate. In a sauté pan, heat some oil and add the cashews, cumin, black pepper, ginger, asafoetida, turmeric, and chili. Stirring constantly, cook for 1 minute. Pour all of this into the rice and mix well. Serve the Pongal with either a coconut chutney or sambhar and some fried poppadum.

DADDOJANAM (SOUTH INDIAN CURD RICE)

The greatest childhood memory I have of comfort food involves a type of snake gourd called *padval* in the style of a *koora* (the Telugu word for a vegetable bhaji)--roasted simply with mustard seeds, fresh coconut, simple spices, and curry leaves – mixed with plain steamed rice and homemade plain yogurt. I would cherish the bhaji all through the meal because there was only so much to go around. But when I still had some left on my plate, the traditional final course comprised of curd rice mixed judiciously with each bite with the *padval koora*.

LEVEL: Basic

YIELD: approximately 4 servings

INGREDIENTS
- 1 cup medium grained white rice, like Puerto Rican rice
- 2 cup water
- 2 cups plain yogurt
- 2 green chile like serrano, chopped
- 1 tablespoon fresh ginger, minced
- 6 curry leaves, chopped
- 2 sprigs chopped fresh cilantro leaves and stems
- 1 tablespoon coconut oil
- 1 teaspoon mustard seeds
- 1 whole red chile
- 1 teaspoon urad dal
- 8 whole curry leaves
- pinch asafoetida
- salt & pepper, in stages and per taste

METHOD

Wash and rinse the rice several times. Cook it according to the instructions. Be sure to add salt in water. In a bowl, combine the yogurt, some water, green chile, fresh ginger, chopped curry leaves, and chopped cilantro. While the rice is still slightly warm, transfer it to a larger bowl and gently mix the yogurt mixture into the cooked rice. Be careful to not break the rice grains completely. Add more water and yogurt depending on how thin you prefer the rice. Traditionally, it should be the consistency of porridge or oatmeal.

The last step is the tempering or tadka stage. In a small pan, heat the coconut oil and add the mustard seeds, red chile, dal, curry leaves and asafoetida. The mustard seeds and curry leaves will crackle. After 20 seconds or so, pour this entire mixture into the yogurt and rice mixture.

Serve chilled, at room temperature, or slightly warm depending on your preference. Traditionally, it is accompanied with Indian lime or mango pickle and papad.

UMAMI RICE PILAF

> This summer, I began taking cooking demos in the kitchen of our house. These are one-take, real-time cooking videos where I make the entire dish from start to finish with a grand reveal. One episode involved this rice dish which is fragrant and feels like it was pampered, but it wasn't.

LEVEL: Basic

YIELD: approximately 4 servings

INGREDIENTS

1 cup Jasmine or Basmati rice, washed well and soaked in water for 15 minutes, drained well
1 tablespoon fresh ginger, chopped coarsely
3 small radishes, quartered
1 small hot or mild green fresh green chili of your liking, minced. I used serrano.
1 whole star anise
1/4 cup Tamari soy sauce
1 tablespoon extra-virgin olive oil
1.5 cups water
salt & pepper, in stages and per taste

METHOD

Over medium heat, sauté the ginger, chilies, and radish in olive oil. Add salt and soy sauce. Simmer for a minute. Add the rice and mix well. Add the water and mix well. Taste the broth and adjust seasoning as preferred. Cover and reduce heat to low-medium. Rice should be done in 12-15 minutes. Let it rest for 10 minutes, covered. Enjoy as is or as an accompaniment.

Note: You may simply add all ingredients to a rice cooker and follow the directions.

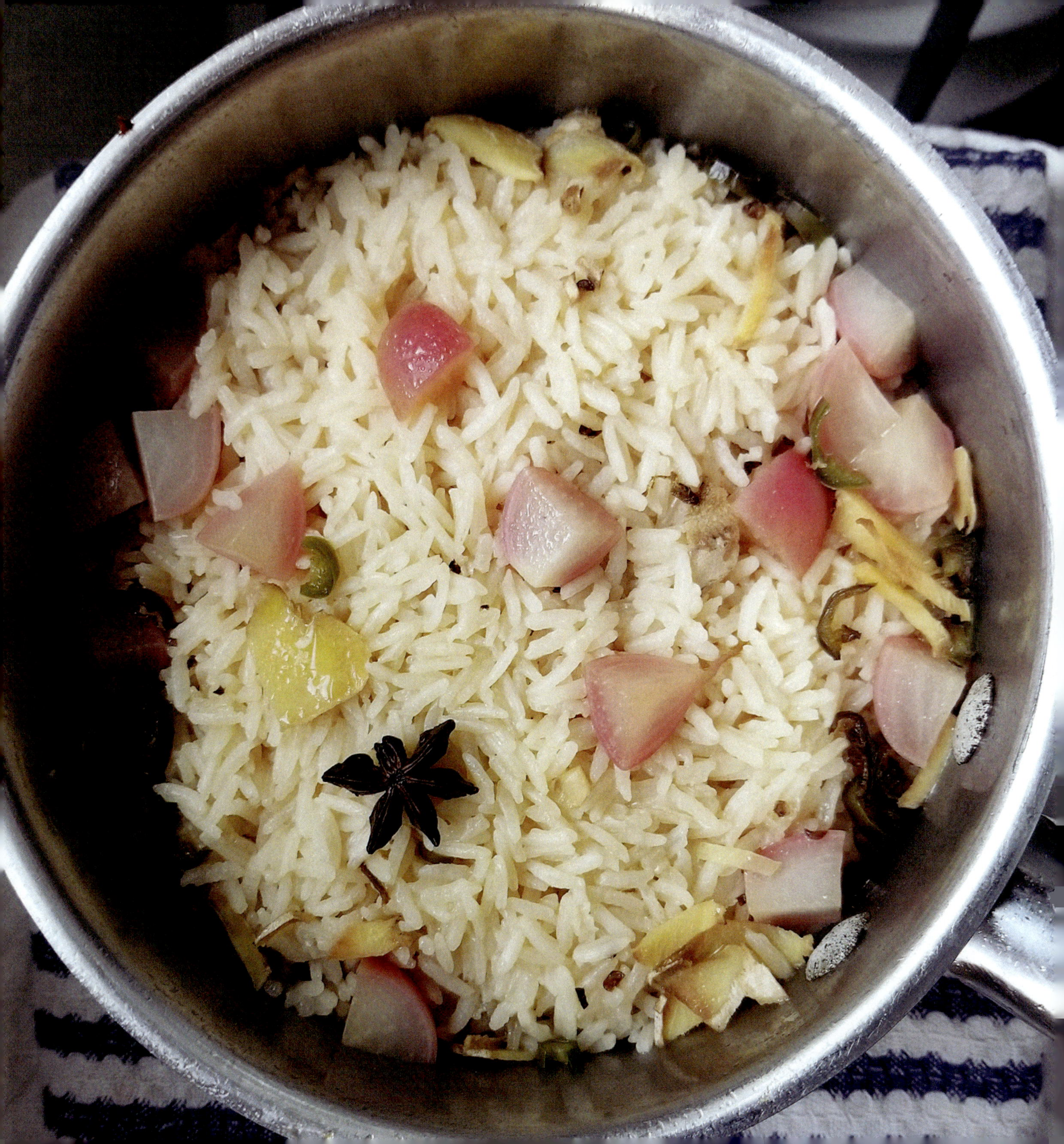

Grains

Whole grains are the powerhouse of the plant world. Can you imagine a world without bread? How about a world without rice or corn? Now can you imagine a world without farro, quinoa, freekeh, bulgur, barley, sorghum? You probably can, but we shouldn't.

HEIRLOOM GRAIN & FIDDLEHEAD FERN FARROTTO

I've used fiddlehead ferns only a few times, but I appreciate their vegetal notes. As a routine "chef performer" on the local morning news station, one holiday season, I was impressed that the host showed a keen interest in the fiddleheads I was using to make this precise version of a risotto except with farro, not rice. The farrotto turned out delicious, so I had to lead this section with this recipe.

LEVEL: Basic

YIELD: approximately 4 servings

INGREDIENTS
1/2 cup farro
1/2 cup wild rice
1/2 cup pearl cous-cous
1 teaspoon minced shallots or red onion
1 teaspoon minced fresh garlic
1 teaspoon lemon zest
1/2 cup heavy cream
1 tablespoon unsalted butter
1 cup dry white wine
vegetable stock, as needed
2 cups fiddlehead ferns (substitute asparagus)
salt & pepper, in stages and per taste

METHOD
Dry toast the farro and wild rice in a sauté pan for 1 minute. In a pot of unsalted water, simmer the farro and wild rice for about 45 minutes. Add the cous-cous and cook for an additional 15 minutes or so until the cous-cous is cooked, but not overcooked. Drain and toss in extra-virgin olive oil so the grains don't stick together. Add 3/4 of the fresh herbs to the panko breadcrumbs and mix. Set aside. Clean the fiddlehead ferns well, blanch in salted water for about 4-5 minutes. Cool in an ice bath. Set aside.

In a sauté pan, add some olive oil and sauté the onions until translucent. Add the garlic and stir well for about 15 seconds. Add the blanched fiddlehead ferns (or asparagus), and the cooked grains. Stir well. Next add the cooked grains and some heavy cream. Taste to make sure it's all well-seasoned. Finish with a pat of butter, the remaining fresh herbs, and the lemon zest.

BULGUR KACHORI

> Kachoris are these perfectly delectable snacks made with coconut, potato, chiles, and cashews. I would eat more than I should have at *Modern Farsan and Food Mart* just on the other side of Santa Cruz West train station. I've tried to replicate the experience while twisting it ever so slightly – now that I'm a trained chef and all.

LEVEL: Intermediate

YIELD: approximately 4 servings

INGREDIENTS
- 2 cups fine bulgur wheat
- 1/4 cup garbanzo flour
- 1 teaspoon smoked paprika
- 1 tablespoon chopped fresh parsley
- 2 cups seasoned hot water or vegetable stock
- 1 cup toasted cashews chopped well
- 1/2 cup soaked golden raisins
- 1/2 cup fresh, unsweetened grated coconut
- 2 tablespoons fresh cilantro, chopped
- 1 teaspoon sesame seeds
- 1/2 teaspoon cayenne pepper
- 1 tablespoon extra-virgin olive oil
- vegetable or peanut oil, as needed
- salt & pepper, in stages and per taste

METHOD

Add the smoked paprika to the bulgur and rub the mixture with the extra-virgin oil until it is a fine crumb. Pour the warm seasoned water or stock over the bulgur and cover immediately with a plastic wrap or tight lid.

Sauté the coconut, sesame, cashew, cayenne, and raisins in some vegetable oil until the coconut is slightly brown. Season with salt and pepper and fold in the cilantro. This mixture should be dry and is the filling.

After 15 minutes, check to see that the bulgur is cooked. Let it cool completely and add the chopped parsley. Using your fingers and palm squeeze the bulgur to break it down. Add the garbanzo flour. Adjust as much flour as needed to be able to form a ball.

Flatten a 1-inch ball in your palm, moistening your fingertips. Add a tablespoon of filling in the center of the flattened bulgur paste. Pull in the sides and form a stuffed kofta. Shape it as desired, but rounds are acceptable.

Deep or shallow fry the koftas in oil. Drain on paper towels and serve with your favorite chutney.

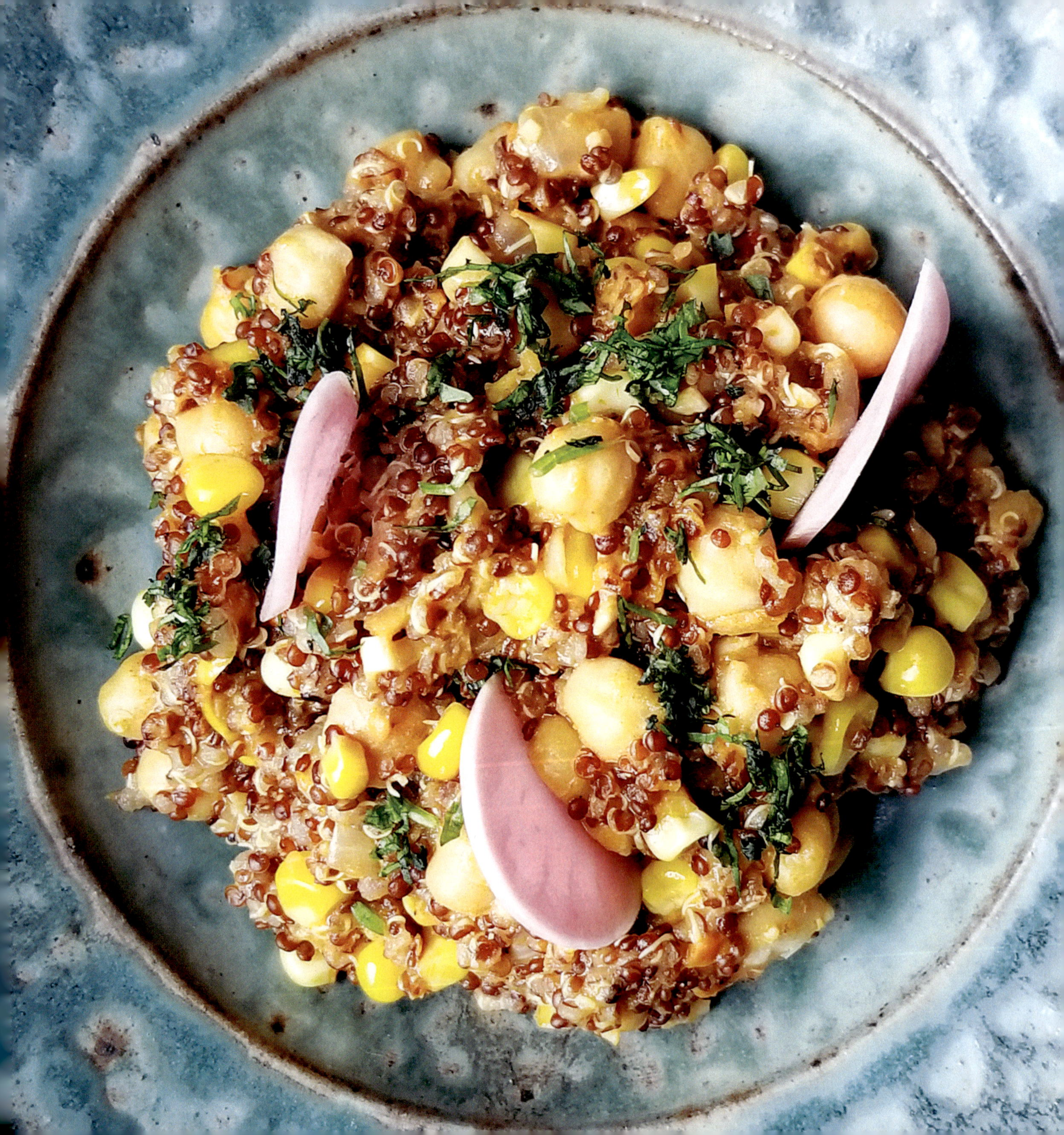

QUINOA, GARBANZO, CORN PILAF

> This pilaf (warm salad) is precisely the kind of dish one can make with hearty grains like corn and quinoa. In my view, the progression of savory to sweet in going from quinoa to corn aptly tells the story of how important grains are in our diet not only for nutritional purposes, but also for a balance of flavor and texture.

LEVEL: Basic

YIELD: approximately 4 servings

INGREDIENTS
- 1 cup diced carrots
- 1 cup diced celery
- 2 cup diced onions
- 1 tablespoon minced garlic
- 1 tablespoon ground cumin
- corn from 2 cobs
- 2 cups fresh tomatoes, chopped
- 2 bay leaves
- 1 cup chopped parsley
- 1 cup quinoa
- 2 cups cooked, ready to eat garbanzo
- 2 cups coconut milk
- extra virgin olive oil, as needed
- coarse salt and black pepper, to taste

METHOD
In a heavy-bottomed saucepan, sauté the carrots, celery, and onions on medium heat in some extra virgin olive oil. Add some salt and pepper to layer flavors. After about 5 minutes, add the bay leaves, garlic, and cumin and cook, stirring for about 2 minutes. Next add the corn and garbanzo and cook for about 10 minutes. Next stir in the tomatoes and cook for about 10 minutes. Now add the quinoa and stir well. Add the coconut milk and stir well. Taste the liquid to make sure it is well seasoned. Add salt as needed. Cover and bring to a low simmer. Cover and cook on medium-low for about 20 minutes. Shut off the flame and keep it covered for about 15 minutes. Fluff with a fork.

FREEKEH TABBOULEH

LEVEL: Basic

YIELD: approximately 4 servings

INGREDIENTS
1.5 cups freekeh
zest and juice of 1 lemon
2 tablespoon fruity, extra-virgin olive oil
1 clove garlic, grated
1 bunch flat-leaf parsley leaves, chopped finely
2 cups ripe cherry tomatoes, halved
1/2 teaspoon za'atar
1 red onion, sliced thinly
1 tablespoon red wine vinegar
water, as needed
salt & pepper, in stages and per taste

METHOD
Soak the garlic in the vinegar and lemon juice in a large glass bowl. Cook the freekeh according to the instructions on the packaging in salted water. Drain well. Add one tablespoon of olive oil to the cooked freekeh and stir in the za'atar. Add the tomatoes, parsley, and remaining olive oil to the garlic in the bowl and mix well. Add salt and pepper, as desired. Fold in the za'atar-spiced freekeh and refrigerate for 30 minutes before stirring well and serving.

SHIITAKE & THYME GRITS

LEVEL: Basic

YIELD: approximately 4 servings

INGREDIENTS
8 oz. yellow corn grits
2 tablespoon unsalted butter
1 small yellow onion or shallot, minced
1 bay leaf (fresh, if available)
1/4 cup shiitake mushrooms, chopped finely
1 tablespoon fresh thyme, picked, chopped coarsely
1 cup half and half or heavy cream
2 cups water, more as needed
salt & pepper, in stages and per taste

METHOD
Melt the butter in a heavy-bottomed saucepan or sauce pot. Add the onions (or shallots), bay leaf, fresh thyme, and mushrooms, and sauté until the butter browns and ingredients exude a nutty aroma. Season with salt and pepper. Add the heavy cream and two cups of water. Season this broth very well. Once it begins to simmer slightly, reduce the heat to a low medium and whisk in the grits slowly, stirring constantly. Stir in a uniform rounded motion using a whip. Continue stirring until the mixture starts thickening. You may need to add more water if the grits are getting too thick before being fully cooked. The process takes about an hour including resting the grits.

TOASTED BARLEY & MIREPOIX STEW

Beef and Barley, move aside. There is a new stew in town. This recipe is a good illustration of soup-making fundamentals. When it's all done, this is as hearty a stew as any other.

LEVEL: Basic

YIELD: approximately 4 servings

INGREDIENTS

1/2 cup barley, washed well, dried well
2 cups onion, small diced
1 cup carrots, small diced
1 cup celery, small diced
2 cloves garlic, minced
2 sprigs fresh thyme, leaves chopped
1 sprig fresh rosemary, leave whole
1 bay leaf (fresh, if available)
2 quarts vegetable stock
1/2 cup red bliss potatoes, medium diced
1/2 cup green or field peas, shucked
1/4 cup fresh parsley, chopped
2 tablespoons extra-virgin olive oil
salt & pepper, in stages and per taste

METHOD

In a heavy bottomed pan, dry toast the barley for about 15 minutes. Alternatively, you may spread it on a baking sheet and toast in a 350F oven for the same amount of time. Typically, I like to see my food cooking, so I prefer to do this on a stove top.

In a medium sized pot, heat the olive oil and sauté the onion, carrot, and celery for 10 minutes on medium heat until the onions start to brown a bit. Add the garlic, chopped thyme, rosemary sprig, bay leaf, and toasted barley. Mix the ingredients and season with some salt and pepper. Add the stock and a bit more seasoning. Cover the pot and reduce the heat to medium-low. Periodically check on the stew to make sure you have enough liquid in the pot. If needed, add more stock or water. The total cook time on the barley is about an hour. Forty-five minutes into the cooking process, add the potatoes and peas. The barley and potatoes will naturally thicken the stew. Once you are pleased with the seasoning, doneness of the barley, and thickness of the stew, remove the bay leaf and rosemary sprig. Mix in the chopped parsley.

Serve with some steamed white rice or crusty bread.

SORGHUM ROTI & DAL

In parts of India, sorghum is referred to as *jowar*. I have a vague recollection of my mother making a steamed dish simply with salt, cracked wheat, and a grain that could very well have been sorghum. We ate it simply with plain homemade yogurt and lime pickle. The sorghum roti is the perfectly hearty and nutritious pick-up tool for a dal. It is a lifeline and staple meal for hard-working folks in India.

LEVEL: Basic

YIELD: approximately 4

INGREDIENTS
1 cup sorghum flour (aka jowar flour)
1 tablespoon extra-virgin or vegetable oil
3/4 cup warm water, more or less
pinch or two of salt
4 cups of masala dal (page 162) or dal makhani (page 283)

METHOD
In a bowl, mix the salt and flour. Rub the oil in-to the flour using the palm of your hand until you reach a small crumb. Make a well and add 1/2 cup water into the well. Bring in the flour into the warm water and mix well. Add more water as needed to form a uniform dough. Adjust the amount of flour or water as needed to achieve a consistency that feels a bit like masa for tortillas. Knead the dough well. Cover and allow the dough to come to room temperature. Make medium sized balls. Sprinkle some sorghum flour on your work surface and roll out gently. You may also use a tortilla press to flatten the dough.

Cook the roti on a hot cast-iron or non-stick pan. Cook on one side for about 2 minutes. While it's still on the first side, sprinkle some water on the uncooked side. Flip the roti and cook on the other side until you see dark spots on that side. If available, flip the roti onto an open flame to puff it up. If an open flame is not available, simply cook it on the pan back on the original side until you see dark spots and the dough is completely opaque. If desired, spread some oil or butter before storing in an airtight container as you would tortillas.

Serve with your favorite version of Indian-style legumes.

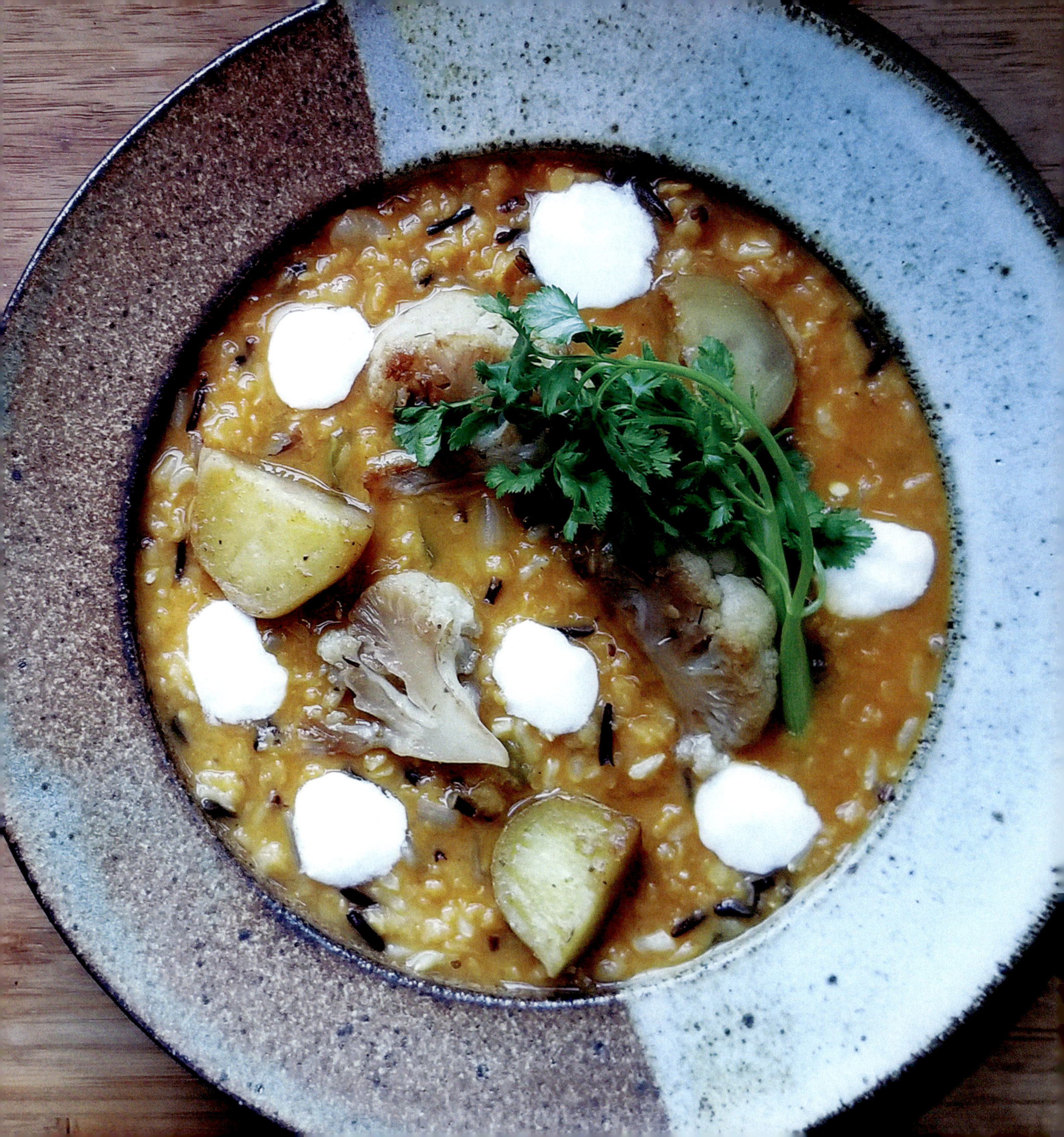

BUCKWHEAT CRÊPE

LEVEL: Basic

YIELD: approximately 8

INGREDIENTS
1 cup buckwheat flour
1/4 cup all-purpose flour
1 egg
1/2 cup milk or buttermilk, plus more if needed
2 tablespoons butter, melted and cooled
pinch or two of salt
butter for cooking the crêpes

METHOD
Sift the flours into a bowl. Add the salt and mix well. Whisk the egg and milk together. In a bowl or in a mixer on low speed, whisk in the egg-milk mixture into the flour mixture until just mixed together. Do not overwork the batter. Slowly drizzle in the melted butter until fully incorporated. Cover the batter and let it rest for at least 30 minutes. If resting for beyond that amount of time, refrigerate the batter. Make the crêpes as you would any other. Serve them either as is or consider filling them with your favorite savory filling like, say, exotic mushroom duxelle or a roasted tomato and goat cheese compote.

ROASTED CORN SALSA

LEVEL: Basic

YIELD: approximately 8 servings

INGREDIENTS
4 ears of corn, husk removed
1/2 cup ripe grape or cherry tomatoes
1 jalapeño or serrano pepper, minced
1 small red bell pepper, small diced
1 poblano pepper, small diced
zest and juice of 1 lemon
zest and juice of 1 lime
3 cloves garlic, minced
1 teaspoon white balsamic vinegar
extra-virgin olive oil, as needed
3 sprigs fresh cilantro, leaves and stems chopped
coarse salt and black pepper, to taste

METHOD
Preheat an oven to 375F. Brush the corn with olive oil, season with salt and pepper and roast for 45 minutes on a baking sheet. Rotate the corn for even roasting. While the corn is roasting, steep the garlic in the combined vinegar and citrus juices and zest. After the roasted corn has cooled a bit, take the kernels off the cob with a knife and use the back of the knife to extract the corn "milk." In a glass or non-reactive bowl, combine all the ingredients. Taste it for balance of acidity, salt, and spice. Adjust as desired. Store in a refrigerator and shake periodically to re-circulate the flavors.

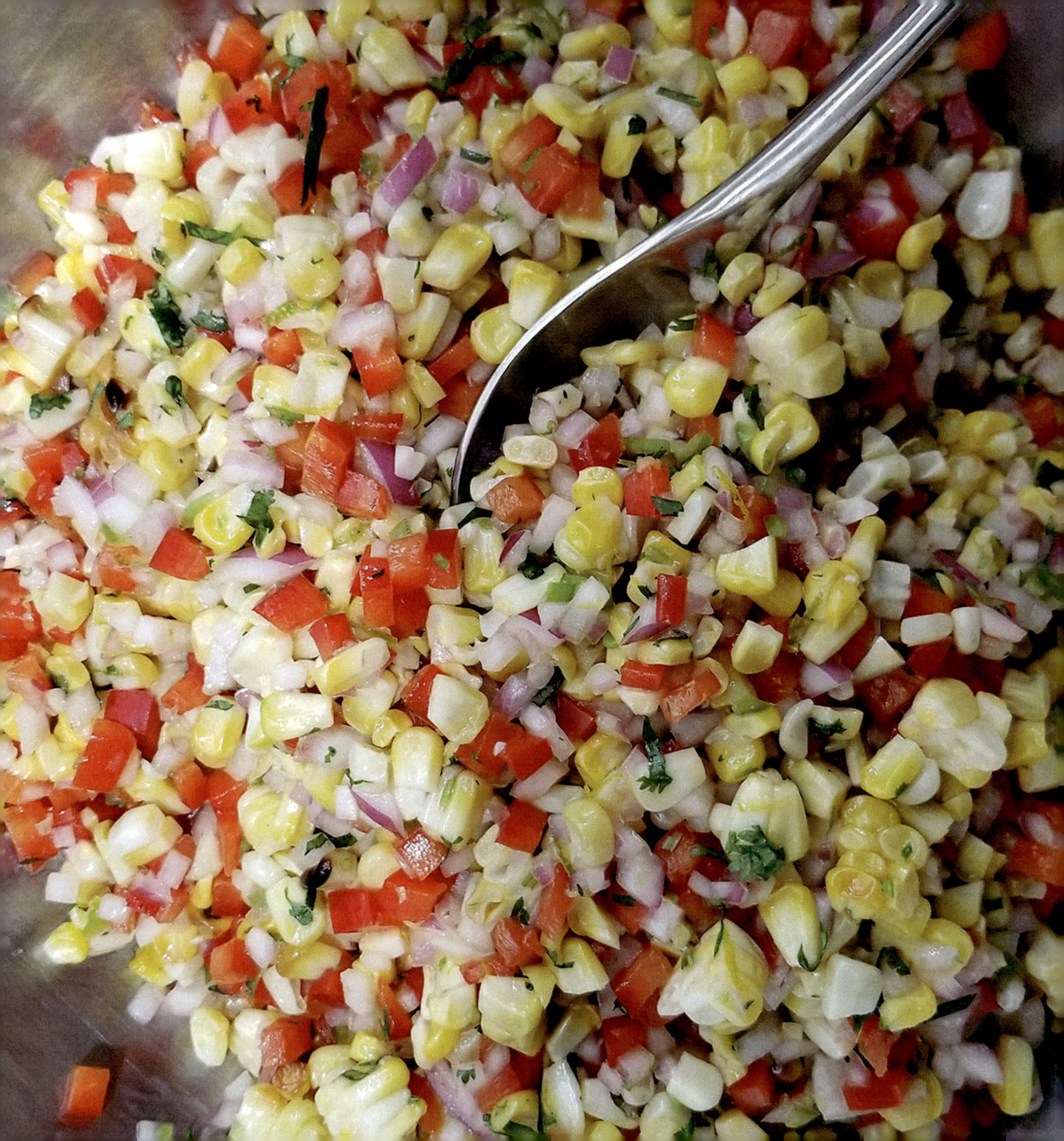

WILD RICE & CRANBERRY

Wild rice is the grain obtained from one of four species of grasses. This dish could very well be served as a warm salad with the addition of greens and maybe nuts. In fact, adding a roasted hard squash like acorn or butternut completes this as a fantastic accompaniment to any holiday table.

LEVEL: Basic

YIELD: approximately 4 servings

INGREDIENTS
2 cups assorted wild rice
1 bay leaf
1 sprig fresh thyme
enough water to cook the rice
1/4 cup fresh cranberries (if available)
1/2 cup dried cranberries
1/4 cup toasted walnuts
your favorite dressing, as much as needed
1/4 cup assorted fresh herbs like basil and mint
salt & pepper, in stages and per taste

METHOD
In salted water, add the bay leaf and fresh thyme spring to some salted water and cook the wild rice. Note that wild rice does not contain too much starch and will not expand much, so you can use more water than on the package directions. I use about a 3:1 water to rice ratio. Ten minutes in, add the fresh cranberries, if using. After the rice is cooked (about 30 minutes), drain it well and discard the bay leaf and thyme.

As the rice is cooking, soak the dried cranberries in warm water to rehydrate. Drain the liquid and use in desserts or dressings.

In a bowl, mix the cooked rice, both kinds of cranberries, toasted walnuts and dressing to your liking. Finish with the fresh herbs and serve at warm or at room temperature.

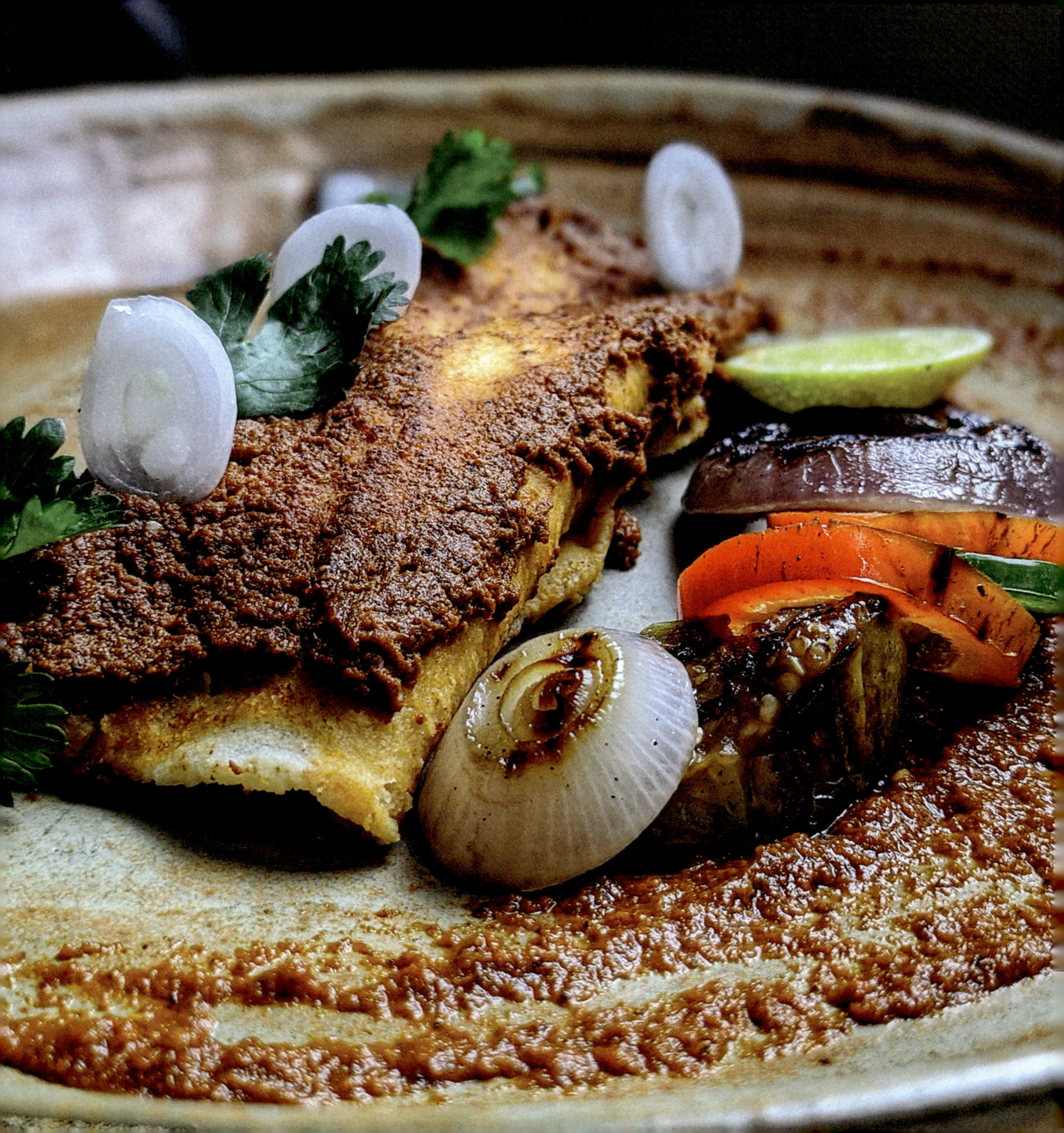

Legumes

Beans, peas, and lentils form the main source of plant protein for much of the vegetarian world. But every cuisine I can think of has found a place for legumes. Peanuts are legumes. Indian, Latin, and to some degree Italian cuisines have done a tremendous job of incorporating legumes as the star of staple dishes. One could dedicate an entire book to the wonderful world of legumes. Maybe I will, someday.

MUNG BEAN & TURMERIC BOWL

Mung beans are extremely nutritious. As is turmeric. So, on paper, this would seem like nutrition for the sake of nutrition. However, there's a reason turmeric appears in so many Indian dishes. It provides an earthy umami that is uniquely deep. The grated coconut takes this dish distinctively to the Indian South.

LEVEL: Basil

YIELD: approximately 4 servings

INGREDIENTS
1 cup cooked sprouted or rehydrated mung beans, cooked in salted turmeric water
1 inch piece fresh turmeric, sliced thinly
1/4 cup grated fresh, unsweetened coconut
1 shallot, sliced thinly
1/4 cup roasted peanuts
1 cup fresh kale, washed and dried
1/2 teaspoon cumin seed
1/2 inch piece fresh ginger, minced
1 green chile, minced (optional)
zest and juice of 1/2 lemon or lime
1 teaspoon coconut oil
salt & pepper, in stages and per taste

METHOD
Heat the coconut oil over medium heat and add the cumin seed, ginger, and fresh turmeric. After a minute, add the shallot and green chile and cook for another minute or two. Next add cooked mung beans, fresh coconut, and peanuts. Stir the mixture and heat for a couple of minutes. Season with salt and pepper, as preferred, and cool a bit but not completely. Add the zest and juice of the lime to the kale and massage with a touch of salt and pepper. Finally, mix the kale with the mung bean mixture (while still slightly warm) and let sit for 5 minutes before serving.

LIMA & CORN SUCCOTASH

> At the end of the day, this is a modest succotash. However, the addition of fresh thyme and white wine give it a professional depth, which is both enjoyable and versatile. Although a staple in low-country cuisine, I feel as though the non-vegetarian protein used traditionally takes away from highlighting the plant-based ingredients.

LEVEL: Basic

YIELD: approximately 4 servings

INGREDIENTS

1 cup lima beans (either rehydrated and cooked in salted water or canned/drained)
1/2 cup fresh corn off the cob
1 medium onion, small diced
2 stalks scallions, sliced thinly
1/2 cup green bell pepper, small diced
1/2 cup red bell pepper, small diced
1/2 teaspoon paprika
2 cloves garlic, minced
1 sprig, fresh thyme, leaves chopped
1 sprig fresh flatleaf parsley, chopped
1 bay leaf (fresh, if available)
1 tablespoon extra-virgin olive oil, or unsalted butter
1/4 cup dry white wine
water or vegetable stock, as needed
salt & pepper, in stages and per taste

METHOD

In a sauté pan, heat the oil and cook the onions and peppers until slightly translucent (about 5 minutes). Add the bay leaf, garlic, and thyme and stir around for 1 minute. Next add the corn and lima beans, and cook for 3 minutes. Add the paprika and season with salt and pepper. Add the white wine and cook for 1 minute. If the mixture is too dry, add some water or vegetable stock to pick up all the flavor bits from the bottom of the pan. Taste the succotash for seasoning level. Finish with the parsley and scallions and serve immediately.

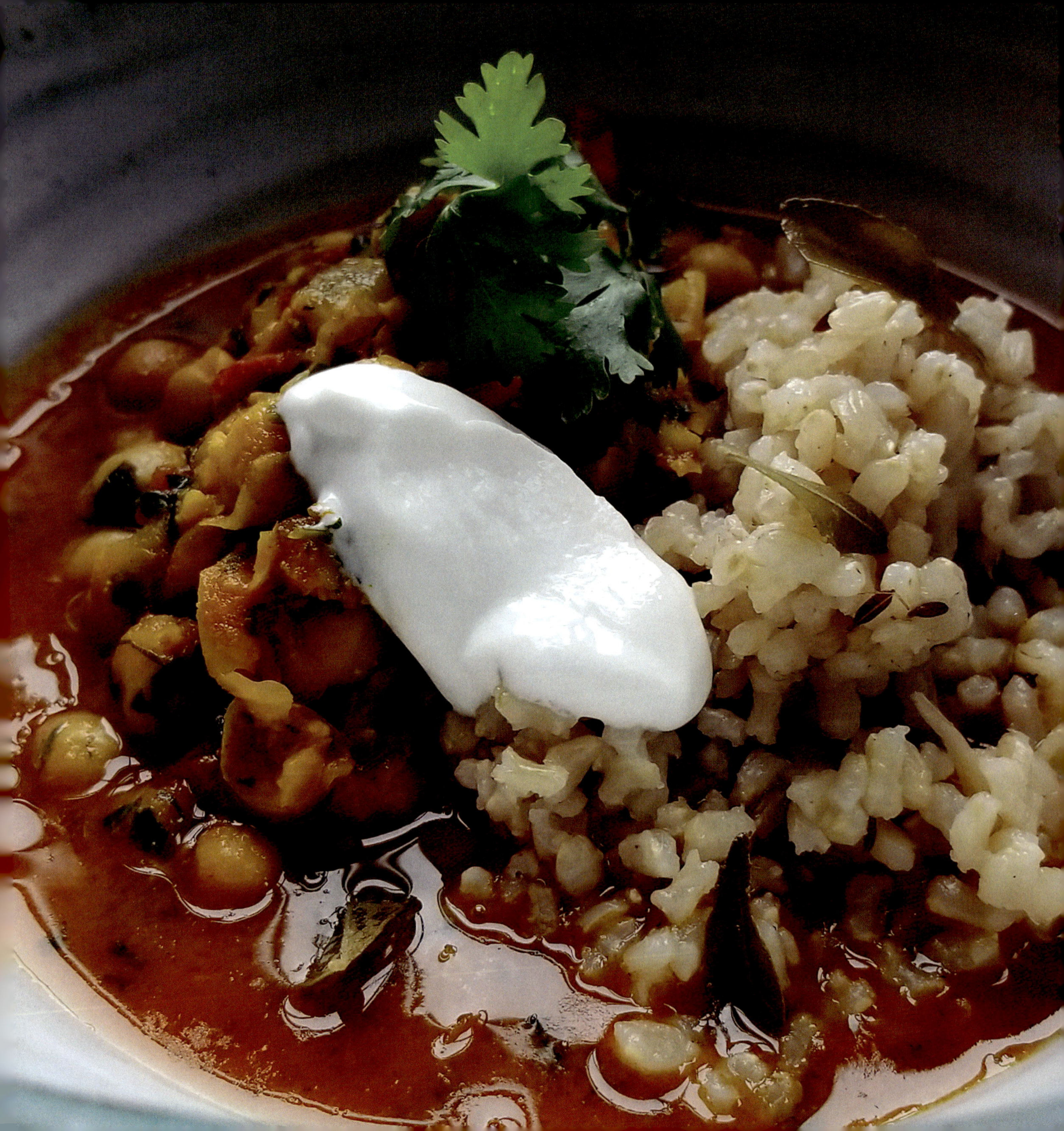

CHOLE MASALA

> This dish also goes by the name *chana masala*. This was one of my father's favorite dishes, but it was rarely made at home. He would order it from *Surang Restaurant*, a Santa Cruz West, Mumbai institution.

LEVEL: Intermediate

YIELD: approximately 4 servings

INGREDIENTS

2 cups dried Kabuli chana or dried garbanzo peas
water for cooking the chickpeas
1 medium sized onion, finely chopped
1 medium sized tomato, finely chopped
3 garlic cloves, minced
1 inch ginger, half minced, the other half sliced thinly for garnish
1 teaspoon turmeric powder
1/2 teaspoon red chili powder
1/4 teaspoon garam masala
1/2 teaspoon dry mango powder or pomegranate seed
2 to 3 green chilies, minced
2 black cardamom pods
1 inch cinnamon stick broken into pieces
4 black peppercorns
2 whole cloves
1 bay leaf
1/4 teaspoon carom seeds (ajwain)
1 teaspoon cumin seeds
1 teaspoon coriander seeds
1 teaspoon fennel seeds
1 teaspoon Kashmiri chili powder
1 cup water or the stock from cooking peas
2 tablespoon vegetable oil
1/4 cup fresh cilantro, chopped
wedges of lime or lemon
salt & pepper, in stages and per taste

METHOD

Preparing the Peas

Soak the peas overnight, starting with plenty of warm water. Strain the liquid, and using a pressure cooker (or standard boiling), cook the re-hydrated peas in water, salt, and half a teaspoon of turmeric powder until soft, but not overcooked. Drain well and reserve the liquid.

The Chole Masala

In a dry skillet, gently toast the cardamom, cinnamon, peppercorn, cloves, bay leaf, carom, cumin seed, coriander seed, fennel seeds, and Kashmiri chili powder for 10 minutes or until you can sense the aroma of the toasting spices. Grind to a fine blend using a spice grinder. This is the masala.

In a heavy-bottomed saucepan, heat the oil and brown the onions. Add the minced ginger, garlic, and green chilies, and cook for a minute. Next add the remaining ground turmeric, cumin, coriander, red chili powder, and mango powder. Cook for 2 minutes, stirring frequently. Add the tomatoes, some salt, and pepper. Stew this spiced mixture for 10 minutes until the tomatoes break down. Now add the cooked peas, the cooking liquid, and the masala. Cover and stew on a medium-low heat for 30 minutes, stirring periodically. Garnish with chopped cilantro, sliced fresh ginger and wedges of lime or lemon.

RAJMA (NORTH-INDIAN RED BEANS)

> This dish held me through the first 5 years in this country. In the early days, I would use simply garam masala that I had brought with me from India, but soon after, I began becoming more confident with spices. Think of rajma and rice as red beans and rice, but with a deeper flavor. And all accomplished without a roux or meat. Today, rajma is a staple of North Indian cuisine. The addition of heavy cream and butter is optional and may be substituted with vegetable oil. Some versions use whole black cardamom for a distinctively smokey flavor. I recommend that as well.

LEVEL: Intermediate

YIELD: approximately 4 servings

INGREDIENTS
- 2 cups dried red kidney beans, washed well, soaked overnight in ample water
- 1 large onion, minced
- 3 medium tomatoes, finely chopped
- 4 medium garlic cloves
- 1/2 inch piece of fresh ginger
- 2 fresh green chilies, minced
- 1 teaspoon coriander powder
- 1/2 teaspoon Kashmiri red chili powder
- 1/2 teaspoon turmeric powder
- 1 pinch asafoetida powder
- 1/2 teaspoon garam masala
- 1/2 teaspoon cumin seeds
- 1 teaspoon dry fenugreek leaves
- 2 tablespoons unsalted butter
- 2 tablespoons heavy cream
- enough water to cook the beans
- 2 sprigs fresh cilantro, chopped
- salt & pepper, in stages and per taste

METHOD
Cook the re-hydrated beans in enough water with a pinch of turmeric and salt. You may use a pressure cooker as well. The beans should be fully cooked. Strain the cooked beans and reserve the cooking liquid.

In a heavy-bottomed pan, melt the butter, add the cumin seeds, and cook for 30 seconds. Next add the onions and brown on medium heat. This may take several minutes. Next, add the ginger, garlic, and green chiles. Cook for 5 minutes. Now add the remaining spices and cook for 2 minutes before adding the tomatoes. Season with salt and pepper, cover, and stew on low for 10 minutes or until the tomatoes break down and start creating a sauce. Now add the cooked beans and enough of the water used to cook the beans to barely cover the mixture. Cook on medium for 45 minutes until the beans start breaking down. Using a ladle or spatula, smash to break down some of the beans. This gives a great depth of flavor and naturally thickens the beans. Finish with heavy cream by mixing it uniformly into the mixture. Garnish with chopped cilantro.

CANNELLINI CASSOULET

Cassoulet is a slow-cooked casserole-style stew containing various proteins and white beans. A popular dish that is said to have originated in the Languedoc region of southwest France was historically a rustic and homey dish. Now, one may find renditions in the finest restaurants. I think the assorted mushrooms and potato are a more than adequate replacement for traditional proteins.

LEVEL: Intermediate

YIELD: approximately 4 servings

INGREDIENTS

1 cup dried cannellini beans, rinsed and soaked overnight starting in warm water
1 large onion, medium diced
2 stalks celery, medium diced
2 small carrots, medium diced
1 tablespoon tomato paste
1 medium ripe tomato, small diced
4 cloves garlic, sliced thinly
vegetable stock, as needed
2 bay leaves
4 sprigs fresh thyme
1 sprig fresh rosemary
2 sprigs flatleaf parsley
1 teaspoon whole peppercorns
1 whole garlic clove
1 Yukon gold potato, large diced with skin
1 turnip, large diced with skin
1 cup assorted exotic mushrooms (like oyster, chanterelle, etc.)
1/4 cup extra-virgin olive oil
1 cup seasoned breadcrumbs, toasted golden brown
water, as needed
salt & pepper, in stages and per taste

METHOD

Place 1 garlic clove, the whole peppercorns, 1 bay leaf, 1 parsley sprig, 2 thyme sprigs in a cheesecloth and tie into a bundle. This is a *bouquet garni*. Cook the beans in salted water, a bay leaf, the sprig of rosemary and 2 thyme sprigs. This should be about 45 minutes. Do not overcook. Drain and hold. In a heavy-bottomed pot on medium heat, heat the olive oil and roast the onions, carrots, and celery for about 20 minutes. Next add the garlic mushrooms and cook for another 5 minutes before adding the tomato paste. Roast for another 5 minutes until a fond forms on the bottom of the pot. Season with salt and pepper in stages. Now add the potato and turnip, and mix gently. Now add the *bouquet garni*, fresh tomatoes, cooked beans and enough stock to just cover the contents of the pot. Scrape the bottom of the pot to release the fond. Season the broth as desired. Cover the pot and cook on low for 15 minutes before cooking for an additional 15 minutes uncovered. Serve with a sprinkle of the toasted breadcrumbs.

MISR WAT

The omnipresent *wat* in any Ethiopian array of dishes, typically on a large injera. Classically, red lentils with simple but distinctive spices make this a special heart and soul-warming protein-packed dish. The cardamom is prominent, more so than in most Indian dishes. The first time I ate this was at Meskerem Restaurant in Adams Morgan, Washington D.C. Since then, I make it routinely at home and crave it more than even masala lentils, probably because how focused the spices are.

LEVEL: Basic

YIELD: approximately 4 servings

INGREDIENTS
1 cup red lentils, washed well
4 cups water or vegetable stock
1 tablespoon Berbere spice (page 77)
1/2 teaspoon cardamom powder
2 tablespoons extra-virgin olive oil
1 small green chile, minced
5 cloves garlic, minced
1 medium onion, minced
1 medium ripe tomato, small dice
salt & pepper, in stages and per taste

METHOD
In a heavy-bottomed pot, heat the oil and add the spices. Stir frequently for about 1 minute before adding the onions to the spiced oil. After the onions brown, add the garlic and green chile. Stir for a minute. Season with some salt and pepper. Next add the tomato and stew for 5 minutes or until the tomatoes begin breaking down. Now add the lentils and stir everything well. Add the water and taste the broth. Adjust the salt level as desired. Cook the lentils uncovered on a low simmer, stirring periodically. If the mixture gets too thick, add a touch more water. At the end of the day, the texture must be on the thicker side to be able to pick it up with some delicious injera. The lentils should cook in about 30 minutes, but follow the cook time directions on the packaging.

PINTO, GREEN CHILE & TORTILLA STEW

> I've become very familiar with the legendary Hatch chiles from New Mexico. First, it was in my mystery basket at the premier Chefs' Taste Challenge Competition in New Orleans. Next, I helped the New Mexico Department of Agriculture showcase it and many other agricultural products from New Mexico at the Produce Marketing Association (PMA) annual summit in Orlando. I made a traditional green chile stew for the summit that was critically applauded. This is my elevated, vegetarian take on a green chile stew.

LEVEL: Basic

YIELD: approximately 4 servings

INGREDIENTS
1 cup dried pinto beans, rinsed and soaked overnight starting in warm water
1 large onion, medium diced
4 cloves garlic, minced
1 sprig fresh thyme
1 bay leaf
2 cups medium hot Hatch chiles (substitute Anaheim or Poblano, if necessary)
3 tomatillos, diced
1 teaspoon ground cumin
1 teaspoon dried Mexican oregano
3 corn tortillas, chopped
1 medium ripe tomato, chopped
vegetable stock, as needed
1 cup fresh cilantro, chopped
1/4 cup extra-virgin olive oil
salt & pepper, in stages and per taste

METHOD
In a heavy-bottomed pot, heat the oil and brown the garlic. Add the onions, green chile, and tomatillos and stew for 10 minutes. Next add the spices, bay leaf, thyme sprig, and beans. Stir well and cook for 10 minutes on medium heat. Next add the chopped tortilla and brown for 5 minutes or so. Finally, add the fresh tomato and enough stock to cover the ingredients in the pot. Taste the broth and adjust the salt and pepper, as desired. Cover the pot and cook for about an hour or until the beans are cooked. Uncover the pot the last 15 minutes to allow for evaporation and natural thickening. Finish by folding in the fresh cilantro. Serve with fresh avocado, a wedge of lime, and crisp tortilla strips.

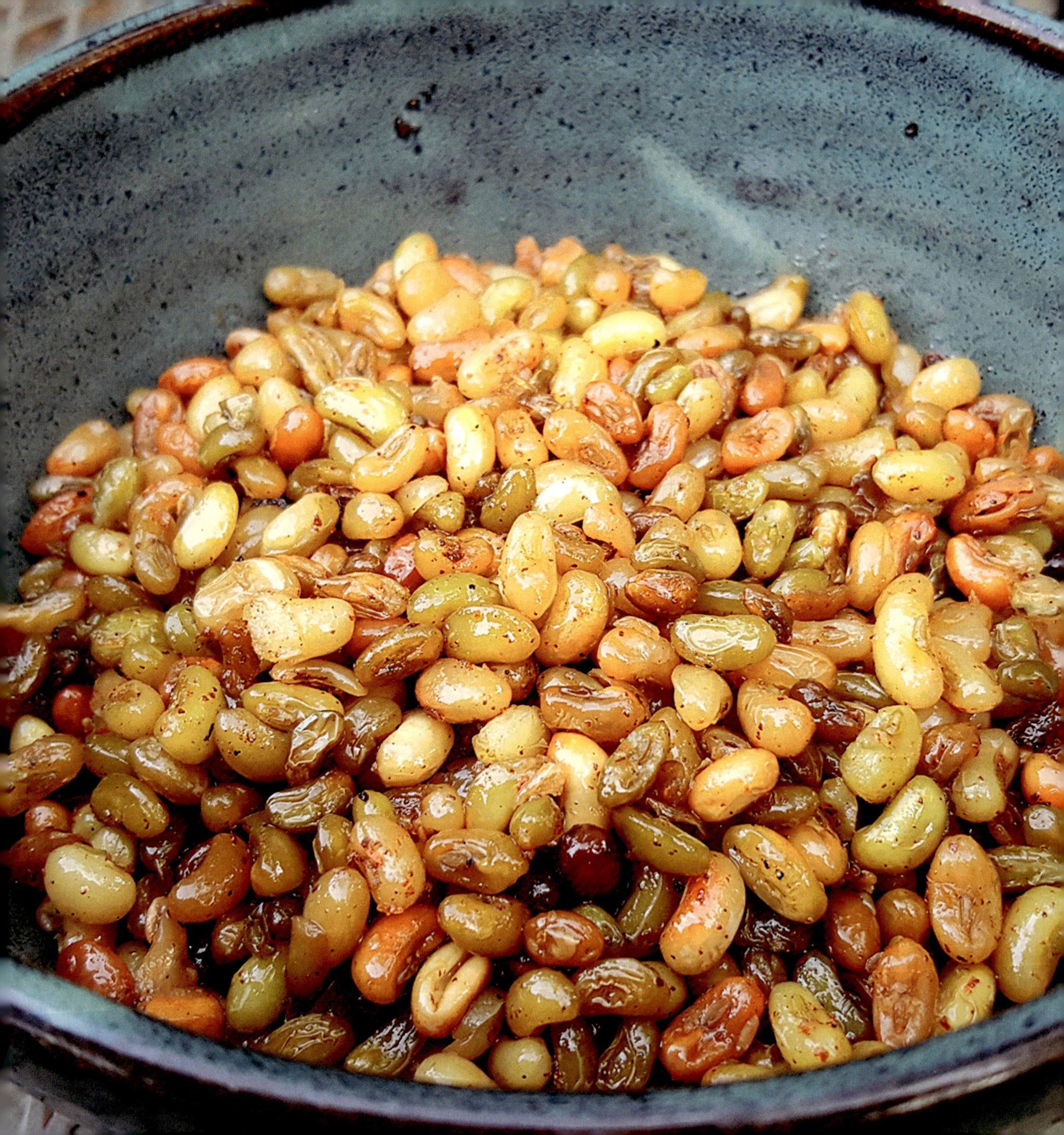

FIELD PEA & ASPARAGUS PURLOO

> Low-country Purloo (or pilau) is a simple yet deep-souled rice dish that can be traced to African roots. There is a plethora of rice dishes from all over the world that seem to be rooted in an ancestral parent. While it's not clear as to which rice dish comes closest to preserving the tradition of such an ancestral dish, a well-made purloo eats like it's been around since the beginning of time. Getting stuck on this sticky pulao is easy.

LEVEL: Basic

YIELD: approximately 4 servings

INGREDIENTS

2 cups asparagus tips and tender stems, 1/2 inch pieces, blanched in salted water
1 cup field peas (like sea Island red peas or common cowpeas), cooked in salted water
1 medium onion, diced
1 bay leaf
4 cloves garlic, minced
2 cups medium-grain rice like Carolina Gold
1/2 cup dry white wine
8 cups asparagus stock made from the trims
1/2 cup, sliced scallions
2 tablespoons chives, sliced thinly
1/4 cup extra-virgin olive oil
wedges of lemon for garnish
salt & pepper, in stages and per taste

METHOD

The cooking method is not unlike that of making khichidi. We make the rice and essentially fold in the cooked asparagus and field peas. By cooking the rice in an asparagus stock made from all the tough ends, we can create a deeper connection with the folded-in asparagus.

Wash the rice a few times and drain well. In a heavy bottomed pan, brown the onions and garlic in olive oil before adding the rice and bay leaf. Coat the rice well with the olive oil and cook on low until most of the moisture in the pan evaporates. Deglaze with the white wine and after 30 seconds, add the stock. Season the broth with salt and pepper, cover, reduce the flame to low, and cook the rice according to the instructions on the packaging. Once the rice is cooked, gently fold in the cooked asparagus, cooked peas, and scallions. Return the cover to the pan and let stand for 15 minutes so more of the liquid is absorbed by the rice and peas. Serve garnished with the chopped chives and a wedge of lemon.

SMOKED BLACK-EYED PEAS & MUSTARD GREENS

Greens and black-eyed peas may be a New Year's Day tradition that ushers in the promise of prosperity and health. But smoking the peas elevates the pairing into the hallowed clouds of 'cue without the guilt.

LEVEL: Basic

YIELD: approximately 4 servings

INGREDIENTS

1 cup dried black-eyed peas, rinsed and soaked overnight starting in warm water
1 lb. mustard greens, washed and chopped with stems on
1 teaspoon dried mustard
1 medium onion, minced
1 jalapeño, diced (optional)
2 cloves garlic, minced
2 tablespoons white balsamic or apple cider vinegar
1 tablespoon brown sugar
1 tablespoon liquid smoke (only if you don't have a smoker)
1 bay leaf
vegetable stock, as needed
1/4 cup extra-virgin olive oil
salt & pepper, in stages and per taste

METHOD

Rinse the soaked black-eyed peas, coat with some olive oil, salt, pepper and a small amount of stock. Transfer to a shallow pan and smoke at 225F for an hour (skip this step if you don't have a smoker).

In a heavy-bottomed pot, sauté the onions and garlic in olive oil. When the onions are golden brown, add the dried mustard and jalapeno and cook for a minute. Next, add the (smoked) peas and smoking juices, greens, bay leaf, liquid smoke (if not smoking the peas), brown sugar, vinegar and cook for five minutes. Season with salt and pepper. Now add enough vegetable stock to cover the ingredients. Taste the broth and adjust the amount of vinegar, heat, and sweet. If needed, add more liquid smoke for the desired smokiness. Cover the pot and cook on low for 45 minutes or until the peas are cooked. Uncover the pot and strain the solids. Transfer the pot licker to a shallow pan and reduce on medium heat by half the volume. Combine the solids and reduced pot licker for the finished disk.

DAL MAKHANI

> The queen of all legume dishes. Even though the title literally translates to "buttery beans" and my recipe below uses butter and even cream, I don't think the dairy is absolutely necessary. When cooked low and slow, the urad dal and red beans explode to reveal their naturally buttery and creamy texture. So, one could theoretically leave the dairy out altogether and use a plant-based oil. Regardless of which version you make, you will become addicted to this beautifully balanced dish.

LEVEL: Intermediate

YIELD: approximately 4 servings

INGREDIENTS

- 1 cup black gram (whole urad dal), soaked for 2 hours in warm water
- 1 cup dried red kidney beans, soaked overnight starting in warm water
- 1 medium onion, finely minced
- 2 green chilies, minced
- 1 inch piece fresh ginger
- 4 cloves garlic
- 2 medium ripe tomatoes, small diced
- 1/2 teaspoon cumin seeds
- 3 whole cloves
- 2 whole green cardamom pods
- 1 black cardamom
- 1 inch piece cinnamon stick
- 1 bay leaf (fresh, if available)
- 1/2 teaspoon Kashmiri red chili powder
- 1/2 teaspoon freshly grated nutmeg
- 1/2 teaspoon dried fenugreek leaves
- water, as needed
- 1/4 cup heavy cream
- 2 tablespoons unsalted butter
- freshly chopped cilantro, as desired
- salt & pepper, in stages and per taste

METHOD

In a mortar and pestle or food processor, make a paste of the ginger and garlic. Melt the butter in a heavy bottomed pan and fry the whole spices for two minutes on medium heat. Next add the ginger-garlic paste and sauté for a minute before adding the finely minced onions and green chilies. Cook on a low heat for about 15 minutes until the onions start melting. Season with salt and pepper along the way. Now add the tomatoes and cook for 5 minutes before adding the beans and remaining spices. Stir well and add water to cover the beans by about an inch. Season the broth with salt, as desired. Cover and simmer the beans on medium-low heat for about 2 hours, stirring periodically. Once the beans are cooked and soft, simmer for an additional 30 minutes uncovered. This will thicken the dish naturally. The desired texture at the end is one that is silky and creamy. Finish the dish with the heavy cream and mix well. Serve with freshly chopped cilantro, and if desired, a pat of butter that melts into the warm serving.

Pasta

For every time I've asserted that I may have been Italian in my former life, I am essentially stating my undying love for pasta. My penultimate comfort food (second only to Daddojanam) is spaghetti or capellini with garlic, olive oil, and fresh herbs. Here, I give some of my favorite forms of pasta. You will notice that there are no filled pastas. Heresy, I'm sure. Oh well.

SPAGHETTI CARBONARA

Have I mentioned that, likely, I was Italian in my previous life? Well, even if that may not be true, I love good Italian food. In this version, we encourage you to make fresh spaghetti, which is not nearly as intimidating as it may seem. It is like making bread or pizza dough at home. Doing it once will only inspire one to do it again, and again. A key ingredient that we will omit is guanciale, pancetta, or any sort of meat. But we will be able to generate a smoky depth, nevertheless, with the addition of a commonly available ingredient.

LEVEL: Intermediate
YIELD: approximately 4 servings

INGREDIENTS
1 lb. spaghetti (preferably, fresh)
2 eggs yolks, beaten
1/2 cup heavy cream
1/4 cup freshly grated Parmigiana Reggiano
1 clove garlic, minced
1/2 teaspoon smoked paprika
salt & pepper, in stages and per taste

METHOD
In a large bowl, whisk the eggs, cream, smoked paprika, some salt, and ground black pepper. Cook the pasta just past al dente in salted water. Reserve a cup of starchy pasta water and while it is warm, slowly temper the egg and cream mixture. This cooks the eggs enough. Hold this mixture just warm enough to not curdle the sauce. Add the warm, drained, cooked pasta into the sauce that is in the bowl and coat the noodles well with the sauce. Be careful to not break up the pasta. Taste for pasta for salt and pepper and re-season as desired. It should be well-seasoned. Fold in the grated cheese and serve immediately.

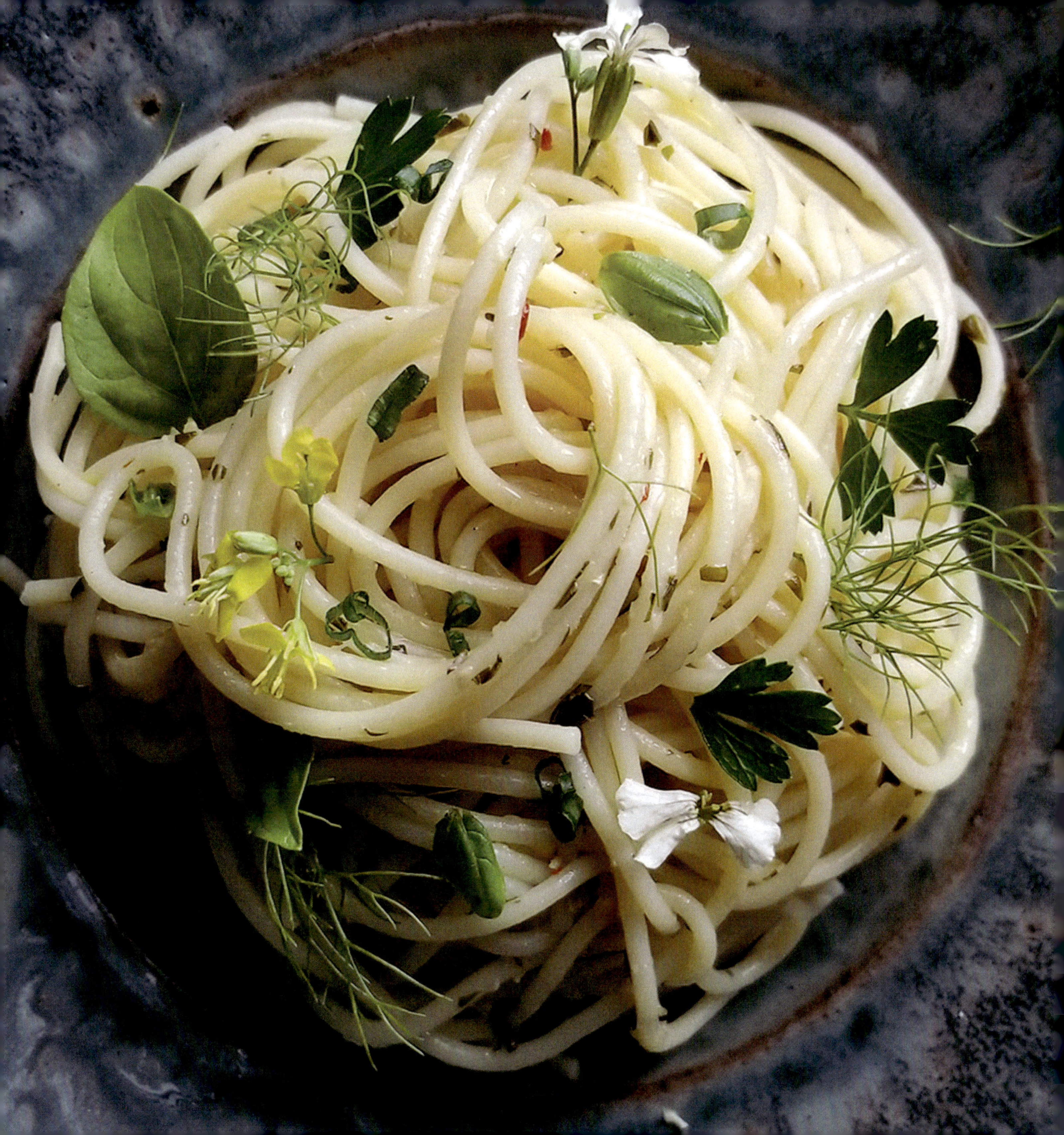

PUMPKIN GNOCCHI PARISIENNE WITH GORGONZOLA, WALNUTS, AND SAGE

Gnocchi Parisienne is essentially dumplings made from a savory *pâte à choux* dough (think éclairs or profiteroles) which have been blanched in salted water and then depending on how one likes it, sautéed in butter or extra virgin olive oil. Thus, it is a canvas which accepts a wide variety of flavors. This version infused the batter (paste, really) with pureed pumpkin. When I made my first traditional gnocchi (which uses potatoes), I thought they were a bit dense. At Canoe in Downtown Toronto, I made a version of gnocchi Parisienne with ricotta and thyme

LEVEL: Intermediate

YIELD: approximately 4 servings

INGREDIENTS
1.5 cups water
3 oz. unsalted butter
3 oz. pumpkin puree
1.5 tablespoon, coarse salt
2 cups all-purpose flour, sifted
2 tablespoons Dijon mustard
1 tablespoon chives, chopped
1 tablespoon parsley, chopped
1 teaspoon dried sage
1/2 teaspoon freshly grated nutmeg
1/2 teaspoon cinnamon
1/4 cup toasted walnuts
5 large eggs
extra-virgin olive oil, as needed
1 tablespoon Gorgonzola cheese
1/4 cup sage leaves with stems
salt & pepper, in stages and per taste

METHOD
Melt the butter. Add the water and some of the salt in a heavy-bottomed saucepan. Bring the liquid to a simmer. Whisk in the flour until it comes together. This takes about 3 minutes. Take it off the stove and let it cool.

In a stand-up mixer with the paddle attachment, whip the flour mixture so it cools down a bit. Add the mustard and pumpkin puree. Grate in the nutmeg. Add the cinnamon and dried sage. Add the remaining salt, and with the mixer on low, add one egg at a time. Finish with the fresh herbs. Either fill a piping bag with the mixture and squeeze/cut with a knife into boiling salted water or use an ice-scream scoop to scoop 1 oz. portions into boiling salted water. Two minutes after the gnocchi rise to the top, drain and cool them.

To finish the dish, melt some olive oil in a pan and add the sage leaves until they crisp up. Remove and hold the leaves and in the same oil, sauté the gnocchi until they are golden brown and serve with some crumbles of a high-quality Gorgonzola, fried sage, and walnuts.

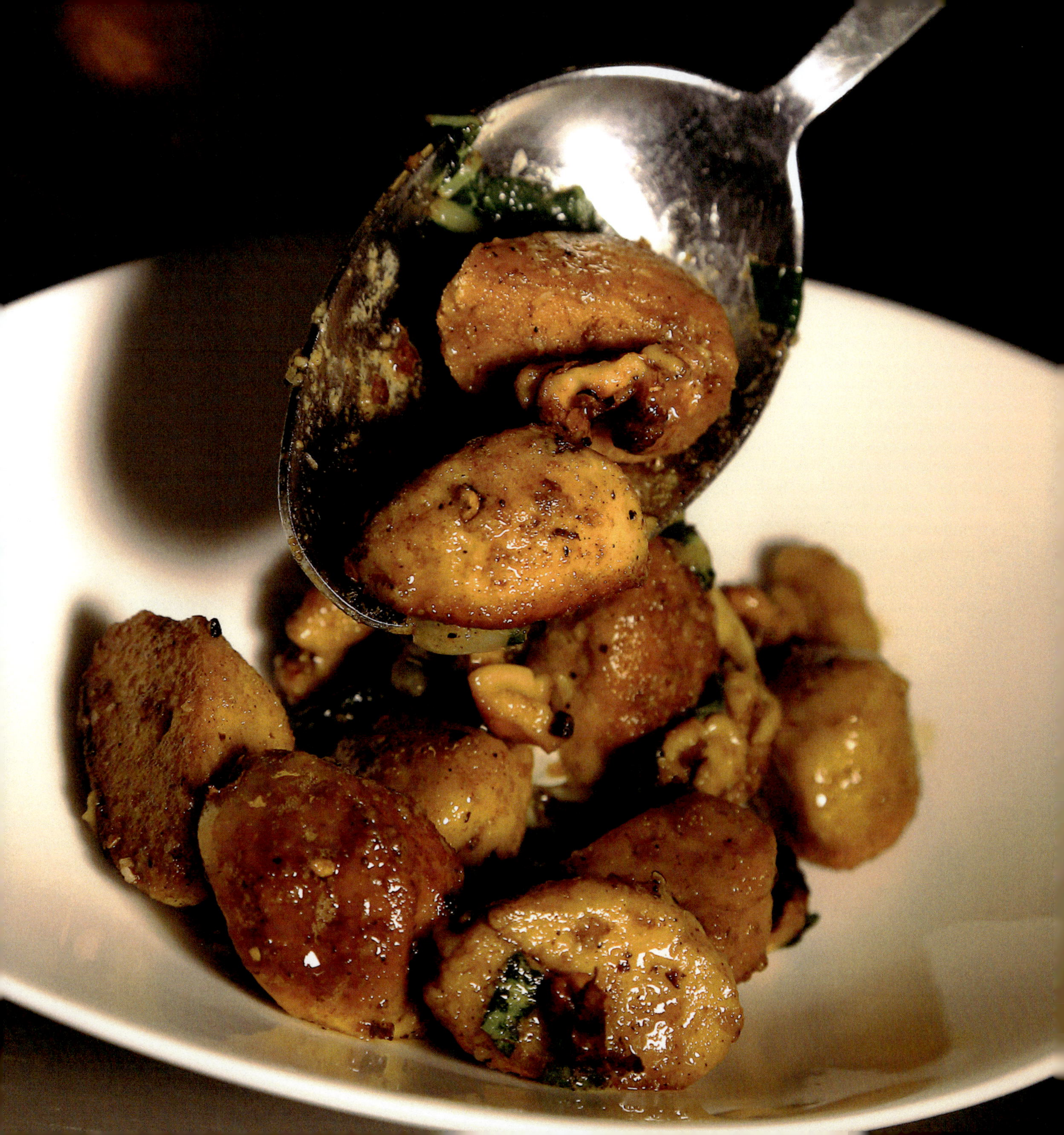

TAGLIATELLE BOLOGNESE

Pasta and Sauce are meant to be married for eternal harmony. Simply plopping sauce on top of cooked pasta doesn't do justice to what is possible when the two become one in a sauté pan, for a couple of minutes. This dish is especially well-suited for that type of finish. In my view, a traditional Bolognese is as defined as it is vague. Without the pasta, the Bolognese is just chili--not that there's anything wrong with that. Always add some pasta water to the pan during the sauté stage because it is the bridge between the two worlds of pasta and sauce.

LEVEL: Basic

YIELD: approximately 4 servings

INGREDIENTS
1 lb. fresh or dry tagliatelle pasta
1 cup firm tofu
1 cup tempeh
1 large onion, minced
2 stalks celery, small dice
2 small carrots, small dice
1/2 teaspoon freshly grated nutmeg
5 cloves garlic, sliced thinly
1 cup canned San Marzano tomatoes
1 sprig rosemary leaves, chopped
2 sprigs fresh thyme leaves, chopped
1 cup dry white wine
1 cup milk or half and half
1 bay leaf
1/2 cup extra-virgin olive oil
water to cook the pasta
1/2 cup freshly grated Parmigiana Reggiano
salt & pepper, in stages and per taste

METHOD
Chop up the tofu and tempeh, spread on a baking sheet and roast in the oven for 30 minutes. While that is happening, in a heavy-bottomed pan, heat the olive oil and begin sweating the onions, carrots, and celery. Cook for 15 minutes before adding the fresh herbs, bay leaf, and garlic. Cook for an additional 5 minutes and deglaze with the wine. Cook the mixture for 5 minutes before adding the toma-toes. Season with some salt and pepper and simmer on medium-low.

Remove the roasted tofu and tempeh and break down to a crumb in a food processor. Add this crumb to the simmering sauce. Stirring periodically, cook this fortified sauce for another 30 minutes before adding the dairy and freshly grated nutmeg. Stir well, taste, and re-season as desired.

Cook the pasta according to the instructions. Just before the pasta is al dente, ladle some of the pasta water to the sauce, drain the pasta, and add it to the sauce. Cook the pasta and sauce for a minute or two before folding in the freshly grated cheese.

SPAGHETTI WITH LEMON AND RAPINI

> Jenneffer and I both love this combination. I'm used to bitter food groups, and the addition of fresh citrus to a bitter vegetable is pure genius. The flavors can get a bit one-note, which is why the addition of spice and garlic provide the necessary relief.

LEVEL: Basic

YIELD: approximately 4 servings

INGREDIENTS
- 1 lb. spaghetti, dried or fresh
- 2 cups rapini leaves and tender stems, chopped
- 1 shallot, minced
- 4 cloves garlic, sliced thinly
- 1 teaspoon crushed red pepper
- zest and juice of 2 lemons
- 1/4 cup extra-virgin olive oil
- 1/4 cup freshly grated Pecorino Romano (optional)
- enough water to cook the pasta
- salt & pepper, in stages and per taste

METHOD

In a wide pan, heat the olive oil on medium heat and add the garlic. Cook the garlic in the oil for 2 minutes until it begins browning slightly. Add the shallot and crushed red pepper and cook for 2 minutes. Next, add the chopped rapini and season with salt and pepper. Cook the rapini until the stems are tender and cooked enough to your liking. Hold this mixture on warm and begin cooking the pasta in salted water. Two minutes away from the al dente stage, ladle some of the starchy pasta water into the rapini mixture and add the lemon juice. A minute out from the al dente stage recommended on the packaging (if using dried pasta), drain the pasta well and add to the rapini and lemon sauté. Coat the pasta well and continue cooking in the pan for another minute or so before serving with lemon zest and grated cheese.

Note: If using fresh pasta, the cooking time is significantly shorter, so you will need to be quick and have completed the rapini-lemon sauce prior to adding the pasta to the pan.

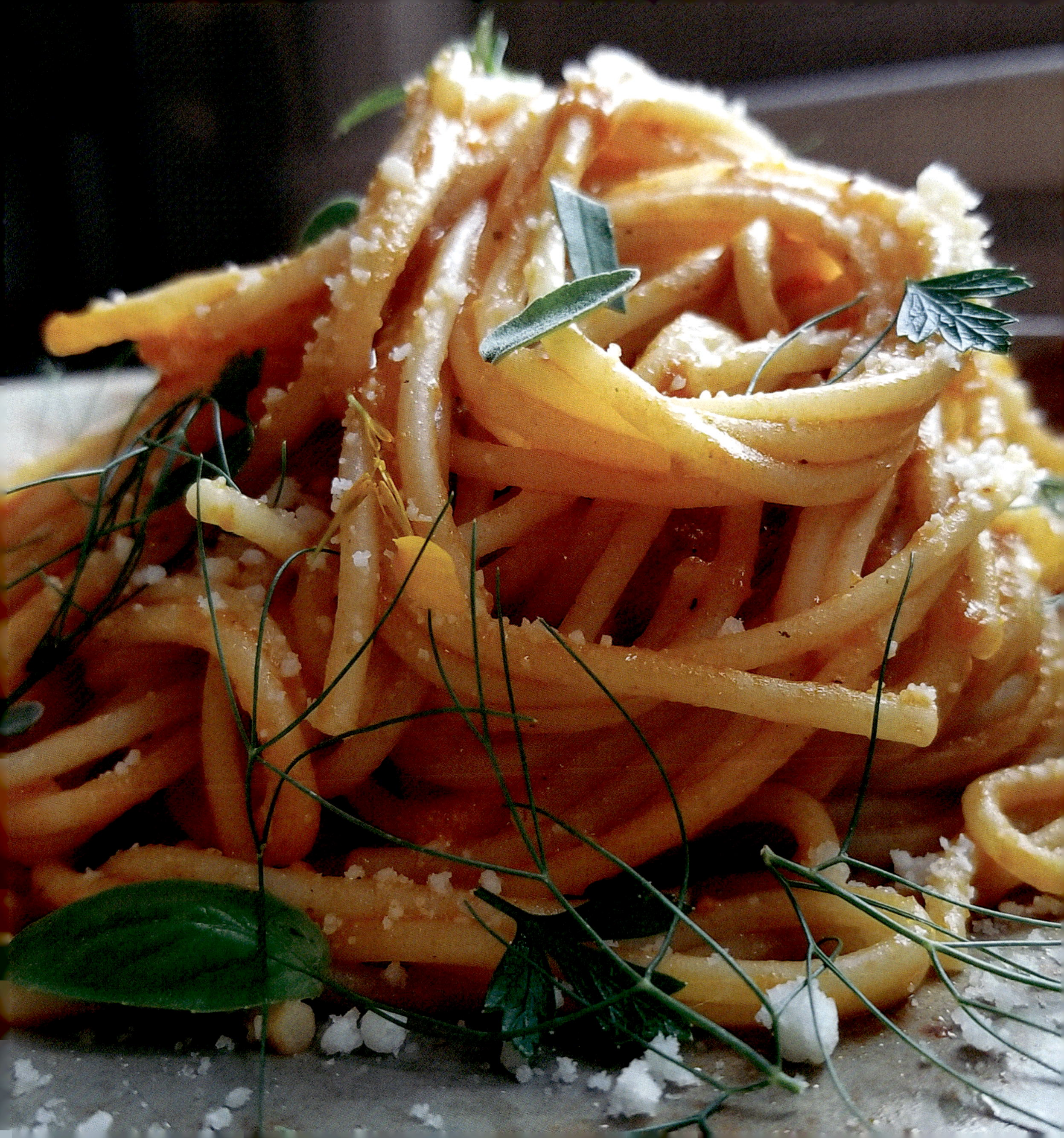

BUCATINI FRA DIAVOLO

> *Brother Devil* (fra diavolo) sounds sinful, but there's nothing errant about a spicy pasta dish. I don't know if Marcela Hazan would have approved of transforming her perfect sauce in this manner, but I've meant as an homage to the versatility of her sauce. The bucatini noodle is interesting enough with the hole through the center, but a bright and spicy sauce with the usual herbaceous and aromatic accents makes this a thoroughly enjoyable Roman-style pasta dish.

LEVEL: Basic

YIELD: approximately 4 servings

INGREDIENTS
1 lb. bucatini, dried
1 teaspoon Calabrian chiles, chopped
1 teaspoon red chili flakes
2 cups Marcela Hazan inspired marinara sauce (page 116)
6 garlic cloves, minced
1/4 cup finely chopped basil
1/4 cup finely chopped flat-leaf parsley
1/4 cup freshly grated Parmigiana Reggiano
a pat of unsalted butter
1/2 cup extra-virgin olive oil
water for cooking pasta
salt & pepper, in stages and per taste

METHOD
First, we will make the base sauce. In a sauté pan, heat the olive oil and cook the garlic on medium heat until it browns slightly. Add the chile flakes and Calabrian chiles. Cook for a few seconds before adding the marinara sauce.

Cook the pasta in salted water and, a minute away from being al dente, ladle some pasta water into the tomato sauce. Drain the pasta well and add it to the sauce. Maintain a medium-low temperature to continue cooking the paste to the al dente stage or the desired doneness. Be sure to gently mix the pasta around so it cooks evenly and doesn't stick to the pan. Taste the sauce and pasta one more time before finishing by mixing in the cheese and fresh herbs. Note that this dish should be spicy, so there is a lot of variability as to exactly how spicy one desires. Serve with some garlic rubbed grilled or oven roasted bread.

PASTA ALLA NORMA

Eggplant, tomato, garlic, olive oil, chiles – what's not to like? For my money, this Catanian (Sicily) staple beats an eggplant parmigiana for its focused and mature flavors any day and all day. The pasta can be left out altogether and what remains is a testament to the world-wide popularity of Italian cuisine.

LEVEL: Basic

YIELD: approximately 4 servings

INGREDIENTS
1 lb. penne or ziti pasta
2 medium Italian eggplant
1 sprig fresh thyme
1 cup basic marinara sauce or Marcela Hazan Inspired sauce (page 116)
4 cloves garlic, sliced thinly
1/2 teaspoon crushed red pepper flakes or Calabrian chile (more or less)
1/2 cup freshly grated Pecorino Romano
1/4 cup extra-virgin olive oil
1/4 cup fresh ricotta or buffalo mozzarella (optional)
1/2 cup fresh basil leaves, coarse chopped without bruising
water for cooking pasta
salt & pepper, in stages and per taste

METHOD
Wash the eggplant and cut them into 3/4-inch pieces. Toss in some olive oil, salt, pepper, and the sprig of thyme. Roast in a 375F degree oven for about 30 minutes. Turn over the eggplant once during the roasting process.

In a wide sauté pan, heat some extra-virgin olive oil and brown the garlic on medium heat before adding the crushed pepper and roasted eggplant. Season as desired with salt and pepper and hold warm until the pasta is ready.

Cook the pasta in salted water, add a ladle or two of the pasta cooking water to the pan sauce. Drain the pasta well at the al dente stage before tossing into the eggplant sauce. Cooking the pasta in the sauce for another minute before mixing in the half of the basil and Pecorino. Serve with dollops of ricotta, a touch more grated cheese, and fresh basil.

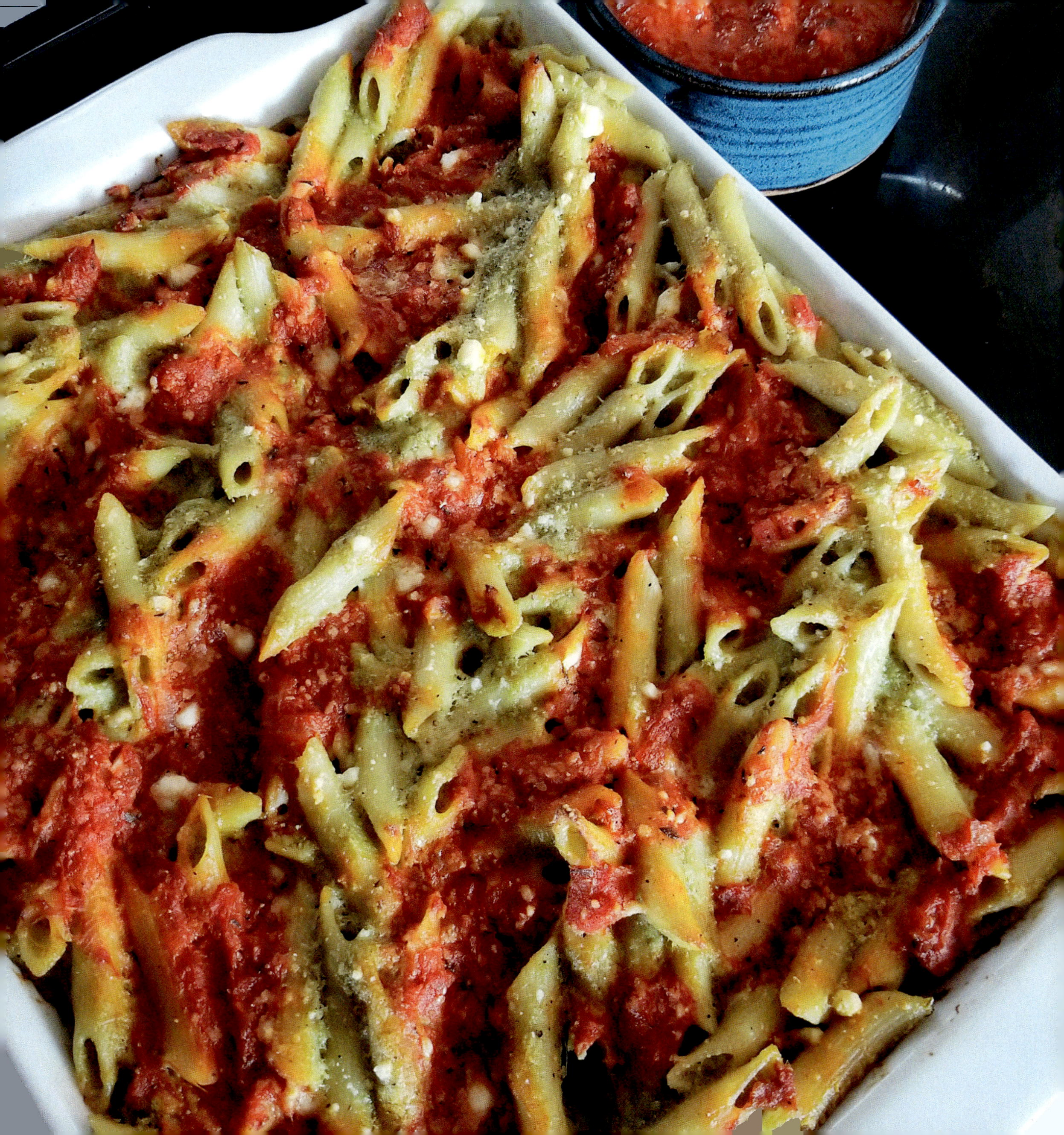

PASTA WITH WILD AND EXOTIC MUSHROOMS

I could very well have named this dish *pasta alla funghi*. The choice of noodle is important because we're going to leave the mushrooms in larger pieces. Over the years, I've discovered that mushrooms are not everyone's cup of tea. Speaking of mushroom tea, I am reminded of that time, Jenneffer and I indulged in local mushroom tea in Negril, Jamaica. The jagged edges of that memory remain as a distinctive vibration for both us.

LEVEL: Basic

YIELD: approximately 4 servings

INGREDIENTS
1 lb. noodle-style pasta, fresh or dried
3 cups assorted wild and exotic mushrooms, cut or torn into uniform sized pieces
1 shallot, sliced thinly
1 sprig rosemary
1 sprig fresh thyme
2 cloves garlic, minced
1/2 cup dry white wine
1/4 cup heavy cream
1 tablespoon unsalted butter
1 teaspoon white truffle oil (optional)
water to cook the pasta
salt & pepper, in stages and per taste

METHOD
In a heavy-bottomed sauté pan, melt the butter and brown the shallots and garlic. Add the rosemary and thyme sprig and cook for a minute. Next add the mushrooms and roast in the pan for 5 minutes, stirring periodically. Deglaze with the white wine and cook for 2 minutes before adding the heavy cream. Hold for the pasta.

Cook the pasta in salted water for a minute less than the al dente stage, following the cooking directions on the box. If using fresh pasta, plan to do this for about 4 minutes. Ladle some pasta water to the mushroom cream sauce and have the pan on medium-low. Taste, then adjust the salt and pepper levels before mixing in the truffle oil. Drain the pasta well and fold it into the sauce. Coat the pasta well and cook to the desired doneness, perhaps just past al dente. Garnish with freshly grated cheese and chopped fresh herbs. Make certain that every portion has a good representation of mushrooms.

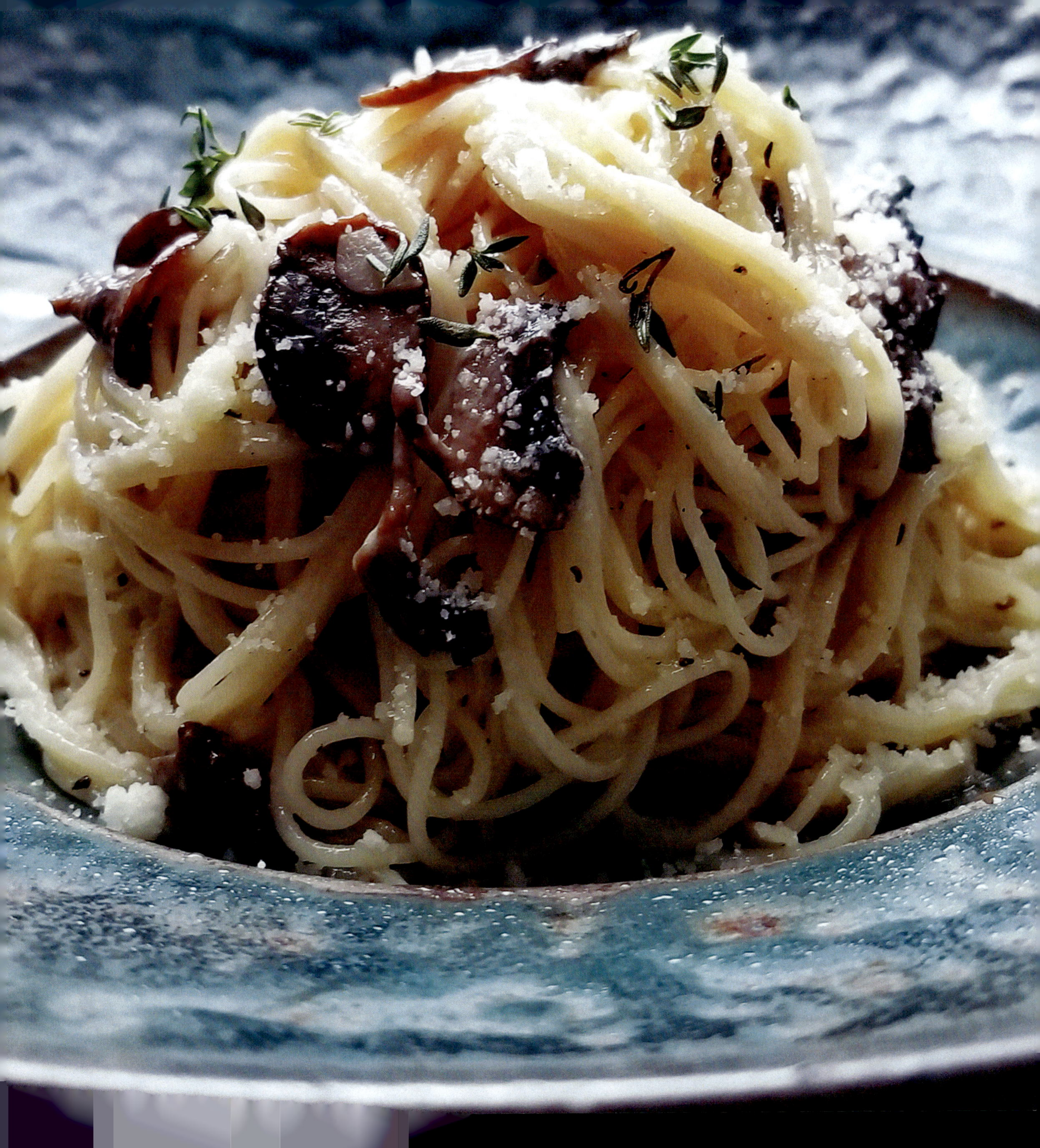

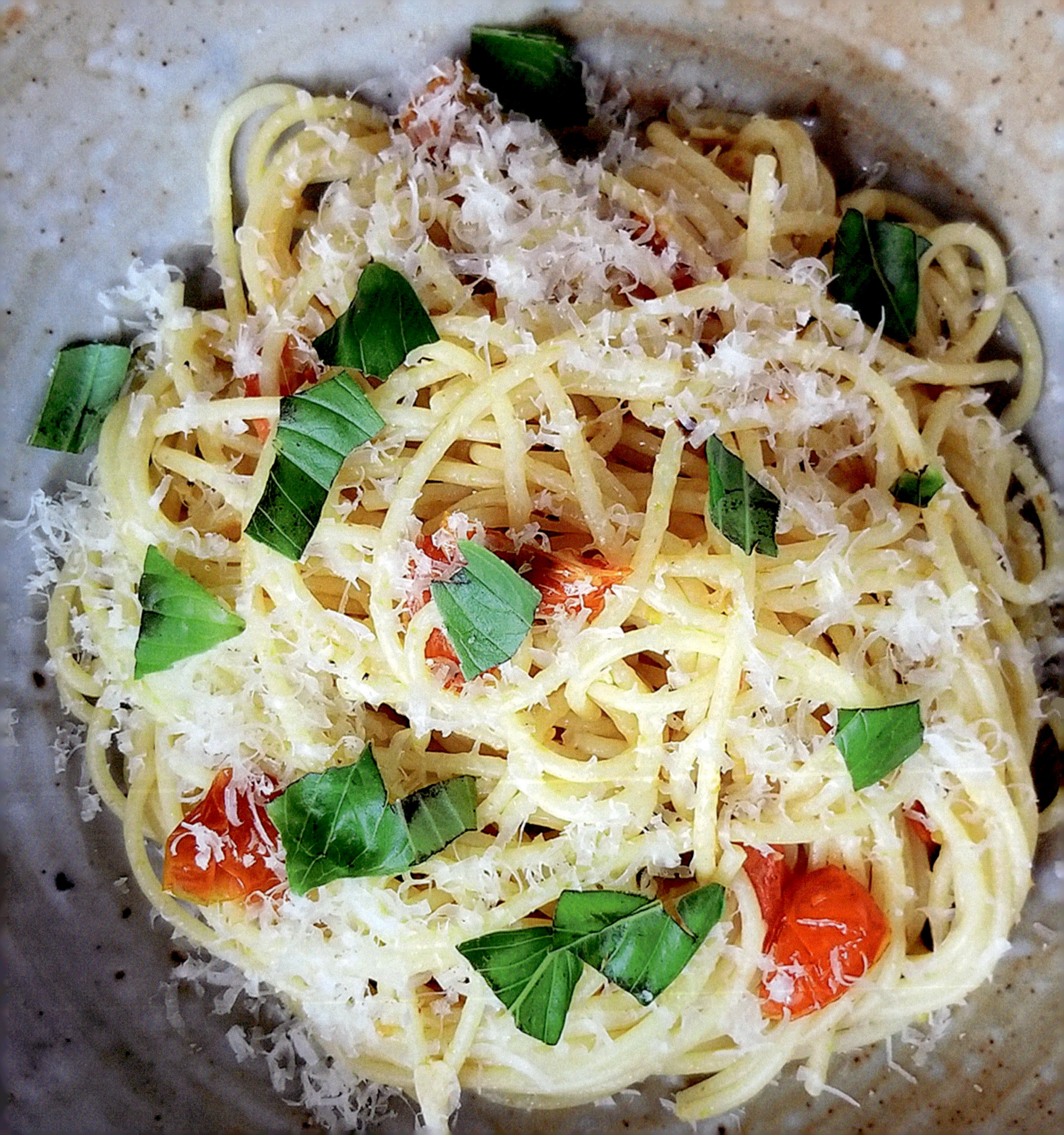

CAPELLINI WITH CREAMY LEMON & GARLIC

> Capellini (angel hair) cooks itself if you look at it the wrong way, so timing is everything in this dish. I've found that par-cooking the pasta and holding it and some pasta water produce the best results. The fresh acidity of the lemon makes the angel hair noodles sing in gratitude to the food gods. I could eat this dish three times a week.

LEVEL: Basic

YIELD: approximately 4 servings

INGREDIENTS

1 lb. dried capellini (angel hair) pasta
1 shallot or red onion, minced
5 cloves garlic, shaved thinly
1 teaspoon red chile flakes (optional)
leaves from 1 sprig of fresh thyme
zest and juice from 3 lemons
1/2 cup heavy cream
2 tablespoons unsalted butter
1/4 cup freshly grated Pecorino Romano
1/4 cup flatleaf parsley, chopped finely
1/4 cup toasted and seasoned breadcrumbs
water to cook pasta
salt & pepper, in stages and per taste

METHOD

Most of the time in this pasta is spent making the sauce. Melt the butter and brown the garlic slightly before adding the shallot and red chile flakes. Cook until the shallot is translucent before adding the lemon juice, zest, and cream. Cook on low, adjusting the salt and pepper. Hold. Cook the pasta in lightly salted water. Be sure to cook for only a minute. Add some of the pasta water to the lemon cream sauce. Drain the pasta well and add to the sauce. Coat the pasta well with the sauce and hold a medium-low heat, switching it off as soon as the pasta is al dente. Note that capellini cooks fast. Sprinkle in the fresh parsley and grated cheese. Serve portions with a sprinkle of the toasted breadcrumbs on top.

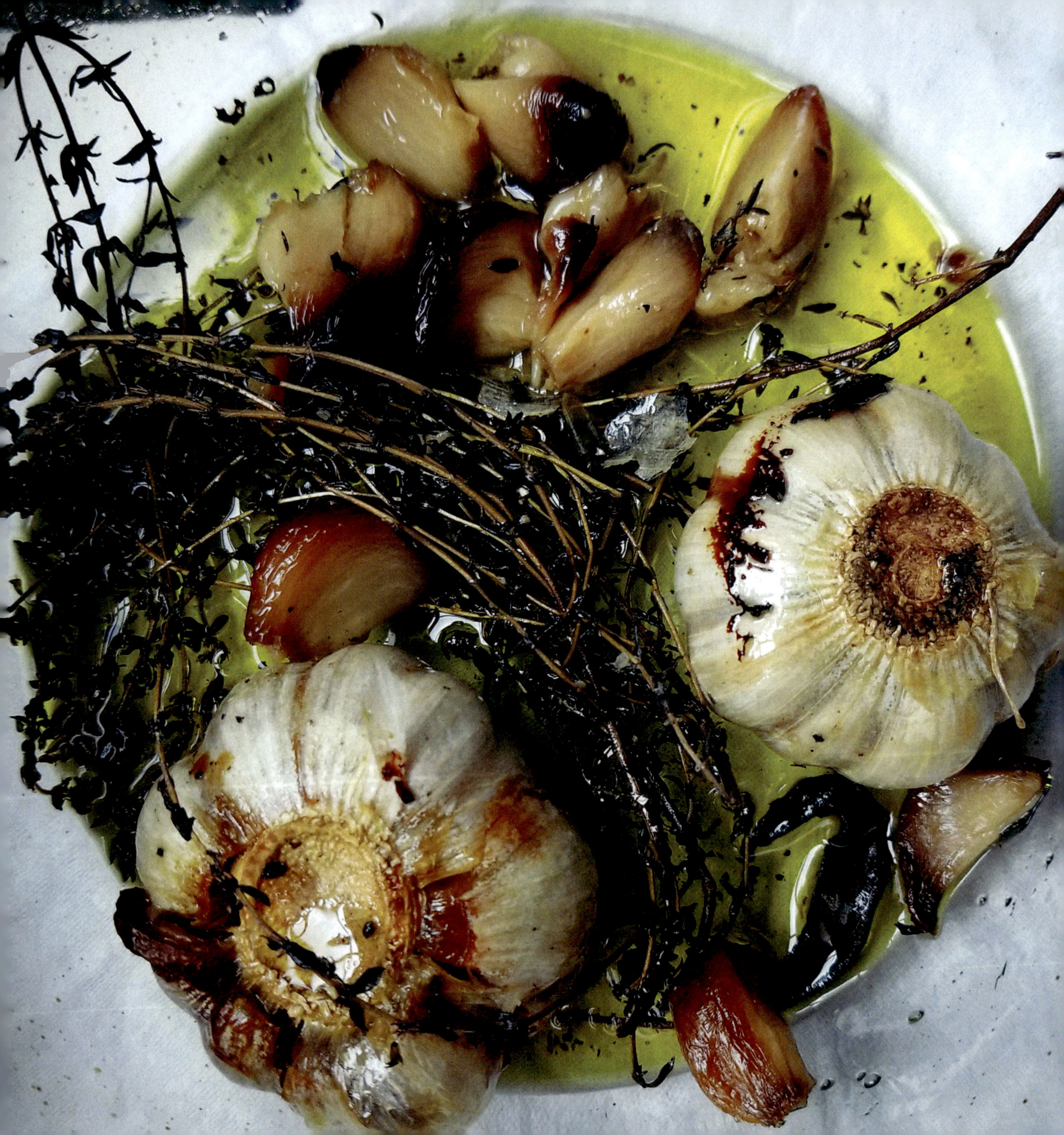

ROASTED FENNEL AND BUTTERNUT SQUASH LASAGNA

> What do roasted fennel, garlic, thyme, roasted tomatoes, and pasta have in common, you may wonder. They are the ingredients in a pasta dish I learnt in culinary school under Chef Tony Adams, a wildly talented chef and instructor. In fact, while in the teaching restaurant Machon at the Orlando Culinary Academy, I worked with Chef Adams on a 9-course tasting menu for Jenneffer, a dining guest at Machon. After culinary school, I made a version of this dish for Jenneffer that I presented to her on one of our dates and she tells me that she ate it in the car on her ride back home. Food is love. The end.

LEVEL: Intermediate

YIELD: approximately 4 servings

INGREDIENTS
- 3 cups butternut squash, medium diced
- 2 bulbs fennel with stems, diced
- 6 cloves garlic
- 4 sprigs fresh thyme
- 3 cups Marcela Hazan inspired marinara (page 116)
- 1 cup truffled gorgonzola cream (see recipe on page 120)
- lasagna pasta sheets, as needed, fresh or dried
- 2 cups fresh ricotta
- water to cook pasta, if using dried sheets
- extra-virgin olive as needed for roasting
- salt & pepper, in stages and per taste

METHOD

Preheat an oven to 375F and spread the butternut and fennel on two separate baking sheets. Toss each in extra-virgin olive oil, two sprigs of thyme each, and 3 cloves of garlic each. Season with salt and pepper and roast for 30 minutes. Remove and let cook. Chop up the roasted garlic and pick the roasted thyme leaves for the lasagna. Coarsely chop up the roasted fennel and mix in the chopped roasted garlic and thyme.

While the vegetables are roasting, cook the pasta sheets, according to the directions if using a dried lasagna product. If you are using fresh or no-bake pasta sheets, of course, skip this step. Prepare an appropriately sized baking pan for the lasagna buy brushing it with a coat of extra-virgin olive oil.

Alternate layers of marinara, pasta, butternut, pasta, gorgonzola cream mixed with some marinara, roasted fennel, etc. Be sure to end with marinara dotted with ricotta. Bake at 375F, first covered for 30 minutes, then uncovered for 30 minutes

Allow the pasta to rest for at least 30 minutes before portioning and serving.

PENNE A LA PROVENÇAL

France has embraced pasta as well as Italy has embraced low and slow braises. Actually, both cuisines would argue fervently that they've contributed more to world cuisine than the other. And they would both be justified, except that Spain, Greece, and Portugal may take issue. And that is the nature of the power of food. Human migration carries with it culinary traditions that require adaptation to the relocated terroir and availability (or lack thereof) of traditional ingredients. All anthropology and history aside, this is a clean and vibrant pasta dish fitted for the warmer months.

LEVEL: Basic

YIELD: approximately 4 servings

INGREDIENTS
1 lb. dry penne pasta
1 cup pitted kalamata olives, soaked and rinsed in cold water to remove the excess salt
1/2 cup Spanish capers, soaked and rinsed in cold water to remove the excess salt
3 cloves garlic, minced
1 bulb of fresh fennel, sliced and caramelized on low heat in extra virgin olive oil
zest of 1 lemon
1 cup wild and exotic mushrooms
1 cup dry white wine
1/2 cup chopped fresh basil
1/2 cup chopped fresh parsley
1/2 cup heavy cream
1 oz. unsalted butter
extra virgin olive oil, as needed
1/2 cup freshly grated Pecorino Romano (optional)
salt & pepper, in stages and per taste

METHOD
Cook the pasta in salted water for about a minute under the recommended al dente time specified on the box. Strain and coat lightly with extra virgin olive oil. Reserve some of the pasta water. In a large sauté pan, sauté the cooked fennel and exotic mushrooms for a few minutes. Add the garlic, lemon zest, olives, and capers. Deglaze with the white wine and cook for a minute. Add the almost cooked pasta and toss to coat uniformly. Add some of the pasta water and continue cooking for about a minute. Add the heavy cream, fresh herbs, and butter. Test the seasoning by tasting the sauce. Cook on low heat for an additional 45 seconds or so. Finish with the grated pecorino Romano cheese, if desired. Serve immediately.

Curries

Here we go. It's still a matter of personal consternation when my food is assumed to be exclusively Indian. Clearly, it can be influenced by Indian cuisine, but I would hope that, by now, that stereotype has been relegated to the backrow. One doesn't find a lot of "curries" *per se* in India, but thanks to the British, the word "curry" has become synonymous with a dish of a certain style and flavor profile. There is no denying the bold and deep flavor achieved in a proper curry.

SQUASH & GREEN BEAN KERALA CURRY

LEVEL: Intermediate

YIELD: approximately 4 servings

INGREDIENTS

2 cups butternut or acorn squash, medium diced
2 cups green beans, picked and cut into one-inch pieces
one large onion, small diced
one-inch piece of fresh ginger, minced
4 cloves garlic, minced 10 fresh curry leaves
1 tablespoon black mustard seeds
1 teaspoon cumin seeds
3 whole red chili peppers
2 small fresh green chilies
1/2 fresh coconut, grated
1/2 teaspoon asafetida
1 cup coconut milk
1 medium tomato, chopped
1 teaspoon garam masala (page 73)
vegetable stock, as needed
water for blanching the green beans
1/2 bunch fresh cilantro, chopped
1/4 cup extra-virgin or vegetable oil
salt & pepper, in stages and per taste

METHOD

Coat squash in some oil, salt and pepper and roast in a 350F oven for 30 minutes. While the squash is roasting, blanch the green beans in salted water for a few minutes until just shy of being cooked. Shock in cold water to stop the cooking. Next we will make the base for the curry sauce. In heavy-bottomed pan, add some oil and heat to medium. Add the asafoetida, mustard seeds, cumin seed, red and green chili and fry for two minutes. Next add the fresh coconut and fry for 5 minutes, stirring frequently. Transfer all these ingredients to a food processor, add some water, and process to a smooth paste. This is the chutney. In a saucepan, add the remaining oil and sauté the onions, garlic and ginger. After about 10 minutes, add the curry leaves. Next add the tomato and stew for about 10 minutes and add the garam masala. Add the processed paste and coconut milk to the stewed mixture. Reduce the heat to medium low. Season to your liking. Stir periodically to not break the sauce. Add the roasted squash and green beans and cook on low for 5 minutes. Sprinkle cilantro and serve alongside steamed rice.

WATER CHESTNUT AND BAMBOO SHOOTS BENGALI CURRY

The first time I ate authentic Bengali food was when Satish and Vandana treated Jenneffer and me to the restaurant Oh! Calcutta at Nehru Place in New Delhi. It is where I first ate properly cooked banana flower. Anyone who thinks they've had typical Indian food, will concede after trying this dish that Indian cuisine is not just about flavors from the North or the South. India also has a West and as in this case, an East.

LEVEL: Intermediate

YIELD: approximately 4 servings

INGREDIENTS

1 cup canned water chestnuts, rinsed and drained
1 cup canned bamboo shoots
1/2 cup canned hearts of palm, rinsed and drained
3 medium onions, minced
1 tablespoon fresh ginger, minced
1 tablespoon fresh garlic, minced
7 curry leaves (optional)
2 tablespoons mustard seeds
1/2 cup fresh grated coconut
2 green chilies, diced (with seeds)
1 tablespoon cumin seeds
1/2 tablespoon coriander seeds
1 tablespoon ground turmeric
1/2 cup mustard oil
1/2 cup coconut milk
1 cup crushed tomatoes
2 tablespoons vegetable oil
cilantro, fresh, as needed
vegetable stock, as needed
salt & pepper, in stages and per taste

METHOD

Dry roast (on low heat) the coconut, mustard seeds, curry leaves, coriander, cumin, and green chilies in a pan until the coconut starts to brown. Blend in a processor. Fry the blended mixture in mustard oil. Add the onions, turmeric, ginger, and garlic. Stir for a couple of minutes. Add tomatoes, stock, and coconut milk. Season and simmer on a low heat for 15-20 minutes. Blend smoothly or leave it chunky depending on preference.

In a shallow pan, sauté the chestnuts, bamboo, and hearts of palm in the vegetable oil for 5 minutes. Add enough curry sauce to barely cover. Simmer on low to finish the curry. Garnish with fresh cilantro. Served with steamed white rice.

JERK-SPICED TARO, PLANTAIN, AND CAPSICUM CURRY

This dish came to me because the distinctive flavors of jerk draw me in, but I know that the warm spices are not for the meek. One needs appropriate accomplices to pull off a proper jerk-style curry. The grounded starch of taro root coupled with the airy starch of green plantain work well with the assorted capsicum and balancing quality of coconut milk.

LEVEL: Intermediate

YIELD: approximately 4 servings

INGREDIENTS
1 cup taro root, washed, peeled, medium diced
1 cup green plantain, peeled, medium diced
1/2 cup jerk paste (page 85), more or less
1 red bell pepper, cored, sliced into 1/4 inch slices
1 green bell pepper, cored, sliced into 1/4 inch slices
1 yellow bell pepper, cored, sliced into 1/4 inch slices
2 cloves garlic, minced
1 medium red onion, sliced thinly
1 sprig fresh thyme
1 bay leaf
2 cups coconut milk
juice of 1 lime
1/4 cup chopped fresh cilantro
water, as needed
extra virgin olive oil, as needed
pinch of sugar, more or less
salt & pepper, in stages and per taste

METHOD
In a saucepan, heat some oil and fry the garlic and onions until the garlic browns slightly. Next add the taro, plantain, and sprig of thyme, and cook for 5 minutes. Now add the jerk paste and fry for 2-3 minutes before adding the peppers. Stir all the ingredients well. Add the bay leaf and some water. Season with some salt, pepper, and sugar. Find a balance to tame the jerk spices a bit before adding the coconut milk. Cover and simmer on a low heat to not break the coconut milk. As soon as the vegetables are cooked to your preference, switch off the flame and stir in the lime juice and fresh cilantro. Serve alongside steamed white or brown rice.

CARAMELIZED ONION AND BLACK GRAM CURRY

When I close my eyes, I can taste these flavors because they take me back to my childhood. Even though there is a small amount of gravy associated with this curry, I can vividly remember picking up meticulously portioned amounts of this bhaji with warm chapatis. That's because there was only so much to go around, of everything. Curry leaves are the only things that should have the word "curry" in them. I am only half-joking because the origins of the word "curry" may be traced back to "kari," a Tamil word for a sauce or soup to be eaten with rice. And these distinctive leaves from the tree in the Rutaceae family are used generously in many South Indian dishes.

LEVEL: Intermediate

YIELD: approximately 4 servings

INGREDIENTS

2 cups black gram (Kabuli chana), washed well and soaked overnight
3 medium red onions, sliced thinly
1 tablespoon fresh ginger, minced
4 cloves garlic, minced
2 fresh green chiles, diced, more or less
1 bay leaf
5 fresh curry leaves (if available)
1 teaspoon turmeric powder
1/2 teaspoon Kashmiri red chile powder
1/4 grated fresh coconut
1 teaspoon black mustard seeds
1/2 teaspoon whole cumin seeds
1 medium tomato, small diced
vegetable stock, as needed
1 tablespoon garam masala (page 73)
extra virgin olive oil, as needed
salt & pepper, in stages and per taste

METHOD

Rinse and cook the overnight-soaked black gram in salted water with 1/2 teaspoon turmeric powder for 1 hour. Strain and keep a cup of the cooking liquid. In a wide Strain and keep a cup of the cooking liquid. In a wide pan, heat the olive oil and start caramelizing the onions on low-medium heat, stirring periodically. This take a while, up to 45 minutes. Remove the onions and hold. In the same pan, increase the heat to medium and fry the mustard and cumin seeds for 30 seconds or until the mustard seeds begin to pop. Next add the ginger, garlic, and green chile, and sauté for a minute or so until the garlic begins to brown a bit. Now add the curry leaves and tomato. Stew down a bit and add the red chile powder, remaining turmeric powder, and fresh coconut. Cook for a couple of minutes, taste and adjust the salt and pepper. Now add the cooked gram and stir well, adding a bit of the cooking water to ensure the mixture is not too dry. Cover the pan and cook on medium for about 30 minutes. Finish by folding in the caramelized onions and garam masala. Serve alongside a flatbread or steamed rice.

ROASTED VEGETABLE & TOFU TIKKA MASALA

This British interpretation of so much of what they loved about Indian food has now become representative of Indian cuisine the world over. I'm no prude, especially when I espouse the virtues of cross-pollinating culinary ideas to make the world a more delicious place. But to think that the curry houses in England represent all of the diversity and complexity of Indian cuisine is to suggest that a pizzeria in North America represents all Italian cuisine – you know...in Italy.

LEVEL: Intermediate

YIELD: approximately 4 servings

INGREDIENTS
- 3 cups of assorted roasted seasonal vegetables
- 1/2 cup firm tofu, cut into cubes
- 2 cloves garlic, minced
- 1/2 inch piece of fresh ginger, minced
- 4 curry leaves
- one small onion, chopped
- one small green bell pepper, chopped
- 2 cups tikka masala sauce (page 108)
- 1/2 teaspoon Kashmiri red chile powder, more or less
- 1/2 cup heavy cream
- water, as needed
- extra virgin olive oil, as needed
- pinch of sugar, more or less
- salt & pepper, in stages and per taste

METHOD
Over medium heat, fry the ginger, garlic, and curry leaves for two minutes. Next add the onions and bell pepper. Cook this for about 5 minutes. Now add the tofu and cook for two minutes before adding the cooked vegetables. Now add the tikka masala sauce and a bit of water to thin it out. Stir everything for a minute or so. Now add the heavy cream, red chili powder, some sugar, salt, and pepper. Stir well and simmer on low for two or three minutes. Taste the sauce and adjust all the seasonings as desired. Serve alongside your favorite flatbread. Perhaps some naan and some steamed white rice.

BRASSICA & CHICKPEA VINDALOO

A vindaloo showcases the brightness of Portuguese flavors coupled with the warmth of Indian spices and hospitality. Typically, this is a gravy-forward dish. And even less so with the addition of so much body that the garbanzo and brassica vegetables provide. So, the key is to balance the sauce perfectly ahead of time, roast the vegetables perfectly, and harmonize them with the other ingredients over a low simmer. This version is so much more interesting than a traditional version that showcases a single protein.

LEVEL: Intermediate

YIELD: approximately 4 servings

INGREDIENTS

- 1 cup cooked garbanzo
- 1 cup broccoli florets
- 1 cup cauliflower florets
- 1 cup brussels sprouts
- 1 cup chopped green cabbage
- 2 cups vindaloo sauce (page 114)
- 1/2 cup heavy cream or coconut milk
- 6 fresh curry leaves
- 2 green chiles, minced
- 1 teaspoon Kashmiri red chile powder, more or less
- water or vegetable stock, as needed
- 1 sprig fresh mint, leaves chopped
- extra virgin olive oil, as needed
- pinch of sugar, more or less
- salt & pepper, in stages and per taste

METHOD

Preheat an oven to 350F. Roast all the vegetables on a sheet tray by coating them in olive oil, salt, and pepper. Roast the vegetables for 30 minutes. While the vegetables are roasting, heat some oil in a pan and add the curry leaves and green chiles. After a few seconds, once they begin crackling, add the cooked garbanzo and cook for a few minutes. Next add the vindaloo sauce and heavy cream or coconut milk. Add red chile powder depending on your desired heat level. Adjust the flavor or the sauce by adding salt and sugar to balance. It should be spicy, but also balanced in a hint of sweetness. If the sauce is too thick, add some stock or water. Re-season as necessary and hold the sauce on a low simmer. Once the vegetables are roasted to the desired tenderness and caramelization, add them to the curry and stir well. Finish with some chopped mint and serve alongside steamed white rice or your favorite flatbread like naan or paratha.

FENNEL AND EGGPLANT GREEN CURRY

> Anise and aubergine have a natural affinity for each other in my opinion. The fragrance and fresh notes of a Thailand-inspired green curry pairs perfectly with the refreshing qualities of fennel. Certainly, one could add a plant-based protein like tofu, but in this case, I think the harmonious interplay between the eggplant soaking up the gravy flavors and the textural contrast offered by the fennel bulb and seeds is a transcendent experience.

LEVEL: Intermediate

YIELD: approximately 4 servings

INGREDIENTS

One bulb fennel, medium diced, keep the fronds for garnish
3 Japanese eggplant, sliced on a bias into 1/2-inch slices
1 teaspoon fennel seed
1 tablespoon fresh ginger, sliced thinly
2 kaffir lime leaves, sliced very thinly
1 cup green curry concentrate (page 112)
1 cup coconut milk, more or less
water or vegetable stock, as needed
4 mint leaves, torn
2 sprigs cilantro, chopped
4 basil leaves, torn
extra-virgin olive oil, as needed
pinch of sugar, more or less
salt & pepper, in stages and per taste

METHOD

Heat the oil in a heavy bottomed pot and add the fennel seeds and lime leaves. After 15 seconds, add the ginger and garlic. Cook for a minute until the garlic starts browning a bit. Now add the chopped fennel bulb and cook for 5 minutes before adding the eggplant. Stir well and make sure there is enough oil in the pot to ensure the eggplant has a chance to cook. After 10 minutes, add the green curry concentrate and mix well. Add some stock to loosen the sauce a bit. After 5 minutes, add the coconut milk and stir well. Adjust the salt, sugar, and pepper as desired. Simmer on low for 10 minutes. As soon as the eggplant is soft and cooked, turn off the heat and fold in all the fresh herbs (mint, cilantro, and basil). Serve with steamed Jasmine or basmati rice.

JERK SPICED LENTIL KOFTA CURRY

A "kofta" is essentially a croquette, but the breading procedure is not necessarily as complete. Essentially, when we fry something in hot oil, the moisture almost instantaneously turns to steam, and we can see that as the object fries. If the object does not have enough binder, it will usually fall apart in the fryer because of the power of the steam. Essentially, a kofta curry is like a sauce with meatballs. But unlike meatballs, one shouldn't simmer the gravy with the koftas, but instead simply ladle the gravy over them just before serving. Here, the koftas are made with roasted pumpkin, jerk spices, and some potato because frankly, vegetarian koftas are the best.

LEVEL: Intermediate

YIELD: approximately 4 servings

INGREDIENTS
1 Yukon gold potato, boiled
1 cup diced ripe pumpkin or butternut squash, roasted
1 small head of cauliflower, florets and tender stems only, roasted
1 cup cooked lentils, drained well
2 tablespoon jerk paste (page 85)
3 medium red onions, finely minced
1 tablespoon fresh ginger, finely minced
breadcrumbs, as needed
1/2 cup garbanzo flour (use all-purpose flour if you have to)
1 tablespoon fresh garlic, finely minced
1 teaspoon fenugreek leaves
1/4 cup cashews, toasted and ground
1 teaspoon turmeric powder
1 cup tomatoes, diced
1/4 cup heavy cream (optional)
vegetable oil or ghee, as needed
1 teaspoon ground cumin
1 teaspoon ground coriander
pinch of sugar
salt & pepper, in stages and per taste

METHOD
To make the koftas, sauté half the onion, ginger, and garlic in some oil for a few minutes. Next, add the jerk paste and stir for a few minutes. Switch off the heat and transfer the contents of the sauté pan to a mixing bowl with the cooked potatoes, pumpkin, cauliflower, and lentils. Smash to a coarse consistency. Season with salt and add the garbanzo flour. Make lime-sized balls and roll them in the breadcrumbs. Shallow fry them on all sides to a golden brown and hold them warm.

To make the gravy, heat some more oil in a pan and add the remaining onions, ginger, and garlic. Sauté until golden brown on low heat. Add the spices including the fenugreek leaves and stir for 5 minutes. Add the ground cashew and sauté for a bit. Add the tomatoes and a bit of water. Season well and adjust if necessary. Concentrate on low heat, add the heavy cream and sugar towards the last 2 minutes, and purée smoothly. Ladle the sauce over the koftas and serve immediately. It may be accompanied with rice or naan.

MUSHROOM CHETTINAD

> Chettinad cuisine is the cuisine of the Chettinad region of Tamil Nadu state in South India. Characterized by huge flavors, spice, and aroma, it is a celebration of all that spices can bring to a dish. This dish does not have large amounts of gravy and is designed to be picked up, literally, with a flat bread or fried dough. But it is certainly acceptable to accompany it with rice, idli, dosa, or adai. In India, one is trained to use one's hand to eat dishes ranging from rasam & rice to a dry dish like this one.

LEVEL: Intermediate

YIELD: approximately 4 servings

INGREDIENTS

- 2 lbs. assorted mushrooms like cremini, shiitake, oyster, and golden chanterelle
- 1 tablespoon poppy seed
- 1 tablespoon coriander seed
- 1 tablespoon cumin seed
- 1 teaspoon fennel seed
- 3 dry red chilies
- 1 red bell pepper, diced
- 1 cinnamon stick
- 2 cardamom pods
- 3 cloves
- 1/2 cup grated fresh coconut
- 2 teaspoons ginger, minced
- 4 cloves garlic, minced
- vegetable oil, as needed
- 10 fresh curry leaves (if available)
- 2 large onions sliced thinly
- 1 whole star anise
- 4 tomatoes chopped fine or equivalent strained tomatoes
- 1 teaspoon cayenne powder (optional)
- water, as needed
- salt & pepper, in stages and per taste

METHOD

Brush and pat dry the mushrooms. Set aside. In a large pan, add enough vegetable oil to sauté all the whole seeds, red chilies, coconut, cardamom, and cloves over medium heat. Season lightly with salt and pepper. Add the onions and sauté until golden brown. Next, add the ginger and garlic. Stir for about 2 minutes on low to medium low heat. Remove from heat and process it to a uniform paste, adding a bit of water if needed. Set aside. In the same pan, add some more oil, season the mushrooms with pepper, and sauté until golden brown. Remove from the pan. Add the star anise, cinnamon stick, spice paste, red bell pepper, and curry leaves, and sauté for a few minutes. Next add the tomatoes and stew for 5 minutes until the tomatoes break down. Now return the mushrooms to the pan and stir well to coat the mushrooms with everything in the pan. Re-season with salt and pepper. Add a bit of water, cover, and simmer on low for 15 minutes. Garnish with chopped cilantro and some fresh lime juice. Serve with a flatbread or fried bread like puri.

VEGETABLE XACUTI

Indian restaurants do this well – make vegetarian versions of dishes that are not traditionally vegetarian. Xacuti is a great example of a Konkani dish, especially with the use of tamarind and coconut milk. The Konkan coast of India alongside the Arabian Sea has a long and storied tradition of celebrating and developing a cuisine that showcases the agricultural bounty of the reason. One can taste the coast in this dish.

LEVEL: Intermediate

YIELD: approximately 4 servings

INGREDIENTS

1 cup green beans, cleaned and cut into 1 inch pieces
1 cup cauliflower florets
2 medium white or red potatoes, washed, medium diced
1 carrot, medium diced
1/2 cup fresh corn
2 tablespoons xacuti blend (page 76)
2 shallots, sliced thinly
5 curry leaves (if available)
4 cloves garlic, minced
2 green chiles, halved
2 medium tomatoes, chopped
3 whole red chiles
1/4 cup tamarind water
1 cup coconut milk
1/2 cup fresh cilantro, chopped
water for blanching the vegetables
vegetable oil, unsalted butter, or ghee, as desired
salt & pepper, in stages and per taste

METHOD

In a pot with salted water, cook the cauliflower, potatoes, carrot, beans and corn. Drain well and hold. In a heavy-bottomed pan, heat some oil, butter, or ghee and add the garlic, red chiles, green chiles, and curry leaves. Cook for a minute before adding the shallots. Cook until the shallots brown a bit before adding the xacuti blend and cook for 2-3 minutes. Deglaze with the tamarind water and tomatoes. Simmer for a few minutes before adding the cooked vegetables. Mix well, taking care not to break up the vegetables too much. Now add the coconut milk and stir well. Taste the sauce and adjust the seasoning as preferred. It should be a zesty and punchy sauce with some spice, but balanced and well-rounded because of the coconut milk. Simmer for 5 minutes or so before finishing with the fresh cilantro. Serve alongside chapati or steamed white rice.

VEGETABLE KORMA

> A korma is a deeply savory curry but is not meant to be pungent. Its roots lie in the cuisines of Central Asia and Turkey. The highlight is the use of yogurt (as a natural meat tenderizer), nuts, and fruit. Mughlai cuisine is elevated and refined. The use of much sought-after ingredients and the delicate balance of spices is a hallmark. When I've served kormas on the menus at the restaurant and a guest asks that it be made "Indian hot," I think to myself: It already is. Here, I present a korma with vegetables. The vegetables used should be seasonal and fresh.

LEVEL: Intermediate

YIELD: approximately 4 servings

INGREDIENTS
- 2 tablespoons grated dry or fresh coconut
- 5 whole cloves
- 5 black peppercorns
- 1 cinnamon stick
- 2 teaspoon sesame seeds
- 4 cashew nuts
- 1 large red onion, finely minced
- 2 tomatoes, finely chopped
- 1 cup cauliflower florets, partially boiled or roasted
- 2 russet potato, medium dice, boiled in salted water
- 1/2 cup carrot, thick slices par boiled
- 1/2 cup green pepper, small dice
- 1/2 cup green peas
- 1 teaspoon red chili powder (or cayenne)
- 4 dry chipotle peppers
- 1 teaspoon coriander powder
- 1/2 teaspoon dry roasted cumin powder
- 1 teaspoon cumin seeds
- 1 teaspoon ginger, minced
- 1 teaspoon garlic, minced
- vegetable oil or ghee, as needed
- salt & pepper, in stages and per taste

METHOD

Start by dry-toasting the sesame seeds, cashews, coconut, and dried chipotle peppers. Blend the mixture in a spice grinder. Next, sauté the cinnamon stick, cumin seeds, cloves, peppercorns, and onion in the ghee or vegetable oil for about 5 minutes. Add the blended spice mixture and fry it in the oil (bhuna). Next, add the ginger and garlic and fry for a few minutes. Follow with the ground spices. Season adequately with salt. Sauté the green peppers and add the par-cooked cauliflower, potatoes and tomatoes. Cook for about 10 minutes. Then add the green peas and simmer on low to marry all the flavors. Finish with some chopped cilantro and serve with a wedge of lemon. This dish is best with a flatbread.

VEGETABLE KOLHAPURI

For many summers now, Jenneffer and I travel to India to visit my family in Mumbai, and then we are off gallivanting to some remote destination. We have been to Kanha National Tiger Preserve in the heart of Madhya Pradesh on multiple occasions; it is a thrilling location. On one occasion, on the car trip back to Nagpur airport, we had enough time to have lunch in a modest restaurant. Jenneffer likes pungent food in general and I knew that she had never had this dish before, so I ordered it. It may be her favorite Indian dish to this day. Kolhapuri cuisine is known for its mutton dishes. This vegetarian interpretation makes heavy use of smoky dried red chilies.

LEVEL: Intermediate

YIELD: approximately 4 servings

INGREDIENTS
2 tablespoons grated dry or fresh coconut
5 whole cloves
5 black peppercorns
1 cinnamon stick
2 teaspoons sesame seeds
4 cashew nuts
1 large red onion, finely minced
2 tomatoes, finely chopped
1 cup cauliflower florets, partially boiled or roasted
2 Russet potatoes, medium dice, boiled in salted water
1/2 cup carrot, thick slices par boiled
1/2 cup green pepper, small dice
1/2 cup green peas
1 teaspoon red chili powder (or cayenne)
4 dry chipotle peppers
1 teaspoon coriander powder
1/2 teaspoon dry roasted cumin powder
1 teaspoon cumin seeds
1 teaspoon ginger, minced
1 teaspoon garlic, minced
vegetable oil or ghee, as needed
salt & pepper, in stages and per taste

METHOD
Start by dry-toasting the sesame seeds, cashews, coconut, and dried chipotle peppers. Blend the mixture in a spice grinder. Next, sauté the cinnamon stick, cumin seeds, cloves, peppercorns, and onion in the ghee or vegetable oil for about 5 minutes. Add the blended spice mixture and fry it in the oil (bhuna). Next, add the ginger and garlic and fry for a few minutes. Follow with the ground spices. Season adequately with salt. Sauté the green peppers and add the par-cooked cauliflower, potatoes and tomatoes. Cook for about 10 minutes. Then add the green peas and simmer on low to marry all the flavors. Finish with some chopped cilantro and serve with a wedge of lemon. This dish is best with a flatbread.

KOHLRABI AND TURNIP BASIL CURRY

When it's the season, kohlrabi and turnips grow well in Central Florida. For years, I would simply roast these vegetables and season simply with salt and pepper to be served alongside many of our *big plates*. One day, at the end of dinner service, I made myself a random combination of left-over green curry and some of these roasted vegetables. The idea for this dish may have been born then. Again, one could add a plant-based protein like tofu, but if one must, I recommend using shucked fresh edamame beans instead. Simply fold them into the dish five minutes from the end.

LEVEL: Intermediate

YIELD: approximately 4 servings

INGREDIENTS

3 medium kohlrabi, washed well and cut into wedges
3 medium turnips, washed well and medium diced
1 medium red onion, thinly sliced
1 cup green curry concentrate (page 112)
1/4 cup low sodium sauce
1 cup coconut milk
water or vegetable stock, as needed
2 cups fresh basil leaves, keep the stems
1 inch fresh ginger, sliced thinly
3 cloves fresh garlic
1 fresh green chile, chopped (optional)
extra-virgin olive oil or vegetable oil as needed
granulated sugar, as needed
salt & pepper, in stages and per taste

METHOD

On a sheet tray, coat the basil stems, kohlrabi, and turnips with some oil and season lightly with salt and pepper. Roast in a 350F oven for 30 minutes. While the vegetables are roasting, in a heavy-bottomed saucepan, sauté the ginger and garlic for 2 minutes before adding the green chile and green curry concentrate. Fry the concentrate for a couple of minutes, add half the basil, and, as soon as it wilts, transfer the sauce to a blender. Process it to a smooth texture. By now, the kohlrabi and turnips will have finished roasting. Discard the basil stems. Return the pureed sauce to a pan, add the coconut milk, some sugar, salt, and pepper, as necessary. Simmer on low. When the sauce is at the desired texture (should coat the back of a spoon) and flavor, fold in the roasted vegetables. Finish by chopping the remaining fresh basil and folding it into the sauce. Serve alongside some steamed Jasmine rice or on top of your favorite cooked noodles, preferably a neutral flavored noodle like rice noodles.

EGGPLANT AND COCONUT BHAJI

This is my interpretation of the bhaji I had with my family when we played wedding crashers after the Bombay-Baroda cricket match. To this day, I can taste the warm puri and this bhaji on a balmy evening as a six-year-old. I have no idea how the cooks made it then, but the flavors here bring me a lot of comfort. Frankly, I am not certain that everyone will like this because the texture of freshly grated coconut is off-putting for some. I grew up with that.

LEVEL: Intermediate

YIELD: approximately 4 servings

INGREDIENTS
- 4 cups large diced eggplant
- 2 medium-sized ripe tomatoes, diced
- 1/2 cup unsweetened grated coconut
- 2 Yukon Gold potatoes, washed, skin on, large diced
- 1 tablespoon fresh ginger, minced
- 1 tablespoon fresh garlic, minced
- 2 red onions, medium diced
- 1 teaspoon whole cumin seeds
- 1 teaspoon whole cloves
- 2 tablespoons vegetable oil (or clarified butter)
- 1 tablespoon turmeric powder
- 1 teaspoon cumin powder
- 1 teaspoon coriander powder
- 1 teaspoon red chili powder (or cayenne)
- 1 serrano chili
- 1 cinnamon stick
- 2 bay leaves
- 2 tablespoons chopped fresh cilantro
- salt & pepper, in stages and per taste

METHOD

Coat the eggplant liberally with vegetable or olive oil, season with salt and pepper, and roast on a sheet tray in a 375F oven until they are soft. Turn the eggplant once during this process for even roasting. Remove and set aside. To a wide and shallow roasting pan, add the oil (or clarified butter) and bring to a medium heat. Add the whole spices (cinnamon, cumin seeds, bay leaves, cloves). Stir for 30 seconds and add the onions and ginger. Sauté until the onions are slightly caramelized. Now add the garlic and stir for 30 seconds. The fresh coconut goes in next—stir it for a couple of minutes. Set aside and blend well in a food processor. Boil the potatoes in salted water and drain well. In a sauté pan, add the coconut and spice mixture and stir on medium heat for a couple of minutes. Add the cooked potatoes, the tomatoes, and all the remaining ingredients (except the eggplant and fresh cilantro). Season with salt and pepper. Let the mixture simmer on medium heat until the tomatoes start breaking down. Add the roasted eggplant and stir well. Stew this on medium heat, stirring periodically until the dish is almost dry. Taste and re-season, if necessary. Finish with the fresh cilantro and a wedge of lemon.

WASTE NOT MASSAMAN

> An incredible fusion of Thai and Indian flavors combining the depth of a classic red curry with the warmth of Indian spices. *Massaman* has connections to *mussalman* (a person who follows the Islamic faith).

LEVEL: Intermediate

YIELD: approximately 4 servings

INGREDIENTS

- 1 cup cauliflower core, cut into large pieces
- 1 cup tender broccoli stems, cut into discs
- 2 cups vegetable peels (like potato, carrots, sweet potato, beets, etc.)
- garbanzo flour, as needed
- egg whites from 2 eggs
- 1 cup left over rice or stale bread, if available
- 2 shallots, sliced
- 1 yellow bell pepper, cored and diced
- 2 tablespoons coriander seeds
- 2 teaspoons cumin seeds
- 3 cloves
- 6 green or white cardamom pods
- 6-12 dried red chilies, soaked in hot water for 5 minutes
- 1/2-inch piece of fresh galingale or ginger, chopped
- 1 tablespoon, chopped lemongrass
- 4 cloves garlic, minced
- 5 kaffir lime leaves, chopped
- 5 cilantro stems, finely chopped
- 1/4 cup tamarind water (tamarind concentrate + water)
- 2 cups coconut milk
- 1/2 cup roasted cashew nuts
- 1 cup fresh cilantro, chopped
- extra-virgin olive oil or vegetable oil, as needed
- water, as needed
- light brown sugar, as needed
- salt & pepper, in stages and per taste

METHOD

Waste Not Dumpling

Blanch the cauliflower cores and broccoli stems in salted water until they are just cooked. Drain well. Toss the skins with some olive oil and roast them on a baking sheet at 350F for 30 minutes. Process the toasted skins and cooked cauliflower cores in a food processor. Season as desired before folding in the egg whites and enough garbanzo flour so one achieves the texture of dumplings.

Massaman Curry

Dry toast all the spices and grind to a fine blend in a spice grinder. In a saucepan, heat some oil and sauté the shallot, galangal, garlic, cilantro stems, lemongrass, kaffir lime, and green chile for 5 minutes. Transfer this mixture into a blender along with the ground spices, soaked red chilies, and salt; grind to a smooth paste. In the same pan, add some oil and fry the paste for 2-3 minutes before adding the coconut milk, tamarind water, and some water. Taste and adjust the seasoning of this sauce. Simmer on low. Bring a pot of salted water to a low simmer and drop in scoops of the dumpling mixture. When all the dumplings have risen to the top, scoop out and drain on a sheet tray. Add the cooked dumplings to the sauce and let them sit in the sauce for at least 15 minutes before serving garnished with roasted cashews and steamed white rice or noodles.

Global Fusion

I once received a lot of flak for writing a piece that essentially asserted that all food today is a fusion of parts and pieces derived from and influenced by other food. While I still believe that, here, I illustrate how one may compose globally inspired dishes with no pretentious claim of authenticity. Only earnest attempts to delight.

ROASTED VEGETABLE BISTEEYA WITH HEIRLOOM GRAINS AND MASALA CREAM

Instead of the traditional filo dough, we will use the user-friendly puff pastry.

LEVEL: Intermediate

YIELD: approximately 4

INGREDIENTS
2 cups Moroccan ratatouille (page 96)
1 cup cooked heirloom grains (page 178)
1 tablespoon sesame sherry vinaigrette (page 164)
2-3 fresh basil leaves, chopped
2 sprigs fresh cilantro
1 cup tikka masala sauce (page 108)
1/2 teaspoon ground cinnamon
1/2 teaspoon ground cardamom
1/4 teaspoon red chile powder or cayenne
1/4 cup heavy cream or coconut milk
granulated sugar, as needed
1 teaspoon confectioner's sugar
1 sheet store bought puff pastry
1 egg (optional)
water, as needed
salt & pepper, in stages and per taste

METHOD
If the ratatouille is too wet, place it in a sauté pan and start cooking it on low heat to evaporate the excess water so it intensifies in flavor and becomes dry. Let this mixture cool down to room temperature. Roll out the puff pastry a bit. Place 1/4 cup of dry ratatouille evenly around the sheet. Brush in between the scoops and around the edges with a half and half mixture of egg and water. Bring in the sides and pinch them together form a ratatouille-filled puff pastry turnover. Place each on a baking sheet with the crimped side down, brush uniformly with more egg wash, and bake in a 400F oven for 20 minutes until golden brown. Remove and let cool a bit.

In a small saucepan, combine the tikka masala base, cinnamon, cardamom, cayenne, and heavy cream. Adjust the salt and sugar levels and bring to a low simmer. Stir the ingredients well. This is the masala cream. Combine the cooked grains with sesame dressing, season with salt and pepper, and fold in the chopped basil. Serve the baked bisteeya alongside the grains salad and a generous amount of the masala cream. Garnish with fresh cilantro and a dusting of confectioner's sugar.

ACORN SQUASH TAJINE

> A few months ago, we wandered about and lost ourselves in the maze that is Old Marrakech. Many a tajine was consumed, but the most memorable version was home-cooked by our *Riad*-manager. She created the most beautiful vegetable version with a garnish of caramelized onions and raisins. And the fluffiest cous-cous I've ever had. This version is inspired by that memory.

LEVEL: Intermediate

YIELD: approximately 4 servings

INGREDIENTS

1 medium sized acorn squash, washed, deseeded and large diced
8 cloves garlic, peeled, sliced into slivers
1 tbs. fresh ginger, minced
1 lemon, seeded, cut into wedges
1 large Spanish onion, peeled, sliced
1/4 cup capers
1/2 cup seedless briny green olives, rinsed and halved
2 cinnamon sticks
4 cardamom pods
1 inch saffron threads
4 bay leaves
1 tablespoon ground cumin
1 teaspoon ground coriander
1 teaspoon chopped sliced preserved lemons
1/2 cup extra virgin olive oil
2 cups vegetable stock
1/2 cup chopped flat-leaf parsley
1/2 cup chopped fresh cilantro
salt & pepper, in stages and per taste

METHOD

Preheat an oven to 325 F. In a tajine, Dutch oven, or shallow pot, heat the olive oil on medium heat and sear the acorn squash so they are golden brown. Set aside. In the same oil, sauté the onions until translucent. Add the capers, olives, lemon wedges, preserved lemon, ginger, garlic, and ground spices. Stir for a minute or so. Add the squash back to the pot and deglaze with enough vegetable stock to barely cover the squash and add the saffron threads. Next, add the whole spices and test the seasoning. Depending on how briny the olives and capers might be, you might need some more salt and even pepper. The ultimate flavor profile should be pronounced with olives, lemon, and olive oil. Cover tightly and bake in the oven for about one hour. Remove from the oven and let the tajine rest for about 15 minutes before sprinkling with the chopped parsley and cilantro. Serve with fluffy cous-cous.

ATKILT WAT

A nice representation of the Indian influence on Ethiopian cuisine. The end result is very close to an Indian cabbage masala-type side dish. However, I've tried here to keep it closer to Ethiopian culinary sensibilities.

LEVEL: Basic

YIELD: approximately 4 servings

INGREDIENTS

1/2 head cabbage, cut into medium sized pieces
1 carrot, sliced
1/2 lb. white or Yukon potatoes, medium diced
1 medium onion, diced
1 teaspoon Berbere spice (page 77)
1 teaspoon turmeric
1/2 teaspoon cumin seeds
1 teaspoon mustard seeds
1/4 teaspoon fenugreek seeds
2 cloves garlic, minced
1 teaspoon fresh ginger, minced
1 green chile, minced
1/4 cup fresh cilantro, chopped
water or vegetable stock, as needed
extra virgin olive oil, as needed
salt & pepper, in stages and per taste

METHOD

The directions for the preparation of this dish are as intuitive as they are modest. It is basically a sautéed and shallow-braised dish. Start by heating the oil in a shallow, yet wide pan. First, add the mustard seeds, cumin seeds, and fenugreek seeds. Fry for about 15 second before adding the green chile, ginger, and garlic. Next add the Berbere spice and turmeric, and fry for 15 seconds before adding the onion and cabbage. If the pan gets too dry, add more oil. Season lightly with salt and pepper. After about 10 minutes, add the carrots and potatoes. Stir well and add enough water or vegetable stock to pick up the fond bits and allow for steaming. Cover the pan with a tight-fitting lid and cook for about 20 minutes or until the vegetables are soft, but not mushy. Taste and adjust for salt and pepper before finishing by sprinkling in the fresh cilantro.

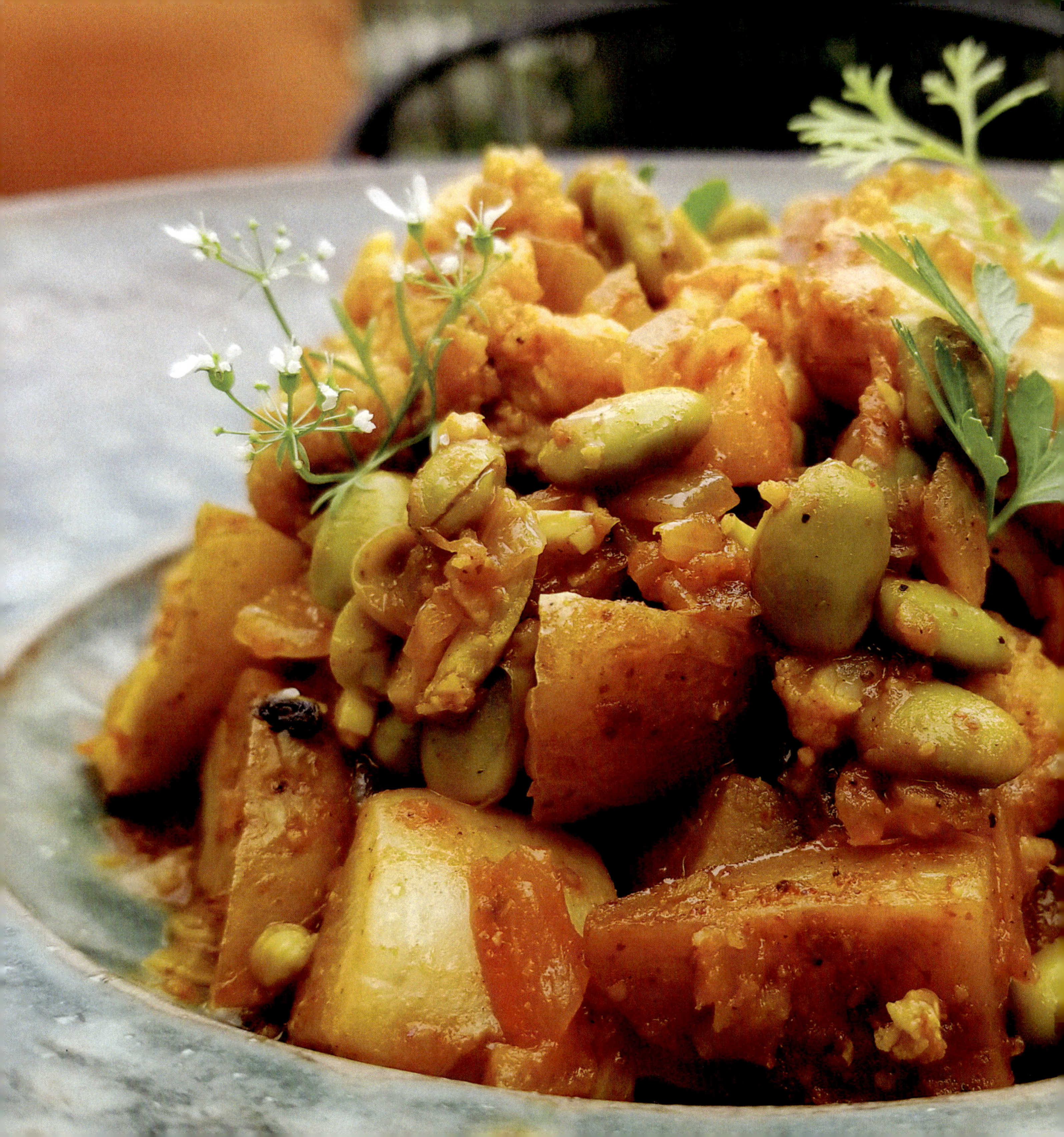

DUXELLE QUINOA BUTTERMILK CRÊPE

A duxelle-filled crêpe isn't the story here. But when one uses duxelle to fill a quinoa buttermilk crêpe, Peru, the American South, India, and France are wrapped together in a fulfilling composition.

LEVEL: Intermediate

YIELD: approximately 4 servings

INGREDIENTS
4 quinoa and buttermilk crêpes (page 201)
3 cups wild and assorted mushrooms, torn or chopped into small pieces
2 shallots, minced
1 tablespoon fresh thyme leaves, chopped coarsely
2 cloves garlic, minced
1 bay leaf
1 cup dry white wine
2 tablespoons fresh tarragon, chopped
2 tablespoons unsalted butter
extra-virgin olive oil, as needed
1/4 cup heavy cream
salt & pepper, in stages and per taste

METHOD
To make the duxelle, melt the butter in a shallow pan and sweat the shallots for a few minutes until translucent. Next add the garlic, thyme, and bay leaf. Stir for a few seconds. Now add the mushrooms and roast in the pan developing some caramelization. Add a touch of salt and pepper. If needed, add a touch of olive oil. Deglaze with wine, scrape the bottom of the pan to mix in the fond, and add the cream. Reduce the temperature to low-medium and cook for as long as it takes to achieve a rather dry, yet creamy mixture. Stir periodically. Finish by folding in the tarragon and discard the bay leaf. Adjust the salt and pepper, as desired.

Once the duxelle cools to room temperature, fill each crêpe as desired and serve with a light fresh salad dressed in an acidic vinaigrette.

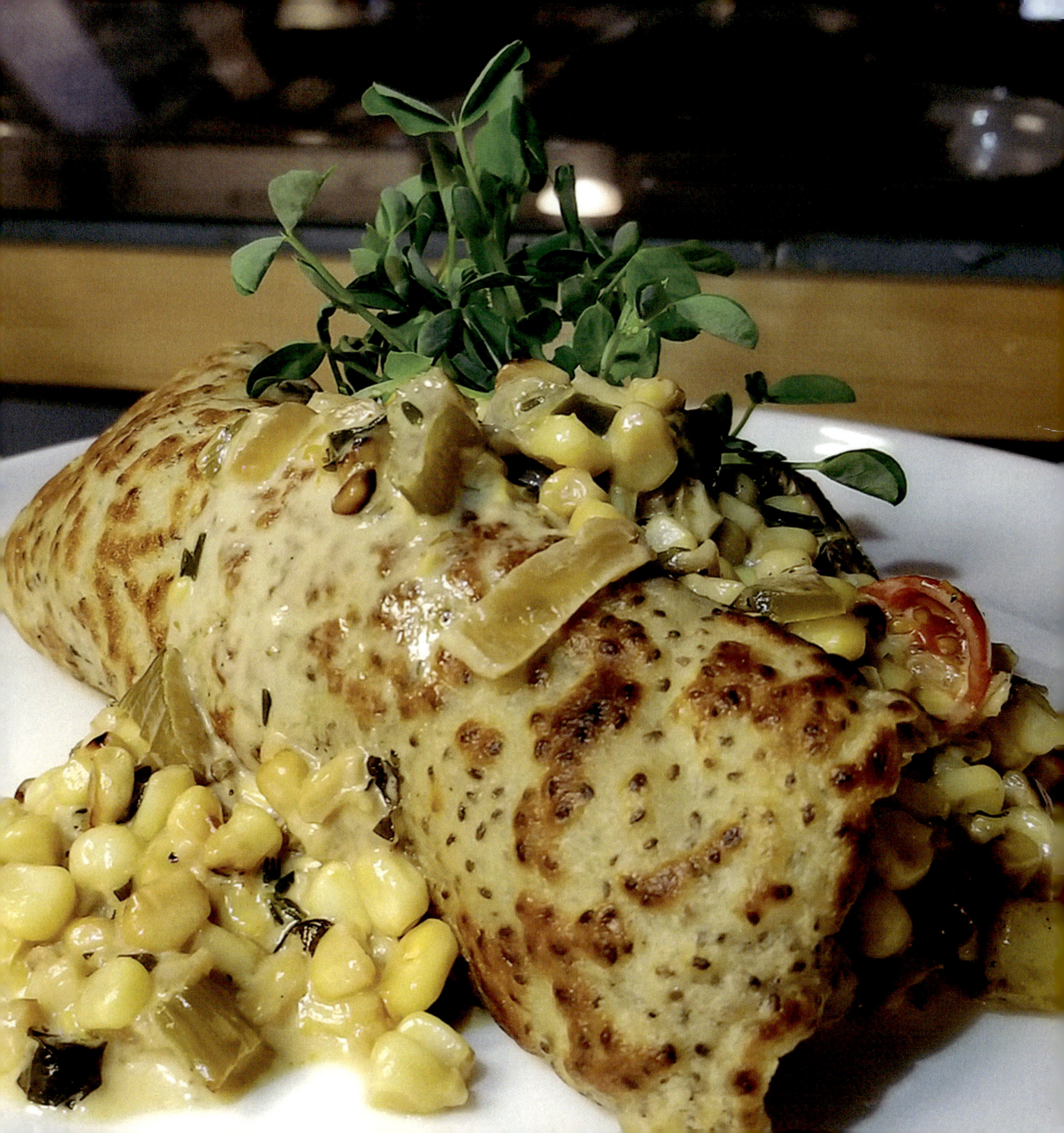

COLLARD GREENS GNOCCHI WITH BLISTERED TOMATOES & FETA

LEVEL: Intermediate

YIELD: approximately 4 servings

INGREDIENTS

2 cups collard greens, leaves only, washed, dried, and torn
1 stick unsalted butter
1.5 cups all-purpose flour
5 large eggs
1 teaspoon smoked paprika
4 cloves fresh garlic, sliced thinly
¼ cup dry white wine
1 tablespoon Dijon mustard
water for cooking gnocchi
20 ripe cherry tomatoes
1 cup feta cheese, crumbled
extra-virgin olive oil, as needed
salt & pepper, in stages and per taste

METHOD

Melt the butter in a saucepan and add the garlic. Cook for a minute or so before adding the smoked paprika, collard greens, and some salt and pepper. Cook for about 3 minutes and deglaze with the wine. Cook for a minute and transfer the mixture to a blender. Puree the mixture and return to the saucepan. With the pureed greens on a low heat, add the flour in stages, stirring with a wooden spoon. It will come together quickly. This is the collard greens pâte à choux. When the dough starts peeling off the sides of the pan and the flour has been completely incorporated (about 3 minutes), transfer the dough to a stand mixer with the paddle attachment or a mixing bowl.

Stir the dough for a few seconds to release the steam before adding the mustard. Next, with the mixer on low (or if doing by hand, stirring gently), add the eggs one at a time. Wait until an egg is incorporated before adding the next. When all the eggs have been mixed in, cool down the mixture a bit before scooping gnocchi with an ice-cream scoop into simmering salted water or use a pastry piping bag and cut 3/4-inch cylinders into the water. Poach the gnocchi until they all rise to the top and have been there for about a minute. Fish them out and hold them on a sheet tray. If necessary, drizzle a small amount of olive oil on the cooked gnocchi to prevent them from sticking together.

The composed dish is very easy to finish. In a hot cast-iron or non-stick pan, add some olive oil, and immediately add the washed and dried, whole, ripe cherry tomatoes. Maintain a high heat to char the tomatoes. Add a touch of salt and pepper. As soon as the tomatoes soften up a bit and have dark spots, remove them and hold. Reduce the heat to medium-low, adding more oil, only if necessary, to brown the gnocchi.

Compose the dish by serving the crisp gnocchi with the charred tomatoes, crumbled feta, fresh basil, drizzle of olive oil and some finishing salt and freshly ground pepper. This is a wonderful springtime dish that will give a pasta primavera a good run for its money.

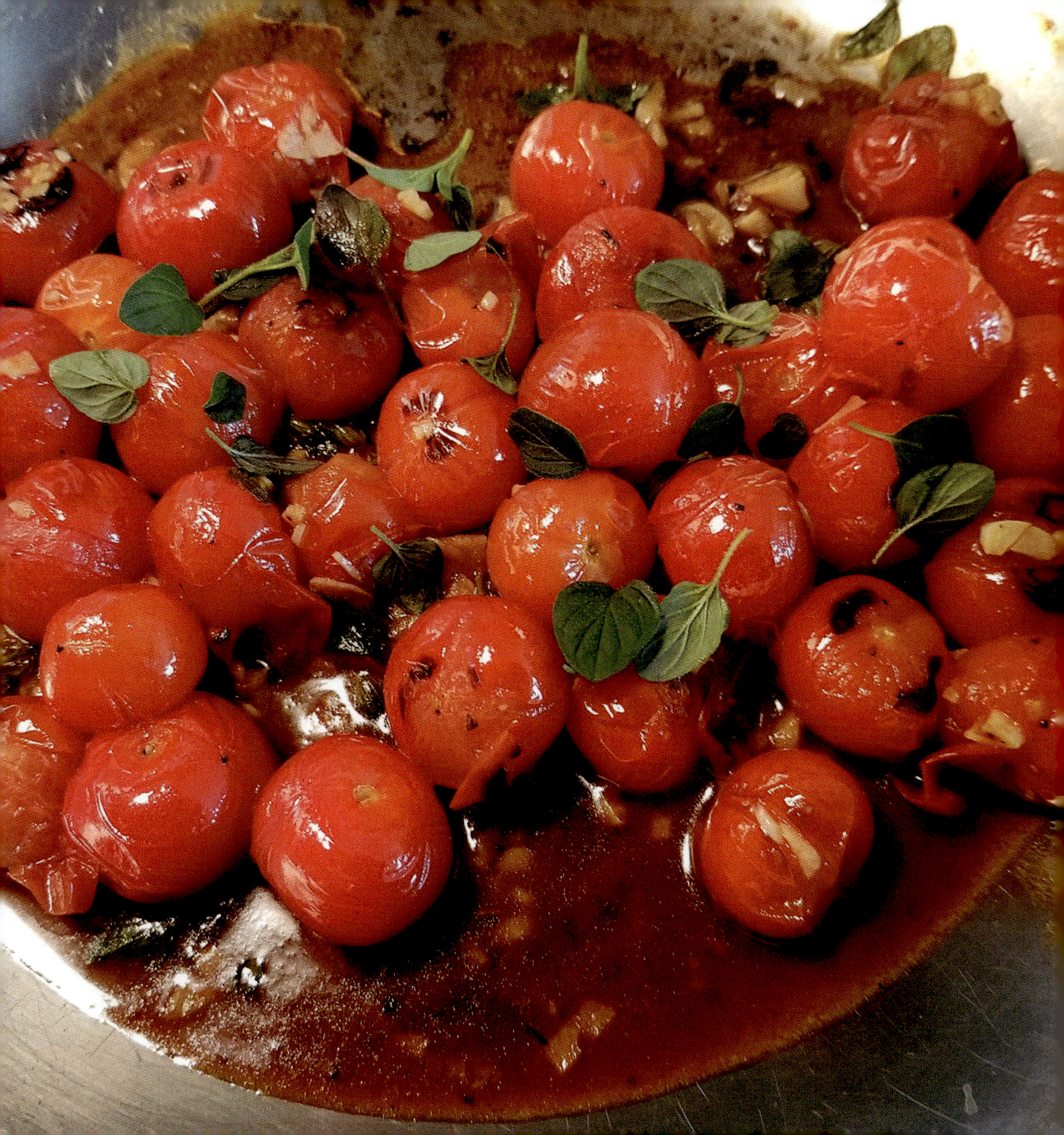

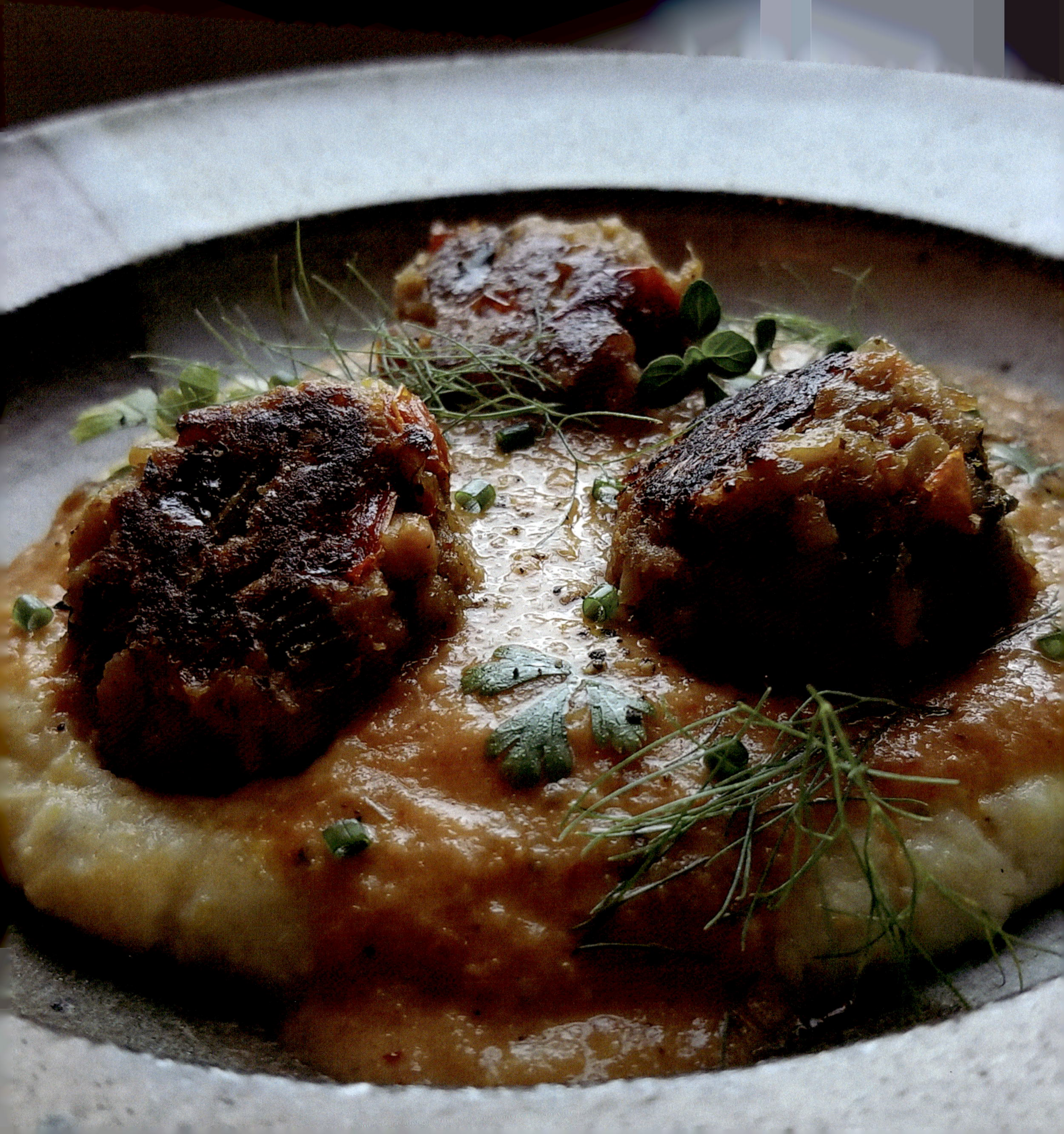

TEMPEH KOFTA ETOUFFEE 'N GRITS

A vegetarian take on a classic dish from the American South. I thought long and hard about the best way to celebrate the creole sauce on top of grits. The kofta holds up to the strong and comforting flavors.

LEVEL: Intermediate

YIELD: approximately 4 servings

INGREDIENTS
8 ounces tempeh (or extra-firm tofu)
1/4 cup almonds, toasted and ground
1 shallot, minced
1/2 inch piece fresh ginger, minced
2 cloves of garlic, roughly chopped
1 green chile, minced
1/4 cup fresh parsley, chopped
1 small potato, boiled
breadcrumbs, as needed
1 teaspoon creole spice blend (page 87)
1/2 cup onion, small diced
1/4 cup celery, small diced
1/4 cup green pepper, small diced
1 bay leaf
2 cups creole sauce (page 107)
1/4 cup heavy cream
water or vegetable stock, as needed
2 tablespoons unsalted butter or vegetable oil, more for cooking the kofta
2 tablespoon flour
4 portions shiitake and thyme grits (page 264)
salt & pepper, in stages and per taste

METHOD
Chop up the tempeh and roast in a 350F oven for 30 minutes. While the tempeh is roasting, sauté the shallot, ginger, and garlic in 1 tablespoon of butter. After a couple of minutes, add the green chile and creole spice blend. Cook for a few seconds before adding the cooked potato. Smash it into the mixture and transfer all the ingredients to a bowl to cool down. After the tempeh comes out of the oven and cools a bit, add it to the same bowl along with the ground almonds and chopped parsley. Mix well. Taste the mixture and season with salt, pepper, and perhaps more creole spices, as desired. Add just enough breadcrumbs to be able to form one-inch balls. These are the koftas. Melt some butter or oil in a heavy bottomed skillet and add the flour. Stir frequently to make a light brown roux. This should take about 15 minutes over medium heat. Add the holy trinity (onions, celery, bell pepper) to the browned roux and cook for another 10 minutes or until the vegetables soften. Add the bay leaf and creole sauce. Cook the sauce for about 10 minutes. Taste and finish with the heavy cream. Warm the grits and loosen it up with some water or stock so it is on the creamy side. Coat the koftas with some olive oil and bake them in the oven to brown or cook them in a non-stick or cast-iron skillet. Serve the dish with grits on the bottom, then some etouffee sauce, and browned koftas on top of the sauce. Garnish with more chopped parsley, if desired.

MUSHROOM BOURGUIGNON

Julia Child may have frowned upon this version of a French classic she made even more famous. But then again, maybe she may have not. We will never know for sure, but I can assure you that I've taken great care in rendering the technique and tradition as purely as I can imagine.

LEVEL: Basic

YIELD: approximately 4 servings

INGREDIENTS

2 lbs. assorted mushroom (like cremini, button, chanterelle, etc.)
1 small carrot, small diced
1/2 cup leeks, sliced
1 medium onion, small diced
1 tablespoon fresh thyme leaves
4 garlic cloves, sliced thinly
1 *bouquet garni*
1/2 cup pearl onions, fresh peeled or frozen thawed
1/2 cup fingerling potatoes, medium diced
2 cups Merlot
1 tablespoon tomato paste
vegetable or mushroom stock, as needed
1/4 cup heavy cream (optional)
1 tablespoon flour
extra-virgin olive oil, as needed
1 tablespoon unsalted butter
salt & pepper, in stages and per taste

Accompaniments: egg noodles, *crème fraîche* or sour cream, chopped parsley or tarragon, crusty baguette

METHOD

In a cast iron skillet, heat the butter and some olive oil together. Sauté the mushrooms and onions until they are roasted and charred in spots. Remove them and hold for later. In the same pan, roast the onions, carrot, and leeks. Once the vegetables are translucent, add the garlic and fresh thyme. Cook for a few seconds before adding the flour. If the skillet is too dry, add more oil. Season lightly with salt and pepper. Next, add the tomato paste and fry until the paste begins getting dark. Now add the potatoes, stir well, and deglaze with wine. Maintain a medium heat so that the cooking is a bit agitated. After a minute or so, add enough mushroom or vegetable stock to barely cover the ingredients. Taste the broth and adjust the seasoning. Submerge the *bouquet garni* into the sauce and simmer, covered on low for about 20 minutes. Return the mushrooms and pearl onions to the skillet and cook on low, uncovered to achieve a thick, dark sauce that is balanced in texture and flavor. Discard the bouquet garni. Mix in the heavy cream to round out the flavors.

Serve over cooked egg noodles, a dollop of *crème fraîche*, some chopped tarragon, and crusty baguette.

SHEPHERD'S PIE

> The only disclaimer here would be that I don't think shepherds are raising soybeans. However, I could very well be mistaken. There is so much natural depth of flavor in this humble, yet supremely comforting dish that I decided only to swap out the protein for a plant-based option. Pro Tip: Caramelize and deglaze.

LEVEL: Intermediate

YIELD: approximately 4 servings

INGREDIENTS

2 cups seitan or tempeh or extra-firm tofu, chopped fine
2 cups onion, small diced
1 cup carrot, small diced
1 cup celery, small diced
2 bay leaves
1 tablespoon fresh rosemary, chopped
1 tablespoon fresh thyme, chopped
1 tablespoon tomato paste
1 cup fresh green peas (frozen if fresh is not available)
1/2 cup dry red wine
1 cup vegetable stock
2 cups milk or half and half
4 cloves garlic, minced
3 medium Yukon gold potatoes
1 egg (optional)
pinch of ground nutmeg, freshly grated, if possible
1 tablespoon fresh parsley, chopped
water for boiling the potatoes
2 tablespoons unsalted butter
salt & pepper, in stages and per taste

METHOD

Boil the potatoes in salted water, starting in cold water. Drain well and spread on a sheet tray and dry out in a low temperature oven for 15 minutes or so. While the potatoes are drying out, heat the milk and one bay leaf. Season with a pinch of freshly grated nutmeg, salt, and pepper. Add a pat of butter to the heated, seasoned milk, Discard the bay leaf. Transfer the cooked and dried potatoes to a bowl and in stages, add the warm milk to the potatoes and mash with a potato masher. Make sure the lumps are non-existent. If using an egg, whisk it and gradually whisk it into the mashed potatoes. In a cast-iron or heavy-bottomed skillet, melt the remaining butter and caramelize the plant protein, browning well. Season with salt and pepper. Remove and hold. In the same skillet, cook the mirepoix (onions, carrots, celery) until soft. Next, add the garlic and cook for a few seconds before adding the tomato paste. Sauté this mixture for a couple of minutes before deglazing with the wine. Return the browned plant protein to the skillet; add the rosemary, thyme, and peas. If the mixture is too dry, add some stock, but it shouldn't be a broth. Transfer this mixture into a baking dish (either family style or individual portions). Spread the warm mashed potatoes on the top and bake at 375F for 20 minutes or until the top is golden brown. Let the pie cool down significantly before finishing with the chopped parsley.

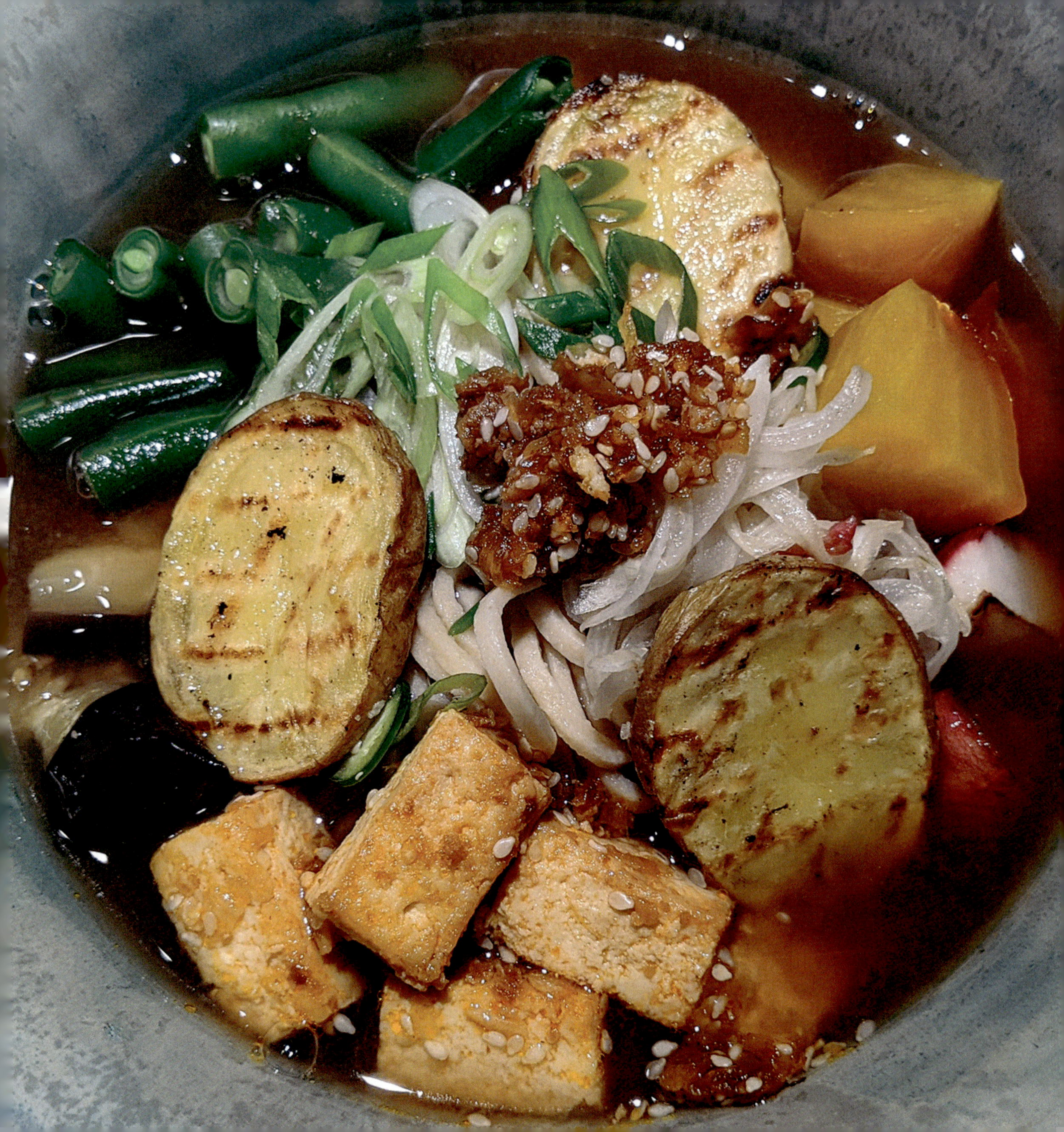

UMAMI RAMEN

> The title of this this version of ramen may be redundant. After all, ramen without umami is just a noodle and broth dish. Too often, vegetarians are left out of this experience, so I wanted to provide canvas to develop umami via plant-based ingredients. The recipe is deceptively straightforward.

LEVEL: Intermediate

YIELD: approximately 4 servings

INGREDIENTS

- 1/4 cup white miso paste
- 1 whole star anise
- 1 medium skin-on white onion, quartered
- 1 *bouquet garni*
- 2 whole heads garlic, cut in half
- 1-inch piece of fresh ginger, cut into slices
- 1/2 cup low sodium tamari soy sauce
- 1 cup Napa or Savoy cabbage, chopped
- 1 cup leeks, sliced
- 2 bay leaves
- 1 sheet kombu (optional)
- 1 carrot, sliced
- 1 cup rehydrated shiitake mushrooms
- 1 cup cremini mushrooms, sliced
- 2 cups sake
- 3 quarts water, more or less
- 1 cup white or brown clamshell or alba mushrooms
- 1 cup Japanese eggplant, sliced and roasted
- 4 eggs, soft boiled
- 1/4 cup scallions, sliced thinly
- few drops of infused oil (page 359) or toasted sesame oil
- 4 portions, ramen-style noodles
- 2 tablespoons vegetable oil
- salt & pepper, in stages and per taste

METHOD

Broth

In a heavy bottomed pot on medium-high heat, heat the oil and brown the onion, garlic heads, ginger, leeks, cabbage, carrot, and cremini mushrooms. There is a fine line between golden brown and burnt. The ingredients have a lot of natural sugars so be careful to not burn the ingredients, especially the garlic. Reduce the heat after you see a fond developing on the bottom of the pot. Deglaze with sake and cook for a couple of minutes. Next add the miso, rehydrated shiitake, kombu, and star anise. Mix well and cook for a minute before adding the soy sauce and enough water to account for a 25% reduction and still yield about 2 quarts of strained broth. Mix all the ingredients well and add the *bouquet garni*. Simmer uncovered on medium low for at least two hours. Adjust the seasonings along the way to achieve the depth and balance of flavor you desire. Strain the broth through a fine mesh or through several layers of cheesecloth. If the broth is weak in flavor, transfer it to a pot and begin reducing it. This will intensify the depth of flavor.

To compose the ramen bowl, arrange the noodles, scallions, alba mushrooms, roasted eggplant, and two halves of a soft-boiled egg in a bowl before ladling in piping hot broth. Be sure to have the noodles in the center of the bowl.

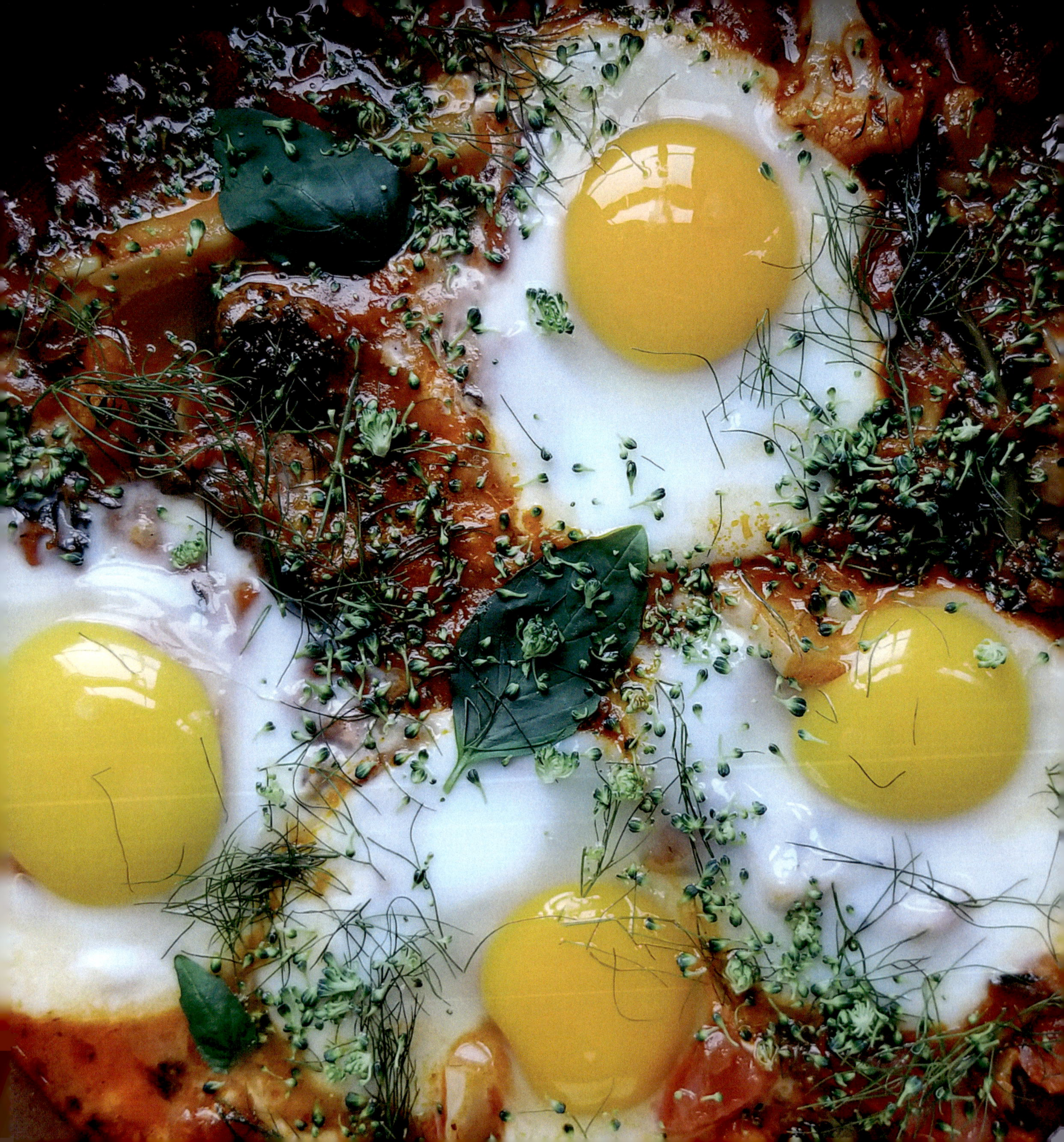

SHAKSHUKA

> This dish is all the rage. It's also fun to say. There are a few keys to a satisfying outcome. The sauce must be well-balanced and devoid of the canned flavor of the tomatoes. The egg whites must be cooked yet the yolks should be runny. Beyond that, this dish can be modified in a wide variety of ways. And although one thinks of this as a brunch/breakfast dish, it really can be enjoyed at any meal.

LEVEL: Basic

YIELD: approximately 4 servings

INGREDIENTS

- 1 medium red onion, sliced thinly
- 1 fennel bulb, medium diced
- 1 red bell pepper, cored, sliced thinly
- 1 yellow bell pepper, cored, sliced thinly
- 1 teaspoon Kashmiri red chile powder, more or less
- 1 cup button or cremini mushrooms, halved
- 1 cup San Marzano tomatoes in sauce, blend
- 4 cloves garlic, sliced thinly
- 1 tablespoon Bāhārat spice (page 78)
- 4 whole eggs
- 1/4 cup fresh flatleaf parsley, chopped
- 1/4 cup extra virgin olive oil
- salt & pepper, in stages and per taste
- crusty baguette-style bread or pita

METHOD

In a cast-iron or other heavy bottomed pan, heat the oil and brown the garlic. Next, add the onions and peppers and cook until they are caramelized well. Next add the mushrooms and cook until they are roasted and just begin to release their inherent water. Reduce the heat a bit and add the Bāhārat spice and red chile powder. Stir well and cook for a couple of minutes before adding the blended tomatoes. Stir well and increase the heat to at least medium to intensify the caramelization and favor. Season with salt and pepper, as desired. Once the sauce has a flavor like a spiced ratatouille, crack open the eggs on the sauce. Take care to not accidentally include any eggshells. Either cover the pan or place in a 350F oven, just long enough to cook the egg whites. Finish with a drizzle of high-quality olive oil and the chopped parsley. Serve immediately, taking care not to break the egg yolks. It is best if the egg yolks are still runny and can be mixed into the warm sauce while enjoying the dish with some crusty bread or warm pita.

BABY AUBERGINE FESENJOON

A uniquely Iranian dish with Persian roots, fesenjoon (also fesenjan) simply demonstrates the expert handling of fruit, fragrance, and decadence all in one dish. It's no wonder that so many North Indian and Pakistani dishes have ancestral roots in the food of Persia. The flavors are uniquely exotic and will inspire you to learn more about Persian food.

LEVEL: Intermediate

YIELD: approximately 4 servings

INGREDIENTS
- 8 baby eggplant, cut a cross-hatch at the base but leave intact
- 2 cloves garlic, minced
- 1/2 inch piece fresh ginger, minced
- pinch of saffron, bloomed in some warm water
- 1 large red onion, sliced thinly
- 1 cup walnuts, toasted and ground
- water or vegetable stock, as needed
- 2 sprigs fresh mint leaves, chopped
- 3/4 cup pomegranate concentrate
- sugar, as needed
- pomegranate seeds for garnish
- extra-virgin olive, as needed
- salt & pepper, in stages and per taste

METHOD
Preheat the oven to 350F. Toss the eggplant in olive oil, salt and pepper and roast on a sheet tray until soft and golden brown (about 45 minutes). In a bowl, mix the ground walnuts in some water to make a walnut paste. Meanwhile, in a pan, heat some more olive oil and fry the onions to a golden-brown stage. Add the garlic and ginger and cook for a couple of minutes. Add the walnut paste, saffron water, and pomegranate concentrate to the pan. Add some stock or water to thin out a bit. Adjust the balance by adding sugar and salt. Simmer on low to intensify the sauce. By now, the eggplants should be ready. Place them carefully in the sauce, spoon some sauce on each, and cover the pan. Stew the eggplant in the sauce for another 10 minutes. Taste the sauce one more time and adjust for seasoning. Finish with fresh pomegranate seeds and the chopped mint. Serve with naan or pulao.

PIEROGI

> Where does an Indian guy come off making pierogi, you ask? Well, you wouldn't be the first, but here's how I see this. It's grounded with a simple dough (not unlike samosa dough) with a filling that's then poached and possibly sautéed. The trick is to ensure that the dumpling is sealed before poaching and that it's rolled out thinly, so it doesn't get too plump after poaching.

LEVEL: Basic

YIELD: approximately 4 servings

INGREDIENTS

1 cup all-purpose flour
1/4 cup water, more or less, more for poaching the pierogi
1 small egg, beaten
2 ounces melted unsalted butter
1 Yukon gold potato, boiled in salted water
1 shallot
1 clove garlic, minced
1/4 cup grated gruyere
1 tablespoon *crème fraîche* or sour cream
pinch of freshly grated nutmeg
1 teaspoon fresh thyme leaves, chopped
1 tablespoon, chopped chives
water for cooking the pierogi
salt & pepper, in stages and per taste

METHOD

Dough

Add some salt to the flour, mix well, and make a well in the middle. Combine the water, beaten egg, and 1 teaspoon of the melted butter. Add this liquid mixture into the well and start pulling in the flour into the liquid. Once they are combined knead the dough for at least 5 minutes until it is smooth and somewhat elastic. Cover the dough and let it rest at room temperature for about an hour.

Filling

While the dough is resting, make the filling. Make sure the boiled potato is well dried as you would for proper mashed potatoes. Add it to a bowl. Sauté the shallot and garlic in a small amount of melted butter and once they are caramelized, add them to the potatoes along with the cheese, nutmeg, thyme, and crème fraîche. Mix all the ingredients well and taste the mixture, adjusting for salt and pepper. The filling should be well seasoned.

Make-Up

The dough should make about 12-16 pierogis depending on the size you prefer. Portion the dough into balls accordingly. Roll out each ball into about a 1/8-inch thick circle. Place at least a teaspoon of filling in the middle. Wet the edges of the circle and close in the dough in a crimped half-moon shape ensuring that you force out the air as you crimp. Once all the pierogis have been formed, cook them in simmering salted water. Once they rise to the top, poach another minute or so before removing them onto a sheet tray with a slotted spoon.

Brown the cooked pierogi in melted butter and serve with caramelized onions, chopped chives, and *crème fraîche* or sour cream.

MOFONGO

Soon after we were married, I surprised Jenneffer with a trip to San Juan, Puerto Rico, and we stayed at the magnificent *El Convento*. I had heard about this dish that was typically Puerto Rican called *mofongo*. How can a dish with a name like that possibly taste bad? We were told that *Raices* was the place to go if we wanted a good mofongo. The staff at *Raices*, dressed in their flowing whites with a turban-like white wrap, were only slightly less enjoyable than the garlicky mofongo. Since then, I've made it many times at the restaurant, always to compliments and gratitude.

LEVEL: Basic

YIELD: approximately 4 servings

INGREDIENTS
2 green plantains, peeled and sliced into 1/2 inch pieces
1 sweet potato, peeled and diced
1/2 teaspoon smoked paprika
2 sprigs fresh cilantro, chopped
1 cup roasted yellow squash, diced
1/2 cup blanched green peas
1 cup roasted cauliflower florets
2 tablespoons cashew nut, toasted and chopped coarsely
6 garlic cloves, minced
2 tablespoon extra-virgin olive oil
1/2 cup homemade sofrito (page 104)
water, as needed
salt & pepper, in stages and per taste

METHOD
Cook the sweet potato and plantains separately in salted water and drain well. In a shallow pan, heat 1 tablespoon of oil and brown the garlic. Remove and hold. In the same pan, fry the sofrito for 5 minutes, add the smoked paprika, and fold in the squash, peas, and cauliflower. Remove from the pan, add the remaining oil, and fry the plantains until golden brown. Set aside. Finally, smash the sweet potato and plantains together and fold in the cashew nuts.

Form a mound of the smashed plantains, sweet potato, and cashew. Arrange all the sautéed vegetables decoratively around the mound and finish with the chopped cilantro.

STUFFED CABBAGE ROLLS

> I heard of this dish from my friend Antonis Valaristos in graduate school, while at the University of Florida. I haven't heard from Antonis in a very long time. I believe he is back home in Greece. I formally made it for the first time in culinary school in the International Cooking course during the section of Eastern European cuisine. I next saw it while preparing (unsuccessfully) for the prestigious ACF-Certified Master Chef Practical Exam. I see a traditional version and raise it to a sinfully vegetarian version. I hope you like what I've done.

LEVEL: Intermediate

YIELD: approximately 4 servings

INGREDIENTS
- 6-8 large leaves of Savoy cabbage
- 1 cup onion, small diced
- 1/2 cup carrot, small diced
- 1/2 cup celery, small diced
- 1 red bell pepper, roasted, deseeded, and peeled, small diced
- 1 bay leaf
- 3 cloves garlic, minced
- 1 medium sized cauliflower, riced on a grater
- 1 cup cooked lentils, drained well
- 1/2 cup toasted pine nuts
- 1/2 teaspoon smoked paprika
- 1/2 teaspoon dried marjoram
- 1/2 teaspoon dried sage
- 1/2 teaspoon cayenne pepper (optional)
- pinch of freshly grated nutmeg
- 1 teaspoon tomato paste
- 1/2 cup dry white wine
- 2 cups Marcela Hazan inspired marinara (page 116)
- water for blanching the cabbage leaves
- 2 tablespoons extra-virgin olive oil
- salt & pepper, in stages and per taste

METHOD

Blanch the cabbage leaves in lightly salted water until they are pliable. Remove and allow to dry on a sheet tray. Dry the cabbage leaves and cut out any thick veins. Chop up the veins finely. To make the filling, sauté the mirepoix (onion, carrot, celery) in the olive oil until the vegetables are soft. Next add the garlic and bay leaf. Season with some salt and pepper. Add the tomato paste and fry for 2 minutes. Next, add the riced cauliflower, cook, and brown well for at least 10 minutes. Next, add the wine to deglaze and adjust the seasonings. Add the paprika, marjoram, sage, and cayenne. Cook for another 15 minutes until the mixture is dry. Transfer to a bowl and add the nutmeg, toasted pine nuts, chopped roasted red pepper, and any chopped cabbage veins.

Place 1/4 cup of filling in the middle of each blanched leaf. Roll it up, tucking in any exposed sides just like a burrito. Make all the stuffed cabbage leaves first. In a baking dish, spread a layer of marinara and place the cabbage rolls evenly spaced. Pour the remaining sauce over the rolls and bake in a 375F oven for about 30 minutes. Let them cook before serving each roll with adequate roasted sauce.

CHILAQUILES

I've labeled the level of this dish as being "easy." That's a bit deceptive because it's the assembly that's easy. Truth be told, it is also easy to mess up. Ultimately, timing is everything. Also, one spends a good amount of time creating the base components of this vegetarian version.

LEVEL: Basic

YIELD: approximately 4 servings

INGREDIENTS
8 homemade corn tortillas (page 200) or store-bought tortillas
1 cup cooked and cumin spiced black beans
1 cup vegetable stock
2 cups tomatillo salsa (page 100)
1 cup shredded queso Oaxaca or other stringy melting cheese
1/4 cup crema or sour cream
queso fresco or queso añejo, as preferred
oil for frying the tortillas
several sprigs of fresh cilantro
whole jalapeños, grilled or pan roasted, sliced (optional)
salt, as needed

METHOD
Cut the fresh tortillas into wedges and fry them until crisp. Warm 1 cup of the tomatillo salsa with the stock and beans. When the mixture is on a low simmer, mix in the fried tortillas and cover immediately and let the mixture sit for a few minutes. Portion out this mixture into appropriate portions, sprinkle some cheese on each, and bake in the oven just until the cheese melts. Spoon a bit more of the fresh tomatillo salsa on each portion, some queso fresco, and fresh cilantro. Serve immediately with the grilled jalapeno (if using) alongside.

HEN OF THE WOODS MOUSSAKA

> Non-vegetarian moussaka is well known, but this earthy and full-bodied variation is a delicious alternative. In general, dishes like moussaka are conducive to many variations. Whoever thought of topping off a meat dish with a fluffy, soufflé-like crust was a genius. And the eggplant provides a deliciously savory addition to what might otherwise be a ho-hum dish. I hope that someday I will have the opportunity to share this dish in person with my Hellenic friends from graduate school.

LEVEL: Intermediate

YIELD: approximately 4 servings

INGREDIENTS
- 4 lbs. eggplant, partially skinned
- flour, for dusting
- 2 medium onions, minced
- 3 cups hen of the woods or similar mushrooms
- 4 cloves garlic, minced
- 1/2 lb. peeled tomatoes
- 1.5 cups white wine
- 2 bay leaves
- 1 tablespoon tomato paste
- 1 tablespoon fresh oregano
- 2 tablespoon flat leaf parsley
- 1/2 cup breadcrumbs
- 5 oz. or so melted butter
- 5 oz. all-purpose flour
- 1/2 gallon milk
- pinch of nutmeg
- 4 egg yolks
- extra virgin olive oil, as needed
- 1-3 oz. of grated Kefalotyri (substitute with parmigiana or pecorino)
- salt & pepper, in stages and per taste

METHOD

Slice eggplants lengthwise and season lightly with salt. Let them sit for 30 minutes, squeeze out excess liquid, and pat dry. Dust lightly with flour and sauté in olive oil. Drain on paper towels. In a pan, sauté onions until translucent. Add the mushrooms and brown them. Add oregano, white wine, tomato paste, peeled tomato, and parsley. Simmer until thick. Make a (light brown) roux by heating the butter and flour until it is thick and slightly brown. Add cold milk, bay leaves, and stir to dissolve the roux. Simmer until you achieve a smooth creamy sauce without the starchiness. Temper with egg yolks and fold in the cheese. Season with freshly grated nutmeg, salt and pepper (this is a thick Mornay sauce). Add more herbs if desired and set aside. In a buttered or oiled pan, sprinkle some seasoned breadcrumbs. Place a layer of the eggplants topped with a layer of the meat stew. Repeat layers until all is used ensuring that the last layer is eggplant. Pour the thick Mornay sauce over the top and bake uncovered at 350-375 F until very hot throughout and the sauce is set and browned (approx. 55-60 minutes). Let it cool for at least 15 minutes before cutting and serving.

SINFULLY VEGETARIAN BREAD PUDDING

> My friend Jim Jackson is tired of savory bread puddings and whips out his impression of *puddin' pop* Bill Cosby at the mere mention. My friend Jim Jackson is also a great amateur baker. I don't get it. This dish began as a versatile catch-all for parts and pieces of vegetables and herbs without just imagining a soup. Since, it has become a versatile component of many a sinfully vegetarian composed dish.

LEVEL: Basic

YIELD: approximately 4 servings

INGREDIENTS
- 1 cup carrot, diced
- 1 cup bell pepper, diced
- 1 cup red onion, diced
- 1 cup celery, diced
- 10 ounces medium mushrooms, quartered or rough chopped (use your favorite kind)
- 12 ounces bread (stale bread is best), cut into ½ inch cubes
- 10 ounces half and half
- 10 ounces goat cheese (you may substitute white cheddar or gruyere)
- 2 cups fresh basil, chopped
- 2 tablespoons fresh thyme, chopped plus 2 sprigs
- 1 cup fresh flat leaf parsley, chopped
- 3 cloves garlic, minced
- 2 bay leaves
- 3 eggs
- extra-virgin olive oil, as needed
- salt & pepper, in stages and per taste

METHOD
Toss the mushrooms in some extra virgin olive oil with the thyme sprigs. Season them lightly with salt and pepper and roast on a baking sheet in a 400-degree oven for about 20 minutes. Let the mushrooms cool and discard the thyme sprigs. On medium heat, sauté the onions, carrots, celery, and peppers in a saucepan with some extra virgin olive oil for about 5 minutes. Add the garlic and bay leaves and stir for 30 seconds so the garlic doesn't burn. Add the dairy and half of the goat cheese (reserve the other half of the cheese for later). After the liquid simmers for 10 minutes, remove from the heat, let cool a bit, and temper the 3 eggs in a bowl in stages. Finish with fresh herbs and season the liquid with salt and pepper until well-seasoned. Pour this warm dairy-egg mixture over the bread that has been torn into 1/2-inch pieces. Add the roasted mushrooms and the remaining goat cheese (in dollops). Mix well and pour this mixture into a (non-stick) baking dish that has been sprayed with a baking spray or greased with butter. Bake at 350F for about an hour. Let it cool down completely before serving (see below for serving instructions).

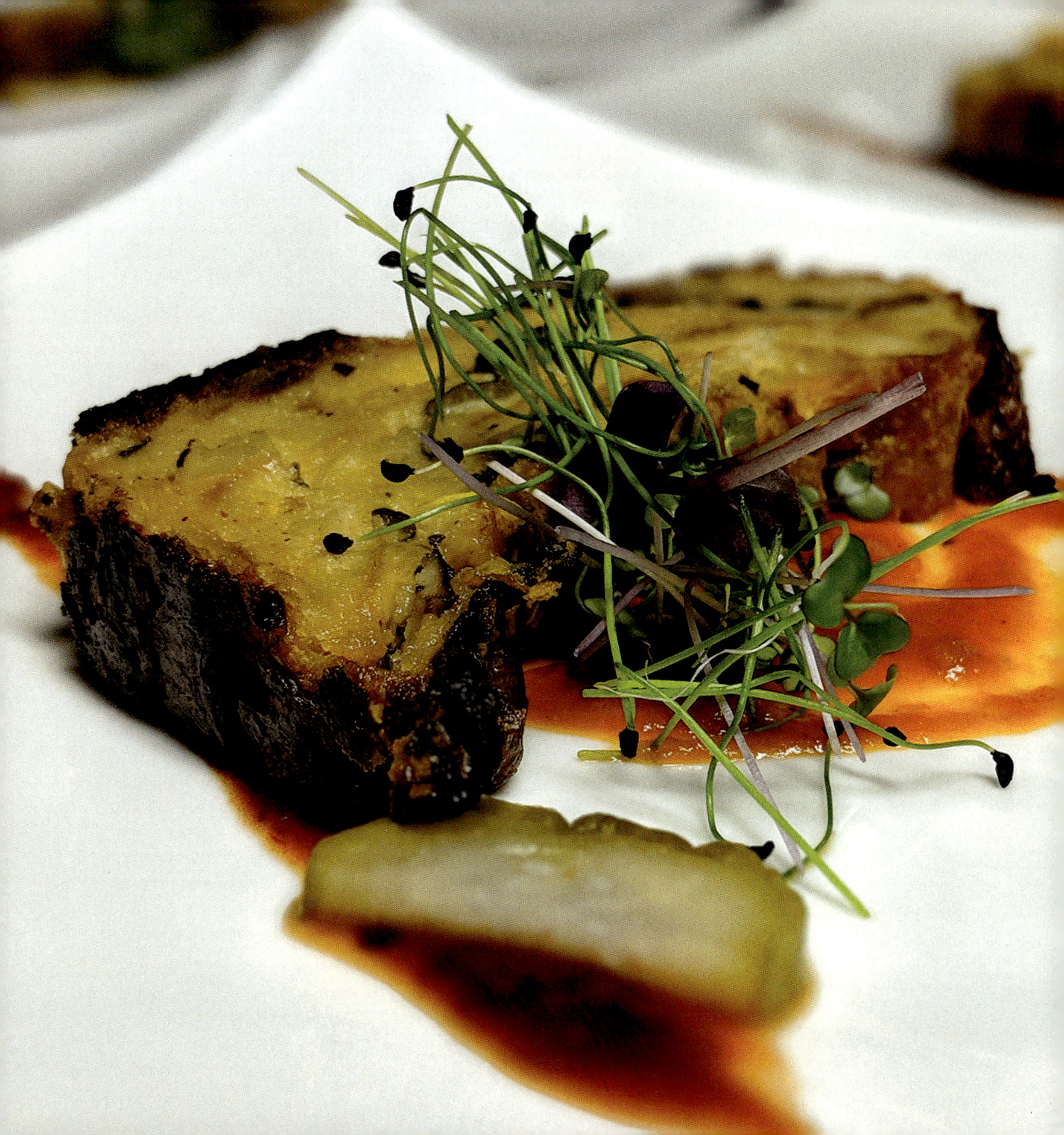

NIGHTSHADE BARBECUE

> Simply adding a barbecue sauce doesn't constitute barbeque, in my humble opinion. There has to be an infusion of smoke, either by actively smoking or by grilling over wood, resulting in a smokey flavor. Many vegetables lend themselves to smoking. At the restaurant, we were smoking tomatoes since the beginning and they became somewhat of a sensation when unsuspecting diners would suddenly discover one in an otherwise balanced salad. Simply grilling vegetables (marinated or otherwise) is not vegetable barbecue and I'm willing to listen to a counter argument.

LEVEL: Intermediate

YIELD: approximately 4 servings

INGREDIENTS
8 small white potatoes
2 large green tomatoes
4 Japanese eggplant
4 red bell peppers, cored
4 yellow bell peppers, cored
1 tablespoon paprika
1/4 cup light brown sugar
1/2 teaspoon cayenne pepper
2 teaspoons ground mustard
1 teaspoon coriander power
1/2 teaspoon cumin powder
1 teaspoon garlic powder
1 teaspoon onion powder
1/2 teaspoon cinnamon powder
1/2 cup ketchup
1/4 cup apple cider vinegar
1/4 cup honey
1 tablespoon Dijon mustard
1 teaspoon hot sauce (page 344), more or less
vegetable oil, as needed
applewood or cherrywood chips, pre-soaked
vegetable oil, as needed
salt & pepper, in stages and per taste

METHOD
Cut the vegetables into uniform sized pieces that will cook at a similar rate. In a bowl, mix the dry ingredients along with some salt and pepper. This is the dry rub. Coat the vegetables with oil and rub in the dry rub onto them. Place on a baking sheet and in a smoking environment at 200F for about two hours. The potatoes and eggplant should be tender.

While the vegetables are smoking, combine the ketchup, vinegar, honey, Dijon, and hot sauce in a saucepan. Adjust the salt level and simmer on low to harmonize the combined flavors. It should be thick enough to coat the back of a spoon. Halfway into the smoking step, begin dabbing the vegetables with the sauce on a soft brush. Be careful to not brush off the spices on the vegetables. Repeat the process a couple more times as the vegetables are smoking. Once you are happy with the level of smoking and doneness on the vegetables, remove them from the smoker, and if needed, brush them one more time with the sauce before serving as a main feature or accompaniment during a feast, summer cookout, or beach picnic.

MISO & EDAMAME POT PIE

> The key to this dish is to season every component to develop deep and comforting flavor in the sauce. The filling can made in many ways, but I've created this version so as to harmonize Japanese and French flavors.

LEVEL: Intermediate

YIELD: approximately 4 servings

INGREDIENTS
2 cups shelled edamame
3 stalks celery, medium diced
1 large Spanish onion, medium diced
3 carrots, peeled, medium diced
1/2 cup white miso paste
3 bay leaves
3 tablespoons fresh thyme, chopped
2 tablespoons fresh rosemary, chopped
2 tablespoons fresh sage, chopped
5 garlic cloves, minced
1 sheet puff pastry
1 cup flat leaf parsley, chopped
1 quart low sodium vegetable stock, warm
1 cup heavy cream or half and half
2 tablespoons unsalted butter
2 tablespoons all-purpose flour
egg wash
salt & pepper, in stages and per taste

METHOD
In a heavy-bottomed pot, make a blond roux with the butter and flour. Add the onions, celery, carrots and sweat, without browning them. Add the garlic, fresh herbs, miso paste, bay leaves, some salt, and pepper and stir for a minute. Add the warm vegetable stock, heavy cream, and stir well. Simmer until the broth thickens to the desired consistency. It should be thick and coat the back of a spoon. Finally, fold in the edamame. Pour into a baking dish and cover with puff pastry. Brush the pastry with an egg wash and make a slit so the steam can escape during the baking process. Place in the center rack of a preheated 375F oven until the pastry is golden brown (about 30 minutes). Let it rest for at least 20 minutes before serving with more chopped parsley.

BEET AND RADISH TERRINE

> This is a technical dish. I could have used a more traditional cream cheese por goat cheese, but I wanted to keep the dish vegan. In fact, I was to showcase this and many other vegan dishes at the Beard House.

LEVEL: Intermediate

YIELD: approximately 4 servings

INGREDIENTS

2 medium golden beets with tops, washed well
2 medium red beets with tops, washed well
1 medium sized daikon radish, washed well
2 cups small red radish with tops, washed well
1 package silken tofu, drained
agar-agar to cold set 2 cups of liquid (follow the directions on packaging)
1 cup cashews, toasted and ground
1/2 cup vegetable stock
2 shallots, minced
4 cloves garlic, minced
juice and zest of 1 lemon
2 tablespoons unsalted butter
2 tablespoons extra-virgin olive oil
3 sprigs fresh thyme
salt & pepper, in stages and per taste

METHOD

Separate the tops from the roots. Toss the beets and radish with the olive oil, thyme sprigs, salt, and pepper, and roast covered in a 325F oven for an hour. While the roots are roasting, wash the tops well in cold water because they tend to be very sandy. Dry them well. Chop the stems into small pieces. Melt the butter in a pan and brown the shallots and garlic. Add the chopped stems and leaves and cook for about 10 minutes. Season them with salt and pepper and add the lemon zest and juice. In a food processor, blend the greens and add the silken tofu. Add a bit of vegetable stock and bring the puree to a low simmer before adding the agar-agar. Be sure to follow the directions on proportions of liquid to agar-agar for proper cold setting. Taste this puree and adjust the seasoning as you prefer.

By now the root vegetables should be soft. Once they cool, peel the skin off the beets (use gloves when handling the red beets) taking care not to let the red beet juice cross over to the other vegetables. Slice the root vegetables thinly (no more than 1/8-inch thickness) using a mandoline or slicer. Line a terrine mold with plastic and fill the terrine mold, alternating between thin layers of golden beet, puree, red beet, puree, daikon, puree, red radish, puree, red beet, puree, and finishing with golden beet. Be sure to pull the excess plastic to cover the top layer well. Place a medium weight on the terrine and refrigerate for 24 hours before carefully unmolding and slicing slabs of terrine.

Serve with a comforting soup, with grilled bread, or a salad for a refined and nutritious meal.

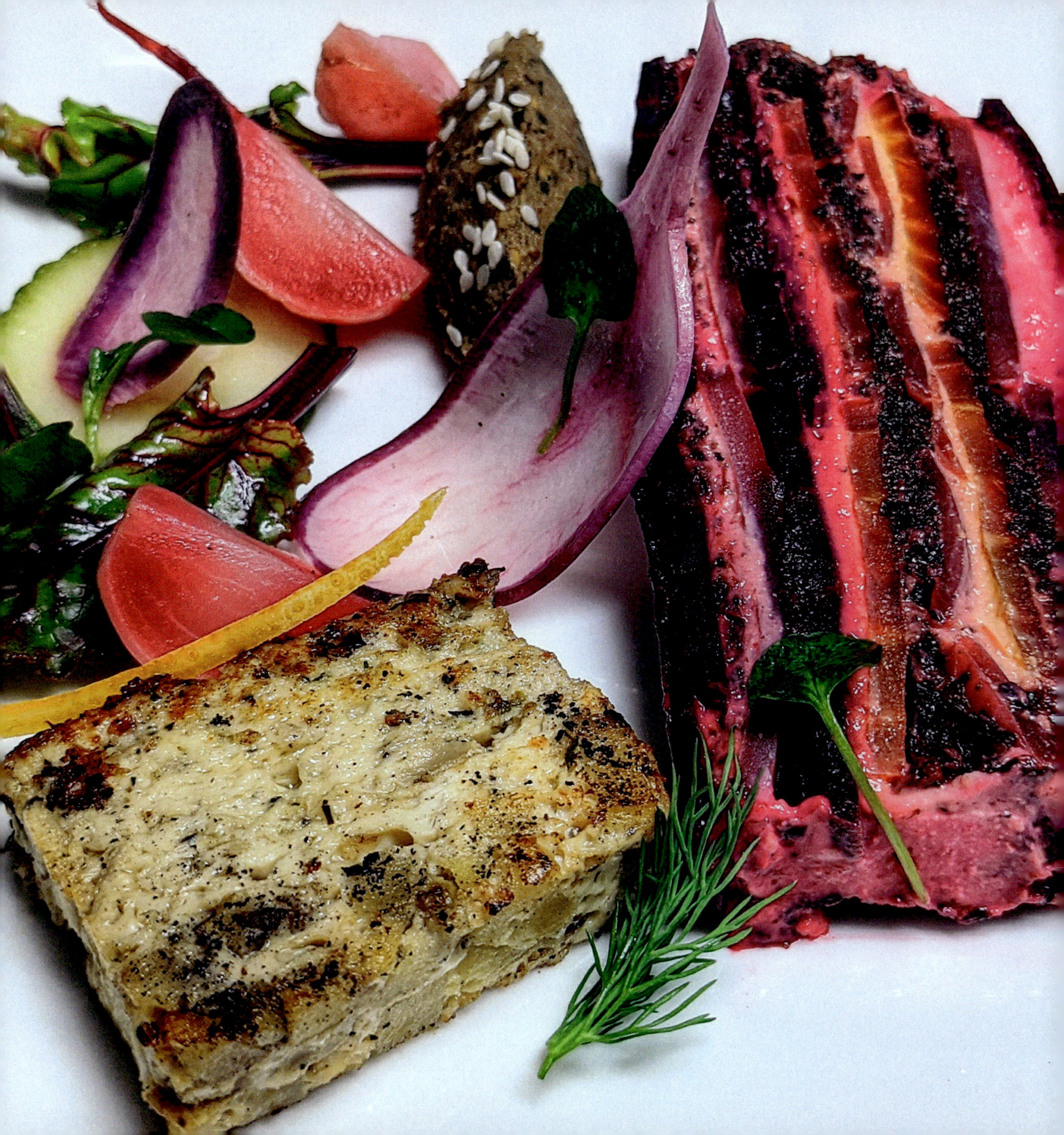

Sides & Condiments

A potpourri of low and medium complexity concoctions. Their role in thoughtful compositions cannot be understated. Their versatility lies in the realization that each one of these gems can be a side at a dinner table or easily be incorporated into a layered composition.

SIGNATURE HOT SAUCE

LEVEL: Basic

YIELD: approximately 2 quarts

INGREDIENTS
6 habaneros, halved
1 large onion, diced
1 tablespoon minced ginger
2 tablespoon minced garlic
2 tablespoon ground cumin
1 tablespoon ground coriander
1 teaspoon ground clove
1 teaspoon ground cardamom
1/2 teaspoon ground cinnamon
2 teaspoon ground turmeric
2 cups crushed tomatoes
1 cup red wine vinegar
1 tablespoon Dijon mustard
1/4 cup light brown sugar
water, as needed
vegetable or canola oil, as needed
salt & pepper, in stages and per taste

METHOD
In a heavy-bottomed stainless pot, sweat the onions until translucent. Add the ginger, garlic, and habanero peppers. Sauté for a minute. Next add all the spices and stir for 30 seconds. Now add the mustard, crushed tomatoes, vinegar, and brown sugar. Add some water if it's too thick. Season with salt and pepper. Simmer on low for about an hour, stirring periodically. After it cools, blend smoothly using a hand blender or food processor. Store in the refrigerator in an airtight container or bottle in mason jars using a proper canning procedure.

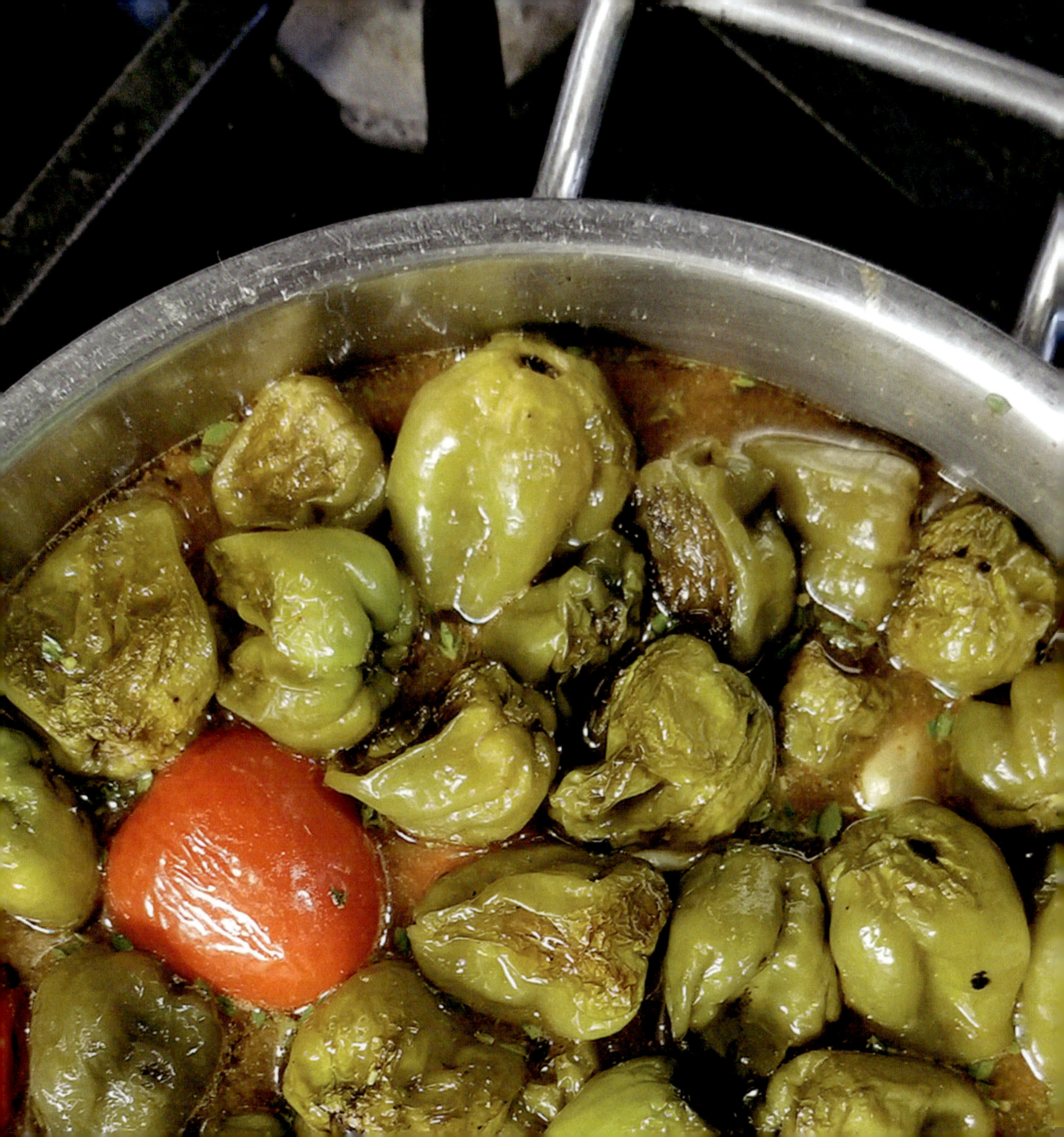

PICKLES

> The first time I learned how to pickle was at Canoe, where they pickled a variety of root vegetables like beets, carrots, and turnips. This version is not designed to create a product for canning, but rather a quickly (24 hours) pickled vegetable that tastes great and is a versatile condiment or accompaniment for a charcuterie or cheese board. The pickling liquid can be re-used upon straining the next day; just bring it to a simmer again.

LEVEL: Basic

YIELD: approximately 6 cups

INGREDIENTS
2 red onions, peeled and sliced lengthwise
6 pickling cucumbers, washed and sliced in half lengthwise
4 red bell peppers, cored and sliced into strips
1 bulb of fennel, cored and sliced into strips
1 jalapeño, sliced in half (optional)
1 cup light brown sugar
1 bay leaf
1 cinnamon stick
2 cloves of garlic
1 teaspoon black peppercorns
1 tablespoon whole coriander seeds
2 cups apple cider vinegar
1 cup red wine vinegar
1 cup white balsamic vinegar water
1 cup water
coarse salt, as preferred

METHOD
The amount of salt depends on the degree of pickling you are seeking. A good approximation is 1/4 cup. Add all the spices, salt, and jalapeño to the vinegars and water. Bring to a low simmer. Make sure the salt and sugar have dissolved. Place all the vegetables in a shallow nonreactive bowl. Pour the simmering liquid onto the vegetables ensuring that they are completely submerged. Refrigerate overnight. The pickles are ready. Strain them and re-use the pickling liquid for the next time.

INDIAN LEMON PICKLE

During the summer months in Mumbai, just before the monsoons roll in, it is hot. Some might say "It's always hot in India," and they would be correct. I felt at home as soon as I landed in Montego Bay, Jamaica, years ago. Many have heard me say for reference, "Mumbai is about the same latitude as parts of Jamaica except a third of the way around the world from each other."

Mumbai: 19.0760° N

Montego Bay: 18.4762° N

By reference, Key West: 24.5551° N

So, yeah, it's always warm in Mumbai. The 30 million residents and concrete jungle only add to the warm and cozy. My mom would buy dozens of lemons and unripe mangoes. We would wash and sun-dry them for days on the terrace of our apartment building in Kalina. After they were devoid of moisture, they were coated in a blend of turmeric, chili powder, fenugreek seeds, sometimes mustard seeds, oil, and salt. Mummy had the perfect blend and they would be stored in special earthenware pickle pots at room temperature in a corner of the kitchen. And we would wait impatiently for them to be ready for consumption. Usually, this took about a month. They lasted for the whole year, even considering that they would be at every dinner table.

LEVEL: Basic

YIELD: approximately 1 quart

INGREDIENTS

- 8 medium sized, thin skinned lemons, quartered, de-seeded
- 2 tsp. ground turmeric
- 1/4 cup vegetable oil
- 1/2 teaspoon cumin seeds
- 1/4 teaspoon fenugreek seeds
- 1 tablespoon Kashmiri chili powder
- 6 cloves garlic, thinly sliced
- 1-inch piece ginger, peeled, sliced thinly
- 1 teaspoon whole black peppercorns
- 1/4 cup coarse salt

METHOD

Wash the lemons well and be sure to dry completely. Rub lemons with salt and turmeric in a bowl and store in a single sterilized glass jar with a tight lid. Cover and store the jar in a dry location. Every day turn the jar back and forth a few times. After 5 days, heat the oil in a pan and add the remaining ingredients until you hear the mustard seeds pop. Pour over the salted lemons and close the lid. Again, store in a dry place making sure you gently re-circulate the contents each day. The pickle is ready in 10 days. Make sure no moisture enters the jar to prevent spoilage.

RICOTTA CHEESE

LEVEL: Basic

YIELD: approximately 1 quart

INGREDIENTS
2 gallons whole milk
juice of 8 lemons and zest of 3 lemons
1/2 cup heavy cream (optional)
cheese cloth or fine strainer
coarse salt, as preferred

METHOD
Line a colander with multiple layers of cheesecloth. Bring the milk to a scald (just shy of boiling) in a heavy-bottomed stainless-steel pot. Add the lemon juice and stir with a wooden spoon. Maintain the heat until the cheese curds begin to coagulate. When the whey clears and most of the solids have coagulated, turn off the heat and pour everything through the cheesecloth-lined colander. Let it drain well until almost dry (this may take up to 30 minutes). Transfer the cheese only to a mixing bowl. If you desire a creamier texture, add some heavy cream. Season and refrigerate.

YOGURT

> In India, my family has made yogurt almost every day. The routine is the same. The milk comes in at 6 a.m. It is pasteurized by boiling. After it cools down, it is combined with leftover yogurt from the previous batch and left at room temperature for an appropriate amount of time. During the summer months, yogurt is done by late evening. During the winter months, it may be left at room temperature overnight.

LEVEL: Basic

YIELD: approximately 3/4 quart

INGREDIENTS
1 quart milk (I prefer whole milk)
1/2 cup plain homemade or store-bought yogurt with live cultures

METHOD
In a heavy-bottomed pot, bring the milk to a scald (just shy of boiling). Let it cool to about 85F. Stir in the yogurt and mix well. Pour the warm mixture into a thermos flask or simply cover with a lid and leave on the kitchen counter in a warm place. The thermos is useful if the ambient temperature is too cold. In about 24 hours, you have yogurt. Retain a cup of this for the next batch. So, you have a starter of sorts.

BALSAMIC REDUCTION

> Balsamic reduction is a good thing. Store-bought balsamic glaze, not so much. Most of us cannot afford a highly prized and valued 50-year-old balsamic vinegar. A good 4+ year old version reduced in a heavy-bottomed pot on a low heat produces a perfectly good alternative. I would never suggest that the two are the same thing because they are not. Some chefs use balsamic reductions as a crutch, but in some cases, it produces a magical counterpoint to a dish. Take the time to make it at home because it doesn't spoil. One must simply survive the strong aroma in the air during the reduction process.

LEVEL: Basic

YIELD: approximately 1/4 of original volume

INGREDIENTS

16 oz. 4-ish year old balsamic vinegar (preferably from Modena)

METHOD

In a pot of water, simmer the stems and trims of the collards. After 30 minutes, the water will be enriched with the flavor of the greens. While the stock is simmering, melt the butter and cook the garlic and onions until they are golden brown. Next add the torn collards and sauté for 5 minutes. Season with salt and pepper and add enough stock to cover the greens by an inch. Submerge the *bouquet garni* into the greens. Cover and simmer for about one hour, adding more stock as necessary. Now add the heavy cream, mix well, and simmer for another 45 minutes on medium-low heat until most of the water has evaporated. Check the seasoning, discard the *bouquet garni* and finished with grated cheese, if desired.

CREAMED COLLARDS

Collard greens are full-flavored. This preparation tempers their assertiveness and results in a familiar yet exotic comfort dish.

LEVEL: Basic

YIELD: approximately 2 quarts

INGREDIENTS

3 bunches collard greens, de-stemmed, cleaned, torn
1 bouquet garni with fresh thyme, peppercorns, bay leaf, and parsley stems)
3 cloves garlic, minced
1 medium red onion, minced
2 cups heavy cream
2 tablespoons unsalted butter
2 cups stock made from the stems and trims of the collards, more or less
water for stock
1/4 cup grated pecorino Romano
salt & pepper, in stages and per taste

METHOD

In a pot of water, simmer the stems and trims of the collards. After 30 minutes, the water will be enriched with the flavor of the greens. While the stock is simmering, melt the butter and cook the garlic and onions until they are golden brown. Next add the torn collards and sauté for 5 minutes. Season with salt and pepper and add enough stock to cover the greens by an inch. Submerge the bouquet garni into the greens. Cover and simmer for about one hour, adding more stock as necessary. Now add the heavy cream, mix well and simmer for another 45 minutes on medium-low heat until most of the water has evaporated. Check the seasoning, discard the bouquet garni and finished with grated cheese, if desired.

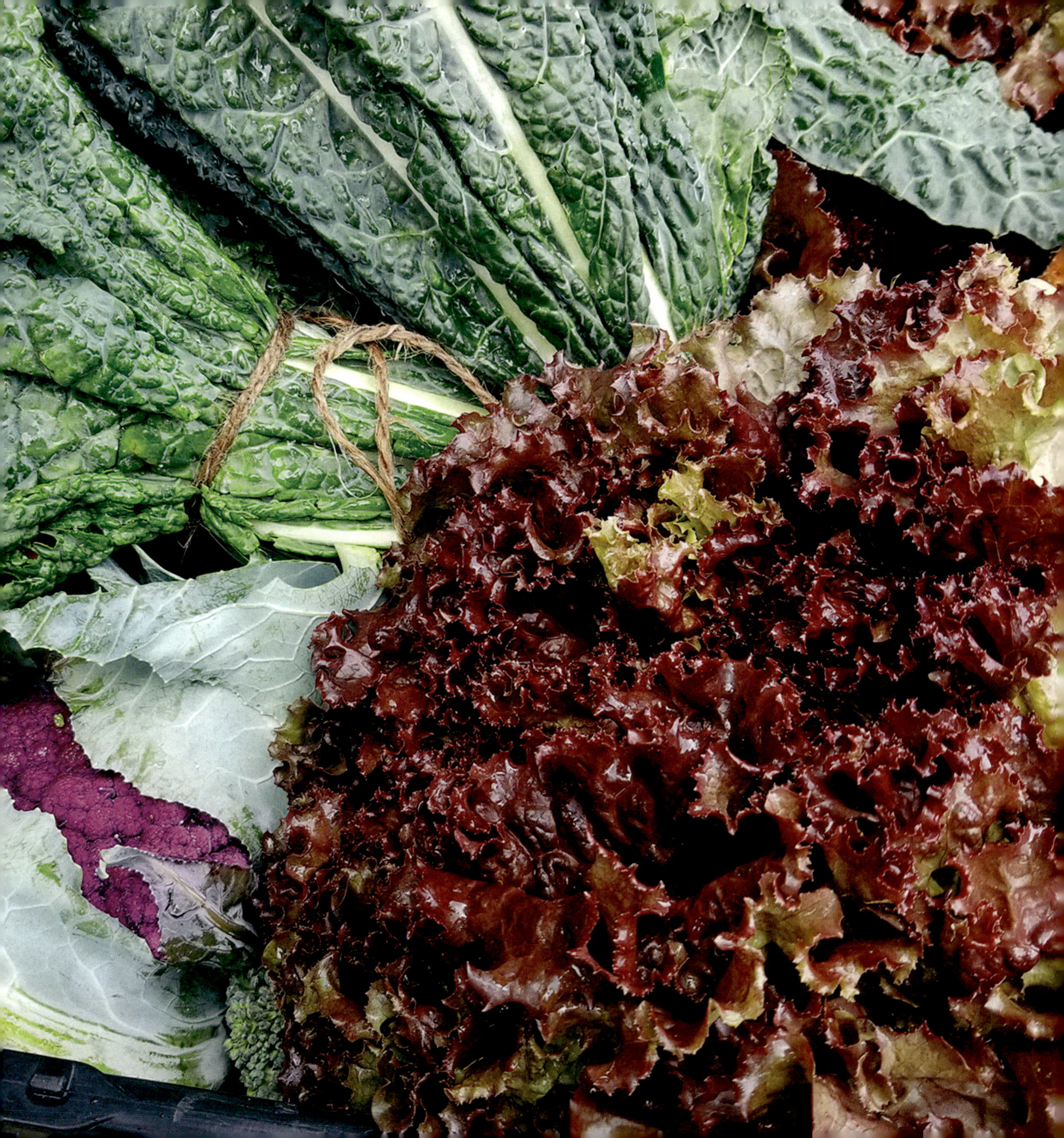

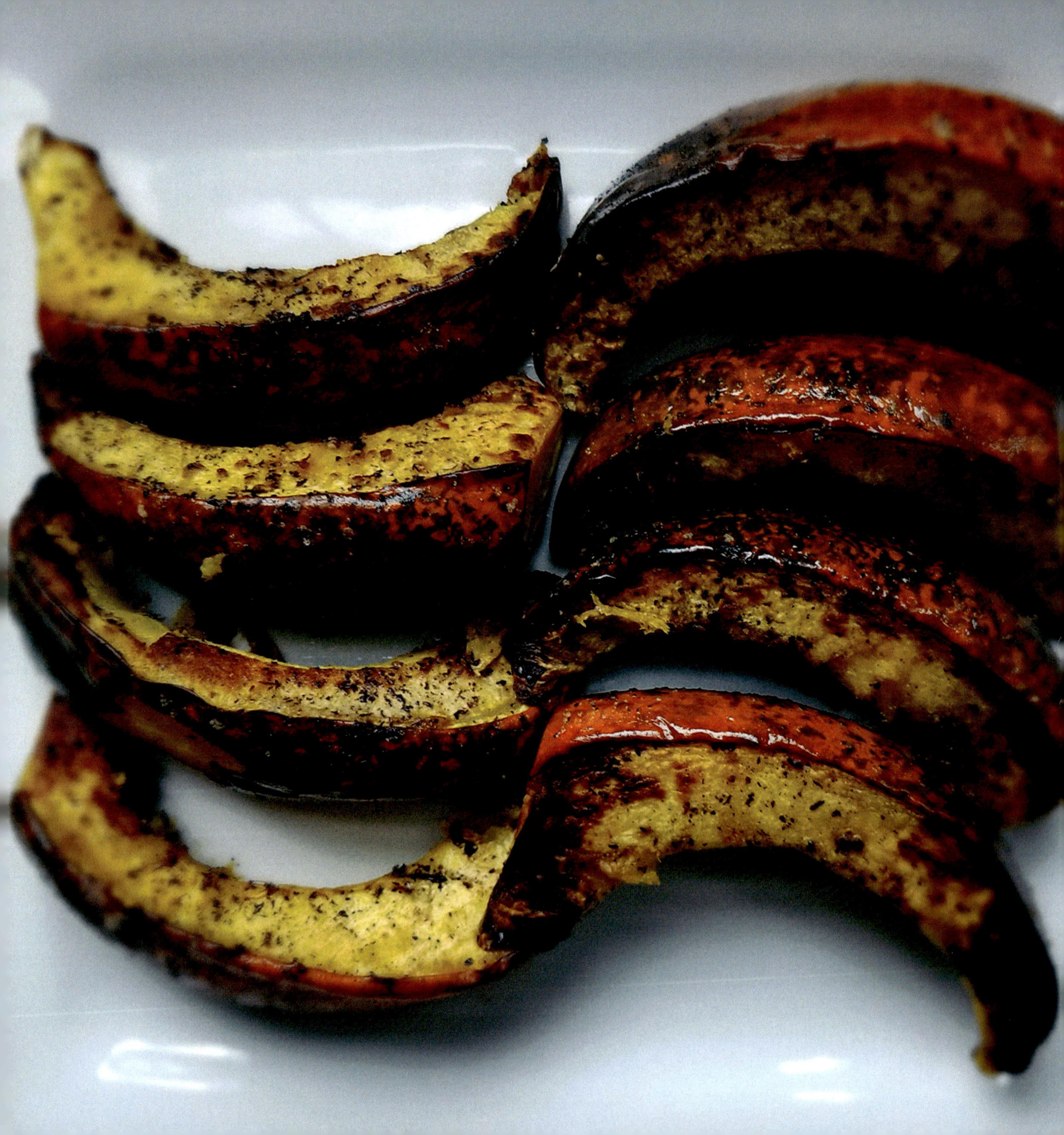

ROASTED ROOT VEGETABLES WITH ROASTED GARLIC & LEMON DRESSING

Since day one, we've roasted a variety of vegetables every single day at the restaurant. We have some dishes that are complemented by other vegetables, but our batch of day-roasted vegetables (squashes, root vegetables, cauliflower, broccoli, to name a few) forms the backbone of our deeply soulful dishes on the menu. In general, roasting is a powerful and easy way to intensify the flavors of ingredients and to develop the natural Maillard reaction, which causes the caramelization of natural sugars and produces the highly desirable golden-brown color and flavor. Mastery of this technique should be in everyone's repertoire.

LEVEL: Basic

YIELD: approximately 8 servings

INGREDIENTS
- 2 medium whole carrots
- 4 small beets
- 6 small radishes
- 2 medium sweet potatoes
- 1 bulb garlic, sliced in half
- 1-inch piece of fresh ginger
- 1 jalapeño (optional)
- 1/2 lemon, de-seeded
- 2 tablespoon extra-virgin olive oil
- 1/2 cup apple cider vinegar
- 1/4 cup honey
- 1 teaspoon Dijon mustard
- salt & pepper, in stages and per taste

METHOD

Wash and dry all the root vegetables. Poke slits with a knife into the beets and sweet potatoes. Coat all the root vegetables, garlic, ginger, and jalapeno with olive oil. Season well with salt and pepper. Spread uniformly on a baking sheet and cover with foil or a lid. Bake in a 330 F oven for 1 hour and 20 minutes. Remove and let cool.

Dressing: In a food processor or blender, combine the roasted garlic cloves (squeezed out), roasted ginger, jalapeno, roasted lemon, vinegar, mustard, honey, salt, pepper and blend smooth. Taste the dressing and adjust the seasoning and thickness. It should be on the thicker side.

Cut up the roasted sweet potatoes, carrots, beets, and radishes (no need to peel any of the vegetables) into wedges and chunks and serve with the dressing as a dipping sauce.

CAULIFLOWER & POTATO GRATIN

> Cauliflower ranks in my top 5 favorite vegetables, and I think roasted cauliflower dressed in extra-virgin olive oil, kosher salt, and freshly ground pepper may be one of the world's great snacks. Forget potato chips--you can't eat just one floret. Here, I take that simple idea of roasted cauliflower but turn it into a composed side dish or even a main course when accompanied by some grilled chicken or lamb chops. The classic potatoes au gratin has no chance against this decadent version of a gratin. Really, at the end of the day, it is a cauliflower casserole and this type of cooking is identifiable, comforting, and old-school.

LEVEL: Basic

YIELD: approximately 8 servings

INGREDIENTS

4 cups cauliflower florets and chopped tender stems
3 Yukon gold potatoes, sliced thinly
1 small red onion, minced
1 tablespoon freshly minced garlic
2 tablespoons fresh thyme leaves
3 tablespoons fresh rosemary, chopped
2 tablespoons fresh flat leaf parsley, chopped
2 whole bay leaves
1/2 quart heavy cream or half and half
1 tablespoons white truffle oil (optional)
1 cup grated Gruyère cheese
1 cup lightly toasted plain panko breadcrumbs
extra virgin olive oil, as needed for roasting and sautéing
3 eggs
salt & pepper, in stages and per taste

METHOD

Preheat an oven to 350 F. Toss the cauliflower in the olive oil and season lightly with salt and pepper. Place on a baking sheet and roast in the oven for about 45 minutes. Turn them over once during the roasting process so that they brown evenly. As the cauliflower is roasting, in a pan with olive oil, add the onions and garlic and sauté for a couple of minutes on medium heat. Add the rosemary, thyme, bay leaves, and stir for a few seconds. Season with salt and pepper. Next, add the heavy cream and the truffle oil (if desired). Whisk the eggs in a stainless bowl and temper them with the hot cream. Discard the bay leaves. Alternate the roasted cauliflower and thinly sliced potato, seasoning well in between the layers in a baking dish and pour the hot cream and egg mixture over it. Ensure everything is coated evenly. Cover with aluminum foil and bake for 30 minutes. Meanwhile, mix the panko breadcrumbs, gruyere cheese, and parsley in a bowl. Remove the foil from the baking dish and sprinkle the breadcrumb mixture evenly over the gratin. Put it back into the oven (uncovered) for another 10-15 minutes or until the cheese melts and the breadcrumbs get golden brown. Let the gratin rest for at least 30 minutes before serving.

RUM-GLAZED APPLES

> My only paid cooking job prior to opening the restaurant was as unofficial tournant at the Princess Wilderness Lodge outside Denali National Park. One of evening prep duties was to make this compote for one of the entrees. Naturally, I would spice it up. Here, I present a more vibrant version of the recipe I was expected to replicate (which I almost always modified).

LEVEL: Basic

YIELD: approximately 8 servings

INGREDIENTS
6 each Fuji apples, washed, cored, cut into wedges
2 cups dark rum
1/2 cup light brown sugar
1 orange
1 vanilla bean, scraped
2 sprigs fresh rosemary
2 sprigs fresh thyme
2 cloves garlic
2 bay leaves
1/4 cup red wine vinegar
1 stick unsalted butter, cubed
water, as needed
salt & pepper, in stages and per taste

METHOD
Sauté the apples in the butter on medium heat. Add some salt and pepper. Add the remaining ingredients and stir/toss to coat the apples evenly. Cover with a lid and cook on low heat for 30 minutes, checking frequently to make sure the apples aren't over caramelizing and that there's still some liquid in the pan. If needed, add some water. Continue cooking on low heat for another 20 minutes or so until the apples are soft, but not mushy. Adjust the seasoning and discard the whole herbs, vanilla bean, bay leaves and garlic cloves. Store the apples in the resulting pan sauce.

BABA GHANOUSH

Many recipes discard the skin because it is purportedly bitter. Nah. And even if it is, that's flavor and nutrition. At the inaugural Chefs' Taste Challenge in New Orleans, I drew eggplant as one of my basket ingredients. I grilled the eggplant whole and used the charred skin to highlight a purée as part of a tasting trio. I was fortunate to win the judge's award and I distinctly recall one of the judges, Izabela Wojcik from the James Beard Foundation commenting that she was intrigued by my bold use of the charred eggplant skin. I recommend using some of the charred skin here as well.

LEVEL: Basic

YIELD: approximately 2 cups

INGREDIENTS
2 large Italian eggplant with minimal seeds
4 garlic cloves, minced
1/2 teaspoon red chile powder
1/2 teaspoon paprika
zest and juice from one lemon
2 tablespoons tahini
1/4 cup extra-virgin olive oil
2 sprigs flat leaf parsley, chopped
salt & pepper, in stages and per taste

METHOD
Preheat an oven to 375F. With a sharp knife, pierce the eggplant in several places, place on a baking sheet, lightly brush with olive oil, season lightly with salt and pepper and roast for 1 hour. Be sure to rotate the eggplant after about 35 minutes. Remove from the oven and let it cool. Cut open both eggplant and scrape any seeds but do not discard the charred skin. Steep the garlic in the lemon juice for 5 minutes. In a food processor, blend the roasted eggplant pulp, chile powder, paprika, charred skin, tahini, orange juice, garlic, salt, and pepper. Taste and adjust the seasoning as desired. With the processor running on low, drizzle in the extra-virgin olive oil and finish by folding in the chopped parsley.

SMOKED TOMATOES & ROASTED GRAPES

> I learned how to roast grapes during my stint at the school's restaurant in my final class in culinary school. I have used that concept ever since. I've used them on scallop dishes, tasting boards, and of course, in salads. Jenneffer had been urging me to do more smoking in the restaurant (I can hear some of you giggle here). She bought me a smoker with John MacConnell's advice one year as a Christmas gift. One of the first items I smoked was some heirloom tomatoes. The rest is history. We smoke all kinds of stuff now: fish, vegetables, meats, shellfish, and even cheese.

LEVEL: Basic

YIELD: approximately 2 cups of each

INGREDIENTS

2 cups, assorted seedless table grapes. cleaned and dried
2 cups ripe grape or cherry tomatoes
1 teaspoon grapeseed oil
1 teaspoon extra-virgin olive oil, as needed
salt & pepper, in stages and per taste

METHOD

Preheat a smoker to 200 F with soaked wood chips (use a wood like cherry or apple wood) Toss the tomatoes in a slight amount of extra virgin olive oil just to coat them lightly. Season lightly with salt and pepper. Place in the center of the rack/grill and smoke for about 45 minutes to an hour. Cool down. The natural smoky jus that forms is delicious and may be used for sauces or vinaigrettes.

Preheat an oven to 300 F. Toss the grapes lightly in grapeseed oil. Do not season them. Place on a baking sheet and roast for about 30 minutes depending on the size of the grapes. They should blister only slightly. Let them cool.

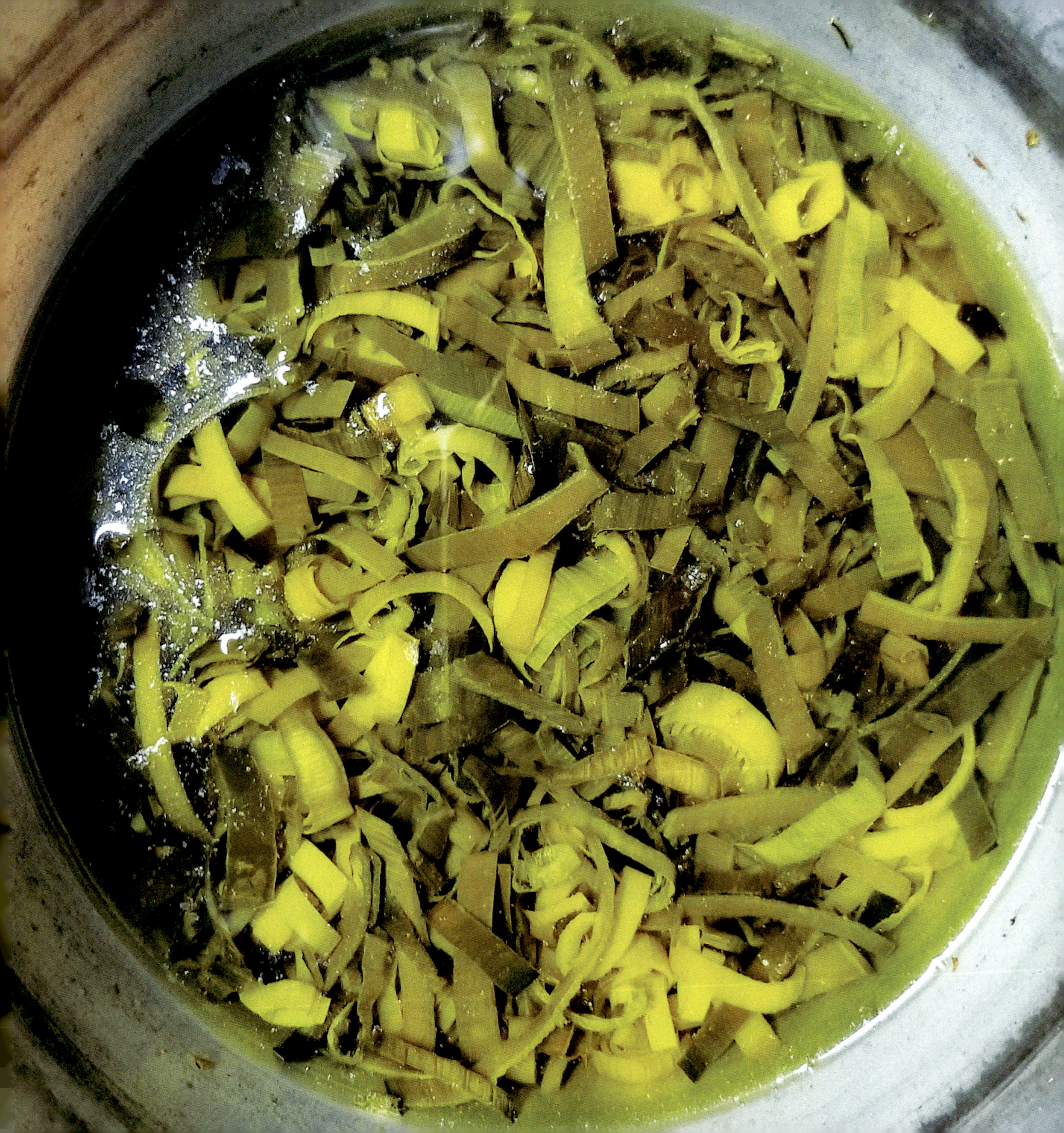

INFUSED OILS (LEEK OIL & GREEN OIL)

> There are essentially two methods of infusing flavor into a neutral oil – cold infusion or warm infusion. Cold infusion is best for delicate flavors like that of gentle herbs. Warm infusion is best when the flavor you desired needs to be agitated with heat: for example, spices and tough ingredients.

LEVEL: Basic

YIELD: approximately 1 quart

INGREDIENTS
1 cup tough leek tops, sliced thinly
1 bunch fresh basil, washed well
1 bunch fresh parsley, washed well
a small amount salted water for blanching the herbs
cold water for shocking the blanched herbs
1 quart grapeseed oil

METHOD

Leek Oil
Of course, the white portion of leeks is a highly prized ingredient. Instead of using the tops for stocks only, here's a great way to extract and preserve tremendous leek flavor and aroma. Slice the toughest part thinly. In a saucepan, gently simmer half a quart of grapeseed oil and the sliced leek tops for 10 minutes. Let the mixture cool completely, before refrigerating for 24 hours. The next day, the oil should be completely infused with leek flavor and aroma. Strain the oil and store in the refrigerator in a squeeze bottle. Drizzle on pastas, soups, crostini, etc. The cooked leek tops may be blended and used in dishes as a flavor element, for example in gnocchi pâte à choux.

Green Oil
Blanch the basil and parsley in hot salted water for 15 seconds before immediately transferring to a bowl of cold water. This step sets the chlorophyll and brightens the color of the herbs. Remove the shocked herbs and squeeze out as much moisture as possible. Transfer the squeezed out basil leaves, parsley leaves, and half quart of grapeseed oil to a high-speed blender. Blend on medium high for at least a minute. Setup a fine cloth or multiple layers of cheesecloth over a bowl. Pour the green oil over the fine cloth and refrigerate. The next day, you should have bright green flavorful oil. As in the case of the leek oil, the green reside may be used in soups, pasta, dough, etc.

COLCANNON

Every St. Patrick's Day, I would showcase my take on Irish (American) delicacies. How could I not prepare this humble, but delicious creation, which speaks to me in in so many ways because it eats like a bhaji I want to pick up with warm *puris*!

LEVEL: Basic

YIELD: approximately 1 1/2 quarts

INGREDIENTS
1 cup green cabbage, chopped
1 cup chopped kale
3 skin on white potatoes, washed and quartered
2 cloves garlic, minced
1 tablespoon fresh thyme, chopped
1 bay leaf (fresh, if available)
pinch of freshly grated nutmeg
water to boil the potatoes
2 tablespoons unsalted butter or extra-virgin olive oil
1 cup milk or unsweetened nut milk
salt & pepper, in stages and per taste

METHOD
Boil the potatoes staring with salted cold water. When the potatoes are half-cooked, grain them. In a wide shallow pan, melt the butter and add the bay leaf, thyme, and garlic. Cook for a minute before adding the cabbage and kale. Sauté until the cabbage starts to caramelize a bit. Cook for about 15 minutes. Next, add the potatoes, milk and additional water, if necessary. Add the nutmeg. Cover the pan and reduce the flame to low-medium. Continue cooking until the potatoes and cabbage are fully cooked. Remove the bay leaf and smash down to a uniform mash. Taste and adjust the seasoning as preferred. Finish with freshly ground black pepper.

MUMBAI POTATOES

At the time of writing this, approximately 5,455 days ago, this was the very first dish I made for Jenneffer. After discovering that we both got our jollies from bold and spice food, I whipped up a version with lots of habanero peppers. Once the toxic pepper fumes had subsided, we sat cross-legged in bed at my modest one-room dwelling, sharing my take on Mumbai potatoes while pretending to watch late night television. Little could we have imagined the beautiful future this moment would blossom into.

LEVEL: Basic

YIELD: approximately 4 servings

INGREDIENTS

1 lb. baby Yukon gold potatoes, halved
1 large onion, sliced thinly
1 thumb-sized piece ginger, grated
2 large garlic cloves
4 large ripe tomatoes, chopped
2 green chilies, sliced thinly
1 teaspoon black mustard seed
1/2 teaspoon cumin seed
2 teaspoon ground coriander
1 teaspoon turmeric
1/2 teaspoon ground cumin
1 teaspoon garam masala
small bunch coriander, chopped
1 sprig curry leaves
extra-virgin olive oil or vegetable oil, as needed
water, as needed
salt & pepper, in stages and per taste

METHOD

Cook the potatoes in salted water until just shy of being completely cooked. Drain well. In a shallow pan, heat some oil and add the mustard seed, cumin seed, curry leaves, ginger, and garlic. Cook for a minute. Next add the onions and cook until light golden brown. Next add all the ground spices and stir around for 30 seconds. Add more oil if the mixture is dry. Now add the tomatoes and season with salt and pepper. Stew the spiced tomato mixture until a bright sauce develops in the pan. Add the par-cooked potatoes, stir well, and cover the pan. Stew the potatoes on low heat for about 20 minutes. Open the pan, taste the sauce, and adjust the seasoning as desired. Finish with the chopped cilantro.

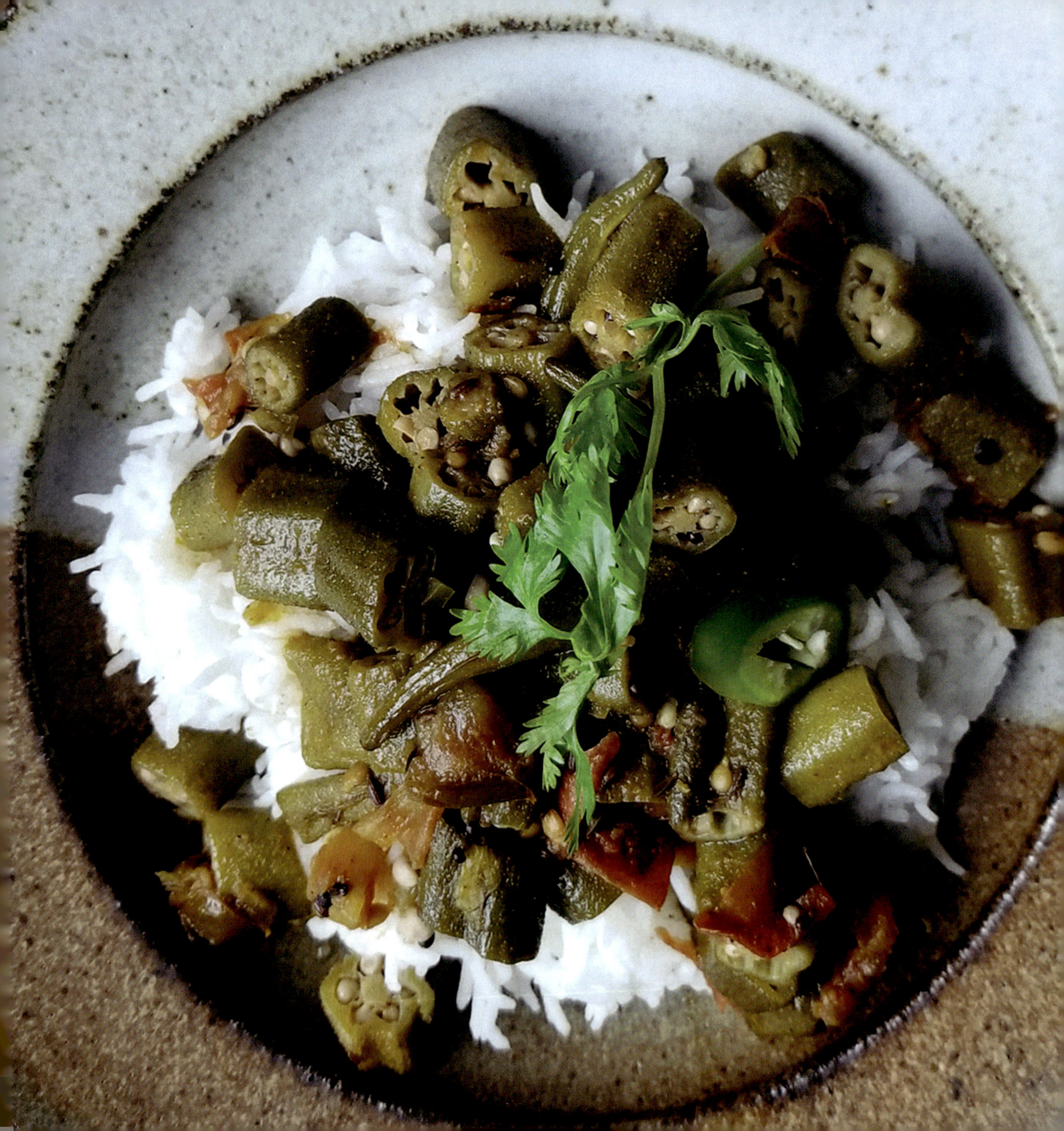

OKRA MASALA

> Indian cuisine embraces okra like few others. People often tell me that they would like okra more if it wasn't for the "slime." Growing up, we had pretty good okra; but when I discovered Emerald okra, the fact that I could eat the okra uncooked and it tasted delicious only meant that using it for a popular Indian preparation would really highlight the okra just as much as the expectedly simple spice combinations.

LEVEL: Basic

YIELD: approximately 4 servings

INGREDIENTS

2 lbs., washed and dried okra (I prefer the "emerald" variety), cut into biased 3/4 inch pieces
2 teaspoons mustard seeds
1 teaspoon cumin seeds
10 fresh curry leaves (usually available in Indian grocery stores)
1 teaspoon turmeric powder
1 teaspoon cumin powder
1 teaspoon coriander powder
1 teaspoon cayenne pepper
1 medium red onion, peeled, sliced thinly
1 teaspoon minced fresh ginger
1 teaspoon minced fresh garlic
1 teaspoon minced fresh jalapeño
1 cup fresh diced tomatoes
1 fresh lemon
1 tablespoon freshly chopped cilantro leaves
1/4 cup vegetable or olive oil
salt & pepper, in stages and per taste

METHOD

In a large skillet, heat the oil on a medium heat, and add the mustard seeds, cumin seeds, and curry leaves until the mustard seeds start popping. Add the ginger and garlic and stir for 20 seconds. Next, add onions and sauté until translucent. Now add all the dry spices and stir for 30 seconds or so. Next, add the okra and stir so that the spices coat all the okra. If needed, add more oil. Cook the okra, stirring occasionally for about 30 minutes or so. Add in the tomatoes and jalapeños. Stir, cover, and let simmer on low heat for an additional 15 minutes, stirring periodically as needed. When the okra is cooked to the desired doneness, remove the lid and "cook off" any additional liquid until the dish is mostly "dry." Finish by squeezing the juice of one lemon and stirring in the fresh cilantro. Serve with any flatbread like naan or pita.

ZESTY CHICKPEAS

> I once garnished my velvety green garbanzo hummus with a za'atar and olive oil roasted garbanzo peas for a restaurant anniversary we spent as guest chefs at the Second Harvest Food Bank of Central Florida.

LEVEL: Basic

YIELD: approximately 2 cups

INGREDIENTS
2 cans garbanzo beans, rinsed or drained well or 1 lb. dried garbanzo soaked overnight
2 sprigs fresh thyme
1 bay leaf
zest of one lemon
1 tablespoon garam masala (page 73)
water, as needed
extra-virgin olive oil, as needed
salt & pepper, in stages and per taste

METHOD
Cook the canned or re-hydrated beans in salted water with the bay leaf until cooked, but not overcooked. Note that the cooking time for re-hydrated beans is significantly longer, about 2 hours. Drain well and transfer to a bowl. Add some extra-virgin olive oil, add the thyme sprigs, some salt, pepper, and the garam masala. Transfer to a baking sheet and roast in an oven at 350F for about 45 minutes. Discard the thyme sprigs and mix in the lemon zest. The beans are ready to snack.

DUCK OR CHICKEN EGG SALAD

LEVEL: Basic

YIELD: approximately 4 servings

INGREDIENTS
6 duck or chicken eggs
2 tablespoons high quality mayonnaise
1 tablespoon Dijon mustard
1/2 cup fresh basil, chopped
1 tablespoon extra virgin olive oil
salt & pepper, in stages and per taste

METHOD
Submerge the eggs in cold water in a heavy bottomed pot and bring to a rapid boil. Switch off the heat and cover immediately with a tight lid. Let the eggs sit for about 15 minutes. Meanwhile in a stainless bowl. mix the remaining ingredients except the fresh basil. Cool the boiled eggs and peel. Rinse the boiled eggs to make sure there are not eggshells. Dice the hard-boiled eggs and fold into the mixture. Test the seasoning to make sure there is a good balance of flavors. Finish by mixing in the fresh basil and serve over grilled bread or in a sandwich with Boston lettuce and a slice of in-season vine-ripened tomato.

TZATZIKI

LEVEL: Basic

YIELD: approximately 3 cups

INGREDIENTS
2 cups of Greek yogurt
1 English cucumber, peeled and grated
1/2 teaspoon paprika
4 cloves of garlic, minced
2 tablespoons lemon juice
2 tablespoon chopped dill
1 tablespoon chopped flatleaf parsley
2 tablespoons extra-virgin olive oil
salt & pepper, in stages and per taste

METHOD
Mix the garlic and lemon juice in a stainless or glass bowl and let sit for 10 minutes. Next mix the remaining ingredients well and season as desired with salt and pepper. Refrigerate and use after the flavors have had a chance to harmonize (at least one hour).

GUACAMOLE

> No matter what else you do, do not skip the step where one steeps the garlic and onions in the fresh citrus juice for a few minutes. Winemaker Andrew Dickson and Jessica Sadowsky once attended a cooking demo I presented at the vaulted Culinary Institute of America, Greystone, NAPA campus. This step during my demo made an impression and I'm told they now use it routinely in their own cooking. By the way, Andrew Lane wines are delicious.

LEVEL: Basic

YIELD: approximately 4 servings

INGREDIENTS
6 semi ripe Haas avocados
juice and zest of 1/2 lime & 1/2 lemon
1/2 teaspoon honey
2 cloves of garlic, minced
1 small red onion, minced
1 jalapeno, minced
1 tablespoon extra-virgin olive oil
1/2 cup ripe in-season tomatoes, diced
1/2 cup fresh cilantro, chopped
salt & pepper, in stages and per taste

METHOD
In a large wooden or stainless mixing bowl, steep the garlic and onions in the combined fresh citrus juice for 5 minutes. Meanwhile, skin and de-seed the avocados. Add them to the bowl. Add all the remaining ingredients except the chopped cilantro. With a fork, "smash" the ingredients to a coarse consistency. Test the seasoning and adjust as necessary. Finish with the fresh cilantro and mix well. Serve immediately.

Sinfully Vegan Degustation in 15 Acts

Evidently, a 100-course meal would not be a stretch using only the ideas in this book. Here, I stay focused on an entire vegan menu without using eggs and dairy as crutches for decadence. Naturally, the portions have to be small (2 ounces on average). This menu is a glimpse into the mind of yours truly. I don't present introductions to the course. Simply titles and recipes. In practice, tweaking and adjusting of flavors is completely plausible. At the end of the day, if you decide to embark on creating this culinary odyssey, I urge you to exercise mis en place, taste everything, and don't serve anything you wouldn't eat yourself. As far as plate presentation goes, less is more. So, avoid crowding the components. Allow the distinct components a chance to be tasted by the diner while believing that the perfect bite is typically a little bit of everything on the plate.

Welcome to the Chef's Table!

CHILLED VICHYSSOISE, WARM MONSOON CORN, TARRAGON OIL

LEVEL: Intermediate

YIELD: approximately 4 tasting servings

INGREDIENTS
1 cup leek whites only, cleaned well, sliced
1 Yukon gold potato, peeled, diced
1 turnip, peeled, diced
1 parsnip, peeled, chopped
1 sprig fresh thyme
1 fresh bay leaf
pinch of nutmeg
2 cloves fresh garlic, minced
1 cup monsoon corn (page 236)
tarragon oil (see and adapt recipe on page 359)
2 tablespoons extra-virgin olive oil
1 cup coconut cream
1 cup water
salt & pepper, in stages and per taste

METHOD
In a heavy saucepan, melt the leeks on medium heat in the olive oil. Season with salt. Add the garlic, thyme sprig, and bay leaf. Cook for a minute and add the potato, turnip, and parsnip. Stir well and add the stock. Season with salt a bit more and cover the pan. Reduce the heat to low-medium and cook for about 25 minutes or until the vegetables are soft and falling apart. Discard the bay leaf and thyme sprig. Finish the vichyssoise by mixing in the coconut cream and adjusting the salt. Allow to cool a bit and blend to a very smooth and velvety consistency. Allow it to cool a bit more before refrigerating. Whisk well and serve chilled with a dollop of monsoon corn and several drops of tarragon oil.

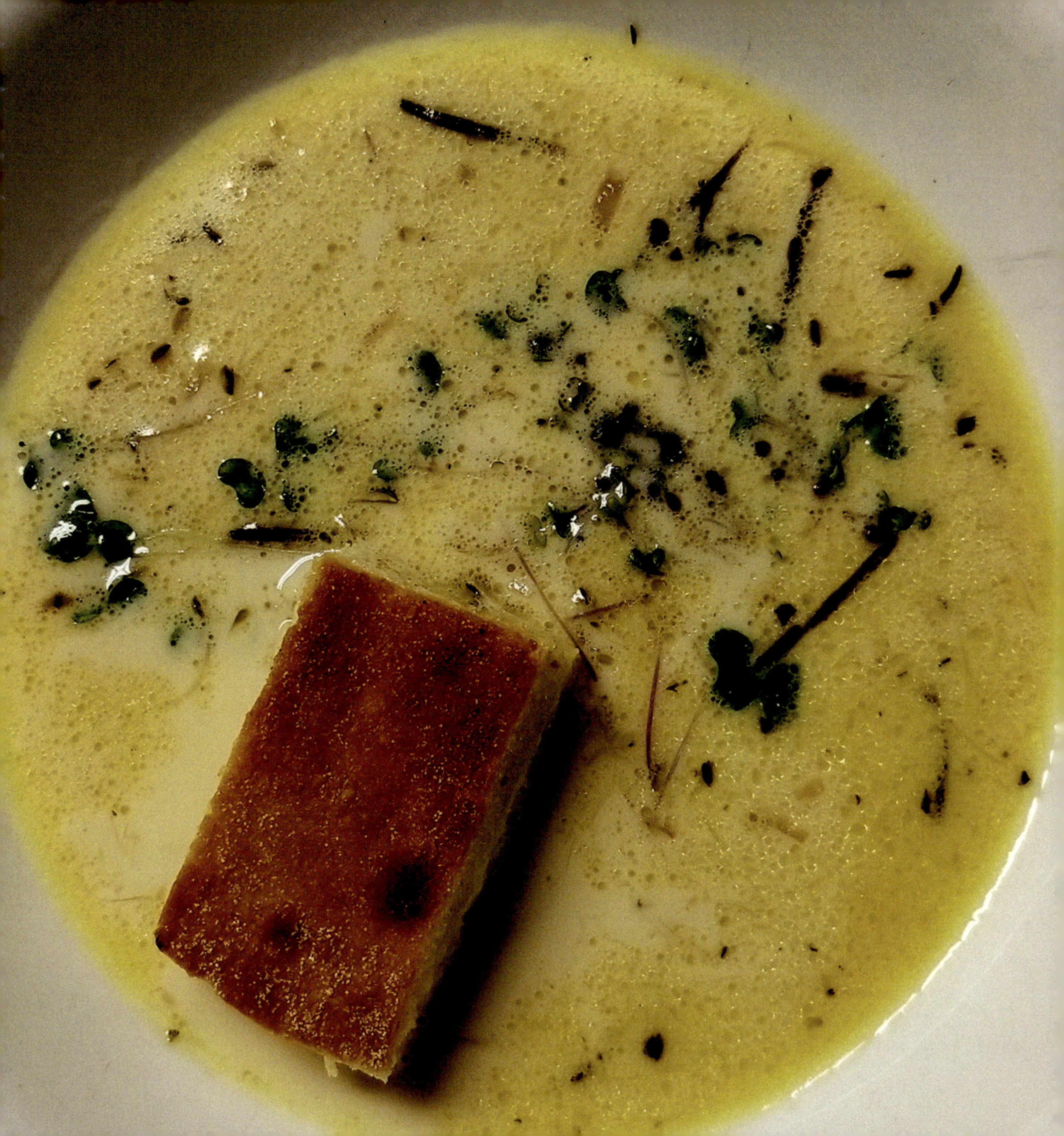

TOMATO TERRINE, WATERMELON SALSA, TEXTURED BASIL

LEVEL: Pro

YIELD: approximately 4 tasting servings

INGREDIENTS

4 vine ripened or otherwise ripe heirloom tomatoes, different colors, cut into wedges
3/4 cup neutral vegetable stock
2 tablespoons agar-agar
1 cup ripe watermelon, small diced
1/4 cup seedless cucumber, small diced
1 teaspoon jalapeno, no seeds, minced (optional)
zest and juice of 1 lemon
1 teaspoon shallot, minced
medium sized basil leaves, washed and dried
1 tablespoon fresh basil, thin strips, held green
extra-virgin olive oil, as needed
salt & pepper, in stages and per taste

METHOD

Tomato Terrine

Season the stock appropriately with salt and pepper. Heat and hold hot. Remove the seeds and pulp from the tomato wedges and gently press out the juice from the pulp through a mesh. Lay out the pressed tomato wedges and season them with salt, pepper, and a touch of high quality extra-virgin olive oil. Next, add the agar-agar to about 1/2 cup tomato juice and mix well. Hold this mixture for about 10 minutes. Meanwhile, prepare a baking dish or terrine mold with plastic ensuring that you have enough excess overhang on all sides, which will be folded over once the terrine has been layered. Smooth out the plastic to remove wrinkles as this will affect the texture of the terrine.

Add the agar-agar and tomato juice mixture to the hot stock and dissolve by whisking well. The layering of the terrine starts by pouring a thin layer of stock on the bottom. Refrigerate and allow it to set. Meanwhile, pat the tomato wedges dry. After the layer of stock sets, begin layering the dry tomato wedges on top of the tomato gelée, ensuring you are pressing gently between layers and using different colors for layers. Continue until you have all the layers. Press down and pour enough only slightly warm stock onto the terrine. Bring the overhanging edges together. Place the terrine on a baking sheet and refrigerate. After the gelée sets again, weight down the terrine under uniform weight and store refrigerated overnight. When you are ready to serve this course, remove terrine from the mold (you may have some juices leech out; this is normal), peel off the plastic and slice appropriately thick slices with a sharp knife. Present with the layers showing.

Watermelon Salsa

Soak the minced shallot in the lemon juice and zest for 10 minutes. Next, carefully mix all the ingredients, and drizzle some high quality olive oil.

Textured Basil

Heat some olive oil in a pan and shallow fry the whole, dried basil leaves turning over to ensure uniform frying and crisping. Drain on a paper towel. Season lightly with salt. Once cooled, very carefully sprinkle the fresh sliced basil onto the fried basil leaves.

EXOTIC MUSHROOMS & EGGPLANT INVOLTINI, ROASTED GARBANZO, ARRABIATTA

LEVEL: Intermediate

YIELD: approximately 4 tasting servings

INGREDIENTS

2 cups assorted exotic mushrooms, cleaned and torn or cut into uniform sizes
1 medium eggplant with few seeds, trimmed and sliced into 1/8-inch-long slices
4 cloves garlic, two whole, two sliced thinly
1 shallot, minced
1 sprig fresh thyme
1/4 cup roasted cashews, ground
1 cup cooked garbanzo beans, drained well
1 tablespoon Tuscan spice blend (see recipe on page 81)
2 cups San Marzano tomatoes from a can, puree in a blender
2 tablespoons Calabrian red chiles (substitute 2 chile de arbol)
extra-virgin olive oil, as needed
salt & pepper, in stages and per taste

METHOD

Involtini

Preheat an oven to 325F. Brush the slices of eggplant with olive oil, season with salt and pepper, and coat the whole garlic and thyme sprig with olive oil. Roast the eggplant slices with the thyme and garlic on them in the oven until the eggplant is soft and pliable. Check after 30 minutes. Remove from the oven and allow the eggplant to cool.

In a sauté pan, heat some extra virgin oil and cook the shallots for a couple of minutes before adding the mushrooms. Keep the heat high enough to obtain some caramelization on the mushrooms. Once the mushrooms are soft enough, stop cooking them, and transfer to a food processor along with the cashew, roasted garlic cloves, and roasted leaves from the thyme sprig. Add a bit of salt and pepper. Pulse a few times to essentially form a wet mushroom crumb. This will be the filling for the involtini.

Roasted Garbanzo

Rinse the cooked garbanzo, toss in extra virgin olive oil, Tuscan spice blend, salt, and pepper. Transfer to a baking sheet and roast at 325F for 30 minutes. This can be done concurrently with the roasting of the eggplant provided you have room in the oven.

Arrabiatta

Heat some extra virgin oil in a saucepan. Brown the sliced garlic in the oil for two minutes. Next add the hot chiles and fry for another minute. Finally add the tomato puree and stew on medium low, stirring periodically, for about 30 minutes or until the canned flavor of the tomato is gone. During this process, the sauce should naturally thicken.

RADISH HOLLOW, TIGER'S MILK, ROASTED GARLIC

LEVEL: Basic

YIELD: approximately 4 tasting servings

INGREDIENTS

4 medium sized red radish
1/2 cup leche de tigre, more or less (page 106)
4 cloves garlic
1 sprig fresh thyme
extra-virgin olive oil, as needed
salt & pepper, in stages and per taste

METHOD

Radish Hollow & Roasted Garlic

Wash the radish well and pat dry. Carefully trim the bottom end of each radish so it will be stable when paced on that side as the base. Brush with a bit of olive oil and season with salt and pepper. Meanwhile, toss the four garlic cloves in olive oil, salt, pepper and the chopped-up thyme sprig. Place in a piece of foil and close around the contents to form a pouch. Place the radish and garlic pouch in a 300F oven for 45 minutes. Allow the roasted radish and garlic to cool. With a small, sharp knife or a melon baller, scoop out the radish to form fillable bowls. Use the scooped-out radish in salads or salsas.

Tiger's Milk

See recipe on page 106. It's better to make more than you need because barring natural separation, it will keep well in the refrigerator for a week.

Assemble the final dish by placing each radish bowl on its base, carefully pushing in one roasted garlic clove and filling the bowl 3/4 of the way with leche de tigre. Garnish as you see fit with a fresh herb or crumb. It should be evident that this course is to be consumed in one bite for both function and flavor.

FRENCH FENNEL SOUP, THYME AND CASHEW TOAST

LEVEL: Basic

YIELD: approximately 4 tasting servings

INGREDIENTS

2 fennel bulbs, cleaned, cored, sliced thinly, keep the fronds
1 clove garlic, minced
1 bay leaf
1 tablespoon fresh thyme chopped coarsely
1/2 teaspoon soy sauce
1 teaspoon Dijon mustard
3 cups stock made from the fennel tops or plain vegetable stock
1/4 cup dry red wine
1/4 cup raw cashews soaked in water for at least 6 hours
1 cup water for the cashews
1/2 teaspoon white miso
1/2 teaspoon lemon juice
1/4 teaspoon tapioca starch
4 slices baguette
extra-virgin olive oil, as needed
salt & pepper, in stages and per taste

METHOD

French Fennel Soup

In a heavy-bottomed saucepan, heat the extra-virgin oil on low-medium heat and begin sweating the fennel. This is the most time-consuming part of the dish. On a low heat, begin caramelizing and melting the fennel to a light golden brown, while stirring periodically. This may take up to an hour. Next add the garlic, bay leaf, and half of the thyme. Cook for 1 minute and deglaze with the red wine. Cook for another 2 minutes before adding in the Dijon mustard and stock. Check the seasoning and simmer on low until you have the desired thickness and consistency. Discard the bay leaf.

Thyme and Cashew Toast

Drain the cashews and reserve the soaking water. In a food processor, blend the cashews, miso, lemon juice, tapioca, and some salt, using just enough water to facilitate a smooth, spreadable spread. Lightly brush the baguette slices with olive oil and pre-toast in a toaster or oven until light golden brown. Fill a portion of soup into av oven safe bowl. Spread a generous amount of cashew spread on one side of each toast. Cut into smaller pieces, if necessary, and place as a cover on the soup. Bake until the cashew spread has dark spots and is bubble. Allow the soup to cool sufficiently before serving.

BLUE CORN JOHNNY CAKE, ACKEE HASH, LILY ESCABÈCHE

LEVEL: Intermediate

YIELD: approximately 4 tasting servings

INGREDIENTS
1/2 cup all-purpose flour
1/2 cup blue corn flour
1/4 teaspoon active dry yeast
1 teaspoon baking powder
2 teaspoons granulated sugar
1/4 cup warm unsalted soymilk, more or less
1/2 cup ackee fruit, canned (drained & rinsed)
1/2 red bell pepper, small diced
2 cloves garlic, minced
1 teaspoon fresh thyme, chopped
1 green chile, chopped
2 shallots, sliced thinly
1 small red onion, sliced thinly
3 stalks scallions, whites and greens sliced thinly on a bias
1/4 teaspoon red chile flakes
1/4 cup red wine vinegar
zest and juice of 1 lime
1 teaspoon granulated sugar
1/4 cup warm water
extra-virgin olive oil, as needed
salt & pepper, in stages and per taste

METHOD

Blue Corn Johnny Cake
Dissolve a pinch of salt in the warm water and whisk in the yeast. Allow the yeast to bloom for 10 minutes. Mix the corn meal, flour, baking powder, and some salt and pepper. Make a well and add the yeasty water. Whisk well. It will be dry. Slowly combine as much soymilk as needed to form a semi-thick batter. Do not overmix. Cover and let rest for 15 minutes. Heat some oil in a non-stick or cast-iron skillet. Ladle 2 ounces of batter over the hot oil to pan fry. Turn when you see the edges browning. Cook through and hold warm.

Ackee Hash
Sauté half the sliced shallots and all the garlic in some olive oil. Add the green chile, thyme and bell pepper and cook for 5 minutes before adding the drained ackee. Season with salt and pepper. The canned ackee is already cooked, so simply sauté, develop flavor, and hold the hash.

Lily Escabèche
Combine the red wine vinegar, lime juice and zest, red chile flakes, remaining sugar, and some salt and pepper; whisk well to dissolve the salt and sugar. Mix the sliced onions, remaining shallot, and scallions together and pour the pickling liquid onto the mixture. Mix well and press down to make sure the lily slices are being cured. Set aside for at least an hour, mixing periodically before using.

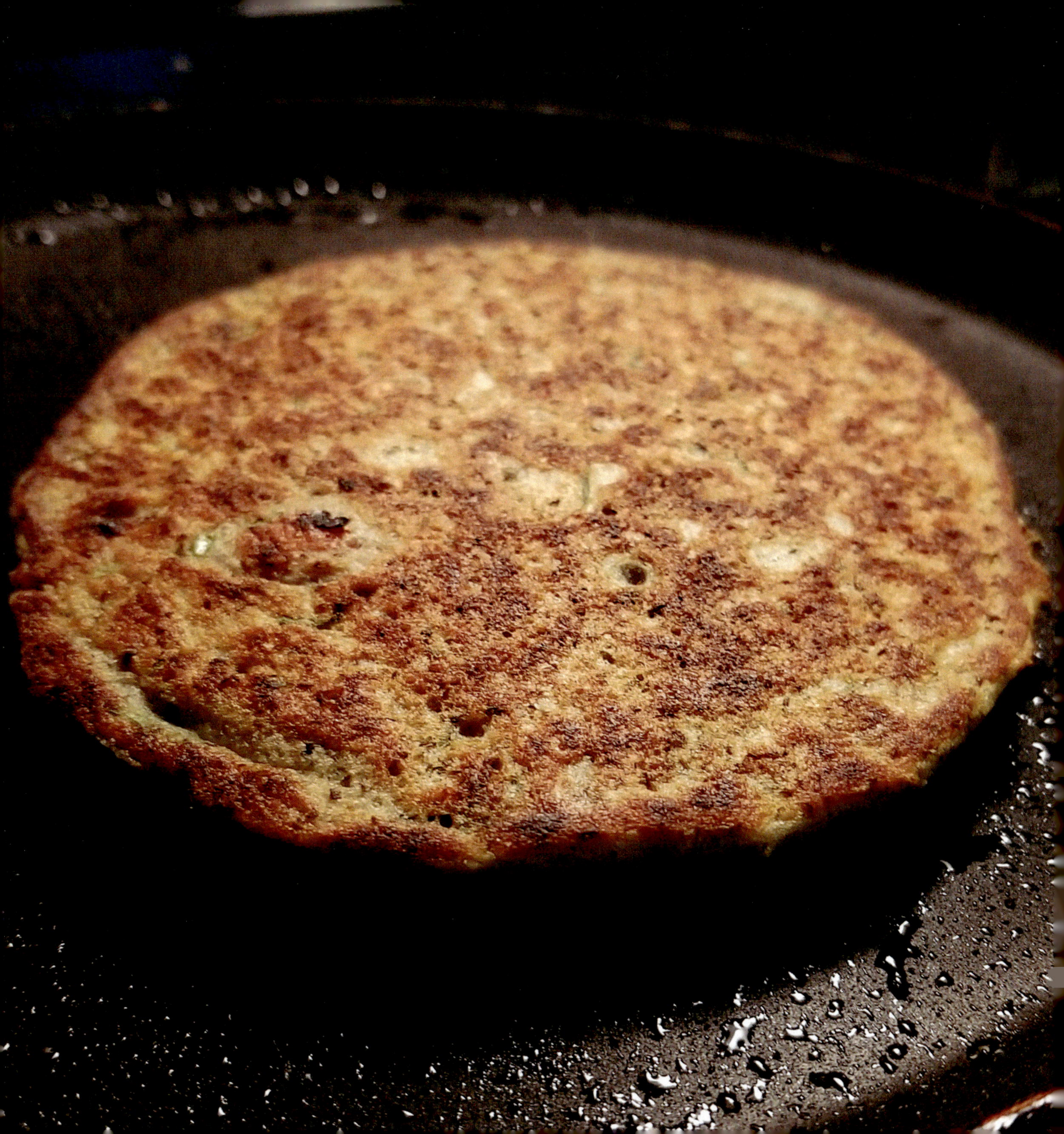

GRILLED LETTUCE HEARTS, HERB TRUFFLE VINAIGRETTE, CRISP SHALLOTS

LEVEL: Basic

YIELD: approximately 4 tasting servings

INGREDIENTS

2 cups assorted lettuce hearts, cleaned and dried
2 tablespoons herb truffled vinaigrette (page 166)
2 shallots, sliced thinly
corn starch
oil for frying
extra-virgin olive oil, as needed
salt & pepper, in stages and per taste

METHOD

Cut the lettuce hearts lengthwise with core intact so you have a flat side to grill on. In a bowl, coat the lettuce with olive oil, salt, and pepper. Grill for about 5 minutes over medium heat, turning over once and hold warm. As the lettuce is grilling, make the vinaigrette and lightly coat the shallots with corn starch, salt, and pepper. Fry until golden brown. Dress the grilled lettuce in the vinaigrette and serve immediately with sprinkles of crisp shallot and drops of vinaigrette.

LENTIL GUMBO, CHARRED OKRA, SCALLION RICE

LEVEL: Intermediate

YIELD: approximately 4 tasting servings

INGREDIENTS

2 tablespoons onion, minced
1 tablespoon celery, minced
1 tablespoon bell pepper, minced
1/4 cup brown lentils
1/2 teaspoon tomato paste
2 tablespoons vegetable oil
1 tablespoon all-purpose flour
3 cloves garlic, minced
vegetable stock, as needed
2 bay leaf
1 teaspoon fresh thyme leaves
1 teaspoon creole spice blend (page 87)
1 teaspoon flat leaf parsley, chopped
1/2 cup thinly sliced okra
oil for frying the okra
1/4 teaspoon cayenne pepper
1/2 cup sliced scallions
1/4 cup white rice, washed well and drained
salt & pepper, in stages and per taste

METHOD

Lentil Gumbo

Heat a tablespoon of oil in a saucepan and add the flour. Stirring over medium heat, form a brown roux. Add the onion, celery, and pepper, and mix well. Cook the vegetables until a bit soft. Add half of the minced garlic, lentils, 1 bay leaf, thyme, creole blend, salt, and pepper. Stir well, coating the lentils with the other ingredients. Next add the tomato paste and fry for about a minute.

Add enough stock to help cook the lentils and cover the pan. Cook on low-medium until the lentils are cooked and soft. Using a ladle or potato masher, break down the stew to release the flavors and thicken it naturally. Finish with the parsley, check and adjust the seasoning, and discard the bay leaf.

Charred Okra

Fry the okra at approximately 325F until it basically stops bubbling. Transfer to a plate lined with enough paper towels. Season with the cayenne pepper and salt. Hold in a warm, dry area until serving to maintain the crisp texture.

Scallion Rice

Instead of plain white rice and scallions as garnish, why not serve the gumbo with scallion rice, which stands on its own. In a small pan, heat a small amount of oil and sauté half the scallions with the other half of the garlic. After a few minutes, add the rice and stir well, coating the rice with the scallion-infused oil. Add the appropriate amount of vegetable stock, salt, and pepper. Cover and cook according to the directions for the rice variety. Allow the rice to absorb all the liquid before fluffing with a fork and finishing with the other half of the scallions.

CELERIAC TOTS, BLOODY MARY ROMESCO, CELERY RELISH

LEVEL: Intermediate

YIELD: approximately 4 tasting servings

INGREDIENTS
1 medium russet potato, peeled
1 medium celeriac (celery root), peeled
1 teaspoon all-purpose flour
1 teaspoon fresh thyme, chopped
1/2 teaspoon onion powder
1/2 teaspoon garlic powder
1 tablespoon V8
1 teaspoon Tabasco
1/2 teaspoon celery salt
1/2 teaspoon prepared horseradish
1/2 teaspoon Worcestershire (without anchovies)
1 teaspoon jalapeno, chopped
1/2 cup standard romesco sauce (page 98)
1 celery stalk, small diced
1 shallot, small diced
1/4 cup seedless cucumber, small diced
juice and zest of 1 lemon
1 teaspoon honey
1/2 teaspoon Dijon mustard
1/4 cup tender celery leaves
oil, for frying tots
water for boiling potato and celeriac
salt & pepper, in stages and per taste

METHOD

Celeriac Tots

Parboil the potato and celeriac, whole; while starting in cold, lightly salted water. Do not cook completely, only about halfway for about 7 minutes. Drain well and cool. Pat them both dry and using a box grater, finely shred both in a bowl. Transfer the mixture to a clean towel or multiple layers of cheesecloth and wring out as much moisture as you can. In a dry bowl, to the dried-out potato and celeriac mixture, add the onion powder, garlic powder, fresh thyme, flour, some salt and pepper. Mix well. Form the mixture into small cylinders (tot shapes) and fry to a golden brown. Shake off excess oil, season with salt as preferred, and hold warm.

Bloody Mary Romesco

In a bowl, combine the standard romesco, V8, Tabasco, celery salt, jalapeno, and Worcestershire (if using). Mix well and re-adjust the seasoning as preferred.

Celery Relish

In a bowl, combine the mustard, honey, lemon juice and zest. Add the shallots and let them sit in the liquid for 10 minutes before adding the cucumber, celery, salt, pepper, and gently folding in the tender celery leaves. Serve immediately while the celery leaves are still vibrant and fresh.

BEET SORBET

LEVEL: Basic

YIELD: approximately 4 tasting servings

INGREDIENTS

1 small red beet, peeled and diced
1 tablespoon cane sugar
water, as needed
1 teaspoon lime juice and zest
1/4 cup almond milk

METHOD

Cook the beets in a small amount of water until soft. Drain and reserve the liquid. Make a simple syrup by dissolving equal parts water and the cane sugar. Cool the syrup. Blend the cooked beets in a blender by adding some of the cooking liquid as needed to facilitate blending. Cool the puree. Finally, just before churning in an ice-cream or sorbet maker for about 30 minutes or so, blend the cooled beet puree, lime juice and zest, simple syrup and almond milk to a smooth puree. Refrigerate the churned sorbet for at least an hour before serving.

JERKED SWEET POTATO, COCONUT THYME VELOUTÉ, CALAMONDIN MARMALADE

LEVEL: Intermediate

YIELD: approximately 4 tasting servings

INGREDIENTS
1 large sweet potato, peeled, cut into 1/2-inch disks
1 tablespoon jerk marinade (page 85)
1 can coconut cream
1 teaspoon shallot, minced
2 sprigs fresh thyme
1 bay leaf, fresh if available
1 teaspoon all-purpose flour
1/2 cup vegetable stock
1/4 cup calamondin, sliced in half
water, as needed
1/4 cup light brown sugar
1 teaspoon apple cider vinegar
1/4 teaspoon garam masala (page 73)
2 tablespoons, extra-virgin olive oil
1 tablespoon vegetable oil
salt & pepper, in stages and per taste

METHOD

Jerked Sweet Potato

Marinate the sweet potato disks in olive oil, salt, pepper, and the jerk marinade. Set aside for at least two hours or, preferably, marinate overnight. Allow to come to room temperature. Either in a smoker or in an oven at 250F, roast low and slow until tender. This may take up to 2 hours depending on the insulation of your smoker or oven.

Coconut Thyme Velouté

Heat the vegetable oil and add the flour. Whisking frequently, make a blond roux (about 5 minutes). Add the shallot, thyme sprigs, bay leaf and cook for a few minutes until the shallot is translucent. Add the vegetable stock and whisk well. Season with some salt and pepper. After the liquid reduces by half, add the coconut cream and mix well. Reduce the heat to low-medium and simmer for about 10 minutes. Taste and re-season with salt and pepper, as desired. Strain the sauce through a fine mesh and hold the sauce warm.

Calamondin Marmalade

Cook down the calamondin, brown sugar, vinegar, some water, garam masala, some salt and pepper until you have a marmalade. You may need to adjust the sugar if the fruit is too acidic. Cool down.

REVERSE-SEARED CABBAGE, PINE NUT RELISH, GRILLED ASPARAGUS

LEVEL: Intermediate

YIELD: approximately 4 tasting servings

INGREDIENTS

4 wedges of red cabbage, being careful to leave the core on each
4 ounces pine nuts, toasted
1 bulb garlic
1 tablespoon cup parmigiana Reggiano, grated
1 tablespoon fresh thyme leaves
1 tablespoon lemon juice and zest
1/2 cup extra-virgin olive oil
water for par-steaming the cabbage
8 medium sized asparagus spears, trimmed, bottoms partially peeled
salt & pepper, in stages and per taste

METHOD

Reverse Seared Cabbage

Steam the cabbage for 10 minutes. Pat the edges dry. Drizzle some olive oil, add salt and pepper, and place on a baking sheet. Roast in a 275F oven for an hour, flipping the sides once halfway during the roasting process. Preheat a cast-iron skillet on medium-high heat. When it begins smoking a bit, sear the cabbage wedges for about 45 seconds on each side. If needed, sprinkle some coarse salt and freshly ground black pepper and serve warm.

Pine Nut and Roasted Garlic Relish

Drizzle half the extra-virgin olive oil on the garlic, cover with aluminum foil, and roast in the oven at 325F. After an hour, you should have roasted garlic. Store the oil in the pouch for grilling the asparagus. Squeeze out the roasted garlic cloves and combine with the pine nuts, remaining extra-virgin olive oil, light amount of salt, pepper, the cheese, and the thyme leaves. Set aside.

Grilled Asparagus

Coat the asparagus with extra-virgin olive oil, salt, and pepper, and grill until just done. Toss the grilled asparagus in the lemon juice and zest. Serve warm.

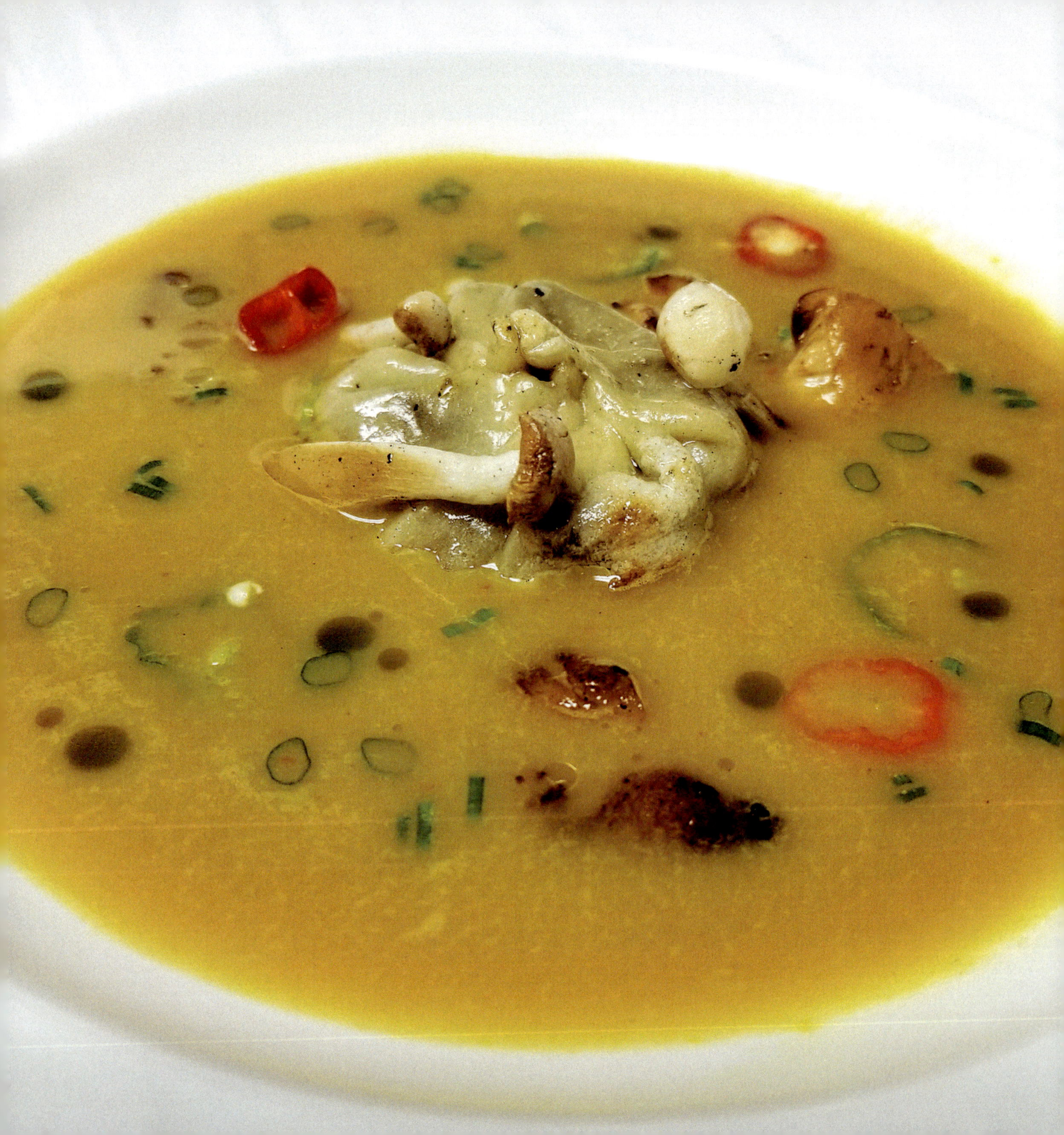

EDAMAME MOMO, SZECHUAN THUKPA, DOODLE

LEVEL: Intermediate

YIELD: approximately 4 tasting servings

INGREDIENTS

1/2 cup shelled edamame (soybeans), cooked in lightly salted water
1 medium onion, slice 3/4 thinly, mince the remaining 1/4
1 tablespoon garlic, minced
2 tablespoons ginger, grated
1 teaspoon green chile, sliced thinly
1/4 cup carrot, sliced thinly
1 teaspoon low sodium soy sauce
few drops of honey
1/2 teaspoon Szechuan peppercorns, coarsely crushed
1 teaspoon turmeric
1/2 teaspoon red chili powder
2 tablespoons olive oil, more or less
1 cup unbleached all-purpose flour
1/3 cup warm water, more or less
2 cups vegetable stock
1 medium length daikon radish, peeled and spiralized
1 tablespoon rice wine vinegar
salt & pepper, in stages and per taste

METHOD

Edamame Momo

Follow the directions for making the momos following the recipe on page xxx. This version will be substituting the cabbage with the cooked soybeans. Use only half the ginger and garlic. The minced onion is for the momo filling.

Szechuan Thukpa

Heat half the olive oil and add the Szechuan peppercorns. Cook for about a minute to infuse the oil with the peppercorn flavor. Next add the sliced onions, remaining ginger and garlic and sauté for 2 minutes. Next add the green chiles. Cook for 30 seconds and add the vegetable stock. Simmer for 5 minutes before adding the soy sauce and honey. Taste and adjust the seasonings as desired.

Doodle (Daikon Noodle)

Soak the spiralized daikon and hold in lukewarm water for 15 minutes. The doodles are ready to be used. When ready to use, drain well and mix in a tablespoon of rice wine vinegar.

CAULIFLOWER MANCHURIAN, GREEN PEANUT HUMMUS, STEM STEM PAKORA

LEVEL: Intermediate

YIELD: approximately 4 tasting servings

INGREDIENTS
2 cups cauliflower florets
1/4 cup manchurian sauce (page 90)
1/2 cup soaked and boiled green peanuts (skin off, if possible)
2 cloves garlic, minced
1 teaspoon tahini
1/4 teaspoon dry toasted cumin powder
1/4 teaspoon paprika
1 tablespoon lemon juice and zest
1 tablespoon scallions, shaved thinly
1/2 cup cilantro stems, chopped, keep leaves for garnish
1 small red onion or shallot, sliced thinly
1/4 cup garbanzo flour, more or less
1/2 teaspoon garam masala (page 73)
water, as needed
oil, for frying the pakora, more for sautéing the cauliflower
2 tablespoons extra-virgin olive oil
salt & pepper, in stages and per taste

METHOD

Cauliflower Manchurian
Blanch the cauliflower in salted water for 5 minutes. Drain well and pat dry. In a skillet, heat some vegetable oil and sauté half the scallions for a minute. Add the blanched cauliflower and begin browning on all sides while adding some salt and pepper. After 5 minutes, add the manchurian sauce and coat the florets in the sauce. Reduce the heat to low-medium and begin glazing the cauliflower in the sauce. Poke a small sharp knife through the thickest part of a floret. If it passes through easily, transfer the manchurian glazed cauliflower to a bowl, toss in the remaining scallions, and hold warm.

Green Peanut Hummus
Steep the minced garlic in the lemon juice and zest for 10 minutes. Meanwhile, process the boiled peanuts in a food processor. With the processor running on low, add the tahini, garlic in lemon juice and zest, toasted cumin, paprika, some salt, and pepper, and drizzle in just enough extra-virgin olive oil to achieve a smooth and velvety texture for the hummus.

Cilantro Stem Pakora
Follow the directions for making pakora on page 125.

CARAMELIZED ONION BISTEEYA, FAVA RENDANG, CARDAMOM CASHEW CRUMB

LEVEL: Pro

YIELD: approximately 4 tasting servings

INGREDIENTS
1 large red onion, sliced thinly
1/2 cup golden raisins
1 clove garlic, minced
1 teaspoon, minced fresh ginger
1 teaspoon ras el hanout spice blend (page 80)
1 teaspoon red wine vinegar
1 small ripe tomato, chopped
filo dough, as needed (ensure that it is vegan)
1/2 cup cooked fava beans (substitute lima beans if unavailable)
1/4 cup raw cashew nuts (pieces are fine)
1/4 teaspoon ground cardamom
pinch of ground cinnamon
1 teaspoon confectioner's sugar
1 cup rendang sauce (page 113)
water, as needed
1/2 cup coconut milk
granulated sugar, as needed
extra-virgin olive oil, as needed
salt & pepper, in stages and per taste

METHOD

Caramelized Onion and Raison Bisteeya

The method to make the bisteeya is like that described in the method on page xxx. The difference is that this version is even more authentic because it requires that filling be inside several layers of filo dough that are brushed with olive oil. I recommend making 4 individual portions and packaging the filling inside covered filo purses. Brush the pastry with olive oil before baking to a golden brown in the oven, following the directions on the filo package.

Fava Rendang

Warm the rendang sauce in a saucepan. Add the cooked fava beans, coconut milk, sugar, salt, and pepper to find the balance. The beans offer protein and a creamy textural complement to the crisp pastry.

Cardamom Cashew Crumb

Toast the cashews in a dry pan. Allow it to cool before pulsing in a food processor along with the cardamom, cinnamon, and a pinch of salt to a semi-coarse crumb. Fold in the confectioner's sugar.

Glossary
(Words Matter)

Agar-Agar Vegetarian substitute for traditional gelatin, made from red sea algae; also, a binder.
Aquafaba Leftover liquid after cooking chickpeas; whip with cream of tartar for vegan mayo
Arancini Italian snack of cooked rice, which is breaded and fried; may also be filled.
Bhaji Indian term used to represent vegetables; may also represent a cooked-vegetable dish without gravy.
Biryani Layered rice dish traditionally made in a clay pot which is sealed with dough.
Blistered Result of cooking quickly on high heat, so as to brown and tear the protective skin.
Braise Classical French cooking technique involving browning and slow-cooking in a moist medium.
Cassoulet Hearty French stew involving proteins and white beans cooked slowly in a earthenware pot.
Char Siu Cantonese-style roasting method involving long strips; skewered and cooked over an open fire.
Chettinad Region in the South Indian state of Tamil Nadu; cuisine characterized by spices and bold flavors.
Chowder Type of stew made with milk or cream thickened with a blond roux (equal parts oil and flour).
Coulis Sauce made by puréeing vegetables or fruits; the ingredients may be cooked or uncooked.
Curry Colonial stereotype of gravy-style dishes inspired from cuisines of the Indian subcontinent.
Dal Ubiquitous term used in India for a preparation of legumes. Usually, dal is a purée or stew.
Demi Sauce made by reducing approximately half the volume in order to intensify flavors.
Duxelle Savory mixture of finely chopped mushrooms, herbs, shallots, wine, and sometimes, cream.
Emulsion Stable mixture of liquids that don't normally mix. Ingredients like mustard enable emulsions.
Etouffee Cajun/Creole dish, often served with rice. Made using a method known as "smothering".
Fra Diavolo Spicy Italian red sauce made with or without tomato. Translates to "brother devil" in Italian.
Gazpacho Iberian (Spain) cold soup made with raw fresh vegetables.
Grain Small, hard seed with or without the hull - wheat, rice corn, oats, sorghum, millet, rye, millet, etc.
Gratin Culinary technique (also style of dish) involving browning of a crust using breadcrumbs, cheese, etc.
Gumbo Roux-based soup containing the "holy trinity" of onions, celery, and bell pepper. Typically, with okra.
Heirloom Old cultivar or plant, not hybrid. Typically handed down through multiple generations.
Kofta Meatball or meatball-style item found in many dishes from the Indian subcontinent and Middle East.
Korma Creamy sauce typically containing gentle spices, nuts, cream and/or yoghurt.
Legume Also known as *pulse*. Seed or other part of certain plants - beans, peanuts, lentils, peas, etc.
Marinade Sauce typically made with oil, citrus, herbs, etc. Meant to infuse flavor into items before cooking.
Masa Harina Dough flour made from ground nixtamalized corn – used to make tortillas.

Glossary
(Words Matter)

Masala Typically a blend of spices. Also used in names of dishes to suggest specific combinations of spices.
Massaman Decadent gravy-based dish from Thailand with a significant Indian influence.
Mirepoix Flavor base made by cooking onions, carrots, and celery in butter or oil- vegetables in a 4:2:1 ratio.
Mis en Place Everything in Place – having all the preparation ready and organized makes for a better outcome.
Mole Traditional, regional sauce from Mexico (Puebla and Oaxaca) made with chiles, fruits, and nuts.
Momo Steamed dumpling from the Himalayan regions of the Indian subcontinent.
Nightshade Family of flowering plants including those that yield tomatoes, eggplant, and bell peppers.
Pakora Fried fritter popular in India typically bound by garbanzo flour.
Pistou Cold sauce or condiment from Provençe, France made with garlic, olive oil, and commonly, basil.
Provençal Relating to things or people from the Provençe region of France.
Pulao Sometimes referred as *pilau* – a rice dish made with a flavorful broth and vegetables.
Purloo Also *perloo*. Regionalized rice dish from the Southern United States and parts of the Caribbean.
Reverse Sear First cook the inside on low and uniform heat. Then sear the outside over high heat.
Roux Mixture of fat and flour to make thickened sauces.
Seitan Hydrated and cooked wheat gluten. Used as a vegan substitute for meat.
Socarrat Crust formed in the bottom of the pan when cooking rice. Intentional outcome for paella.
Sofrito Aromatic condiment common in Latin American. Also refers to beginning step of sauce-making.
Spice Aromatic or pungent ingredient typically obtained from roots, seeds, or barks. Used to flavor food.
Succotash Traditional preparation made with corn, lima beans, onions, garlic, and sometimes, herbs.
Sustainable The ability to maintain levels without compromising the ability to do so in the future.
Tadka The Indian method of tempering. Typically, when dried herbs and spices are cooked quickly in hot oil.
Tajine Traditional Algerian and Moroccan dish as well the earthenware utensil in which the dish is cooked.
Tandoori Indian dish prepared by cooking the marinated skewered ingredients in a clay oven – tandoor.
Tempeh Product made from fermented soybeans – said to have originated in Indonesia.
Umami Sense of taste referring to something being savory. Said to be one of the five senses of taste.
Vichyssoise Thick puréed soup made typically with potatoes, leeks, and heavy cream. Served cold or warm.
Vinaigrette Mixture of oil and an acidic liquid. Classically in a 3:1 ration of oil to vinegar. Often for salads.
Waste Not Movement to reduce food waste with the intent to make food systems more sustainable.
Wat Stew - traditional in many North African cuisines.
Xacuti Traditional gravy-based dish from Goa made with spices, white poppy seeds, coconut, and red chiles.

Index

A

adobo 86, 116, 147, 212, 230
advocacy 14
agar-agar 384
aquafaba 63, 384
arancini 67, 135, 384
arepa 230

B

banh mi 217
barley 56, 68, 265
beet 130, 182, 213, 342, 377
berbere 77
beurre blanc 48, 119
bhaji 182, 206, 223, 245, 257, 304, 314, 360
biryani 59, 245
biscuit 205
bloom 62, 108, 114, 186, 238, 372
bolognese 69, 288
bouquet garni 63, 277, 326, 329, 349, 350
bourguignon 326
burrito 234, 335
butternut 158, 270, 299, 301, 308

C

cabbage 43, 129, 211, 216, 218, 233, 306, 318, 329, 335, 360, 379, 381
cajun 87, 384
carbonara 284
cashew 28, 142, 223, 242, 245, 256, 261, 308, 311, 312, 315, 342, 369, 371, 383
cassoulet 68, 277, 384

chutney 18, 88, 95, 99, 103, 125, 129, 131, 136, 142, 150, 201, 206, 212, 213, 222, 225, 226, 228, 230, 233, 238, 256, 261, 301
coconut milk 64, 106, 113, 150, 252, 263, 301, 302, 303, 306, 307, 310, 313, 315, 316, 383
corn 117, 139, 142, 156, 200, 201, 203, 220, 226, 234, 236, 247, 256, 260, 263, 264, 268, 273, 279, 310, 336, 366, 372, 374, 384, 385
creole 67, 87, 384
crêpe 94, 201, 268, 320
culinary school 22, 24, 25, 27, 40, 58, 106, 108, 164, 186, 193, 197, 247, 299, 335, 357
cutlet 142

D

daddojanam 257
dal 161, 162, 206, 225, 249, 257, 266, 283, 384
demi 118, 212, 217, 231
duxelle 56, 69, 384

E

edamame 68, 69, 70, 248, 250, 313, 341, 381
eggplant 38, 61, 96, 97, 102, 144, 206, 232, 244, 255, 292, 307, 314, 329, 332, 337, 340, 356, 369, 385
Emeril Lagasse 114, 144
empanada 233
emulsion 384
etouffee 69, 384

F

farro 24, 151, 178, 209, 260
fennel 56, 73, 75, 76, 80, 81, 82, 117, 143, 144, 180, 182, 275, 299, 300, 307, 309, 331, 346, 371
fesenjoon 332
fra diavolo 291
freekeh 260, 264

G

garbanzo 18, 28, 64, 102, 125, 127, 142, 220, 222, 225, 226, 228, 232, 261, 263, 275, 306, 308, 315, 364, 369, 382, 385
gazpacho 155
gnocchi 68, 69, 193, 286
gnudi 68, 193
grain 178, 384
gratin 69, 384
grits 25, 48, 135, 264, 325
gumbo 144, 244, 375

H

Health 35
heirloom 68, 178, 384

I

injera 96, 194, 278

J

jambalaya 244
James Beard 9, 10, 12, 13, 14, 15, 17, 18, 19, 55, 212, 356, 390
jerk 85, 303, 308, 378

K

kofta 261, 308, 325
korma 69, 70, 384

L

leche de tigre 106, 212, 370
legume 31, 38, 39, 40, 42, 49, 55, 63, 160, 162, 266, 272, 384
lentil 157, 160, 162, 194, 211, 246, 250, 272, 278, 308, 335, 375, 384

M

Maillard 353
marinara 135, 197, 291, 292, 299, 335
masala 32, 62, 73, 108, 131, 142, 191, 213, 222, 223, 225, 226, 228, 238, 249, 266, 275, 276, 278, 301, 304, 305, 316, 318, 361, 364, 378, 382
Mathematics 10, 14, 26, 32, 33, 390
mirepoix 265
mise en place 25, 58
mole 67, 385
momo 129
muhammara 92, 218
Mumbai 10, 12, 17, 18, 49, 58, 68, 69, 90, 186, 193, 213, 223, 225, 228, 231, 233, 275, 312, 347, 361, 390
mushroom 118, 201, 220, 231, 234, 246, 268, 294, 326, 369

N

naan 96, 102, 192, 218, 305, 306, 308, 332, 363
nightshade 69, 385

O

oak 52, 53, 55, 57
okra 144, 363, 375, 384

P

paella 241, 245, 385
pakora 125, 220, 222, 382
Paratha 191
pav
 bhaji 68, 223
pickle 191, 256, 257, 266, 346, 347
pierogi 333
pistou 99, 100, 174
plantain 117, 232, 303

poutine 68, 231
Provençe 81, 152, 385
pulao 242, 281, 332
purloo 69, 281, 385

Q

quinoa 39, 64, 148, 151, 178, 201, 260, 263, 320

R

rajma 276
ramen 84, 329
roti 266
roux 384, 385

S

saag 67, 110
salsa 88, 155, 201, 203, 212, 222, 225, 230, 234, 246, 336
samosa 18, 131, 228, 333
seitan 65, 385
shakshuka 331
smoking 43, 121
socarrat 241
sofrito 67, 104, 385
spice 4, 5, 6, 9, 14, 66, 67, 73, 385, 390
squash
  butternut 38, 43, 57, 96, 130, 158, 270, 299, 301, 308, 317, 334
Stetson 6, 14, 32, 390
succotash 273
Szechuan 70, 82, 381

T

tadka 161, 385
tajine 186, 317

tamarind 105, 112, 113, 161, 212, 222, 225, 226, 228, 238, 249, 255, 310, 315
tandoori 74
tannins 50, 51, 52, 53, 55, 56, 158
tempeh 65, 147, 209, 211, 216, 217, 232, 234, 244, 288, 325, 327
terrine 69, 70, 368
terroir 48, 51, 53, 75, 300
tikka masala 108, 305
tofu 64, 65, 74, 140, 147, 288, 305, 307, 313, 325, 327, 342
tortilla 200, 234, 266, 279, 336, 384

U

umami 52, 53, 55, 60, 62, 84, 112, 272, 329

V

vichyssoise 67, 70, 385
vinaigrette 70, 385
vindaloo 114, 306

W

waste not 69, 315, 385
wat 278, 318
wild rice 270

X

xacuti 67, 69, 76, 310, 385

Y

yeast 50, 51, 56, 57, 186, 192, 194, 197, 217, 238, 372

Author Biography

HARI PULAPAKA

Hari Pulapaka is a full-time, tenured Associate Professor of Mathematics at Stetson University (DeLand, FL) and co-founder, co-owner of Cress Restaurant. Born and raised in Mumbai, Hari has been in the United States since 1987. After completing a Ph.D. in Mathematics at the University of Florida in 1995, a professional midlife crisis led to a fast-paced, top-of-the-class graduation from culinary school in 2004 while teaching full-time. Hari has published many research papers in the areas of Graph Theory and Number Theory and is an award-winning chef with four James Beard Award semifinalist nods as Best Chef-South and multiple Food & Wine People's Best Chef recognitions. Hari won the inaugural Chefs Taste Challenge in New Orleans and his cuisine helped rate Cress Restaurant as the top-rated restaurant in the inaugural ZAGAT Orlando Guide with a food score of 29/30. In 2015, Hari published his first book-a memoir-food advocacy-cookbook of sorts titled *Dreaming in Spice*. Upon invitation, Hari has, by invitation, cooked at the James Beard House in New York City on many occasions and most recently, was a featured chef at the 2018 James Beard Awards in Chicago. In 2016, Hari was recognized as a GRIST 50 fixer for his innovative and active work in the area of food waste reduction. Hari has helped develop food waste reduction related teaching materials for the James Beard Foundation as part of a full-use kitchen curriculum. Hari was an invited chef at the inaugural official JBF Chefs Boot Camp for Policy and Change and is an active leader & chef advisor for the Monterey Bay Aquarium Seafood Watch Program and the JBF Smart Catch Program. Hari is a Certified Executive Chef of the American Culinary Federation and qualified for and attempted one of the toughest culinary certification exams: The Certified Master Chef (CMC) Exam in 2017. Hari is a Paul Harris Fellow of the Rotary Foundation of Rotary International.

Chef Hari is founder and CEO of Global Cooking School, LLC, a company that is dedicated to offer a wide swathe of educational and consulting services aimed at making food more delicious, thoughtful, nutritious, and inclusive.

When he is not cooking, teaching a wide variety of undergraduate Mathematics, or supervising Undergraduate Research, Hari writes and speaks frequently on food-related matters. Hari is married to Jenneffer, a podiatric surgeon who not only specializes in diabetic limb salvage but is also a certified sommelier, and co-owner of Cress Restaurant. They live in DeLand, Florida with a few non-human family members.

DeLand, Florida
United States of America